Lecture Notes in Computer Science 5387

Commenced Publication in 1973
Founding and Former Series Editors:
Gerhard Goos, Juris Hartmanis, and Jan van Leeuwen

Roberto Bruni   Karsten Wolf (Eds.)

Web Services and Formal Methods

5th International Workshop, WS-FM 2008
Milan, Italy, September 4-5, 2008
Revised Selected Papers

 Springer

Volume Editors

Roberto Bruni
University of Pisa, Computer Science Department
Largo Bruno Pontecorvo 3, 56127 Pisa, Italy
E-mail: bruni@di.unipi.it

Karsten Wolf
Universität Rostock, Institut für Informatik
Albert-Einstein-Str. 21, 18059 Rostock, Germany
E-mail: karsten.wolf@uni-rostock.de

Library of Congress Control Number: Applied for

CR Subject Classification (1998): D.2.4, C.2.4, C.2, F.3, C.4, K.4.4

LNCS Sublibrary: SL 2 – Programming and Software Engineering

ISSN   0302-9743

ISBN 978-3-642-01363-8 Springer Berlin Heidelberg New York

Typesetting: Camera-ready by author, data conversion by Scientific Publishing Services, Chennai, India
Printed on acid-free paper   SPIN: 12663354   06/3180   5 4 3 2 1 0

Preface

This volume contains the proceedings of the 5th International Workshop on Web Services and Formal Methods (WS-FM 2008) held during September 4–5, 2008 in Milan, Italy, co-located with the 6th International Conference on Business Process Management (BPM 2008). Previous editions of the workshop were held in Pisa, Italy (WS-FM 2004), Versailles, France (WS-FM 2005), Vienna, Austria (WS-FM 2006) and Brisbane, Australia (WS-FM 2007).

The aim of the workshop series is to bring together researchers working on web services and formal methods in order to catalyze fruitful collaboration. Web service (WS) technology provides standard mechanisms and protocols for describing, locating and invoking services available all over the web. Existing infrastructures already enable providers to describe services in terms of their interface, access policy and behavior, and to combine simpler services into more structured and complex ones. However, research is still needed to move WS technology from skilled handcrafting to well-engineered practice. Formal methods can play a fundamental role in the shaping of such innovations. For instance, they can help us define unambiguous semantics for the languages and protocols that underpin existing WS infrastructures, and provide a basis for checking the conformance and compliance of bundled services. The WS-FM series has a strong tradition of attracting submissions on formal approaches to enterprise systems modeling in general, and business process modeling in particular. Potentially, this could have a significant impact on the on-going standardization efforts for WS technology.

The main topics of the workshop include: formal approaches to service-oriented analysis and design, to enterprise modeling and business process modeling; WS coordination and transactions frameworks; formal comparison of different models proposed for WS protocols and standards; types and logics for WS; goal-driven and semantics-based discovery and composition of WS; model-driven development, testing, and analysis of WS; security, performance and quality of services; innovative application scenarios for WS.

The Program Committee included experts from industry and academia, who helped us to select 13 contributed papers out of 39 submissions. As a way to guarantee the fairness and quality of the selection phase, each submission was reviewed five Program Committee members, at least. The 13 presentations were grouped into four sessions on "Analysis, Test, and Verification," "Choreographies and Process Calculi," "Transactions and Interoperability" and "Workflows and Petri Nets." The program also included one invited talk by Mario Bravetti from the University of Bologna, for which an invited paper also appears in this volume.

Starting from 2007, the workshop has taken over the activities of the online community formerly known as the "Petri and Pi" Group, which allowed to bring closer the community of workflow-oriented researchers with that of process calculi-oriented researchers. Those interested in the subject can still join the active mailing list on "Formal Methods for Service-Oriented Computing and Business Process Management" (FMxSOCandBPM) available at

http://www.cs.unibo.it/cgi-bin/mailman/listinfo/fmxsocandbpm

We would like to express our gratitude to all members of the Program Committee and additional referees for the great work done in the review phase. We want to thank Andrei Voronkov for providing the EasyChair system, which was used to manage the submissions, to carry the review process including the electronic Program Committee meeting, and also to assemble the proceedings. Finally, we thank the Politecnico di Milano for hosting WS-FM 2008 and especially the local organizers of BPM 2008, Barbara Pernici and Danilo Ardagna, who helped us greatly.

February 2009   Roberto Bruni
                                                 Karsten Wolf

Organization

Steering Committee

Wil van der Aalst	Eindhoven University of Technology, The Netherlands
Mario Bravetti	University of Bologna, Italy
Marlon Dumas	University of Tartu, Estonia
José-Luiz Fiadeiro	University of Leicester, UK
Gianluigi Zavattaro	University of Bologna, Italy

Program Chairs

Roberto Bruni	University of Pisa, Italy
Karsten Wolf	Universität Rostock, Germany

Program Committee

Farhad Arbab	CWI, The Netherlands
Matteo Baldoni	University of Turin, Italy
Alistair Barros	SAP Research Brisbane, Australia
Boualem Benatallah	University of New South Wales, Australia
Karthik Bhargavan	Microsoft Research Cambridge, UK
Eduardo Bonelli	Universidad Nacional de Quilmes, Argentina
Michael J. Butler	University of Southhampton, UK
Paolo Ciancarini	University of Bologna, Italy
Francisco Curbera	IBM Hawthorne Heights, USA
Gero Decker	HPI Potsdam, Germany
Francisco Duran	University of Malaga, Spain
Schahram Dustdar	University of Vienna, Austria
Andreas Friesen	SAP Research Karlsruhe, Germany
Stephen Gilmore	University of Edinburgh, UK
Reiko Heckel	University of Leicester, UK
Dan Hirsch	Intel Argentina, Argentina
Nickolas Kavantzas	Oracle Inc., USA
Alexander Knapp	LMU Munich, Germany
Frank Leymann	University of Stuttgart, Germany
Mark Little	RedHat, UK
Fabio Martinelli	CNR Pisa, Italy
Hernan Melgratti	University of Buenos Aires, Argentina
Shin Nakajima	National Institute of Informatics, Japan
Manuel Nunez	Complutense University of Madrid, Spain

Julian Padget	University of Bath, UK
Giuseppe Pozzi	Politecnico Milano, Italy
Rosario Pugliese	University of Florence, Italy
Antonio Ravara	Technical University of Lisbon, Portugal
Steve Ross-Talbot	pi4tech
Natalia Sidorova	Eindhoven University of Technology, The Netherlands
Christian Stahl	Humboldt University Berlin, Germany
Emilio Tuosto	University of Leicester, UK
Hagen Voelzer	IBM Zurich, Switzerland
Daniel Yankelevich	Pragma Consultores, Argentina
Prasad Yendluri	Software AG, USA

External Reviewers

Cristina Baroglio
Frederic Boussinot
Carmen Bratosin
Owen Cliffe
Pedro R. D'Argenio
James Davenport
Dirk Fahland
Carla Ferreira
Andreas Friesen
David de Frutos-Escrig
Maxime Gamboni
Simon Gay
Stephen Gilmore
Katharina Goerlach
Paul Jackson
Christian Koehler
Natallia Kokash
Oliver Kopp
Ivan Lanese
Alessandro Lapadula
Tammo Lessen

Niels Lohmann
Issam Maamria
Manuel Mazzara
Mercedes G. Merayo
Leonardo Gaetano Mezzina
Ganna Monakova
Hamid Motahari
Hyder Nizamani
Olivia Oanea
Luca Padovani
Gian Luca Pozzato
Michael Reiter
Abdolbaghi Rezazadeh
Fernando Rosa-Velardo
Gustavo Rossi
Matthias Schmalz
Helen Schonenberg
Meng Sun
Francesco Tiezzi
Vasco T. Vasconcelos

Table of Contents

On the Expressive Power of
Process Interruption and Compensation*
(Extended abstract)

Mario Bravetti and Gianluigi Zavattaro

Dipartimento di Scienze dell'Informazione, Università di Bologna,
Mura A.Zamboni 7, I-40127 Bologna, Italy
{bravetti,zavattar}@cs.unibo.it

Abstract. The investigation of the foundational aspects of linguistic mechanisms for programming long running transactions (such as the scope operator of WS-BPEL) has recently renewed the interest in process algebraic operators that *interrupt* the execution of one process, replacing it with another one called the *compensation*. We investigate the expressive power of two of such operators, the *interrupt* operator of CSP and the *try-catch* operator for exception handling. We consider two non Turing powerful fragments of CCS (without restriction and relabeling, but with either replication or recursion). We show that the addition of such operators strictly increases the expressive power of the calculi. The calculi with replication and either interrupt or try-catch turn out to be *weakly* Turing powerful (Turing Machines can be encoded but only non-deterministically). The calculus with recursion is weakly Turing powerful when extended with interrupt, but it is Turing complete (Turing Machine can be modeled deterministically) when extended with try-catch.

1 Introduction

The investigation of the foundational aspects of the so-called service composition languages (see, e.g., WS-BPEL [OAS03] and WS-CDL [W3C04]) has recently attracted the attention of the concurrency theory community. In particular, one of the main novelties of such languages is concerned with primitives for programming *long running transactions*. These primitives permit, on the one hand, to interrupt processes when some unexpected failure occur and, on the other hand, to activate alternative processes responsible to *compensate* those activities that, even if completed, must be undone due to the failure of other related activities.

Several recent papers propose process calculi that include operators for process interruption and compensation. Just to mention a few, we recall StAC [BF04], cJoin [BMM04], cCSP [BHF03], π_t [BLZ03], SAGAS [BMM05], web-pi [LZ05], ORC [MC07], SCC [BB+06], COWS [LPT07], and the Conversation Calculus [VCS08]. This huge amount of calculi, including process interruption and compensation as first-class operators, is the pragmatic proof that traditional

---

* Research partially funded by EU Integrated Project Sensoria, contract n. 016004.

basic process calculi (that do not include neither process interruption nor compensation) are not completely adequate when one wants to perform a formal investigation of long running transactions, or of fault and compensation handling in languages for service composition.

The aim of this paper is to formally investigate the expressiveness boundary between traditional process calculi and the mechanisms for process interruption and compensation. Instead of performing our investigation on yet another new calculus, we consider standard CCS [Mil89] extended with process interruption and compensation operators taken from the tradition of either process algebras or programming languages. Namely, we consider the *interrupt* operator of CSP [Hoa85] and the *try-catch* operator for exception handling from languages such as C++ or Java. The interrupt operator $P \triangle Q$ executes P until Q executes its first action; when Q starts executing, the process P is definitely interrupted. The try-catch operator $\text{try} \, P \, \text{catch} \, Q$ executes P, but if P performs a *throw* action it is definitely interrupted and Q is executed instead.

We have found these operators particularly useful because, even if very simple, they are expressive enough to model the typical operators for programming long running transactions. For instance, we can consider an operator $\text{scope}_x(P, F, C)$ corresponding to a simplified version of the *scope* construct of WS-BPEL. The meaning of this operator is as follows. The main activity P is executed. In case a fault is raised by P, its execution is interrupted and the fault handler F is activated. If the main activity P completes, but an outer scope fails and calls for the compensation of the scope x, the compensation handler C is executed.

If we assume that the main activity P communicates internal failure with the action $\overline{throw}$[1] and completion with $\overline{end}$, and the request for compensation corresponds with the action $\overline{x}$, we can model the behaviour of $\text{scope}_x(P, F, C)$ with both the interrupt:

$$P \triangle (f.\text{F}) \mid throw.\overline{f} \mid end.x.\text{C}$$

and the try-catch operator:

$$\text{try} \, P \, \text{catch} \, F \mid end.x.\text{C}$$

where the vertical bar means parallel composition.

Even if the two considered operators are apparently very similar, we prove an important expressiveness gap between them. More precisely, we consider two non Turing complete fragments of CCS, that we call $CCS_!$ and CCS_{rec}, corresponding to CCS without restriction and relabeling, but with replication or recursion, respectively. We have chosen these two language because, even if not Turing complete, they are expressive enough to model communicating processes (performing input and output operations as in standard service communication) with an infinite behaviour described by means of the two traditional operators of process

---

[1] We use the typical notation of process calculi: an overlined action (e.g. $\overline{a}$) is complementary with the corresponding non-overlined one (e.g. action a), and complementary actions allows parallel processes to synchronize.

algebras: recursion as in CCS [Mil89] or replication as in π-calculus [MPW92]. We extend these calculi with either the interrupt operator (obtaining the calculi that we call $CCS_!^\triangle$ and $CCS_{rec}^\triangle$, respectively) or the try-catch operator (obtaining $CCS_!^{\mathtt{tc}}$ and $CCS_{rec}^{\mathtt{tc}}$, respectively). We prove that the four obtained extensions are strictly more expressive than the two original basic calculi. The two extensions $CCS_!^\triangle$ and $CCS_!^{\mathtt{tc}}$ of the calculus with replication, as well as the calculus $CCS_{rec}^\triangle$ with recursion and interrupt, are *weakly* Turing powerful. By weakly Turing powerful, we mean that Turing Machines can be modeled but only in a nondeterministic manner, i.e., a Turing Machine terminates if and only if the corresponding modeling in the calculus has a terminating computation. On the other hand, the calculus $CCS_{rec}^{\mathtt{tc}}$ with recursion and try-catch is Turing complete as it permits also the deterministic modeling of Turing Machines.

In order to prove these results we investigate the decidability of *convergence* and *termination* in the considered calculi. By convergence we mean the existence of at least one terminating computation, by termination we mean that all computations terminate. For the weakly Turing powerful calculi, we first prove that convergence is undecidable showing the existence of a nondeterministic modeling of Random Access Machines (RAMs) [Min67], a well known register based Turing complete formalism. Then, we prove that termination is decidable resorting to the theory of well structured transition systems [FS01]. The decidability of termination proves the impossibility to model deterministically any Turing powerful formalism. On the other hand, for the Turing complete calculi we present a deterministic modeling of RAMs.

The most significant technical contribution of this paper concerns the proof of decidability of termination in $CCS_{rec}^\triangle$. This because, while proving decidability of termination in $CCS_!^{\mathtt{tc}}$ is done by resorting to the approach in [BGZ03], proving termination in $CCS_{rec}^\triangle$ requires introducing an order over terms with an unbounded nesting depth of the interrupt operators. For this reason we need to resort to a completely different technique which is based on devising a particular transformation of terms into *trees* (of unbounded depth) and considering an ordering on such trees. The particular transformation devised must be "tuned" in such a way that the ordering obtained is: from the one hand a well quasi ordering (and to prove this we exploit the Kruskal Tree theorem [Kru60]), from the other hand strongly compatible with the operational semantics. Obtaining and proving the latter result is particularly intricate and it also requires us to slightly modify the operational semantics of the interruption operator in a termination preserving way and to technically introduce different kinds of trees on subterms and contexts in order to interpret transitions on trees.

The paper is structured as follows. In Section 2 we define the considered calculi. In Section 3 we show the undecidability of convergence in $CCS_!^\triangle$ and $CCS_!^{\mathtt{tc}}$ (hence the same trivially holds also in $CCS_{rec}^\triangle$ and $CCS_{rec}^{\mathtt{tc}}$). In Section 4 we show the undecidability of termination in $CCS_{rec}^{\mathtt{tc}}$. Section 5 is dedicated to showing decidability of termination for $CCS_!^{\mathtt{tc}}$ and $CCS_{rec}^\triangle$ (hence the same trivially holds also for $CCS_!^\triangle$). In Section 6 we draw some conclusive remarks. Due to space limitation the proofs are omitted, the details are available in [BZ08].

Table 1. The transition system for finite core CCS (symmetric rules of PAR and SUM omitted)

$$\alpha.P \xrightarrow{\alpha} P \qquad \frac{P \xrightarrow{\alpha} P'}{P|Q \xrightarrow{\alpha} P'|Q}$$

$$\frac{P \xrightarrow{\alpha} P'}{P+Q \xrightarrow{\alpha} P'} \qquad \frac{P \xrightarrow{\alpha} P' \quad Q \xrightarrow{\overline{\alpha}} Q'}{P|Q \xrightarrow{\tau} P'|Q'}$$

2   The Calculi

We start considering the fragment of CCS [Mil89] without recursion, restriction, and relabeling (that we call finite core CCS or simply finite CCS). After we present the two infinite extensions with either replication or recursion, the new *interrupt operator*, and finally the *try-catch* operator.

Definition 1 (finite core CCS). *Let Name, ranged over by x, y, ..., be a denumerable set of channel names. The class of finite core CCS processes is described by the following grammar:*

$$P ::= \mathbf{0} \quad | \quad \alpha.P \quad | \quad P+P \quad | \quad P|P \qquad\qquad \alpha ::= \tau \quad | \quad x \quad | \quad \overline{x}$$

The term $\mathbf{0}$ denotes the empty process while the term $\alpha.P$ has the ability to perform the action α (which is either the unobservable τ action or a synchronization on a channel x) and then behaves like P. Two forms of synchronization are available, the output $\overline{x}$ or the input x. The sum construct $+$ is used to make a choice among the summands while parallel composition $|$ is used to run parallel programs. We denote the process $\alpha.\mathbf{0}$ simply with α.

For input and output actions α, i.e. $\alpha \neq \tau$, we write $\overline{\alpha}$ for the complementary of α; that is, if $\alpha = x$ then $\overline{\alpha} = \overline{x}$, if $\alpha = \overline{x}$ then $\overline{\alpha} = x$. The channel names that occur in P are denoted with $n(P)$. The names in a label α, written $n(\alpha)$ is the set of names in α, i.e. the empty set if $\alpha = \tau$ or the singleton $\{x\}$ if α is either x or $\overline{x}$.

Table 1 contains the set of the transition rules for finite core CCS.

Definition 2 (CCS!). *The class of CCS! processes is defined by adding the production $P ::= !\alpha.P$ to the grammar of Definition 1.*

The transition rule for replication is

$$!\alpha.P \xrightarrow{\alpha} P|!\alpha.P$$

We consider a guarded version of replication in which the replicated process is in prefix form. We make this simplification in order to have a finitely branching transition system, that allows us to apply directly the theory of well structured transition system in order to prove the decidability of termination. Nevertheless, the proof discussed in Section 5 can be extended also to general replication exploiting an auxiliary transition system which is finitely branching and termination equivalent to the initial transition system. This transition system can be obtained using standard techniques (see, e.g., [BGZ03, BGZ08]).

Definition 3 (CCS_{rec}). *We assume a denumerable set of process variables, ranged over by X. The class of CCS_{rec} processes is defined by adding the productions $P ::= X \mid recX.P$ to the grammar of Definition 1. In the process $recX.P$, $recX$ is a binder for the process variable X and P is the scope of the binder. We consider (weakly) guarded recursion, i.e., in the process $recX.P$ each occurrence of X (which is free in P) occurs inside a subprocess of the form $\alpha.Q$.*

The transition rule for recursion is

$$\frac{P\{recX.P/X\} \stackrel{\alpha}{\longrightarrow} P'}{recX.P \stackrel{\alpha}{\longrightarrow} P'}$$

where $P\{recX.P/X\}$ denotes the process obtained by substituting $recX.P$ for each free occurrence of X in P, i.e. each occurrence of X which is not inside the scope of a binder $recX$. Note that $CCS_!$ is equivalent to a fragment of CCS_{rec}. In fact, the replication operator $!\alpha.P$ of $CCS_!$ is equivalent to the recursive process $recX.(\alpha.(P|X))$.

We now introduce the extensions with the new *process interruption* operator.

Definition 4 ($CCS_!^{\triangle}$ and $CCS_{rec}^{\triangle}$). *The class of $CCS_!^{\triangle}$ and $CCS_{rec}^{\triangle}$ processes is defined by adding the production $P ::= P \triangle P$ to the grammars of Definition 2 and Definition 3, respectively.*

The transition rules for the interrupt operator are

$$\frac{P \stackrel{\alpha}{\longrightarrow} P'}{P \triangle Q \stackrel{\alpha}{\longrightarrow} P' \triangle Q} \qquad \frac{Q \stackrel{\alpha}{\longrightarrow} Q'}{P \triangle Q \stackrel{\alpha}{\longrightarrow} Q'}$$

We complete the list of definitions of the considered calculi presenting the extensions with the new *try-catch* operator.

Definition 5 ($CCS_!^{tc}$ and CCS_{rec}^{tc}). *The class of $CCS_!^{tc}$ and CCS_{rec}^{tc} processes is defined by adding the productions $P ::= \mathtt{try}\,P\,\mathtt{catch}\,P$ and $\alpha ::= \mathtt{throw}$ to the grammars of Definition 2 and Definition 3, respectively. The new action $\mathtt{throw}$ is used to model the raising of an exception.*

The transition rules for the try-catch operator are

$$\frac{P \stackrel{\alpha}{\longrightarrow} P' \quad \alpha \neq \mathtt{throw}}{\mathtt{try}\,P\,\mathtt{catch}\,Q \stackrel{\alpha}{\longrightarrow} \mathtt{try}\,P'\,\mathtt{catch}\,Q} \qquad \frac{P \stackrel{\mathtt{throw}}{\longrightarrow} P'}{\mathtt{try}\,P\,\mathtt{catch}\,Q \stackrel{\tau}{\longrightarrow} Q}$$

We use $\prod_{i \in I} P_i$ to denote the parallel composition of the indexed processes P_i, while we use $\prod_n P$ to denote the parallel composition of n instances of the process P (if $n = 0$ then $\prod_n P$ denotes the empty process $\mathbf{0}$).

In the following we will consider only closed processes, i.e. processes without free occurrences of process variables. Given a closed process Q, its internal runs $Q \longrightarrow Q_1 \longrightarrow Q_2 \longrightarrow \ldots$ are given by its reduction steps, (denoted with $\longrightarrow$), i.e. by those transitions $\longrightarrow$ that the process can perform in isolation, independently of the context. The internal transitions $\longrightarrow$ correspond to the transitions labeled with τ, i.e. $P \longrightarrow P'$ iff $P \xrightarrow{\tau} P'$. We denote with $\longrightarrow^+$ the transitive closure of $\longrightarrow$, while $\longrightarrow^*$ is the reflexive and transitive closure of $\longrightarrow$.

A process Q is *dead* if there exists no Q' such that $Q \longrightarrow Q'$. We say that a process P *converges* if there exists P' s.t. $P \longrightarrow^* P'$ and P' is dead. We say that P *terminates* if all its internal runs terminate, i.e. the process P cannot give rise to an infinite computation: formally, P *terminates* iff there exists no family $\{P_i\}_{i \in \mathbf{N}}$, s.t. $P_0 = P$ and $P_j \longrightarrow P_{j+1}$ for any j. Observe that *process termination* implies *process convergence* while the vice versa does not hold.

3 Undecidability of Convergence in $\mathrm{CCS}_!^{\triangle}$ and $\mathrm{CCS}_!^{\mathrm{tc}}$

We prove that $\mathrm{CCS}_!^{\triangle}$ and $\mathrm{CCS}_!^{\mathrm{tc}}$ are powerful enough to model, at least in a nondeterministic way, any Random Access Machine [SS63] (RAM), a well known register based Turing powerful formalism.

A RAM (denoted in the following with R) is a computational model composed of a finite set of registers $r_1, \ldots, r_n$, that can hold arbitrary large natural numbers, and by a program composed by indexed instructions $(1 : I_1), \ldots, (m : I_m)$, that is a sequence of simple numbered instructions, like arithmetical operations (on the contents of registers) or conditional jumps. An internal state of a RAM is given by $(i, c_1, \ldots, c_n)$ where i is the program counter indicating the next instruction to be executed, and $c_1, \ldots, c_n$ are the current contents of the registers $r_1, \ldots, r_n$, respectively. Given a configuration $(i, c_1, \ldots, c_n)$, its computation proceeds by executing the instructions in sequence, unless a jump instruction is encountered. The execution stops when an instruction number higher than the length of the program is reached. Note that the computation of the RAM proceeds deterministically (it does not exhibit non-deterministic behaviors).

Without loss of generality, we assume that the registers contain the value 0 at the beginning and at the end of the computation. In other words, the initial configuration is $(1, 0, \ldots, 0)$ and, if the RAM terminates, the final configuration is $(i, 0, \ldots, 0)$ with $i > m$ (i.e. the instruction I_i is undefined). More formally, we indicate by $(i, c_1, \ldots, c_n) \to_R (i', c_1', \ldots, c_n')$ the fact that the configuration of the RAM R changes from $(i, c_1, \ldots, c_n)$ to $(i', c_1', \ldots, c_n')$ after the execution of the i-th instruction ($\to_R^*$ is the reflexive and transitive closure of $\to_R$).

In [Min67] it is shown that the following two instructions are sufficient to model every recursive function:

- $(i : Succ(r_j))$: adds 1 to the contents of register r_j;
- $(i : DecJump(r_j, s))$: if the contents of register r_j is not zero, then decreases it by 1 and go to the next instruction, otherwise jumps to instruction s.

Our encoding is nondeterministic because it introduces computations which do not follow the expected behavior of the modeled RAM. However, all these computations are infinite. This ensures that, given a RAM, its modeling has a terminating computation if and only if the RAM terminates. This proves that *convergence* is undecidable.

In this section and in the next one devoted to the proof of the undecidability results, we reason up to a structural congruence $\equiv$ in order to rearrange the order of parallel composed processes and to abstract away from the terminated processes $\mathbf{0}$. We define $\equiv$ as the least congruence relation satisfying the usual axioms $P|Q \equiv Q|P$, $P|(Q|R) \equiv (P|Q)|R$, and $P|\mathbf{0} \equiv P$.

Let R be a RAM with registers $r_1, \ldots, r_n$, and instructions $(1 : I_1), \ldots, (m : I_m)$. We model separately registers and instructions.

The program counter is modeled with a message $\overline{p}_i$ indicating that the i-th instruction is the next to be executed. For each $1 \leq i \leq m$, we model the i-th instruction $(i : I_i)$ of R with a process which is guarded by an input operation p_i. Once activated, the instruction performs its operation on the registers and then updates the program counter by producing $\overline{p_{i+1}}$ (or $\overline{p_s}$ in case of jump).

Formally, for any $1 \leq i \leq m$, the instruction $(i : I_i)$ is modeled by $[\![(i : I_i)]\!]$ which is a shorthand notation for the following processes:

$$[\![(i : I_i)]\!] \quad : \quad !p_i.(\overline{inc_j}.\overline{loop} \mid \overline{p_{i+1}}) \qquad\qquad \text{if } I_i = Succ(r_j)$$

$$[\![(i : I_i)]\!] \quad : \quad !p_i.(\ \tau.(\overline{loop} \mid \overline{dec_j}.loop.loop.\overline{p_{i+1}}) \ + \atop \tau.\overline{zero_j}.ack.\overline{p_s} \ ) \qquad \text{if } I_i = DecJump(r_j, s)$$

It is worth noting that every time an increment operation is performed, a process $\overline{loop}$ is spawned. This process will be removed by a corresponding decrement operation. The modeling of the $DecJump(r_j, s)$ instruction internally decides whether to decrement or to test for zero the register.

In case of decrement, if the register is empty the instruction deadlocks because the register cannot be actually decremented. Nevertheless, before trying to decrement the register a process $\overline{loop}$ is generated. As we will discuss in the following, the presence of this process prevents the encoding from converging. If the decrement operation is actually executed, two instances of process $\overline{loop}$ are removed, one instance corresponding to the one produced before the execution of the decrement, and one instance corresponding to a previous increment operation.

In case of test for zero, the corresponding register will have to be modified as we will discuss below. As this modification on the register requires the execution of several actions, the instruction waits for an acknowledgment before producing the new program counter $\overline{p_s}$.

We now show how to model the registers using either the interruption or the try-catch operators. In both cases we exploit the following idea. Every time the register r_j is incremented, a dec_j process is spawned which permits the subsequent execution of a corresponding decrement operation. In case of test for zero on the register r_j, we will exploit either the interruption or the try-catch operators in order to remove all the active processes dec_j, thus resetting the register. If the register is not empty when it is reset, the computation of the encoding does not reproduce the RAM computation any longer. Nevertheless, such "wrong" computation surely does not terminate, thus we can conclude that we faithfully model at least the terminating computations. Divergence in case of "wrong" reset is guaranteed by the fact that if the register is not empty, k instances of dec_j processes are removed with $k > 0$, and k instances of the process $\overline{loop}$ (previously produced by the corresponding k increment operations) will never be removed.

As discussed above, the presence of $\overline{loop}$ processes prevents the encoding from converging. This is guaranteed by considering, e.g., the following divergent process

$$LOOP \ : \ loop.(\overline{l} \mid !l.\overline{l})$$

Formally, we model each register r_j, when it contains c_j, with one of the following processes denoted with $[\![r_j = c_j]\!]^\triangle$ and $[\![r_j = c_j]\!]^{\mathrm{tc}}$:

$$[\![r_j = c_j]\!]^\triangle \ : \ (!inc_j.dec_j \mid \textstyle\prod_{c_j} dec_j \,)\triangle(zero_j.\overline{nr_j}.\overline{ack})$$

$$[\![r_j = c_j]\!]^{\mathrm{tc}} \ : \ \mathtt{try} \ (!inc_j.dec_j \mid \textstyle\prod_{c_j} dec_j \mid zero_j.\mathtt{throw}) \ \mathtt{catch} \ (\overline{nr_j}.\overline{ack})$$

It is worth observing that, when a test for zero is performed on the register r_j, an output operation $\overline{nr_j}$ is executed before sending the acknowledgment to the corresponding instruction. This action is used to activate a new instance of the process $[\![r_j = 0]\!]$, as the process modeling the register r_j is removed by the execution of either the interruption or the try-catch operators. The activation of new instances of the process modeling the registers is obtained simply considering, for each register r_j, (one of) the two following processes

$$!nr_j.[\![r_j = 0]\!]^\triangle \qquad !nr_j.[\![r_j = 0]\!]^{\mathrm{tc}}$$

We are now able to define formally our encoding of RAMs as well as its properties.

Definition 6. *Let R be a RAM with program instructions $(1 : I_1), \ldots, (m : I_m)$ and registers $r_1, \ldots, r_n$. Let also Γ be either $\triangle$ or $\mathtt{tc}$. Given the configuration $(i, c_1, \ldots, c_n)$ of R we define*

$$[\![(i, c_1, \ldots, c_n)]\!]_R^\Gamma =$$
$$\overline{p_i} \mid [\![(1 : I_1)]\!] \mid \ldots \mid [\![(m : I_m)]\!] \mid \textstyle\prod_{\sum_{j=1}^n c_j} \overline{loop} \mid LOOP \mid$$
$$[\![r_1 = c_1]\!]^\Gamma \mid \ldots \mid [\![r_n = c_n]\!]^\Gamma \mid !nr_1.[\![r_1 = 0]\!]^\Gamma \mid \ldots \mid !nr_n.[\![r_n = 0]\!]^\Gamma$$

the encoding of the RAM R in either $CCS_!^\triangle$ or $CCS_!^{\mathrm{tc}}$ (taking $\Gamma = \triangle$ or $\Gamma = \mathtt{tc}$, respectively). The processes $[\![(i : I_i)]\!]$, $LOOP$, and $[\![r_j = c_j]\!]^\Gamma$ are as defined above.

The following proposition states that every step of computation of a RAM can be mimicked by the corresponding encoding. On the other hand, the encoding could introduce additional computations. The proposition also states that all these added computations are infinite.

Proposition 1. *Let R be a RAM with program instructions $(1 : I_1), \ldots, (m : I_m)$ and registers $r_1, \ldots, r_n$. Let also Γ be either $\triangle$ or $\mathtt{tc}$. Given a configuration $(i, c_1, \ldots, c_n)$ of R, we have that, if $i > m$ and $c_j = 0$ for each $1 \leq j \leq n$, then $[\![(i, c_1, \ldots, c_n)]\!]_R^\Gamma$ is a dead process, otherwise:*

1. *if $(i, c_1, \ldots, c_n) \to_R (i', c_1', \ldots, c_n')$ then we have $[\![(i, c_1, \ldots, c_n)]\!]_R^\Gamma \to^+ [\![(i', c_1', \ldots, c_n')]\!]_R^\Gamma$*

2. *if $[\![(i, c_1, \ldots, c_n)]\!]_R^\Gamma \longrightarrow Q_1 \longrightarrow Q_2 \longrightarrow \cdots \longrightarrow Q_l$ is a, possibly zero-length, internal run of $[\![(i, c_1, \ldots, c_n)]\!]_R^\Gamma$ then one of the following holds:*
   - *there exists k, with $1 \leq k \leq l$, such that $Q_k \equiv [\![(i', c_1', \ldots, c_n')]\!]_R^\Gamma$, with $(i, c_1, \ldots, c_n) \to_R (i', c_1', \ldots, c_n')$;*
   - *$Q_l \longrightarrow^+ [\![(i', c_1', \ldots, c_n')]\!]_R^\Gamma$, with $(i, c_1, \ldots, c_n) \to_R (i', c_1', \ldots, c_n')$;*
   - *Q_l does not converge.*

Corollary 1. *Let R be a RAM. We have that the RAM R terminates if and only if $[\![(1, 0, \ldots, 0)]\!]_R^\Gamma$ converges (for both $\Gamma = \triangle$ and $\Gamma = \mathtt{tc}$).*

This proves that convergence is undecidable in both $CCS_!^\triangle$ and $CCS_!^{\mathtt{tc}}$. As replication is a particular case of recursion, we have that the same undecidability result holds also for $CCS_{rec}^\triangle$ and $CCS_{rec}^{\mathtt{tc}}$.

4   Undecidability of Termination in $CCS_{rec}^{\mathtt{tc}}$

In this section we prove that also termination is undecidable in $CCS_{rec}^{\mathtt{tc}}$. This result follows from the existence of a deterministic encoding of RAMs satisfying the following stronger soundness property: a RAM terminates if and only if the corresponding encoding terminates.

The basic idea of the new modeling is to represent the number c_j, stored in the register r_j, with a process composed of c_j nested try-catch operators. This approach can be adopted in $CCS_{rec}^{\mathtt{tc}}$ because standard recursion admits recursion in *depth*, while it was not applicable in $CCS_!^{\mathtt{tc}}$ because replication supports only recursion in *width*. By recursion in width we mean that the recursively defined term can expand only in parallel as, for instance, in $recX.(P|X)$ (corresponding to the replicated process $!P$) where the variable X is an operand of the parallel composition operator. By recursion in depth, we mean that the recursively defined term expands also under other operators such as, for instance, in $recX.(\mathtt{try}\,(P|X)\,\mathtt{catch}\,Q)$ (corresponding to an unbounded nesting of try-catch operators).

Let R be a RAM with registers $r_1, \ldots, r_n$, and instructions $(1 : I_1), \ldots, (m : I_m)$. We start presenting the modeling of the instructions which is similar to the encoding presented in the previous section. Note that here the assumption on registers to all have value 0 in a terminating configuration is not needed. We encode each instruction $(i : I_i)$ with the process $[\![(i : I_i)]\!]$, which is a shorthand for the following process

$$
\begin{aligned}
[\![(i : I_i)]\!] &: recX.p_i.\overline{inc_j}.\overline{p_{i+1}}.X && \text{if } I_i = Succ(r_j) \\
[\![(i : I_i)]\!] &: recX.p_i.(\ \overline{zero_j}.\overline{p_s}.X \ + \ \overline{dec_j}.ack.\overline{p_{i+1}}.X\ ) && \text{if } I_i = DecJump(r_j, s)
\end{aligned}
$$

As in the previous section, the program counter is modeled by the process $\overline{p_i}$ which indicates that the next instruction to execute is $(i : I_i)$. The process $[\![(i : I_i)]\!]$ simply consumes the program counter process, then updates the registers (resp. performs a test for zero), and finally produces the new program counter process $\overline{p_{i+1}}$ (resp. $\overline{p_s}$). Notice that in the case of a decrement operation, the instruction process waits for an acknowledgment before producing the new program counter process. This is necessary because the register decrement requires the execution of several operations.

The register r_j, that we assume initially empty, is modeled by the process $[\![r_j = 0]\!]$ which is a shorthand for the following process (to simplify the notation we use also the shorthand R_j defined below)

$$
\begin{aligned}
[\![r_j = 0]\!] &: \ recX.\big(zero_j.X \ + \ inc_j.\text{try } R_j \text{ catch}\,(\overline{ack}.X)\big) \\
R_j &: \ recY.\big(dec_j.\text{throw} \ + \ inc_j.\text{try } Y \text{ catch}\,(\overline{ack}.Y)\big)
\end{aligned}
$$

The process $[\![r_j = 0]\!]$ is able to react either to test for zero requests or increment operations. In the case of increment requests, a try-catch operator is activated. Inside this operator a recursive process is installed which reacts to either increment or decrement requests. In the case of an increment, an additional try-catch operator is activated (thus increasing the number of nested try-catch). In the case of a decrement, a failure is raised which removes the active try-catch operator (thus decreasing the number of nested try-catch) and emits the acknowledgment required by the instruction process. When the register returns to be empty, the outer recursion reactivates the initial behavior.

Formally, we have that the register r_j with contents $c_j > 0$ is modeled by the following process composed of the nesting of c_j try-catch operators

$$
\begin{aligned}
[\![r_j = c_j]\!] \ : \ &\text{try} \\
&\quad\big(\text{try} \\
&\qquad\big(\cdots \\
&\qquad\quad \text{try } R_j \text{ catch}\,(\overline{ack}.R_j) \\
&\qquad \cdots\big) \\
&\quad \text{catch}\,(\overline{ack}.R_j)\big) \\
&\text{catch}\,(\overline{ack}.[\![r_j = 0]\!])
\end{aligned}
$$

where R_j is as defined above. We are now able to define formally the encoding of RAMs in CCS^{tc}_{rec}.

Definition 7. *Let R be a RAM with program instructions $(1 : I_1), \ldots, (m : I_m)$ and registers $r_1, \ldots, r_n$. Given the configuration $(i, c_1, \ldots, c_n)$ we define with*

$$[(i, c_1, \ldots, c_n)]_R \; \dot{=} \; \overline{p_i} \mid [(1 : I_1)] \mid \ldots \mid [(m : I_m)] \mid [r_1 = c_1] \mid \ldots \mid [r_n = c_n]$$

the encoding of the RAM R in CCS^{tc}_{rec}.

The new encoding faithfully reproduces the behavior of a RAM as stated by the following proposition. In the following Proposition we use the notion of *deterministic* internal run defined as follows: an internal run $P_0 \longrightarrow P_1 \longrightarrow \ldots \longrightarrow P_l$ is deterministic if for every process P_i, with $i < l$, P_{i+1} is the unique process Q such that $P_i \longrightarrow Q$.

Proposition 2. *Let R be a RAM with program instructions $(1 : I_1), \ldots, (m : I_m)$ and registers $r_1, \ldots, r_n$. Given a configuration $(i, c_1, \ldots, c_n)$ of R, we have that, if $i > m$ then $[(i, c_1, \ldots, c_n)]_R$ is a dead process, otherwise:*

1. *if $(i, c_1, \ldots, c_n) \to_R (i', c'_1, \ldots, c'_n)$ then we have $[(i, c_1, \ldots, c_n)]_R \to^+ [(i', c'_1, \ldots, c'_n)]_R$*
2. *there exists a non-zero length deterministic internal run $[(i, c_1, \ldots, c_n)]^{\Gamma}_R \longrightarrow Q_1 \longrightarrow Q_2 \longrightarrow \cdots \longrightarrow [(i', c'_1, \ldots, c'_n)]^{\Gamma}_R$ such that $(i, c_1, \ldots, c_n) \to_R (i', c'_1, \ldots, c'_n)$.*

Corollary 2. *Let R be a RAM. We have that the RAM R terminates if and only if $[(1, 0, \ldots, 0)]_R$ terminates.*

This proves that termination is undecidable in CCS^{tc}_{rec}.

5   Decidability of Termination in $CCS^{tc}_!$ and $CCS^{\triangle}_{rec}$

In the RAM encoding presented in the previous section natural numbers are represented by chains of nested try-catch operators, that are constructed by exploiting recursion. In this section we prove that both recursion and try-catch are strictly necessary. In fact, if we consider replication instead of recursion or the interrupt operator instead of the try-catch operator, termination turns out to be decidable.

These results are based on the theory of well-structured transition systems [FS01]. We start recalling some basic definitions and results concerning well-structured transition systems, that will be used in the following.

A *quasi-ordering*, also known as pre-order, is a reflexive and transitive relation.

Definition 8. *A well-quasi-ordering (wqo) is a quasi-ordering $\leq$ over a set S such that, for any infinite sequence $s_0, s_1, s_2, \ldots$ in S, there exist indexes $i < j$ such that $s_i \leq s_j$.*

Transition systems can be formally defined as follows.

Definition 9. *A transition system is a structure $TS = (S, \to)$, where S is a set of states and $\to \subseteq S \times S$ is a set of transitions. We write $Succ(s)$ to denote the set $\{s' \in S \mid s \to s'\}$ of immediate successors of S. TS is finitely branching if all $Succ(s)$ are finite.*

Well-structured transition system, defined as follows, provide the key tool to decide properties of computations.

Definition 10. *A* well-structured transition system with strong compatibility *is a transition system $TS = (\mathcal{S}, \rightarrow)$, equipped with a quasi-ordering $\leq$ on $\mathcal{S}$, such that the two following conditions hold:*

1. **well-quasi-ordering***: $\leq$ is a well-quasi-ordering, and*
2. **strong compatibility***: $\leq$ is (upward) compatible with $\rightarrow$, i.e., for all $s_1 \leq t_1$ and all transitions $s_1 \rightarrow s_2$, there exists a state t_2 such that $t_1 \rightarrow t_2$ and $s_2 \leq t_2$.*

In the following we use the notation $(\mathcal{S}, \rightarrow, \leq)$ for transition systems equipped with a quasi-ordering $\leq$.

The following theorem (a special case of a result in [FS01]) will be used to obtain our decidability results.

Theorem 1. *Let $(\mathcal{S}, \rightarrow, \leq)$ be a finitely branching, well-structured transition system with strong compatibility, decidable $\leq$ and computable Succ. The existence of an infinite computation starting from a state $s \in \mathcal{S}$ is decidable.*

The proof of decidability of termination in $CCS_{rec}^{\triangle}$ is not done on the original transition system, but on a termination equivalent one. The new transition system does not eliminate interrupt operators during the computation; in this way, the nesting of interrupt operators can only grow and do not shrink. As we will see, this transformation will be needed for proving that the ordering that we consider on processes is strongly compatible with the operational semantics. Formally, we define the new transition system $\overset{\alpha}{\longmapsto}$ for $CCS_{rec}^{\triangle}$ considering the transition rules of Definition 3 (where $\overset{\alpha}{\longmapsto}$ is substituted for $\overset{\alpha}{\longrightarrow}$) plus the following rules

$$\frac{P \overset{\alpha}{\longmapsto} P'}{P \triangle Q \overset{\alpha}{\longmapsto} P' \triangle Q} \qquad \frac{Q \overset{\alpha}{\longmapsto} Q'}{P \triangle Q \overset{\alpha}{\longmapsto} Q' \triangle \mathbf{0}}$$

Notice that the first of the above rules is as in Definition 4, while the second one is different because it does not remove the $\triangle$ operator.

As done for the standard transition system, we assume that the reductions $\longmapsto$ of the new semantics corresponds to the τ–labeled transitions $\overset{\tau}{\longmapsto}$. Also for the new semantics, we say that a process P terminates if and only if all its computations are finite, i.e. it cannot give rise to an infinite sequence of reductions $\longmapsto$.

Proposition 3. *Let $P \in CCS_{rec}^{\triangle}$. Then P terminates according to the semantics $\longrightarrow$ iff P terminates according to the new semantics $\longmapsto$.*

We now separate in two subsections the proofs of decidability of termination in $CCS_{!}^{tc}$ and in $CCS_{rec}^{\triangle}$.

5.1   Termination Is Decidable in $(CCS_!^{tc}, \longrightarrow)$

The proof for $CCS_!^{tc}$ is just a rephrasal of the proof of decidability of termination in CCS without relabeling and with replication instead of recursion reported in [BGZ08].

We define for $(CCS_!^{tc}, \longrightarrow)$ a quasi-ordering on processes which turns out to be a well-quasi-ordering compatible with $\longrightarrow$. Thus, exploiting Theorem 1 we show that termination is decidable.

Definition 11. *Let* $P \in CCS_!^{tc}$. *With* $Deriv(P)$ *we denote the set of processes reachable from* P *with a sequence of reduction steps:*

$$Deriv(P) = \{Q \mid P \longrightarrow {}^*Q\}$$

To define the wqo on processes we need the following structural congruence.

Definition 12. *We define* $\equiv$ *as the least congruence relation satisfying the following axioms:* $P|Q \equiv Q|P$ $P|(Q|R) \equiv (P|Q)|R$ $P|0 \equiv P$

Now we are ready to define the quasi-ordering on processes:

Definition 13. *Let* $P, Q \in CCS_!^{tc}$. *We write* $P \preceq Q$ *iff there exist* n, P', R, $P_1, \ldots, P_n$, $Q_1, \ldots, Q_n$, $S_1, \ldots, S_n$ *such that* $P \equiv P' | \prod_{i=1}^{n} \mathtt{try}\, P_i \,\mathtt{catch}\, S_i$, $Q \equiv P' | R | \prod_{i=1}^{n} \mathtt{try}\, Q_i \,\mathtt{catch}\, S_i$, *and* $P_i \preceq Q_i$ *for* $i = 1, \ldots, n$.

Theorem 2. *Let* $P \in CCS_!^{tc}$. *Then the transition system* $(Deriv(P), \longrightarrow, \preceq)$ *is a finitely branching well-structured transition system with strong compatibility, decidable* $\preceq$ *and computable* $Succ$.

Corollary 3. *Let* $P \in CCS_!^{tc}$. *The termination of process* P *is decidable.*

5.2   Termination Is Decidable in $(CCS_{rec}^{\triangle}, \longmapsto)$

According to the ordering defined in Definition 13, we have that $P \preceq Q$ if Q has the same structure of nesting of try-catch operators and it is such that in each point of this nesting Q contains at least the same processes (plus some other processes in parallel). This is a well-quasi-ordering in the calculus with replication because, given P, it is possible to compute an upper bound to the number of nesting in any process in $Deriv(P)$. In the calculus with recursion this upper bound does not exist as recursion permits to generate nesting of unbounded depth (this e.g. is used in the deterministic RAM modeling of Section 4). For this reason, we need to move to a different ordering inspired by the ordering on trees used by Kruskal in [Kru60]. This allows us to use the Kruskal Tree theorem that states that the trees defined on a well quasi ordering is a well quasi ordering.

The remainder of this section is devoted to the definition of how to associate trees to processes of $CCS_{rec}^{\triangle}$, and how to extract from these trees an ordering for $(CCS_{rec}^{\triangle}, \longmapsto)$ which turns out to be a wqo.

We take $\mathcal{E}$ to be the set of (open) terms of $CCS_{rec}^{\triangle}$ and $\mathcal{P}$ to be the set of $CCS_{rec}^{\triangle}$ processes, i.e. closed terms. $\mathcal{P}_{seq}$ is the subset of $\mathcal{P}$ of terms P such that either $P = \mathbf{0}$ or $P = \alpha.P_1$ or $P = P_1 + P_2$ or $P = recX.P_1$, with $P_1, P_2 \in \mathcal{E}$. Let $\mathcal{P}_{int} = \{P \triangle Q \mid P, Q \in \mathcal{P}\}$.

Given a set E, we denote with E^* the set of finite sequences of elements in E. We use ";" as a separator for elements of a set E when denoting a sequence $w \in E^*$, ϵ to denote the empty sequence and $len(w)$ to denote the length of a sequence w. Finally, we use w_i do denote the $i - th$ element in the sequence w (starting from 1) and $e \in w$ to stand for $e \in \{w_i \mid 1 \le i \le len(w)\}$.

Definition 14. *Let $P \in \mathcal{P}$. We define the flattened parallel components of P, $FPAR(P)$, as the sequence over $\mathcal{P}_{seq} \cup \mathcal{P}_{int}$ given by*

$$FPAR(P_1|P_2) = FPAR(P_1); FPAR(P_2)$$
$$FPAR(P) = P \ if \ P \in \mathcal{P}_{seq} \cup \mathcal{P}_{int}$$

Given a sequence $w \in E^*$ we define the sequence $w' \in E'^*$ obtained by filtering w with respect to $E' \subseteq E$ as follows. For $1 \le i \le len(k)$, $w'_i = w_{k_i}$, where $k \in \{1, \ldots, len(w)\}^*$ is such that k is strictly increasing, i.e. $j' > j$ implies $k_{j'} > k_j$, and, for all h, $w_h \in E'$ if and only if $h \in k$. In the following we call $FINT(P)$ the sequence obtained by filtering $FPAR(P)$ with respect to $\mathcal{P}_{int}$ and $FSEQ(P)$ the sequence obtained by filtering $FPAR(P)$ with respect to $\mathcal{P}_{seq}$.

In the following we map processes into ordered trees (with both a left to right ordering of children at every node and the usual son to father ordering).

Definition 15. *A tree t over a set E is a partial function from $\mathbf{N}^*$ to E such that $dom(t)$ is finite, is closed with respect to sequence prefixing and is such that $\vec{n}; m \in dom(t)$ and $m' \le m$, with $m' \in \mathbf{N}$, implies $\vec{n}; m' \in dom(t)$.*

Example 1. $(\epsilon, l) \in t$ denotes that the root of the tree has label $l \in E$; $(1; 2, l) \in t$ denotes that the second son of the first son of the root of the tree t has label $l \in E$.

Let $\mathcal{P}_{rint} = \{\triangle Q \mid Q \in \mathcal{P}\}$ be a set representing compensations.

Definition 16. *Let $P \in \mathcal{P}$. We define the tree of P, $TREE(P)$, as the minimal tree $TREE(P)$ over $\mathcal{P}_{seq}^* \cup \mathcal{P}_{rint}$ (and minimal auxiliary tree $TREE^{odd}(P')$ over $\mathcal{P}_{seq}^* \cup \mathcal{P}_{rint}$, with $P' \in \mathcal{P}_{int}$) satisfying*

$$(\epsilon, FSEQ(P)) \in TREE(P)$$
$$(\vec{n}, l) \in TREE^{odd}(FINT(P)_i) \ implies \ (i; \vec{n}, l) \in TREE(P)$$

$$(\epsilon, \triangle Q) \in TREE^{odd}(P' \triangle Q)$$
$$(\vec{n}, l) \in TREE(P') \ implies \ (1; \vec{n}, l) \in TREE^{odd}(P' \triangle Q)$$

Example 2. The tree of the process $a + b|((recX.(a.X|c))\triangle Q)|c|((a|c)\triangle S)$ for some processes Q and S is $\{(\epsilon, a + b; c), (1, \triangle Q), (1; 1, recX.(a.X|c)), (2, \triangle S), (2; 1, a; c)\}$.

In the following, we define the ordering between processes by resorting to the ordering on trees used in [Kru60] applied to the particular trees obtained from processes by our transformation procedure. In particular, in order to do this we introduce the notion of injective function that strictly preserves order inside trees: a possible formal way to express homeomorphic embedding between trees, used in the Kruskal's theorem [Kru60], that we take from [Sim85].

Let t be a tree. We take $\leq_t$ to be the ancestor pre-order relation inside t, defined by: $\vec{n} \leq_t \vec{m}$ iff $\vec{m}$ is a prefix $\vec{n}$ (or $\vec{m} = \vec{n}$). Moreover, we take $\wedge_t$ to be the minimal common ancestor of a pair of nodes, i.e. $\vec{n_1} \wedge_t \vec{n_2} = min\{\vec{m}|\vec{n_1} \leq_t \vec{m} \wedge \vec{n_2} \leq_t \vec{m}\}$.

Definition 17. *We say that an injective function φ from $dom(t)$ to $dom(t')$ strictly preserves order inside trees iff for every $\vec{n}, \vec{m} \in dom(t)$ we have:*

- *$\vec{n} \leq_t \vec{m}$ implies $\varphi(\vec{n}) \leq_{t'} \varphi(\vec{m})$*
- *$\varphi(\vec{n} \wedge_t \vec{m}) = \varphi(\vec{n}) \wedge_{t'} \varphi(\vec{m})$*

Definition 18. *Let $P, Q \in \mathcal{P}$. $P \preceq Q$ iff there exists an injective function φ from $dom(TREE(P))$ to $dom(TREE(Q))$ such that φ strictly preserves order inside trees and for every $\vec{n} \in dom(\varphi)$:*

- *either there exists $R \in \mathcal{P}$ such that $TREE(P)(\vec{n}) = TREE(Q)(\varphi(\vec{n})) = \triangle R$*
- *or $TREE(P)(\vec{n}), TREE(Q)(\varphi(\vec{n})) \in \mathcal{P}^*_{seq}$ and, if $len(TREE(P)(\vec{n})) > 0$, there exists an injective function f from $\{1, \ldots, len(TREE(P)(\vec{n}))\}$ to $\{1, \ldots, len(TREE(Q)(\varphi(\vec{n})))\}$ such that for every $i \in dom(f)$: $TREE(P)(\vec{n})_i = TREE(Q)(\varphi(\vec{n}))_{f(i)}$.*

Notice that $\preceq$ is a quasi-ordering in that it is obviously reflexive and it is immediate to verify, taking into account the two conditions for the injective function in the definition above, that it is transitive.

We redefine on the transition system $(CCS^{\triangle}_{rec}, \longmapsto)$ the function $Deriv(P)$ that associates to a process the set of its derivatives.

Definition 19. *Let $P \in CCS^{\triangle}_{rec}$. With $Deriv(P)$ we denote the set of processes reachable from P with a sequence of reduction steps:*

$$Deriv(P) = \{Q \mid P \longmapsto^* Q\}$$

We are now ready to state our main result, that can be proved by contemporaneously exploiting Higman's Theorem on sequences [Hig52] and Kruskal's Theorem on trees [Kru60].

Theorem 3. *Let $P \in CCS^{\triangle}_{rec}$. Then the transition system $(Deriv(P), \longmapsto, \preceq)$ is a finitely branching well-structured transition system with strong compatibility, decidable $\preceq$ and computable Succ.*

Corollary 4. *Let $P \in CCS^{\triangle}_{rec}$. The termination of process P is decidable.*

As replication is a particular case of recursion, we have that the same decidability result holds also for $CCS^{\triangle}_!$.

6   Conclusion and Related Work

Following a recent trend of research devoted to the investigation of the foundational properties of languages for service oriented computing by means of process calculi including mechanisms for process interruption and compensation (see, e.g., [BF04, BMM04, BHF03, BLZ03, BMM05, LZ05, MC07, BB+06, LPT07, VCS08]), we have investigated the expressive power of two basic operators for process interruption and compensation taken from the tradition of either process algebras or programming languages. Namely, we have considered the *interrupt* operator of CSP [Hoa85] and the *try-catch* construct of languages such as C++ or Java.

We have formalized an expressiveness gap between the traditional input-output communication primitives of process algebras and the considered operators. Formally, we have proved that CCS [Mil89] without restriction and relabeling, and with replication instead of recursion (which is not Turing complete) turns out to be weakly Turing powerful when extended with the considered operators. On the other hand, the same fragment of CCS with recursion instead of replication (which is still non Turing complete) turns out to be weakly Turing powerful when extended with the interrupt operator, while it is Turing complete when extended with try-catch.

It is worth to compare the results proved in this paper with similar results presented in [BGZ03]. In that paper, the interplay between replication/recursion and restriction is studied: a fragment of CCS with restriction and replication is proved to be weakly Turing powerful, while the corresponding fragment with recursion is proved to be Turing complete. This result is similar to what we have proved about the interplay between replication/recursion and the try-catch operator. This proves a strong connection between restriction and try-catch, at least as far as the computational power is concerned. Intuitively, this follows from the fact that, similarly to restriction, the try-catch operator defines a new scope for the special **throw** action which is bound to a specific exception handler. On the contrary, the interrupt operator does not have the same computational power. In fact, the calculus with recursion and interrupt is only weakly Turing powerful. This follows from the fact that this operator does not provide a similar binding mechanism between the interrupt signals and the interruptible processes.

It is worth to compare our criterion for the evaluation of the expressive power with the criterion used by Palamidessi in [Pal03] to discriminate the expressive power of the synchronous and the asynchronous π-calculus. Namely, in that paper, it is proved that there exists no modular embedding of the synchronous into the asynchronous π-calculus that preserves any reasonable semantics. When we prove that termination (resp. convergence) is undecidable in one calculus while it is not in another one, we also prove that there exists no encoding (thus also no modular embedding) of the former calculus into the latter that preserves any semantics sensible to termination (resp. convergence). By semantics sensible to some property, we mean any semantics that distinguishes one process that satisfies the property from one process that does not. If we assume that the termination of one computation is observable (as done for instance in process calculi with explicit termination [BBR08]), we have that any reasonable semantics (according to the notion of reasonable semantics presented in [Pal03]) is sensible to both termination and convergence.

We conclude by mentioning the investigation of the expressive power of the disrupt operator (similar to our interruption operator) done by Baeten and Bergstra in a technical report [BB00]. In that paper, a different notion of expressive power is considered: a calculus is more expressive than another one if it generates a larger set of transition systems. We consider a stronger notion of expressive power: a calculus is more expressive than another one if it supports a more faithful modeling of Turing complete formalisms.

References

[BBR08]   Baeten, J.C.M., Basten, T., Reniers, M.A.: Process algebra (equational theories of communicating processes. Cambridge Tracts in Theoretical Computer Science. Cambridge University Press, Cambridge (2008)

[BB00]   Baeten, J.C.M., Bergstra, J.: Mode transfer in process algebra. Report CSR 00-01, Technische Universiteit Eindhoven. This paper is an expanded and revised version of J. Bergstra, A mode transfer operator in process algebra, Report P8808, Programming Research Group, University of Amsterdam (2000),
          http://alexandria.tue.nl/extra1/wskrap/publichtml/200010731.pdf

[BLZ03]   Bocchi, L., Laneve, C., Zavattaro, G.: A calculus for long running transactions. In: Najm, E., Nestmann, U., Stevens, P. (eds.) FMOODS 2003. LNCS, vol. 2884, pp. 124–138. Springer, Heidelberg (2003)

[BB+06]   Boreale, M., Bruni, R., Caires, L., De Nicola, R., Lanese, I., Loreti, M., Martins, F., Montanari, U., Ravara, A., Sangiorgi, D., Vasconcelos, V.T., Zavattaro, G.: SCC: A Service Centered Calculus. In: Bravetti, M., Núñez, M., Zavattaro, G. (eds.) WS-FM 2006. LNCS, vol. 4184, pp. 38–57. Springer, Heidelberg (2006)

[BZ08]   Bravetti, M., Zavattaro, G.: On the Expressive Power of Process Interruption and Compensation. Technical report,
          http://cs.unibo.it/~zavattar/papers.html

[BMM04]   Bruni, R., Melgratti, H.C., Montanari, U.: Nested Commits for Mobile Calculi: Extending Join. In: TCS 2004: IFIP 18th World Computer Congress, TC1 3rd International Conference on Theoretical Computer Science, pp. 563–576. Kluwer, Dordrecht (2004)

[BMM05]   Bruni, R., Melgratti, H.C., Montanari, U.: Theoretical foundations for compensations in flow composition languages. In: POPL 2005: Proceedings of the 32nd Symposium on Principles of Programming Languages, pp. 209–220. ACM Press, New York (2005)

[BGZ03]   Busi, N., Gabbrielli, M., Zavattaro, G.: Replication vs. Recursive Definitions in Channel Based Calculi. In: Baeten, J.C.M., Lenstra, J.K., Parrow, J., Woeginger, G.J. (eds.) ICALP 2003. LNCS, vol. 2719, pp. 133–144. Springer, Heidelberg (2003)

[BGZ08]   Busi, N., Gabbrielli, M., Zavattaro, G.: On the Expressive Power of Recursion, Replication, and Iteration in Process Calculi. Technical report, http://cs.unibo.it/~zavattar/papers.html Extended version of BGZ03

[BF04]   Butler, M., Ferreira, C.: An operational semantics for StAC, a language for modelling long-running business transactions. In: De Nicola, R., Ferrari, G.-L., Meredith, G. (eds.) COORDINATION 2004. LNCS, vol. 2949, pp. 87–104. Springer, Heidelberg (2004)

[BHF03]   Butler, M., Hoare, T., Ferreira, C.: A trace semantics for long-running transactions. In: Abdallah, A.E., Jones, C.B., Sanders, J.W. (eds.) Communicating Sequential Processes. LNCS, vol. 3525, pp. 133–150. Springer, Heidelberg (2005)

[FS01]   Finkel, A., Schnoebelen, P.: Well-Structured Transition Systems Everywhere! Theoretical Computer Science 256, 63–92 (2001)

[Hig52]   Higman, G.: Ordering by divisibility in abstract algebras. Proc. London Math. Soc. 2, 236–366 (1952)

[Hoa85]   Hoare, T.: Communicating Sequential Processes. Prentice-Hall, Englewood Cliffs (1985)

[Kru60]   Kruskal, J.B.: Well-Quasi-Ordering, The Tree Theorem, and Vazsonyi's Conjecture. Transactions of the American Mathematical Society 95(2), 210–225 (1960)

[LZ05]   Laneve, C., Zavattaro, G.: Foundations of web transactions. In: Sassone, V. (ed.) FOSSACS 2005. LNCS, vol. 3441, pp. 282–298. Springer, Heidelberg (2005)

[LPT07]   Lapadula, A., Pugliese, R., Tiezzi, F.: A Calculus for Orchestration of Web Services. In: De Nicola, R. (ed.) ESOP 2007. LNCS, vol. 4421, pp. 33–47. Springer, Heidelberg (2007)

[Mil89]   Milner, R.: Communication and Concurrency. Prentice-Hall, Englewood Cliffs (1989)

[MPW92]   Milner, R., Parrow, J., Walker, D.: A Calculus of Mobile Processes, Part I + II. Information and Computation 100(1), 1–77 (1992)

[Min67]   Minsky, M.L.: Computation: finite and infinite machines. Prentice-Hall, Englewood Cliffs (1967)

[MC07]   Misra, J., Cook, W.R.: Computation Orchestration. Journal of Software and System Modeling 6(1), 83–110 (2007)

[OAS03]   OASIS. WS-BPEL: Web Services Business Process Execution Language Version 2.0. Technical report, OASIS (2003)

[Pal03]   Palamidessi, C.: Comparing the Expressive Power of the Synchronous and the Asynchronous pi-calculus. In: Mathematical Structures in Computer Science, vol. 13(5), pp. 685–719. Cambridge University Press, Cambridge (2003); A short version of this paper appeared in POPL 1997 (1997)

[SS63]   Shepherdson, J.C., Sturgis, J.E.: Computability of recursive functions. Journal of the ACM 10, 217–255 (1963)

[Sim85]   Simpson, S.G.: Nonprovability of certain combinatorial properties of finite trees. In: Harvey Friedman's Research on the Foundations of Mathematics, pp. 87–117. North-Holland, Amsterdam (1985)

[VCS08]   Vieira, H.T., Caires, L., Seco, J.C.: The Conversation Calculus: A Model of Service-Oriented Computation. In: Drossopoulou, S. (ed.) ESOP 2008. LNCS, vol. 4960, pp. 269–283. Springer, Heidelberg (2008)

[W3C04]   W3C. WS-CDL: Web Services Choreography Description Language. Technical report, W3C (2004)

Modelling and Analysis of Time-Constrained Flexible Workflows with Time Recursive ECATNets

Kamel Barkaoui[1], Hanifa Boucheneb[2], and Awatef Hicheur[1]

[1] CEDRIC-CNAM, 292 Rue Saint-Martin, Paris 75003, France
{barkaoui,hicheur}@cnam.fr
[2] VeriForm-Ecole Polytechnique de Montréal, P.O. Box 6079, Station Centre-ville,
Montral, Québec, Canada, H3C 3A7
hanifa.boucheneb@polymtl.ca

Abstract. We present, in this paper, the Time Recursive ECATNets (T-RECATNets) formalism for the modelling and analysis of time-constrained reconfigurable workflows, which are preponderant in the field of Web services. In a second step, we propose a method for building a specific state class graph in terms of rewrite logic. Therefore, one can verify some properties with respect to time constraints using model checking techniques.

Keywords: Time Petri nets, Recursive Petri nets, Time-constrained Flexible workflows, Rewriting logic.

1 Introduction

Workflow is the automation of a business process, in whole or part, during which documents, information or tasks are passed from one participant to another for action, according to a set of procedural rules. Workflow management is concerned with the coordination, control and communication of work for improving the operational efficiency of business processes [2]. The current trend of business globalisation brings new challenges regarding the flexibility of business processes [1],[11], [14]. On the one hand, the execution of such processes is distributed over multiple workflow engines (within the same organization or over multiple organisations). On the other hand, the structures of these collaborative processes are extremely dynamic, driven by external conditions, changing user requirements and business partners. Indeed, a business partnership is often created dynamically and maintained temporary only for the realization of the required business goal [16]. That's why we need a formalism permitting a faithful description of these flexible and collaborative workflow processes. Moreover, a successful implementation of a workflow system must handle with the temporal specifications and constraints [18]. In real world situations, where processes are both automatic and human, the duration of some tasks can be unpredictable and non-deterministic. This execution time can be estimated by a time interval giving the

R. Bruni and K. Wolf (Eds.): WS-FM 2008, LNCS 5387, pp. 19–36, 2009.
© Springer-Verlag Berlin Heidelberg 2009

minimum and maximum durations or by using a stochastic method (arbitrary time distribution). The objective of this paper is to cope with analysis of time-constrained and flexible workflows. The proposed model, called Time Recursive ECATNets (T-RECATNets for short), inherits all modelling abilities of the Recursive ECATNets (RECATNets for short) introduced in [4]. The RECATNets model offers practical mechanisms for a direct and intuitive support of dynamic creation and suppression of processes. They are well-suited for handling the most advanced workflow patterns (involving cancellation and multiple instances) and for specifying exceptional behaviors [4]. In fact, RECATNets have the ability to express the current state of a concurrent system as a dynamical tree of threads where each thread has its own execution context. Threads in RECATNets are created by a special type of transitions called abstract transitions. A thread of such a tree terminates (a cut step is executed) when it reaches a final marking. T-RECATNets extend the descriptive power of the RECATNets with possibilities to express time constraints explicitly. Indeed, we associate to each transition (abstract or ordinary) of a T-RECATNet a firing time interval specifying possible dates of firings. Moreover, we attach to an abstract transition a cancellation time interval which specifies the minimum and the maximum duration tolerated for a thread created by this abstract transition. So, a thread which takes too much time to complete its execution can be interrupted by the abstract transition which gave birth to it. This feature is useful for modelling interruption (cancellation of running sub-processes) due to deadline constraints. We describe T-RECATNets semantics in terms of rewriting logic [10], which permits the use of the Maude system [12] for purposes of verification and evaluation.

The rest of this paper is organized as follows: Section 2 reminds the concepts of the RECATNets model. Section 3 introduces the time extension of the RECATNets model, namely Time RECATNets (T-RECATNets for short). Section 4 illustrates how the T-RECATNet model can be used in modelling time-constrained collaborative workflows. Section 5 is devoted to the computation of the state class graph of T-RECATNets. In section 6, we discuss some links to related works. The section 7 concludes this paper.

2   Recursive ECATNets Review

The Recursive ECATNets (RECATNets) model [4] is defined on the basis of a sound combination of the classical ECATNets (Extended Concurrent Algebraic Term Nets) [6] formalism and the Recursive Petri Nets (RPNs) [13]. We remind that ECATNets are a kind of algebraic nets combining the expressive power of Petri nets and abstract data types. The places in an ECATNet are associated to a sort and are marked with multisets of algebraic terms. The RECATNets inherit all concepts of the classical ECATNets formalism except that their transitions are partitioned into two types: *elementary transitions* (represented by a simple rectangle. See Fig. 1 (a)) and *abstract transitions* (represented by a double border rectangle. See Fig. 1 (b)). Each abstract transition is associated to a starting marking represented graphically in a frame.

(a) A generic elementary transition

(b) A generic abstract transition

Fig. 1. Transition Types

In a RECATNet, an arc from an input place p to a transition t (*elementary* or *abstract*) is labelled by two algebraic expressions: $IC(p,t)$ and $DT(p,t)$. The expression $IC(p,t)$ specifies the partial condition on the marking of the input place p for the enabling of t. It takes one of the following forms (see Table 1). The expression $DT(p,t)$ specifies the multiset of tokens to be removed from the marking of the input place p when the transition t is fired. Also, each transition t may be labelled by a Boolean expression $TC(t)$ which specifies an additional enabling condition on the values taken by local variables of t (i.e. variables related to all the input places of t). When the expression $TC(t)$ is omitted, the default value is the term *True*.

Table 1. The different forms of the expression $IC(p,t)$ for a given transition t

$IC(p, t)$	Enabling condition
α^0	The marking of the place p must be equal to α (e.g. $IC(p,t) = \emptyset^0$ means the marking of p must be empty).
α^+	The marking of the place p must include α (e.g. $IC(p,t) = \emptyset^+$ means condition is always satisfied).
α^-	The marking of the place p must not include α, with $\alpha \neq \emptyset$.
$\alpha_1 \wedge \alpha_2$	Conditions α_1 and α_2 are both true.
$\alpha_1 \vee \alpha_2$	α_1 or α_2 is true.

The semantics of a RECATNet can be explained informally as follows. In a RECATNet, there is a clear distinction between the firing condition of a given transition t and the tokens which may be destroyed during the firing action of t (respectively specified via the expression $IC(p,t)$ and $DT(p,t)$). A transition t (elementary or abstract) is fireable when several conditions are satisfied simultaneously: (1) Every $IC(p,t)$ is satisfied for each input place p of the transition t and (2) the additional condition $TC(t)$ is true. Moreover, a RECATNet generates during its execution a dynamical tree of threads (denoting the fatherhood relation and describing the inter-thread calls) where each of these threads has its own execution context. All threads of such a tree can be executed simultaneously. A step of a RECATNet is thus a step of one of its threads.

When a thread fires an elementary transition t_{elt}, the tokens $DT(p,t_{elt})$ are removed from each input place p of t_{elt} and simultaneously the tokens $CT(p',t_{elt})$ are added to each output place p' of t_{elt} (in the same manner as transitions of classical ECATNets).

When a thread fires an abstract transition t_{abs}, it consumes the multiset of tokens $DT(p, t_{abs})$ from each input place p of the transition t_{abs} and simultaneously it creates a new thread (called its child) launched with an initial state being the starting marking associated to this abstract transition. Naturally, when an elementary or an abstract transition is fired, appropriate instantiations of the variables appearing in the expressions IC, DT and CT, take place.

A family Υ of Boolean terms is associated to a RECATNet in order to describe the termination states of the threads. These termination states, called *final markings*, are specified by conditions on the marking of the RECATNet places. A family of such final markings is indexed by a finite set whose items are called *termination indices*. Therefore, when a thread reaches a final marking Υ_i (with $i \in I$), it terminates, aborts its whole descent of threads and creates the multiset of tokens $ICT(p', t_{abs}, i)$ in the output place p' of the abstract transition t_{abs} which gave birth to it (in its father thread). Such an event is called a *cut step* and denoted τ_i (with $i \in I$). An arc from an abstract transition t_{abs} to its output place p', labelled by an expression $\langle i \rangle \, ICT(p', t_{abs}, i)$, means that the tokens $ICT(p', t_{abs}, i)$ are produced in the place p' if the marking Υ_i is reached in the terminating thread (where i is the index of this termination). Therefore, the production of tokens in the output place of an abstract transition is delayed until the child thread, generated by the firing of this transition, reaches a final marking. Note that if a cut step occurs in the root of the tree of threads, it leads to the empty tree, denoted by $\bot$, from which neither transition nor cut step can occur.

In what follows, we note $Spec = (\Sigma, E)$ an algebraic specification of an abstract data type associated to a RECATNet (with Σ its set of operations and sorts, E its set of equations). $T_{\Sigma,E}(X)$ denotes the Σ-algebra of the equivalence classes of the Σ-terms with variables in X, modulo the equations E. $CATdas(E, X)$ is the structure of equivalence classes formed from multisets of the terms $T_{\Sigma,E}(X)$ modulo the associative, commutative and identity axioms for the operator $\oplus$ (with the empty multiset $\emptyset$ as the identity element). The operations $\subset$, $-$ represent, respectively, the multiset inclusion and the multiset difference. The next definitions formalize the RECATNets model and its associated states called *extended markings*.

Definition 1 (Recursive ECATNets). *A Recursive ECATNet is a tuple RE-CATNet = (Spec, P, T, sort, Cap, IC, DT, CT, TC, I, Υ, ICT) where:*

- *$Spec = (\Sigma, E)$ is a many sorted algebra where the sorts domains are finite,*
- *P is a finite set of places,*
- *$T = T_{abs} \uplus T_{elt}$, is a finite set of transitions (with $P \cap T = \emptyset$) partitioned into abstract and elementary ones, respectively ($\uplus$ denotes the disjoint union),*
- *$sort : P \rightarrow S$ (with S the set of sorts of Spec),*
- *$Cap : P \rightarrow CATdas(E, \emptyset) \cup \{\infty\}$, (Capacity),*
- *$IC : P \times T \rightarrow CATdas(E, X)^*$, (Input Condition) where*
  $CATdas(E, X)^* = \{\alpha^+ \mid \alpha \in CATdas(E, X)\} \cup \{\alpha^- \mid \alpha \in CATdas(E, X)\}$
  $\cup \, \{\alpha^0 \mid \alpha \in CATdas(E, X)\} \cup \{\alpha_1 \wedge \alpha_2 \mid \forall i \, \alpha_i \in CATdas(E, X)^*\} \cup$
  $\{\alpha_1 \vee \alpha_2 \mid \forall i \, \alpha_i \in CATdas(E, X)^*\},$

- $DT : P \times T \to CATdas(E, X)$, *(Destroyed Tokens)*,
- $CT : P \times T \to CATdas(E, X)$, *(Created Tokens)*,
- $TC : T \to CATdas(E, X)_{bool}$, *(Transition Condition)*,
- *I is a finite set of indices,*
- Υ *is a family, indexed by* I, *of Boolean terms defined in order to describe the termination conditions (i.e. final markings) of threads,*
- $ICT : P \times T_{abs} \times I \to CATdas(E, X)$, *(Indexed Created Tokens)*.

Remark. The termination conditions of threads in a RECATNet can be specified by a system of linear inequalities or equalities on the marking of the RECATNet places. Since the sorts domains of *Spec* (i.e. the underlying algebraic specification of a RECATNet) are assumed to be finite, determining the truth value of a termination condition is thus decidable.

The global state of a RECATNet is described by a dynamical tree of threads called an *extended marking* where each thread is associated to an *ordinary marking* describing its internal context. The places of a thread are marked by multisets of algebraic terms.

Definition 2 (Extended marking). *An extended marking of a RECATNet* $RN = (Spec, P, T, sort, Cap, IC, DT, CT, TC, I, \Upsilon, ICT)$ *is a labelled rooted tree denoted* $Tr = \langle V, M, E, A \rangle$ *such that:*

- V *is the set of nodes (i.e. threads),*
- M *is a Mapping* $V \to CATdas(E, \emptyset)$ *associating an ordinary marking with each node of the tree, such that* $\forall v \in V, \forall p \in P, M(v)(p) \leq Cap(p)$,
- $E \subseteq V \times V$ *is the set of edges,*
- A *is a mapping* $E \to T_{abs}$ *associating an abstract transition with each edge.*

$M(v)$ denotes the marking of a thread v in an extended marking Tr and $M(v)(p)$ denotes the marking of a place p in a thread v. A marked RECATNet (RN, Tr_0) is a RECATNet RN associated to an initial extended marking Tr_0. For each node $v \in V$, $Succ(v)$ denotes the set of its direct and indirect successors including v ($\forall v \in V, Succ(v) = \{v' \in V \mid (v, v') \in E^*\}$ where E^* is the reflexive and transitive closure of E). Moreover, when a node v is not the root thread of an extended marking Tr, we denote by $pred(v)$ its unique predecessor in Tr (i.e. its father thread).

An *elementary step* in a marked RECATNet can be a firing of a transition or a cut step occurence (denoted τ_i with $i \in I$).

Definition 3. *An elementary transition* t_{elt} *is enabled in a thread* v *of an extended marking* Tr *(with* $Tr \neq \perp$) *iff: (1) Every* $IC(p, t_{elt})$ *is satisfied for each input place* p *of the transition* t_{elt}. *(2) The transition condition* $TC(t_{elt})$ *is true. The firing of an elementary transition* t_{elt} *in a thread* v *of* $Tr = \langle V, M, E, A \rangle$ *leads to an extended marking* $Tr' = \langle V', M', E', A' \rangle$ *(denoted* $Tr \xrightarrow{v,\ t_{elt}} Tr'$) *such that:*

- $V' = V$, $E' = E$,
- $\forall e \in E', A'(e) = A(e)$,

- $\forall v' \in V' \setminus \{v\}$, $M'(v') = M(v')$,
- $\forall p \in P$, $M'(v)(p) = M(v)(p) - DT(p, t_{elt}) \oplus CT(p, t_{elt})$.

Definition 4. *An abstract transition t_{abs} is enabled in a thread v of an extended marking Tr (with $Tr \neq \perp$) iff: (1) Every $IC(p, t_{abs})$ is satisfied for each input place p of the transition t_{abs}. (2) The transition condition $TC(t_{abs})$ is true. The firing of an abstract transition t_{abs} in a thread v of $Tr = \langle V, M, E, A \rangle$ leads to an extended marking $Tr' = \langle V', M', E', A' \rangle$ (denoted $Tr \xrightarrow{v, \, t_{abs}} Tr'$) such that:*

- *Let v' be a fresh identifier in the tree Tr',*
- $V' = V \cup \{v'\}$, $E' = E \cup \{(v, v')\}$,
- $\forall e \in E'$, $A'(e) = A(e)$, $A'((v, v')) = t_{abs}$,
- $\forall v'' \in V' \setminus \{v\}$, $M'(v'') = M(v'')$,
- $\forall p \in P$, $M'(v)(p) = M(v)(p) - DT(p, t_{abs})$,
- $\forall p \in P$, $M'(v')(p) = CT(p, t_{abs})$.

Definition 5. *A cut step τ_i is enabled in a thread v of an extended marking Tr (with $Tr \neq \perp$) iff $M(v)$ satisfies the condition of the final marking Υ_i. The occurence of a cut step τ_i in a thread v of $Tr = \langle V, M, E, A \rangle$ leads to an extended marking $Tr' = \langle V', M', E', A' \rangle$ (denoted $Tr \xrightarrow{v, \tau_i} Tr'$) such that:*

- *If v is the root thread of the tree Tr, then $Tr' = \perp$, otherwise:*
- $V' = V \setminus Succ(v')$, $E' = E \cap (V' \times V')$,
- $\forall e \in E'$, $A'(e) = A(e)$,
- $\forall v' \in V' \setminus \{pred(v)\}$, $M'(v') = M(v')$,
- $\forall p \in P$, $M'(pred(v))(p) = M(pred(v))(p) \oplus ICT(p, A(pred(v), v), i)$.

These features of RECATNets will be illustrated in the workflow example given in the following section.

3   Time Recursive ECATNets

In order to describe time constraints in real workflow processes, we have to employ an explicit representation of time in RECATNets. There are several ways for time representation in Petri nets [9]: firing duration (Ramchandani's model), enabling duration (Merlin's model) and holding durations (Van der Aalst's model). The challenge is to include time in an efficient manner which allows meeting time requirements without making the verification more complex. Enabling duration is the most used way as it offers a good compromise between the modelling power and analysis complexity. In enabling duration models, a firing delay is associated with each transition. This delay specifies the time that the transition has to be enabled before it can fire. The firing of a transition takes no time (i.e. tokens are removed and created in the same instant). The delay may be either a *random distribution* function (as in the stochastic Petri nets) or *deterministic* bounds (i.e. bounds of delays are fixed). We focus in this paper on deterministic delay bounds, represented in the model by intervals attached to transitions (as in the Merlin's model).

In a RECATNet, we denote by *firing step*, the firing of an *elementary* or an *abstract* transition or the occurence of a *cut step*. Consequently, to include uniformly time in RECATNets, we associate a *firing interval* to each transition (abstract and elementary) and to each cut step. The firing interval has the same semantics as those of Merlin's model. In a T-RECATNet, a transition t (elementary or abstract) is fireable when t is maintained continuously enabled during some time inside the firing interval of t. The firing in both cases must be done without any additional delay, if the enabling time reaches the upper bound of the firing interval [9]. Unlike abstract and elementary transitions, the execution of a cut step τ_i is immediately executed in a thread of a RECATNet as soon as a final marking Υ_i is reached in this thread (i.e. without delay). Therefore, the firing interval associated to a *cut step* is always considered as null (i.e. $[0, 0]$). Particularly, when an abstract transition t_{abs} is fired, it consumes tokens $DT(p, t_{abs})$ from its input place p and simultaneously it creates a new child thread. It will be useful to provide a mechanism for cancelling the execution of threads. In this sense, we attach a *cancellation interval* to each abstract transition (in addition to its firing interval). Such interval means that a running thread generated by this abstract transition can be cancelled (i.e. aborted together with its all descent of threads) as soon as the lower bound of its cancellation interval is reached. This abortion must be immediately done at the expiration of this cancellation interval.

Definition 6 (Time Recursive ECATNet). *A Time Recursive ECATNet is a tuple T-RECATNet = (RECATNet, Is, Δ) such that:*

- *$Is : T \cup \{\tau_i \mid i \in I\} \rightarrow \mathbb{Q}^+ \times (\mathbb{Q}^+ \cup \{\infty\})$ (where $\mathbb{Q}^+$ is the set of positive rational numbers) is the static firing interval function. Is associates a firing interval to each transition (elementary or abstract) and to each cut step of a RECATNet,*
- *$\Delta : T_{abs} \rightarrow \mathbb{Q}^+ \times (\mathbb{Q}^+ \cup \{\infty\})$ is the static cancellation interval function. Δ associates a cancellation interval to each abstract transition of a RECATNet.*

$\downarrow Is(t)$ and $\uparrow Is(t)$ denote, respectively, the lower and the upper bounds of the firing interval $Is(t)$ (i.e. the earliest and the latest firing time of the transition t). In a similar manner, $\downarrow \Delta(t)$ and $\uparrow \Delta(t)$ denote, respectively, the lower and the upper bounds of the cancellation interval $\Delta(t)$. Fig.2 shows how both time intervals attached to an abstract transition are managed. If an abstract transition t_f becomes enabled at instant θ_0, it will fire at any instant θ_1 in interval $[\theta_0 + \downarrow Is(t_f), \theta_0 + \uparrow Is(t_f)]$ unless it is disabled. If t_f is fired at some instant θ_1, the thread generated by its firing will be cancelled at any time θ_2 in interval $[\theta_1 + \downarrow \Delta(t_f), \theta_1 + \uparrow \Delta(t_f)]$ or by the execution of a cut step τ_i in this thread (i.e. a final marking Υ_i is reached).

In the rest of the paper, we denote by $TCut = T_{abs} \cup T_{elt} \cup \{\tau_i \mid i \in I\}$, the set of transitions (elementary and abstract) and cut steps of a T-RECATNet and by $v.t$ an element t of $TCut$ enabled in a thread v of an extended marking Tr. Also,

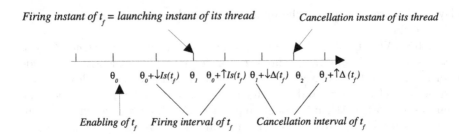

Fig. 2. Firing interval and cancellation interval of an abstract transition

we denote by $En(Tr)$ the set of all *elementary* transitions, *abstract* transitions and *cut steps* enabled in an extended marking Tr. If an extended marking Tr' results from the firing of a transition or a cut step t_f in a thread v of an extended marking Tr, we denote by $New(Tr', v.t_f)$ the set of all transitions and cut steps considered to be *newly enabled* in Tr'. We consider in the next definitions that a transition is *newly enabled*, if it remains enabled after its firing. We define the *newly enabledness* notion of transitions or cut steps in the context of extended markings as follows.

Definition 7. *Consider a firing* $Tr = \langle V, M, E, A \rangle \xrightarrow{v,t_f} Tr' = \langle V', M', E', A' \rangle$. *The elements of* $TCut$ *which are newly enabled in* Tr' *after the firing of* t_f *in a thread* v *of* Tr *are obtained as follows:*

- *If* $t_f \in T_{elt}$, *only the corresponding thread* v *may have newly enabled transitions or cut steps. An element* t *of* $TCut$ *is newly enabled in* v *after the firing of* t_f, *iff* t *is enabled in the marking* $M'(v)$ *and either* $t = t_f$ *or* t *is not enabled in the marking* $M(v) - DT(p, t_f)$.
- *If* $t_f \in T_{abs}$, *only the created thread* v' *obtained in* V' *and the corresponding thread* v *are concerned: an element* t *of* $TCut$ *is newly enabled in* v *after the firing of* t_f, *iff* t *is enabled in the marking* $M'(v)$ *and either* $t = t_f$ *or* t *is not enabled in* $M(v)$.
- *If* $t_f \in \{\tau_i \mid i \in I\}$, *a cut step occurring in a thread* v *different from the root, only the thread* $pred(v)$ *is concerned: an element* t *of* $TCut$ *is newly enabled in* $pred(v)$ *iff* t *is enabled in* $M'(pred(v))$ *and* t *is not enabled in* $M(pred(v))$.

From a semantic point of view, if a transition t becomes enabled in a thread v, the bounds of its firing interval $Is(t)$ decrease synchronously with time until $v.t$ (i.e. the transition t enabled in v) is fired or disabled. Note that $v.t$ cannot be fired before $\downarrow Is(t)$ reaches 0 and must be fired as soon as $\uparrow Is(t)$ reaches 0, unless it is disabled by the firing of another element of $TCut$. When an abstract transition t_{abs} is fired, the cancellation interval of t_{abs} (i.e. $\Delta(t_{abs})$) is associated to the created thread v. The bounds of this interval decrease synchronously with time until a cut step is executed in the created thread v. The execution of a cut step τ_i in v (denoted $v.\tau_i$) is done as soon as a final marking Υ_i (with $i \in I$) is reached. Also, a running thread v may be cancelled as soon as the lower bound of its cancellation interval reaches 0. Such cancellation must be done as soon as $\uparrow \Delta(t_{abs})$ reaches 0. This cancellation is specified as a special type of cut step denoted $\tau*$ (i.e. the index of this cut step is $\langle * \rangle$).

Each reachable state s of a T-RECATNet is defined as a triplet $s = (Tr, In, Id)$ where: Tr is an extended marking (defined in a similar manner as for untimed RECATNets) and In is the set of cut steps $\tau*$ due to expiration of cancellation delays. Note that the elements of In are of the form $v.\tau*$ with v a thread of Tr generated by an abstract transition. Also, Id is a firing interval function $(Id : En(Tr) \cup In \rightarrow \mathbb{Q}^+ \times (\mathbb{Q}^+ \cup \{\infty\}))$. The function Id associates thus to each element $v.t$ enabled in Tr, and each cut step $v.\tau*$ of In the time interval in which it can be fired. $\downarrow Id(v.t)$ and $\uparrow Id(v.t)$ denote, respectively, the lower and the upper bounds of the interval $Id(v.t)$.

The state of a T-RECATNet evolves either by *time progression* or by *firing steps* (firing of transitions or cut steps execution). Let $s = (Tr, In, Id)$ and $s' = (Tr', In', Id')$ be two states of the model.

Given θ in $\mathbb{R}^+$, a nonnegative reel number, we write $s \xrightarrow{\theta} s'$, iff state s' is reachable from state s after a *time progression* of θ time units (s' is also denoted $s + \theta$), i.e.:

- $\exists\, \theta \in \mathbb{R}^+, \forall\, v.t \in En(Tr) \cup In, \theta \leq \uparrow Id(v.t)$,
- $Tr' = Tr$,
- $In' = In$,
- $\forall\, v'.t' \in En(Tr') \cup In', Id'(v'.t') = [\downarrow Max(Id(v'.t') - \theta, 0), \uparrow Id(v'.t') - \theta]$

We write $s \xrightarrow{v.t} s'$ iff state s' is immediately reachable from state s by *firing* of a transition or a cut step t in a thread v of the extended marking Tr, i.e.:

- $v.t \in En(Tr) \cup In$,
- $\downarrow Id(v.t) = 0$,
- Tr' is the successor of Tr by $v.t$ in the untimed underlying model (i.e. $Tr \xrightarrow{v.t} Tr'$),
- In' is computed from In, such that:
    1. In the case $v.t$ is the firing of an elementary transition t: $In' = In$,
    2. In the case $v.t$ is the firing of an abstract transition t in a thread v: add $v'.\tau*$ to In where v' is the identifier of the thread generated by the firing of t in v (i.e. $In' = In \cup \{v'.\tau*\}$).
    3. In the case $v.t$ is a cut step t occurring in v: eliminate from In cut steps $v''.\tau*$ related to threads removed from Tr by the firing of $v.t$ (i.e. $In' = In \setminus \{v''.\tau * \mid v'' \in Succ(v)\}$),
- $\forall v'.t' \in En(Tr') \cup In'$,

$$Id'(v'.t') = \begin{cases} Is(t') & \text{if } v'.t' \in New(Tr', v.t) \\ \Delta(t) & \text{if } t \in T_{abs} \text{ and } v'.t' \in In' \text{ and } v'.t' \notin In \\ Id(v'.t') & \text{otherwise} \end{cases}$$

The semantic of a T-RECATNet model is defined by the timed transitions system (state space) $(S, s_0, \rightarrow)$, where: $s_0 = (Tr_0, \emptyset, Id_0)$ is the initial state of the model $(Id_0(v.t) = Is(t)$, for all $v.t \in En(Tr_0))$, $S = \left\{ s \mid s_0 \xrightarrow{*} s \right\}$ is the set of reachable states of the model ($\xrightarrow{*}$ is the reflexive and transitive closure of the relation $\rightarrow$).

4 Workflow Modelling Using Time Recursive ECATNets

We propose in our T-RECATNets based approach for modelling flexible and collaborative workflows to introduce two types of tasks in these processes: *Elementary tasks* (represented by elementary transitions) and *abstract tasks* (represented by abstract transitions). The execution of an abstract task dynamically generates a new (lower-level) plan of actions in a workflow process. When a plan reaches a final marking, it terminates and the whole descent of action plans generated by it are aborted (i.e. a cut step is executed). This ability offers a natural way to introduce *flexibility* in workflow planning and execution. In fact, a dynamical tree of action plans describes the structure of a workflow process where all plans can be executed simultaneously. The root plan of such a tree represents the principal process by which the whole specified workflow starts and terminates. The exceptions that may occur during the execution of a workflow can be reflected by the execution of cut steps or by the firings of abstract transitions. So, a workflow process may handle exceptions, respectively, by terminating the current process or generating a new action plan. Note that with the introduced time concept, it is possible to model both the starting time and ending time of such action plans (i.e. threads) and so to specify exception handling related to time-constraint violations. The descriptive power of T-RECATNets appears, also, adequate in describing both the distributed execution of collaborative processes over multiple process engines and their inter-process interaction. The event flows which coordinate and link up together these distributed sub-processes are reflected by the firing of *abstract transitions* (i.e. call for a sub-process) or the execution of *cut steps* (i.e. termination of a sub-process and result return to the caller). Moreover, the T-RECATNets model allows us to describe advanced data structures and to integrate the data flow related to workflows through their algebraic specification, in a natural way. We illustrate the suitability of T-RECATNets in modelling time-constrained and reconfigurable workflow processes in the particular field of Web services composition and orchestration through the example of Fig. 3. This net depicts a simplified *online computer shopping* workflow. In the graphical representation of the T-RECATNet, the name of a transition is followed by its firing interval. In addition, a cancellation interval associated to an abstract transition t_{abs} is noted $(\tau* : \Delta(t_{abs}))$. For more clarity, both intervals are only represented if they are different from $[0, \infty[$. Also, $IC(p,t)$ (or $DT(p,t)$) is omitted, when $IC(p,t) = DT(p,t)$.

In this workflow example the main company which offers the online shopping service coordinates the execution of the different web services supported by its collaborating partners. Let us note that the initial state of this net is a tree containing only the root process with a token $(code, listCmd)$ in the place *CustomerOrder*. This token represents the waiting order which contains, respectively,

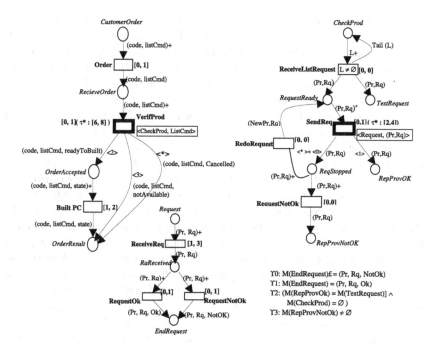

Fig. 3. Time-Constrained Online computer shopping workflow

the order ID number and the list of requested computer components. The workflow process starts by the firing of the transition *"Order"*. Then, the abstract transition *"VerifProd"* invokes the service *Check products* to check the availability of the requested computer components. When the service *Check products* is initialized, the task *"ReceiveListRequest"* looks for the name of the providers offering each requested component (i.e. for each element of the list *L*). This transition produces, at each firing, a couple (Pr, Rq) which corresponds, respectively, to the name of the provider and the associated requested component. Note that $Pr = FindIn(Rq, ListProvider)$ where the function $FindIn$ returns the first provider from the constant list $ListProvider$ associated to the product Rq. Next, the abstract task *"SendRequest"* initialises (at each firing) a new instance of the service *Research in stock providers*. The number of running instances of this invoked service depends on the number of requested products. Each instance (i.e. thread of the tree) represents the local execution of the invoked service in the environment of the associated provider Pr. The termination of one instance is indicated by a token in *EndRequest* (see Υ_0 and Υ_1). Also, each instance launched by the abstract transition *"SendRequest"* is aborted (there is execution of a cut step τ^*), if its completion takes too much time and exceeds the cancellation interval associated to *"SendRequest"*. Depending on the index of this termination ($\langle 0 \rangle$, $\langle 1 \rangle$, or $\langle * \rangle$), the place *RqProvOk* or *RqStopped*, respectively, is marked in the previous recursion level (after execution of the appropriate cut step). In the case a current request is not satisfied (represented by a token in *RqStopped*), it

can be resubmitted near another provider (by execution of the elementary task
"'RedoRequest"') or terminated (by execution of the elementary task "Request-
NotOk"). Note that $NewRq = FindNextIn(Rq, Pr, ListProvider)$ where the
function $FindNextIn$ returns the next provider from $ListProvider$ not already
checked (i.e. different from Pr) and associated to the product Rq. The whole
product verification sub-process launched by the transition "verifProd" terminates, reducing the tree of threads to its root process, (1) if one of the requested
computer components is not available i.e. failure of the commit (Υ_3 reached), (2)
if all the requested computer components are available i.e. success of the commit
(Υ_2 reached) or (3) if there is expiration of the cancellation delay associated to
this process i.e. enforced termination. Then, depending on the index of this ter-
mination ($\langle 2 \rangle$, $\langle 3 \rangle$ or $\langle * \rangle$) the outputs of the abstract transition "VerifProd" are
created in the root process. We can see that such a construction describes, ade-
quately, the flexible structure of the workflow example where multiple instances
of some part of the process can be created dynamically and cancelled e.g. if a
deadline violation is detected. Moreover, the modularity is a natural feature of
T-RECATNets. For instance, in the depicted workflow we can add a sub-process
for checking the credit card of the customer, created with the initialization of
the product verification sub-process. It is sufficient to add such a sub-net and
modify the starting marking of the abstract transition "VerifProd".

In Fig. 4, we present a particular timed trace of our workflow example. The
black node in the depicted tree of threads denotes the thread in which the following step is fired. $(\theta; t)$ denotes a firing step where t (a transition or a cut
step) is fired after θ units of time from the current state. Suppose that the
place $ReceiveOrder$ contains one token $(c01, (L1; L2))$ and the current state is
$s_0 = (Tr_0, \emptyset, Id(v_0.VerifProd) = [0, 1])$. At this state, the transition "Verif-
Prod" can fire immediately but no later than 1 time units. After 1 time units,
we reach the state $s_0 + 1 = (Tr_0, \emptyset, Id(v_0.VerifProd) = [0, 0])$.

At this state, "VerifProd" must be fired immediately (the upper bound of its
firing interval reaches 0). The firing of "VerifProd" leads to the state $s_1 = (Tr_1,$
$\{v_1.\tau*\}, Id(v_1.\tau*) = [6, 8], Id(v_1.ReceiveListRequest) = [0, 0])$. Note that the interval of the cut step $v_1.\tau*$ is set to the cancellation interval of the transition
"VerifProd" which generates the thread v_1. At this state, the transition "ReceiveListRequest" is fired two times in a sequential manner leading to the state
$s_2 = (Tr_2, \{v_1.\tau*\}, Id(v_1.\tau*) = [6, 8], Id(v_1.SendRequest) = [0, 1])$. After 1 time
unit, we reach the state $s_2 + 1 = (Tr_2, \{v_1.\tau*\}, Id(v_1.SendRequest) = [0, 0],$
$Id(v_1.\tau*) = [5, 7])$. At this state, "SendRequest" must be fired leading to the
state $s_3 = (Tr_3, \{v_1.\tau*, v_2.\tau*\}, Id(v_1.\tau*) = [5, 7], Id(v_1.SendRequest) = [0, 1],$
$Id(v_2.ReceiveRq) = [1, 3], Id(v_2.\tau*) = [2, 4])$. The transition "SendRequest" is
again newly enabled in s_3. After a similar firing (i.e. $1; SendRequest$) we reach
a state $s_4 = (Tr_4, \{v_1.\tau*, v_2.\tau*, v_3.\tau*\}, Id(v_1.\tau*) = [4, 6], Id(v_2.\tau*) = [1, 2],$
$Id(v_2.receiveRq) = [0, 2], Id(v_3.\tau*) = [2, 4], Id(v_3.receiveRq) = [1, 3])$. After 1
time unit, the process launched by "SendRequest" may be cancelled or the
transition "receiveRq" may be fired in v_2 (the lower bounds of both $v_2.\tau*$ and
$v_2.receiveRq$ is equal to 0). In case the process is cancelled (i.e. a cut step $\tau*$ is

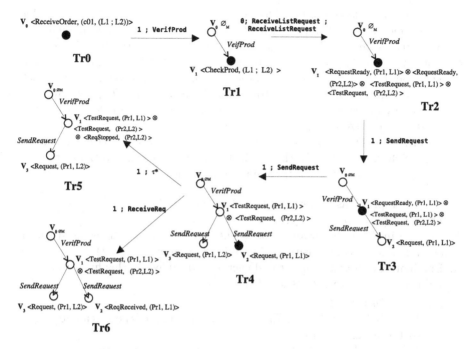

Fig. 4. Some Timed Traces of the workflow example

executed in v_2), we reach the state $s_5 = (Tr_5, \{v_1.\tau*, v_3.\tau*\}, Id(v_1.\tau*) = [3,5]$, $Id(v_3.\tau*) = [1,3]$, $Id(v_3.receiveRq) = [0,2])$.

5   State Class Graph of T-RECATNets

The integration of time in RECATNet increases their modelling power. However due to time density, state spaces are in general infinite. Therefore, the analysis power of techniques based on reachability graphs is greatly reduced. To cope with this, methods based on the state space abstractions have been developed for timed automata and some time extensions of Petri nets as well. Resulting graphs are mainly characterized by their sizes, the condition of their finiteness and the kind of properties they preserve (linear properties (firing sequences), branching properties (execution trees)). The preserved properties are verified by exploring these graphs. Among state space abstractions proposed in the literature, we consider here the *state class graph* (SGC) method [5] for constructing a state space abstraction for T-RECATNets which preserves linear properties. In the state class method, states reachable by the same firing sequence, independently of their firing times, are agglomerated in the same node called state class. In the context of T-RECATNets, a state class is defined as a triplet $c = (Tr, In, F)$ where: Tr is the common extended marking of the states agglomerated in the class, In is the set of cut steps $v.\tau*$ associated to running threads in Tr and F is a formula which characterizes the union of all firing and cancellation domains of these states. Each element $v.t$ enabled in Tr and each element of In is a variable with the same name in F representing its firing delay or cancellation delay.

The initial state class is $c_0 = (Tr_0, \emptyset, F_0)$ where Tr_0 is the initial extended marking and $F_0 = \wedge_{v.t \in En(Tr_0)} \downarrow Is(t) \leq v.t \leq\uparrow Is(t)$. Let $c = (Tr, In, F)$ be a state class and $v.t$ a transition or a cut step t enabled in a thread v of Tr. Such a step $v.t$ can fire from c (i.e. $Next(c, v.t) \neq \emptyset$) iff $v.t \in En(Tr) \cup In$ and can fire before any other enabled transition and cut step, i.e. the following formula is consistent[1]: $F \wedge (\wedge_{v'.t' \in En(Tr) \cup In} v.t \leq v'.t')$.

The firing condition means that there is, at least, a state within the state class in which $v.t$ may fire. In this case, the firing of $v.t$ leads to the state class $c' = (Tr', In', F') = Next(c, v.t)$ computed in 6 steps:

1. Tr' is computed as in untimed RECATNets (i.e. $Tr \xrightarrow{v.t} Tr'$).
2. $F' = F \wedge (\wedge_{v'.t' \in En(Tr) \cup In} v.t \leq v'.t')$
3. Replace in F' each variable $v'.t' \neq v.t$, by $(v'.t' + v.t)$. This substitution actualises delays of transitions (i.e. $old\ v'.t' = new\ v'.t' + v.t$).
4. Eliminate by substitution $v.t$ and each $v'.t'$ disabled by this firing.
5. In' is computed from In, such that:
    (a) $In' = In$ if $t \in T_{elt}$,
    (b) $In' = In \cup \{v'.\tau*\}$ if $t \in T_{abs}$ (v' is the identifier of the thread generated by the firing of t in v),
    (c) $In' = In \setminus \{v''.\tau * \mid v'' \in Succ(v)\}$ if $t \in \{\tau_i \mid i \in I \vee i = *\}$,
6. Add constraint $\downarrow Is(v'.t') \leq v'.t' \leq \uparrow Is(v'.t')$, for each transition $v'.t' \in New(Tr', v.t)$ and the constraint $\downarrow \Delta(t) \leq v'.\tau* \leq \uparrow \Delta(t)$, if $t \in T_{abs}$ and $v'.\tau* \in In'$ and $v'.\tau* \notin In$.

State classes are computed using the implementation of the above firing rule given in [7] and its optimization established in [8]. Formally, the SCG of the model is the structure $(C, c_0, \rightarrow)$, where:

1. $c_0 = (Tr_0, \emptyset, F_0)$ is the initial state class of the model,
2. $\rightarrow$ is the transition relation defined by:
    (a) $\exists v.t,\ c,\ c',\ c \xrightarrow{v.t} c'$ iff $Next(c, v.t) \neq \emptyset \wedge c' = Next(c, v.t)$,
    (b) $C = \left\{c \mid c_0 \xrightarrow{*} c\right\}$, where $\xrightarrow{*}$ is the reflexive and transitive closure of $\rightarrow$, is the set of reachable state classes of the model.

The finiteness property of the SCG of time Petri nets (Merlin's model) is known to be undecidable [5]. However, the finiteness of the SCG of time Petri nets is ensured if the underlying Petri net is finite. This property is also undecidable for T-RECATNets since this class of Petri nets includes time Petri nets. We can show in the same manner as for time Petri nets that the number of state classes sharing the same marking is finite [5]. Therefore, the SCG of T-RECATNet is finite if the underlying RECATNet is finite. We are currently working on

---

[1] A formula F is consistent iff there is, at least, one tuple of values that satisfies, at once, all constraints of F.

sufficient conditions for the underlying RECATNet to be finite. The finiteness problem of RECATNets can be reduced to the finiteness problem of recursive Petri Nets that is known to be decidable [13].

In a previous work [4], we have expressed the semantics of the untimed RE-CATNets in terms of rewriting logic [10], where each RECATNet is defined as a rewrite theory. We extend this rewriting semantics to the SCG of T-RECATNets. Each T-RECATNet is defined as a conditinal rewrite theory where transitions firing and cut steps execution are expressed by conditional rewrite rules as follows. The distributed structure of a SCG is specified by an equational specification. Each class is described by a term $[Tr \mid In \mid Mat]$ where Tr is a term expressing the tree of threads, In is the list of cut steps $v.\tau*$ related to launched threads in Tr and Mat is a multiset of elements describing the time constraints on each enabled transition and cut step in Tr. A thread (node) Th of the tree Tr is described by a term $[S, M_{Th}, t_{abs}, ChildThreads]$, where: S is the thread identifier, M_{Th} represents the internal marking of the thread Th, t_{abs} is the name of the abstract whose firing gave birth to the thread Th and $ChildThreads$ is the multiset of threads generated by this thread Th in the current tree Tr. Moreover, we add two rewrite rules included in each T-RECATNet's rewrite theory for determining the earliest transition or cut step $v.t$ to fire (temporal firing condition) and to complete the computation (i.e. the elements of Mat) of the next state class generated by the firing $v.t$ as in [7].

Since we give a rewriting semantics to T-RECATNets, we can benefit from the use of the LTL (Linear Time Logic) model-checker of the Maude system [12] for verification purpose. For instance, one can check liveness properties and safety properties on the finite generated state class graph related to (finite) workflow schemas. We have generated the SCG of our workflow example, using the version 2.3 of the Maude system under Linux with, as an initial marking, a token $(c01, L1)$ in the source place of the root process. We obtain 35 state classes. In the following, we show the use of the Maude system in checking proper termination of our workflow example. By using the command "search" of Maude, one can explore the reachable state space in different ways. In our example, we can check if starting from the workflow initial marking, it is always possible to reach the workflow final marking (one token in the place $OrderResult$ of the root process which has no child threads). From the obtained result of Fig. 5, we can see that the expected final states (three configurations are possible) can be reached and all correspond to proper termination.

We apply the Maude model-checker to prove the following property ($prop1$) related to our (finite) workflow example (see Fig. 6).

Prop 1 : A verification process (launched by the firing of the abstract transition "*VerifProd*") terminates only if a requested product is not available or if all the requested products are available. This property formulated in LTL terms, [ ] (VerifProcess-Initialised --> <> (product-not-available) or (order-accepted)), is proved to be *not valid*. Indeed, the model-checker returns the expected counterexample, which corresponds to the termination of

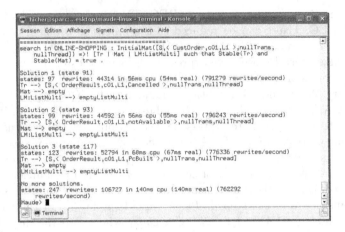

Fig. 5. Proper termination checking of the workflow example under Maude environment

Fig. 6. Verification of workflow properties using Maude LTL Model-Checker

the verification sub-process due to the expiration of the cancellation interval associated to *"VerifProd"*.

6   Related Works

Compared to other classes of high level Petri nets having the ability to model the dynamic creation or suppression of processes like Nested nets [17] and Object Petri nets [19] used for modelling flexible and collaborative workflow systems [15], the T-RECATNets permit advanced descriptions of complex data structures and context conditions checking (i.e. read and inhibitor arcs). Moreover, the hierarchy of created processes in T-RECATNets is unbounded as in Nested nets and RPNs. This is not the case for Object Petri nets objects where the depth of the hierarchy is limited to two levels. Regarding the time extension of T-RECATNets, we choose to associate time intervals to elementary and abstract transitions to describe tasks duration or the availability duration of resources in workflow processes. Indeed the duration of tasks in a workflow cannot be determined before its implementation. The process designers can only estimate the minimum and the maximum duration of each activity at built time.

7   Conclusion

In the present paper, we proposed a time extension to the RECATNets model for the modelling of timed-constrained reconfigurable workflow processes operating on distributed execution environments. This extension is guided by the growing interest in temporal specifications in the workflow management domain. We define their semantics in rewriting logic and show how we can use the Maude Tools in the computation of the state class graph (SCG) for the analysis of the T-RECATNets specifications. Future work will include:

1. Design and verification of inter-organizational workflows exploiting the descriptive power of the T-RECATNets.
2. Evaluation of QoS of workflow tasks using a real time extension of LTL on T-RECATNets [3].

References

1. Van der Aalst, W.M.P., Adams, M., ter Hofstede, A.H.M., Pesic, M., Schonenberg, H.: Flexibility as a Service. BPM Center Report BPM-08-09. BPMcenter.org. (2008)
2. Van der Aalst, W.M.P., Van Hee, K.M.: Workflow Management: Models, Methods, and Systems. MIT Press, Cambridge (2002)
3. Alur, R., Henzinger, T.A.: Real-Time Logics: Complexity and Expressiveness. Inf. Comput. 104, 35–77 (1993)
4. Barkaoui, K., Hicheur, A.: Towards Analysis of Flexible and Collaborative Workflow Using Recursive ECATNets. In: Benatallah, B., ter Hofstede, A., Paik, H. (eds.) BPM Workshops 2007. LNCS, vol. 4928, pp. 206–217. Springer, Heidelberg (2008)
5. Berthomieu, B., Diaz, M.: Modeling and Verification of Time Dependent Systems using Time Petri Nets. IEEE Transactions on Software Engineering 17(3), 259–273 (1991)
6. Bettaz, M., Maouche, M.: How to Specify Non Determinism and True Concurrency with Algebraic Terms Nets. In: Bidoit, M., Choppy, C. (eds.) Abstract Data Types 1991 and COMPASS 1991. LNCS, vol. 655, pp. 164–180. Springer, Heidelberg (1993)
7. Boucheneb, H., Rakkay, H.: A More Efficient Time Petri net State Space Abstraction Preserving Linear Properties. In: Proc. of the seventh International Conference on Application of Concurrency to System Design, pp. 61–70. IEEE Computer Society, Los Alamitos (2007)
8. Boucheneb, H., Barkaoui, K.: Relevant Timed Schedules / Clock Valuation for Constructing Time Petri Net Reachability Graphs. In: Cassez, F., Jard, C. (eds.) FORMATS 2008. LNCS, vol. 5215, pp. 265–279. Springer, Heidelberg (2008)
9. Bowden, F.D.J.: A Brief Survey and Synthesis of the Roles of Time in Petri Nets. In: Mathematical and Computer Modelling, pp. 55–68 (2000)

10. Bruni, R., Meseguer, J.: Semantic foundations for generalized rewrite theories. J. Theor. Comput. Sci. 360(1-3), 386–414 (2006)
11. Casati, F.: A discussion on approaches to handling exceptions in workflows. In: 1998 Conference on Computer-Supported Cooperative Work, Seattle (1998)
12. Clavel, M., Duran, F., Eker, S., Lincoln, P., Marti-Oliet, N., Meseguer, J., Talcott, J.: Maude Manual (Version 2.3). SRI International and University of Illinois at Urbana-Champaign (2007), http://maude.cs.uiuc.edu
13. Haddad, S., Poitrenaud, D.: Recursive Petri nets: Theory and Application to Discrete Event Systems. Acta Informatica 40(7-8), 463–508 (2007)
14. Halliday, J.J., Shrivastava, S.K., Wheater, S.M.: Flexible Workflow Management in the OPENflow System. In: 4th IEEE Int. Enterprise Distributed Object Comp. Conf., pp. 82–92. IEEE Computer Society, Los Alamitos (2001)
15. van Hee, K., Lomazova, I.A., Oanea, O., Serebrenik, A., Sidorova, N., Voorhoeve, M.: Nested Nets for Adaptive Systems. In: Donatelli, S., Thiagarajan, P.S. (eds.) ICATPN 2006. LNCS, vol. 4024, pp. 241–260. Springer, Heidelberg (2006)
16. Sadiq, W., Sadiq, S., Schulz, K.: Model Driven Distribution of Collaborative Business Processes. In: IEEE International Conference on Services Computing, pp. 281–284. IEEE Computer Society, Los Alamitos (2006)
17. Lomazova, I.A.: Modeling Dynamic Objects in Distributed Systems with Nested Petri Nets. J. Fundam. Inform. 51(1-2), 121–133 (2002)
18. Tiplea, F.L., Macovei, G.I.: Timed workflow nets. In: Proc. of IEEE International Symposium on Symbolic and Numeric Algorithms for Scientific Computing, pp. 361–366 (2005)
19. Valk, R.: Object Petri Nets-Using the Nets-within-Nets Paradigm. In: Desel, J., Reisig, W., Rozenberg, G. (eds.) Lectures on Concurrency and Petri Nets. LNCS, vol. 3098, pp. 819–848. Springer, Heidelberg (2004)

Contract Compliance and Choreography Conformance in the Presence of Message Queues*

Mario Bravetti and Gianluigi Zavattaro

Department of Computer Science, University of Bologna, Italy

Abstract. Choreography conformance and contract compliance have been widely studied in the context of synchronous communication. In this paper we approach a more realistic scenario in which the messages containing the invocations are queued in the called service. More precisely, we study the foundational aspects of contract compliance in a language independent way by just taking contracts to be finite labeled transition systems. Then, we relate the proposed theory of contract compliance with choreography specifications à la WS-CDL where activities are interpreted as pairs of send and receive events. An interesting consequence of adopting a language independent representation of contracts is that choreography projection can be defined in structured operational semantics.

1 Introduction

In the context of Service Oriented Computing (SOC) the problem of the specification of service composition is addressed using two main approaches: service *orchestration* and service *choreography*. According to the first approach, the activities of the composed services are coordinated by a specific component, called the orchestrator, that is responsible for invoking the composed services and collect their responses. Several languages have been already proposed for programming orchestrators such as WS-BPEL [OAS]. As far as choreography languages are concerned, the two main representatives are WS-CDL [W3C] and BPEL4Chor [DKL⁺07]. Differently from orchestration languages, choreography languages admit the direct interaction among the combined services without the mediation of the orchestrator. In WS-CDL, the basic activity is the interaction between a sender and a receiver, while according to the BPEL4Chor approach a choreography is obtained as the parallel composition of processes that independently execute send and receive activities.

Given an orchestrator (resp. a choreography), one of the main challenges for the SOC community is the definition of appropriate mechanisms for the (semi)automatic retrieval of services that, once combined with the orchestrator (resp. once reciprocally combined), are guaranteed to implement a correct service composition. The currently investigated approach for solving this

---

* Research partially funded by EU Integrated Project Sensoria, contract n. 016004.

R. Bruni and K. Wolf (Eds.): WS-FM 2008, LNCS 5387, pp. 37–54, 2009.

problem is to associate to each available service a behavioral description that describes the externally observable message-passing behavior of the service itself. In the literature, this description is known with the name of *behavioral signature* [RR02], *contract* [FHR+04], or (in the specific SOC area) *service contract* [CCL+06, BZ07a, LP07, CGP08]. Assuming that services expose their contract, the above problem can be rephrased as follows: given an orchestrator (resp. a choreography) and a set of service contracts, check whether the services exposing the given contracts can be safely combined with the orchestrator (resp. safely reciprocally combined). The proposed theories of contracts solve this problem formalizing the following notions: *contract compliance* (if a set of contracts is compliant then the corresponding services can be safely combined), *contract refinement* (if a service exposes a refinement of the contract of another service then the former is a safe substitute for the latter), and *choreography conformance* (if the contract of a service is conformant with a given role of a choreography then the service can be used to implement that role in any implementation of the choreography).

In [BZ07b] we have investigated the interplay between the above notions of contract compliance, contract refinement and choreography conformance considering synchronous communication. In this paper we consider a more realistic scenario in which services are endowed with queues used to store the received messages.

More precisely, we revisit our previous theory for contract compliance and choreography conformance [BZ07b] as follows. Contracts are specified in a language independent way by means of finite labeled transition systems. In this way, our new contract theory is more general and foundational as we abstract away from the syntax of contracts and we simply assume that a contract language has an operational semantics defined in terms of a labeled transition system. The presence of queues strongly influences the notion of contract compliance, for instance, the following client and service are now compliant (while this was not the case in [CCL+06, BZ07a, LP07, CGP08]):

$$Client = invoke(a); invoke(b) \qquad Server = receive(b); receive(a)$$

In fact, the presence of queues allows the client to perform the invoke operation in a different order w.r.t. the receive order of the server.

As far as the notion of contract refinement is concerned, the main result is that in the presence of queues refinement can be done independently. That is, given a set of compliant contracts $C_1, \cdots, C_n$, each contract C_i can be replaced by any refinement C_i', and the overall system obtained by composition of $C_1', \cdots, C_n'$ is still compliant. In general, in a synchronous setting, independent refinement is not possible [CCL+06]. As an example, consider the two following service behaviors:

$$\begin{aligned} Printer \quad &= receive(docToPrint) \\ PrinterFax &= receive(docToPrint) + \\ &\quad\ receive(docToFax); invoke(faxReceipt) \end{aligned}$$

where + denotes a choice among alternative operations, and the two following client behaviors:

$$PrintClient \quad = invoke(docToPrint)$$
$$PrintFaxClient = invoke(docToPrint)+$$
$$invoke(docToFax); invoke(faxNum); receive(faxReceipt)$$

$Printer$ and $PrintClient$ can be safely combined. The composition is still correct even if we replace either $Printer$ with $PrinterFax$ or $PrintClient$ with $PrintFaxClient$, but it turns out to be incorrect if we apply both replacements. For this reason we have that in a synchronous context $PrintClient$ is not a valid refinement of $Printer$. On the contrary, we will prove that in the presence of message queues the $PrinterFax$ service is always a valid refinement of the $Printer$ service.

The presence of message queues decouples the send event (corresponding to the introduction of one message in a queue) from the receive event (corresponding to its consumption from the queue). Due to this decoupling, we propose a new interpretation of the semantics of a WS-CDL choreography language in which the two events are modeled by two distinct transitions labeled with a send and a receive label, respectively. Another novelty with respect to previous work is that the choice of representing contracts by means of labeled transition systems allows us to define choreography projections in structured operational semantics. As described below, the use of choreography projection is an important step toward the definition of an appropriate notion of conformance.

Conformance is an important notion to be used to retrieve services that, once combined, correctly implement a given choreography. Formally, (as already done for synchronous communication [BZ07b]) we propose to define conformance as the maximal relation among contracts (ranged over by C), roles (ranged over by r), and choreographies (ranged over by H) written $C \vartriangleleft_r H$ such that, given a choreography H with roles $r_1, \cdots, r_n$ and a set of contracts $C_1, \cdots, C_n$ for which $C_1 \vartriangleleft_{r_1} H, \cdots, C_n \vartriangleleft_{r_n} H$, we have that the composition of $C_1, \cdots, C_n$ is a correct implementation of H. As in our previous work [BZ07b] we show that, unfortunately, there exists no such maximal relation. The proof of this negative result is more complex than in [BZ07b] because, due to the presence of message queues, we had to find out a more subtle counterexample. We partially alleviate this negative result showing that we can define a conformance notion with the above properties as follows: C is conformant to the role r of the choreography H if C is a refinement of the contract obtained by projecting the choreography H to the role r.

Due to space limitations, the proofs of our results are not included in this paper but they can be found in [BZ08].

2 The Theory of Contracts

2.1 Contracts

Contracts are defined as labeled transition systems over located action names, representing operations at a certain location over the network.

Definition 1. *A finite connected labeled transition system (LTS) with termi-nation states is a tuple $T = (S, T, L, \longrightarrow, s_0)$ where S is a finite set of states, $T \subseteq S$ is a set of states representing successful termination, L is a set of labels, the transition relation $\longrightarrow$ is a finite subset of $S \times L \times S$, $s_0 \in S$ and it holds that every state in S is reachable (according to $\longrightarrow$ from s_0).*

Note that non-termination states may have no outgoing transitions: in this case they represent internal failures or deadlocks.

We assume a denumerable set of action names $\mathcal{N}$, ranged over by $a, b, c, \ldots$ and a denumerable set Loc of location names, ranged over by $l, l', l_1, \cdots$. The set $\mathcal{N}_{loc} = \{a_l \mid a \in \mathcal{N}, l \in Loc\}$ is the set of located action names. We use $\tau \notin \mathcal{N}$ to denote an internal (unsynchronizable) computation.

Definition 2. *A contract is a finite connected LTS with termination states $(S, T, L, \longrightarrow, S_0)$, where $L = \{a, \overline{a}_l, \tau \mid a \in \mathcal{N}, l \in Loc\}$, i.e. labels are either a receive (input) on some operation $a \in N$ or an invoke (output) directed to some operation $a \in N$ at some location l.*

In the following we introduce a process algebraic representation for contracts by using a basic process algebra with prefixes over $\{a, \overline{a}_l, \tau \mid a \in \mathcal{N}, l \in Loc\}$ and we show that from the LTS denoting a contract we can derive a process algebraic term whose behavior is the same as that of the LTS. The process algebra is a simple extension of basic CCS [Mil89] with successful termination denoted by "**1**": this new term is necessary in order to have two kinds of states without outgoing transitions, those that are successfully terminating (that we denote with the process "**1**") and those that are not (denoted with the traditional null process "**0**").

Definition 3 (Contracts). *We consider a denumerable set of contract vari-ables Var ranged over by X, Y, $\cdots$. The syntax of contracts is defined by the following grammar*

$$C ::= \mathbf{0} \mid \mathbf{1} \mid \alpha.C \mid C + C \mid X \mid recX.C$$
$$\alpha ::= \tau \mid a \mid \overline{a}_l$$

where $recX._{-}$ is a binder for the process variable X denoting recursive definition of processes. The set of the contracts C in which all process variables are bound, i.e. C is a closed term, is denoted by $\mathcal{P}_{con}$.

Besides the already commented recursion operator, we consider the standard prefix $\alpha._{-}$ (with possible prefixes τ, a, and $\overline{a}_l$ denoting internal, input, and output action, respectively) and choice $_{-} + _{-}$ operators. In the following we will omit trailing "**1**" when writing contracts.

The structured operational semantics of contracts is defined in terms of a transition system labeled over $L = \{a, \overline{a}_l, \tau, \mid a \in \mathcal{N}, l \in Loc\}$ and a termination predicate $\sqrt{}$ over states obtained by the rules in Table 1 (plus symmetric rule for choice).

Table 1. Semantic rules for contracts (symmetric rules omitted)

$$\mathbf{1}\surd \qquad\qquad \alpha.C \xrightarrow{\alpha} C$$

$$\frac{C \xrightarrow{\alpha} C'}{C+D \xrightarrow{\alpha} C'} \qquad\qquad \frac{C\surd}{C+D\surd}$$

$$\frac{C\{recX.C/X\} \xrightarrow{\alpha} C'}{recX.C \xrightarrow{\alpha} C'} \qquad\qquad \frac{C\{recX.C/X\}\surd}{recX.C\surd}$$

Note that we use the notation $C\{recX.C/X\}$ to denote syntactic replacement of free occurrences of variable X in C with the same contract C (where, as usual, α-conversion is applied to avoid the possible captures of variable names). The rules for the operational semantics are standard; we simply comment the actual meaning of the termination predicate $\surd$. Informally, a contract C satisfies the predicate if it is the successfully terminating terms $\mathbf{1}$ or it is a more complex term in which there is at least one $\mathbf{1}$ that does not occur inside a prefixed term $\alpha.C$.

We have that the semantics of a contract $C \in \mathcal{P}_{con}$ gives rise to a finite connected LTS with termination states $(S, T, L, \longrightarrow, C)$ where $L = \{a, \overline{a}_l, \tau, \mid a \in \mathcal{N}, l \in Loc\}$ and: S is the set of states reachable from C, T is the subset of S of the states for which the predicate $\surd$ is true and $\longrightarrow$ includes only transitions between states of S. Note that the fact that such a LTS is finite (i.e. finite-state and finitely branching) is a well-known fact for basic CCS [Mil89] (and obviously the additional presence of successful termination does not change this fact).

Definition 4. *A set of process algebraic equations is denoted by $\theta = \{X_i = C_i \mid 0 \leq i \leq n-1\}$, where n is the number of equation in the set, X_i are process variables, and C_i are contract terms (possibly including free process variables). The process algebraic equations θ is closed if only process variables X_i, with $0 \leq i \leq n-1$, occur free in the bodies C_j, with $0 \leq j \leq n-1$, of the equations in the set.*

Definition 5. *Let $\mathcal{T} = (S, T, L, \longrightarrow, S_0)$ be a contract. A contract term $C \in \mathcal{P}_{con}$ is obtained from $\mathcal{T}$ as follows.*

- *Supposed $S = \{s_0, \ldots, s_{n-1}\}$ (i.e. any given numbering on the states S), we first obtain from $\mathcal{T}$ a finite closed set of equations $\theta = \{X_i = C_i \mid 0 \leq i \leq n-1\}$ as follows. Denoted by m_i the number of transitions outgoing from s_i, by α_j^i the label of the $j-th$ transition outgoing from s_i (for any given numbering on the transitions outgoing from s_i), with $j \leq m_i$, and by $s_{succ_j^i}$ its target state, we take $C_i = \sum_{j \leq m_i} \alpha_j^i.X_{succ_j^i} + \{\mathbf{1}\}$, where $\mathbf{1}$ is present only if $s_i \in T$ and an empty sum is assumed to yield $\mathbf{0}$.*
- *We then obtain, from the closed set of equations $\theta = \{X_i = C_i \mid 0 \leq i \leq n-1\}$, a closed contract term C by induction on the number of equations. The base case is $n = 1$: in this case we have that C is $recX_0.C_0$. In the inductive*

case we have that C is inductively defined as the term obtained from the equation set $\{X_i = C_i' \mid 0 \leq i \leq n - 2\}$, where $C_i' = C_i\{recX_{n-1}.C_{n-1}/X_{n-1}\}$.

Definition 6. *A homomorphism from a finite connected LTS with termination states $\mathcal{T} = (S, T, L, \longrightarrow, s_0)$ to a finite connected LTS with termination states $\mathcal{T}' = (S', T', L, \longrightarrow', s_0')$ is a function f from S to S' such that: $f(s_0) = s_0'$ and for all $s \in S$ we have $\{(l, s') \mid f(s) \xrightarrow{l}' s'\} = \{(l, f(s')) \mid s \xrightarrow{l} s'\}$, i.e. the set of transitions performable by $f(s)$ is the same as the set of transitions performable by s when f-images of the target states are considered, and $s \in T$ if and only if $f(s) \in T'$.*

Note that, if f is a homomorphism between finite connected LTSes with finite states then f is surjective: this because all states reachable by $f(s_0)$ must be f-images of states reachable from s_0.

Proposition 1. *Let $\mathcal{T} = (S, T, L, \longrightarrow, s_0)$ be a contract and $C \in \mathcal{P}_{con}$ be a contract term obtained from $\mathcal{T}$. There exists a (surjective) homomorphism from the semantics of C to $\mathcal{T}$ itself.*

2.2   Composing Contracts

Definition 7 (Systems). *The syntax of systems (compositions of contracts) is defined by the following grammar*

$$P ::= [C, \mathcal{Q}]_l \mid P\|P \mid P\backslash L$$
$$\mathcal{Q} ::= \epsilon \mid a^l :: \mathcal{Q}$$

where $L \subseteq \mathcal{N}_{loc}$.

The restriction operator $\_\backslash L$ is a binder for the names in located actions. Formally, if a_l is in L, then L binds a in any action a occurring in the contract located at l and in any action $\bar{a}_l$. The terms in the syntactic category $\mathcal{Q}$ denote message queues. They are lists of messages, each one denoted with a^l where a is the action name and l is the location of the sender. We use ϵ to denote the empty message queue. Trailing ϵ are usually left implicit, and we use :: also as an operator over the syntax: if $\mathcal{Q}$ and $\mathcal{Q}'$ are ϵ-terminated queues, according to the syntax above, then $\mathcal{Q} :: \mathcal{Q}'$ means appending the two queues into a single ϵ-terminated list. Therefore, if $\mathcal{Q}$ is a queue, then $\epsilon :: \mathcal{Q}$, $\mathcal{Q} :: \epsilon$, and $\mathcal{Q}$ are syntactically equal.

A system P is well-formed if: (i) every contract subterm $[C, \mathcal{Q}]_l$ occurs in P at a different location l and (ii) no output action with destination l is syntactically included inside a contract subterm occurring in P at the same location l, i.e. actions $\bar{a}_l$ cannot occur inside a subterm $[C, \mathcal{Q}]_l$ of P. The set of all well-formed systems P is denoted by $\mathcal{P}$. In the following we will just consider well-formed systems and, for simplicity, we will call them just systems. Moreover, we will use the shorthand $[C]_l$ to stand for $[C, \epsilon]_l$.

Given a system P, we use $loc(P)$ to denote the subset of Loc of the locations of contracts syntactically occurring inside P: e.g. $loc([C]_{l_1}\|[C']_{l_2}) = \{l_1, l_2\}$.

Also the operational semantics of systems is defined in terms of a labeled transition system. The labels, denoted with $\lambda, \lambda', \cdots$, are taken from the set $\{a_{rs}, \overline{a}_{rs}, a^+_{r \to s}, a^-_{r \to s}, \tau \mid a \in \mathcal{N}; r, s \in Loc\}$, where: a_{rs} denotes a potential input by a queue where the sender is at location r and the receiver queue is at location s, $\overline{a}_{rs}$ denotes a potential output where the sender is at location r and the receiver queue is at location s, $a^+_{r \to s}$ denotes an insertion in the queue (that actually took place) where the sender is at location r and the receiver queue is at location s, $a^-_{r \to s}$ denotes an extraction from the queue (that actually took place) where the sender (that originally sent the message) is at location r and the receiver queue is at location s, and τ denotes a move performed internally by one contract in the system. We use α−renaming of names bound by the restriction operator $\_\backslash L$; namely, we write $P \equiv_a Q$ if P is α-convertible into Q (or vice-versa), i.e. if Q can be obtained from P by turning subterms $P'\backslash L$ of P into subterms $Q'\backslash L'$ by renaming of located names a_l of L into located names $ren(a)_l$ (yielding L' with the same cardinality) and by correspondingly replacing: (i) each input-related syntactical occurrence of a with $ren(a)$ inside the unique subterm $[C, Q]_l$ of P', if it exists (more precisely occurrences of $a^{l'}$ inside Q are renamed into $ren(a)^{l'}$, independently of the location l', and a input prefixes inside C are renamed into $ren(a)$ input prefixes), and (ii) each syntactical occurrence of $\overline{a}_l$ inside P' with $ren(a)_l$ (obviously a renaming is only allowed if it does not generate a name that is already present as a free name in association with the same location).

The rules in the Table 2 (plus symmetric rules) define the transition system and the termination predicate ($\sqrt{}$) for systems. In Table 2 we assume that $a^l \in Q$ holds true if and only if a^l syntactically occurs inside Q.

Table 2. Semantic rules for contract compositions (symmetric rules omitted)

$$[C, Q]_s \xrightarrow{a_{rs}} [C, Q :: a^r]_s \qquad \dfrac{C \xrightarrow{\overline{a}_s} C'}{[C, Q]_r \xrightarrow{\overline{a}_{rs}} [C', Q]_r} \qquad \dfrac{P \xrightarrow{a_{rs}} P' \quad Q \xrightarrow{\overline{a}_{rs}} Q'}{P \| Q \xrightarrow{a^+_{r \to s}} P' \| Q'}$$

$$\dfrac{C \xrightarrow{\tau} C'}{[C, Q]_l \xrightarrow{\tau} [C', Q]_l} \qquad \dfrac{C \sqrt{}}{[C, \epsilon]_l \sqrt{}} \qquad \dfrac{P \xrightarrow{\lambda} P'}{P \| Q \xrightarrow{\lambda} P' \| Q} \qquad \dfrac{P \sqrt{} \quad Q \sqrt{}}{P \| Q \sqrt{}}$$

$$\dfrac{P \xrightarrow{\lambda} P' \quad \text{if } \lambda = a_{rs}, \overline{a}_{rs} \text{ then } a_s \notin L}{P \backslash L \xrightarrow{\lambda} P' \backslash L} \qquad \dfrac{P \sqrt{}}{P \backslash L \sqrt{}}$$

$$\dfrac{P \equiv_\alpha P' \quad P' \xrightarrow{\lambda} Q}{P \xrightarrow{\lambda} Q} \qquad \dfrac{C \xrightarrow{a} C' \quad \text{if } b^l \in Q \text{ then } b \neq a}{[C, Q :: a^r :: Q']_s \xrightarrow{a^-_{r \to s}} [C', Q :: Q']_s}$$

We will also use the following notations: $P \xrightarrow{\lambda}$ to mean that there exists P' such that $P \xrightarrow{\lambda} P'$ and, given a sequence of labels $w = \lambda_1 \lambda_2 \cdots \lambda_{n-1} \lambda_n$ (possibly empty, i.e., $w = \varepsilon$), we use $P \xrightarrow{w} P'$ to denote the sequence of transitions

$P \xrightarrow{\lambda_1} P_1 \xrightarrow{\lambda_2} \cdots \xrightarrow{\lambda_{n-1}} P_{n-1} \xrightarrow{\lambda_n} P'$ (in case of $w = \varepsilon$ we have $P' = P$, i.e., $P \xrightarrow{\varepsilon} P$). In the following we will adopt the usual notation A^* to denote (possibly empty) sequences over labels in A.

We now define the notion of correct composition of contracts. This notion is the same as in [BZ07a]. Intuitively, a system composed of contracts is correct if all possible computations may guarantee completion; this means that the system is both deadlock and livelock free (there could be an infinite computation, but given any possible prefix of this infinite computation, it can be extended to reach a successfully completed computation).

Definition 8 (Correct contract composition). *A system P is a correct contract composition, denoted $P \downarrow$, if for every P' such that $P \xrightarrow{\;w\;} P'$, with $w \in \{a^+_{r \to s}, a^-_{r \to s}, \tau \mid a \in \mathcal{N}; r, s \in Loc\}^*$, there exists P'' such that $P' \xrightarrow{\;w'\;} P''$, with $w' \in \{a^+_{r \to s}, a^-_{r \to s}, \tau \mid a \in \mathcal{N}; r, s \in Loc\}^*$, and $P'' \sqrt{}$.*

It is interesting to observe that in a correct contract composition, when all contracts successfully terminate, it is ensured that all the sent messages have been actually received. In fact, by definition of the termination predicate $\sqrt{}$ for contract compositions, a system is terminated only if all message queues are empty. Note also that, obviously, contracts that form correct contract compositions still form correct contract compositions if they are replaced by homomorphic ones.

We complete this subsection presenting a simple example of correct contract composition

$$[\overline{a}_{l_3}]_{l_1} \parallel [\overline{b}_{l_3}]_{l_2} \parallel [a.b]_{l_3}$$

composed by three contracts, the first one and the second one that send respectively the message a and b to the third one, and this last contract that consumes the two messages.

2.3   Independent Subcontracts

We are now ready to define the notion of subcontract pre-order. Given a contract $C \in \mathcal{P}_{con}$, we use $oloc(C)$ to denote the subset of Loc of the locations of the destinations of all the output actions occurring inside C.

With $P \xrightarrow{\tau^*} P'$ we denote the existence of a (possibly empty) sequence of τ-labeled transitions starting from the system P and leading to P'. Given the sequence of labels $w = \lambda_1 \cdots \lambda_n$, we write $P \xRightarrow{\;w\;} P'$ if there exist $P_1, \cdots, P_m$ such that $P \xrightarrow{\tau^*} P_1 \xrightarrow{\lambda_1} P_2 \xrightarrow{\tau^*} \cdots \xrightarrow{\tau^*} P_{m-1} \xrightarrow{\lambda_n} P_m \xrightarrow{\tau^*} P'$.

Definition 9 (Independent subcontract pre-order). *A pre-order $\leq$ over $\mathcal{P}_{con}$ is an independent subcontract pre-order if, for any $n \geq 1$, contracts $C_1, \ldots, C_n \in \mathcal{P}_{con}$ and $C'_1, \ldots, C'_n \in \mathcal{P}_{con}$ such that $\forall i. C'_i \leq C_i$, and distinguished location names $l_1, \ldots, l_n \in Loc$ such that $\forall i. oloc(C_i) \cup oloc(C'_i) \subseteq \{l_j \mid 1 \leq j \leq n \wedge j \neq i\}$, we have $([C_1]_{l_1} \parallel \ldots \parallel [C_n]_{l_n}) \downarrow$ implies*

- $([C_1']_{l_1} \parallel \ldots \parallel [C_n']_{l_n}) \downarrow$ and
- $\forall w \in \{a_{r \to s}^+, a_{r \to s}^- \mid a \in \mathcal{N}; r, s \in Loc\}^*.$
  $$\exists P' : ([C_1']_{l_1} \parallel \ldots \parallel [C_n']_{l_n}) \overset{w}{\Longrightarrow} P' \wedge P'\sqrt{} \quad \Rightarrow$$
  $$\exists P'' : ([C_1]_{l_1} \parallel \ldots \parallel [C_n]_{l_n}) \overset{w}{\Longrightarrow} P'' \wedge P''\sqrt{}.$$

We will prove that there exists a maximal independent subcontract pre-order; this is a direct consequence of the queue based communication. In fact, if we simply consider synchronous communication it is easy to prove that there exists no maximal independent subcontract pre-order (see [BZ07a]).

We will show that the maximal independent subcontract pre-order can be achieved defining a more coarse form of refinement in which, given any system composed of a set of contracts, refinement is applied to one contract only (thus leaving the other unchanged). We call this form of refinement *singular subcontract pre-order*. Intuitively a pre-order $\leq$ over $\mathcal{P}_{con}$ is a singular subcontract pre-order whenever the correctness of systems is preserved by refining just one of the contracts. More precisely, for any $n \geq 1$, contracts $C_1, \ldots, C_n \in \mathcal{P}_{con}$, $1 \leq i \leq n, C_i' \in \mathcal{P}_{con}$ such that $C_i' \leq C_i$, and distinguished location names $l_1, \ldots, l_n \in Loc$ such that $\forall k \neq i . l_k \notin oloc(C_k)$ and $l_i \notin oloc(C_i) \cup oloc(C_i')$, we require that $([C_1]_{l_1} \parallel \ldots \parallel [C_i]_{l_i} \parallel \ldots \parallel [C_n]_{l_n}) \downarrow$ implies that the statement in Def. 9 holds for $([C_1]_{l_1} \parallel \ldots \parallel [C_i']_{l_i} \parallel \ldots \parallel [C_n]_{l_n})$. By exploiting commutativity and associativity of parallel composition we can group the contracts which are not being refined and get the following cleaner definition. We let $\mathcal{P}_{conpar}$ denote the set of systems of the form $[C_1]_{l_1} \parallel \ldots \parallel [C_n]_{l_n}$, with $C_i \in \mathcal{P}_{con}$, for all $i \in \{1, \ldots, n\}$.

Definition 10 (Singular subcontract pre-order). *A pre-order $\leq$ over $\mathcal{P}_{con}$ is a singular subcontract pre-order if, for any $C, C' \in \mathcal{P}_{con}$ such that $C' \leq C$, $l \in Loc$ and $P \in \mathcal{P}_{conpar}$ such that $l \notin loc(P)$ and $oloc(C) \cup oloc(C') \subseteq loc(P)$, we have $([C]_l \| P) \downarrow$ implies*

- $([C']_l \| P) \downarrow$ and
- $\forall w \in \{a_{r \to s}^+, a_{r \to s}^- \mid a \in \mathcal{N}; r, s \in Loc\}^*.$
  $$\exists P' : ([C']_l \| P) \overset{w}{\Longrightarrow} P' \wedge P'\sqrt{} \quad \Rightarrow \quad \exists P'' : ([C]_l \| P) \overset{w}{\Longrightarrow} P'' \wedge P''\sqrt{}.$$

The following proposition, which shows that extending possible contexts with an external restriction does not change the notion of singular subcontract pre-order, will be used in the following Sect. 2.4. It plays a fundamental role in eliminating the source of infinite branching in the interaction behavior of the contract composition originated by α-renaming of restriction. We let $\mathcal{P}_{conpres}$ denote the set of systems of the form $([C_1]_{l_1} \parallel \ldots \parallel [C_n]_{l_n}) \backslash L$, with $C_i \in \mathcal{P}_{con}$ for all $i \in \{1, \ldots, n\}$ and $L \subseteq \mathcal{N}_{loc}$.

Proposition 2. *Let $\leq$ be a singular subcontract pre-order. For any $C, C' \in \mathcal{P}_{con}$ such that $C' \leq C$, $l \in Loc$ and $P \in \mathcal{P}_{conpres}$ such that $l \notin loc(P)$ and $oloc(C) \cup oloc(C') \subseteq loc(P)$, we have $([C]_l \| P) \downarrow$ implies*

- $([C']_l \| P) \downarrow$ and
- $\forall w \in \{a_{r \to s}^+, a_{r \to s}^- \mid a \in \mathcal{N}; r, s \in Loc\}^*$.
$$\exists P' : ([C']_l \| P) \xrightarrow{w} P' \wedge P' \sqrt{} \quad \Rightarrow \quad \exists P'' : ([C]_l \| P) \xrightarrow{w} P'' \wedge P'' \sqrt{}.$$

From the simple structure of their definition we can easily deduce that singular subcontract pre-orders have maximum, i.e. there exists a singular subcontract pre-order includes all the other singular subcontract pre-orders.

Definition 11 (Subcontract relation). *A contract C' is a subcontract of a contract C denoted $C' \preceq C$, if and only if for all $l \in Loc$ and $P \in \mathcal{P}_{conpar}$ such that $l \notin loc(P)$ and $oloc(C) \cup oloc(C') \subseteq loc(P)$, we have that $([C]_l \| P) \downarrow$ implies*

- $([C']_l \| P) \downarrow$ and
- $\forall w \in \{a_{r \to s}^+, a_{r \to s}^- \mid a \in \mathcal{N}; r, s \in Loc\}^*$.
$$\exists P' : ([C']_l \| P) \xrightarrow{w} P' \wedge P' \sqrt{} \quad \Rightarrow \quad \exists P'' : ([C]_l \| P) \xrightarrow{w} P'' \wedge P'' \sqrt{}.$$

It is trivial to verify that the pre-order $\preceq$ is a singular subcontract pre-order and is the maximum of all the singular subcontract pre-orders.

In order to prove the existence of the maximal independent subcontract pre-order, we will prove that every pre-order that is an independent subcontract is also a singular subcontract (Theorem 1), and vice-versa (Theorem 2).

Theorem 1. *If a pre-order $\leq$ is an independent subcontract pre-order then it is also a singular subcontract pre-order.*

Theorem 2. *If a pre-order $\leq$ is a singular subcontract pre-order then it is also an independent subcontract pre-order.*

We can, therefore, conclude that there exists a maximal independent subcontract pre-order and it corresponds to the subcontract relation "$\preceq$".

2.4   Input-Output Knowledge Independence

In the following we will show that allowing the subcontract relation to depend on the knowledge about input and output actions of other initial contracts does not change the relation. As a consequence of this fact we will show that input on new types (operations) can be freely added in refined contracts.

Given a set of located action names $I \subseteq \mathcal{N}_{loc}$, we denote: with $\overline{I} = \{\overline{a}_l \mid a_l \in I\}$ the set of output actions performable on those names and with $I_l = \{a \mid a_l \in I\}$ the set of action names with associated location l.

Definition 12 (Input and Output sets). *Given a contract $C \in \mathcal{P}_{con}$, we define $I(C)$ (resp. $O(C)$) as the subset of $\mathcal{N}$ (resp. $\mathcal{N}_{loc}$) of the potential input (resp. output) actions of C. Formally, we define $I(C)$ as follows ($O(C)$ is defined similarly):*

$$I(\mathbf{0}) = I(\mathbf{1}) = I(X) = \emptyset \qquad I(a.C) = \{a\} \cup I(C)$$
$$I(C + C') = I(C) \cup I(C') \qquad I(\overline{a}_l.C) = I(\tau.C) = (recX.C) = I(C)$$

Given a system $P \in \mathcal{P}_{conpres}$, *we define* $I(P)$ *(resp.* $O(P)$*) as the subset of* $\mathcal{N}_{loc}$ *of the potential input (resp. output) actions of* P. *Formally, we define* $I(P)$ *as follows (*$O(P)$ *is defined similarly):*

$$I([C]_l) = \{a_l \mid a \in I(C)\} \qquad I(P\|P') = I(P) \cup I(P') \qquad I(P\backslash L) = I(P) - L$$

In the following we let $\mathcal{P}_{conpres,I,O}$, with $I, O \subseteq \mathcal{N}_{loc}$, denote the subset of systems of $\mathcal{P}_{conpres}$ such that $I(P) \subseteq I$ and $O(P) \subseteq O$.

Definition 13 (Input-Output subcontract relation). *A contract* C' *is a subcontract of a contract* C *with respect to a set of input located names* $I \subseteq \mathcal{N}_{loc}$ *and output located names* $O \subseteq \mathcal{N}_{loc}$, *denoted* $C' \preceq_{I,O} C$, *if and only if for all* $l \in Loc$ *and* $P \in \mathcal{P}_{conpres,I,O}$ *such that* $l \notin loc(P)$ *and* $oloc(C) \cup oloc(C') \subseteq loc(P)$, *we have* $([C]_l\|P) \downarrow$ *implies*

- $([C']_l\|P) \downarrow$ *and*
- $\forall w \in \{a^+_{r \to s}, a^-_{r \to s} \mid a \in \mathcal{N}; r, s \in Loc\}^*$.
  $$\exists P' : ([C']_l\|P) \overset{w}{\Longrightarrow} P' \wedge P'\surd \quad \Rightarrow \quad \exists P'' : ([C]_l\|P) \overset{w}{\Longrightarrow} P'' \wedge P''\surd.$$

Due to Proposition 2, we have $\preceq = \preceq_{\mathcal{N}_{loc},\mathcal{N}_{loc}}$. The following proposition states an intuitive contravariant property: given $\preceq_{I',O'}$, and the greater sets I and O (i.e. $I' \subseteq I$ and $O' \subseteq O$) we obtain a smaller pre-order $\preceq_{I,O}$ (i.e. $\preceq_{I,O} \subseteq \preceq_{I',O'}$). This follows from the fact that extending the sets of input and output actions means considering a greater set of discriminating contexts.

Proposition 3. *Let* $C, C' \in \mathcal{P}_{con}$ *be two contracts,* $I, I' \subseteq \mathcal{N}_{loc}$ *be two sets of input located names such that* $I' \subseteq I$ *and* $O, O' \subseteq \mathcal{N}_{loc}$ *be two sets of output located names such that* $O' \subseteq O$. *We have:*

$$C' \preceq_{I,O} C \quad \Rightarrow \quad C' \preceq_{I',O'} C$$

The following lemma, that will be used to characterize the subcontract relation, states that a subcontract is still a subcontract even if we modify it so to consider only the inputs and outputs already available in the supercontract.

In the following lemma, and in the remainder of the paper, we use the abuse of notation "$C\backslash M$", with $M \subseteq \mathcal{N}$, to stand for "$C\{0/\alpha.C'|\alpha \in M\}$", that denotes the effect of restricting C with respect to inputs in M.

Lemma 1. *Let* $C, C' \in \mathcal{P}_{con}$ *be contracts and* $I, O \subseteq \mathcal{N}_{loc}$ *be sets of located names. We have that both the following hold*

$$C' \preceq_{I,O} C \quad \Rightarrow \quad C'\backslash(I(C') \doteq I(C)) \preceq_{I,O} C$$
$$C' \preceq_{I,O} C \quad \Rightarrow \quad C'\{\tau.0/\alpha.C'' \mid \alpha \in \overline{O(C') - O(C)}\} \preceq_{I,O} C$$

A fundamental result depending on the queue based communication is reported in the following proposition. It states that if we substitute a contract with one of its subcontract, the latter cannot activate outputs that were not included in the potential outputs of the supercontract (and similarly for the system considered as context).

Proposition 4. *Let $C, C' \in \mathcal{P}_{con}$ be contracts and $I, O \subseteq \mathcal{N}_{loc}$ be sets of located names. Let $l \in Loc$ and $P \in \mathcal{P}_{conpres,I,O}$, $l \notin loc(P)$ and $oloc(C) \cup oloc(C') \subseteq loc(P)$ be such that $([C]_l \| P)\downarrow$. We have that both the following hold:*

If $([C'\{\tau.\mathbf{0}/\alpha.C'' \mid \alpha \in \overline{O(C') - O(C)}\}]_l \| P)\downarrow$ then

$$([C']_l \| P) \xrightarrow{w} ([C'_{der}, \mathcal{Q}]_l \| P_{der}) \wedge w \in \{a^+_{r \to s}, a^-_{r \to s}, \tau \mid a \in \mathcal{N}; r, s \in Loc\}^* \Rightarrow$$
$$\forall a_{l'} \in O(C') - O(C).\, C'_{der} \xcancel{\xrightarrow{\overline{a}_{l'}}}$$

If $([C'\backslash(I(C') - I(C))]_l \| P)\downarrow$ then

$$([C']_l \| P) \xrightarrow{w} ([C'_{der}, \mathcal{Q}]_l \| P_{der}) \wedge w \in \{a^+_{r \to s}, a^-_{r \to s}, \tau \mid a \in \mathcal{N}; r, s \in Loc\}^* \Rightarrow$$
$$\forall a \in I(C') - I(C).\, \forall r \in loc(P).\, P_{der} \xcancel{\xrightarrow{\overline{a}_{rl}}}$$

The following propositions permit to conclude that the set of potential inputs and outputs of the other contracts in the system is an information that does not influence the subcontract relation.

Proposition 5. *Let $C \in \mathcal{P}_{con}$ be contracts, $O \subseteq \mathcal{N}_{loc}$ be a set of located output names and $I, I' \subseteq \mathcal{N}_{loc}$ be two sets of located input names such that $O(C) \subseteq I, I'$. We have that for every contract $C' \in \mathcal{P}_{con}$,*

$$C' \preceq_{I,O} C \quad \Longleftrightarrow \quad C' \preceq_{I',O} C$$

Proposition 6. *Let $C \in \mathcal{P}_{con}$ be contracts, $O, O' \subseteq \mathcal{N}_{loc}$ be two sets of located output names such that for every $l \in Loc$ we have $I(C) \subseteq O_l, O'_l$, and $I \subseteq \mathcal{N}_{loc}$ be a set of located input names. We have that for every contract $C' \in \mathcal{P}_{con}$,*

$$C' \preceq_{I,O} C \quad \Longleftrightarrow \quad C' \preceq_{I,O'} C$$

We finally show that the subcontract relation $\preceq$ allows input on new types (and unreachable outputs on new types) to be added in refined contracts. The result, that uses Lemma 1, is a direct consequence (in the case of inputs) of the fact that $C' \preceq_{\mathcal{N}_{loc}, \bigcup_{l \in Loc} I([C]_l)} C$ if and only if $C' \preceq C$, i.e. it exploits the results above about independence from knowledge of types used by other initial contracts.

Theorem 3. *Let $C, C' \in \mathcal{P}_{con}$ be contracts. Both the following hold*

$$C'\backslash(I(C') - I(C)) \preceq C \qquad \Longleftrightarrow \qquad C' \preceq C$$
$$C'\{\tau.\mathbf{0}/\alpha.C'' \mid \alpha \in \overline{O(C') - O(C)}\} \preceq C \qquad \Longleftrightarrow \qquad C' \preceq C$$

3   Contract-Based Choreography Conformance

We first introduce a choreography language similar to those already presented in [BGG+05, CHY07, BZ07b]. The main novelty is that, as we are considering communication mediated by a message queue, in the operational semantics we distinguish between the send and the receive events.

Definition 14 (Choreographies). *Let* Operations, *ranged over by* $a, b, c, \cdots$ *and* Roles, *ranged over by* $r, s, t, \cdots$, *be two countable sets of operation and role names, respectively. The set of Choreographies, ranged over by* $H, L, \cdots$ *is defined by the following grammar:*

$$H \quad ::= \quad a_{r \to s} \quad | \quad H + H \quad | \quad H; H \quad | \quad H | H \quad | \quad H^*$$

The invocations $a_{r \to s}$ *(where we assume* $r \neq s$*) means that role* r *invokes the operation* a *provided by the role* s. *The other operators are choice* $\_ + \_$, *sequential* $\_; \_$, *parallel* $\_|\_$, *and repetition* $\_^*$.

The operational semantics of choreographies considers three auxiliary terms $a_{r \to s}^-$, **1**, and **0**. The first one is used to model the fact that an asynchronous interaction has been activated but not yet completed. The other two terms are used to model the completion of a choreography, which is relevant in the operational modeling of sequential composition. The formal definition is given in Table 3 where we take η to range over the set of labels $\{a_{r \to s}^+, a_{r \to s}^- \mid a \in$ *Operations*, $r, s \in$ *Roles*$\}$ and the termination predicate $\sqrt{}$. The rules in Table 3 are rather standard for process calculi with sequential composition and without synchronization; in fact, parallel composition simply allows for the interleaving of the actions executed by the operands.

Table 3. Semantic rules for choreographies (symmetric rules omitted)

$$a_{r \to s} \xrightarrow{a_{r \to s}^+} a_{r \to s}^- \qquad a_{r \to s}^- \xrightarrow{a_{r \to s}^-} 1 \qquad 1\sqrt{} \qquad H^*\sqrt{}$$

$$\frac{H \xrightarrow{\eta} H'}{H + L \xrightarrow{\eta} H'} \qquad \frac{H\sqrt{}}{H + L\sqrt{}} \qquad \frac{H \xrightarrow{\eta} H'}{H; L \xrightarrow{\eta} H'; L} \qquad \frac{H\sqrt{} \quad L \xrightarrow{\eta} L'}{H; L \xrightarrow{\eta} L'}$$

$$\frac{H\sqrt{} \quad L\sqrt{}}{H | L\sqrt{}} \qquad \frac{H\sqrt{} \quad L\sqrt{}}{H; L\sqrt{}} \qquad \frac{H \xrightarrow{\eta} H'}{H | L \xrightarrow{\eta} H' | L} \qquad \frac{H \xrightarrow{\eta} H'}{H^* \xrightarrow{\eta} H'; H^*}$$

Choreographies are especially useful to describe the protocols of interactions within a group of collaborating services, nevertheless, even if choreography languages represent a simple and intuitive approach for the description of the message exchange among services, they are not yet very popular in the context of service oriented computing. The main problem to their diffusion is that it is not trivial to relate the high level choreography description with the actual implementation of the specified system realised as composition of services that are usually loosely coupled, independently developed by different companies, and autonomous. More precisely, the difficult task is, given a choreography, to lookup available services that, once combined, are ensured to behave according to the given choreography.

In order to formally investigate this problem, we define a mechanism to extract from a choreography the description of the behavior of a given role. Formally, for each role i, we define a labeled transition system with transitions $\xrightarrow{\eta}_i$ (see the rules in Table 4) and termination predicate $\sqrt{}_i$ representing the behavior of the role i. In the following, given a choreography H and one of its role i, with $sem H_i$ we denote the contract term obtained from the labeled transition system $trans \eta_i$ according to the technique defined in Section 2.

Table 4. Projection on the role i of a choreography (symmetric rules omitted)

$$a_{r \to s} \xrightarrow{\overline{a}_s}_r \mathbf{1} \qquad a_{r \to s} \xrightarrow{a}_s \mathbf{1} \qquad a_{r \to s} \sqrt{}_i \text{ if } i \neq r, s$$

$$\mathbf{1}\sqrt{}_i \qquad H^* \sqrt{}_i$$

$$\frac{H \xrightarrow{\eta}_i H'}{H+L \xrightarrow{\eta}_i H'} \qquad \frac{H\sqrt{}_i}{H+L\sqrt{}_i} \qquad \frac{H \xrightarrow{\eta}_i H'}{H;L \xrightarrow{\eta}_i H';L} \qquad \frac{H\sqrt{}_i \quad L \xrightarrow{\eta}_i L'}{H;L \xrightarrow{\eta}_i L'}$$

$$\frac{H\sqrt{}_i \quad L\sqrt{}_i}{H|L\sqrt{}_i} \qquad \frac{H\sqrt{}_i \quad L\sqrt{}_i}{H;L\sqrt{}_i} \qquad \frac{H \xrightarrow{\eta}_i H'}{H|L \xrightarrow{\eta}_i H'|L} \qquad \frac{H \xrightarrow{\eta}_i H'}{H^* \xrightarrow{\eta}_i H';H^*}$$

In this section we discuss how to exploit the choreography and the contract calculus in order to define a procedure that checks whether a service exposing a specific contract C can play the role r within a given choreography.

First of all we need to uniform the choreography and the contract calculus. From a syntactical viewpoint, we have to map the operation names used for choreographies with the names used for contracts assuming $Operations = \mathcal{N}$. We do the same also for the role names that are mapped into the location names, i.e., $Roles = Loc$. Taken these assumptions, we have that the labels of the operational semantics of the choreography calculus are a subset of the labels of the operational semantics of contract systems, i.e. $a^+_{r \to s}$ and $a^-_{r \to s}$.

We are now ready to formalize the notion of correct implementation of a choreography. Intuitively, a system implements a choreography if it is a correct composition of contracts and all of its conversations (i.e. the possible sequences of message exchanges), are admitted by the choreography.

Definition 15 (Choreography implementation). *Given the choreography H and the system P, we say that P implements H (written $P \propto H$) if*

- *P is a correct contract composition and*
- *given a sequence w of labels of the kind $a^+_{r \to s}$ and $a^-_{r \to s}$, if $P \xRightarrow{w} P'$ and $P'\sqrt{}$ then there exists H' such that $H \xrightarrow{w} H'$ and $H'\sqrt{}$.*

Note that it is not necessary for an implementation to include all possible conversations admitted by a choreography. As an example, consider the choreography $reserve_{client \to server}; (accept_{server \to client} + reject_{server \to client})$. We can think of implementing it with the following system

$$[\overline{reserve}_{server}.(accept + reject)]_{client} \parallel [reserve.\overline{accept}_{client}]_{server}$$

where the server is always ready to accept the client's request.

It is interesting to observe that given a choreography H, the system obtained composing its projections is not ensured to be an implementation of H. For instance, consider the choreography $a_{r\to s}$; $b_{t\to u}$. The system obtained by projection is $[\bar{a}_s]_r \parallel [a]_s \parallel [\bar{b}_u]_t \parallel [b]_u$. Even if this is a correct composition of contracts, it is not an implementation of H because it comprises the conversation $b^+_{t\to u}b^-_{t\to u}a^+_{r\to s}a^-_{r\to s}$ which is not admitted by H.

The problem is not in the definition of the projection, but in the fact that the above choreography cannot be implemented preserving the message exchanges specified by the choreography. In fact, in order to guarantee that the communication between t and u is executed after the communication between r and s, it is necessary to add a further message exchange (for instance between s and r) which is not considered in the choreography. We restrict our interest to well formed choreographies.

Definition 16 (Well formed choreography). *A choreography H, defined on the roles $r_1, \cdots, r_n$, is* well formed *if* $[\,[\![H]\!]_{r_1}\,]_{r_1} \parallel \cdots \parallel [\,[\![H]\!]_{r_n}\,]_{r_n} \varpropto H$

As another example of non well formed choreography we consider $a_{l_1\to l_3}; b_{l_2\to l_3}$ which have the following projection $[\bar{a}_{l_3}]_{l_1} \parallel [\bar{b}_{l_3}]_{l_2} \parallel [a.b]_{l_3}$ corresponding to the system described at the end of the subsection 2.2. Among the possible traces of this system we have $a^+_{l_3}b^+_{l_3}a^-_{l_3}b^-_{l_3}$ which is not a correct trace for the above choreography. This example is of interest because it shows that some interesting contract systems are not specifiable as choreographies. This follows from the fact that we have adopted the same approach of WS-CDL that exploits synchronizations as its basic activity. In order to model at a choreographic level the above contract system, we should separate also in the syntax (and not only in the semantics) the send from the receive actions. For instance, we could consider two distinct basic terms $a^+_{r\to s}$ and $a^-_{r\to s}$ for send and receive actions, respectively, and describe the above system with the choreography $a^+_{l_1\to l_3} \mid b^+_{l_2\to l_3} \mid a^-_{l_1\to l_3}; b^-_{l_2\to l_3}$.

We are now in place for the definition of the relation $C \vartriangleleft_r H$ indicating whether the contract C can play the role r in the choreography H.

Definition 17 (Conformance family). *A relation among contracts, roles, and choreographies denoted with $C \vartriangleleft_r H$ is a* conformance relation *if, given a well formed choreography H with roles $r_1, \cdots, r_n$, we have that $[\![H]\!]_{r_i} \vartriangleleft_{r_i} H$ for $1 \le i \le n$ and if $C_1 \vartriangleleft_{r_1} H, \cdots, C_n \vartriangleleft_{r_n} H$ then $[C_1]_{r_1} \parallel \cdots \parallel [C_n]_{r_n} \varpropto H$*

In the case of synchronous communication we proved in [BZ07a] a negative result about conformance: differently from the subcontract pre-orders defined on contracts in the previous Section, there exists no maximal conformance relation. The counter-example used in that paper to prove this negative results does not work in the presence of message queues, but we have found out the following more subtle counter-example. Consider the choreography $H = a_{r\to s} \mid b_{s\to r}$. We could have two different conformance relations, the first one $\vartriangleleft^1$ including (besides the projections) also $a.\bar{b}_r \vartriangleleft^1_s H$ and the second one $\vartriangleleft^2$ including also $b.\bar{a}_s \vartriangleleft^2_r H$. It is easy to see that it is not possible to have a conformance relation that comprises the union of the two relations $\vartriangleleft^1$ and $\vartriangleleft^2$. In fact, the system $[b.\bar{a}_s]_r \parallel [a.\bar{b}_r]_s$ is not a correct composition because the two contracts are both blocked for a never incoming message.

The remainder of the paper is dedicated to the definition of a mechanism that, exploiting the choreography projection and the notion of contract refinement defined in the previous Section, permits to characterize an interesting conformance relation. This relation is called *consonance*.

Definition 18 (Consonance). *We say that the contract C is consonant with the role r of the well formed choreography H (written $C \bowtie_r H$) if $C \preceq [\![H]\!]_r$ where $\preceq$ is the subcontract relation defined in Section 2.*

Theorem 4. *Given a well formed choreography H, we have that the consonance relation $C \bowtie_r H$ is a conformance relation.*

4 Related Work and Conclusion

We have addressed the problem of the definition of suitable notions of contract refinement and choreography conformance for services that communicate through message queues. We have attacked this problem exploiting the approach that we have already successfully adopted for synchronously communicating services [BZ07b]. However, the new theory of contracts is more general than the theory in our previous paper because we represent contracts in a language independent way. On the one hand, this required to significantly revisit our technical contribution, but on the other hand, our results are now more general as they apply to any contract language (for which an operational semantics is defined in terms of a labeled transition system). This choice also influenced the theory for choreography conformance. Now a choreography projection must produce a labeled transition system instead of a contract specified in a given language. We solve this problem defining the projection in structured operational semantics.

It is worth noting that, differently from our previous work, in this paper we do not present an actual way for deciding compliance, refinement, and conformance. This follows from the fact that the presence of message queues make a contract system possibly infinite. In fact, even if contracts are finite state, a contract could repeatedly emit the same message thus introducing an unbounded amount of messages in a queue. Contract systems can be limited to be finite in (at least) two possible ways, either considering bounded buffers or avoiding cycles in contracts.

In the Introduction we have already commented similar contract theories available in the literature [CCL+06, LP07, CGP08] developed for synchronous communication. Similar ideas were already considered also in [FHR+04] where the notion of *stuck-free* conformance is introduced. The unique contract theories for asynchronous communication that we are aware of are by Rajamani and Rehof [RR02] and by van der Aalst and others [ALM+07]. In [RR02] a conformance relation is defined in a bisimulation-like style introducing an ad-hoc treatment of internal and external choices that are included in the calculus as two distinct operators. We try somehow to be more general, avoiding the introduction of two distinct choice operators and by defining our refinement notion indirectly as the maximal contract substitution relation that preserves system correctness. In [ALM+07] the same approach for formalizing compliance and refinement that we have presented in [BZ07b] has been applied to service systems specified using open Workflow Nets (a special class of Petri nets) that communicate asynchronously. As in our works, they prove that contract refinement can be done independently. Moreover, they present an actual way for checking refinement that work assuming that contracts do not contain cycles. As a future work, we plan to investigate whether their decidability technique can be applied also in our different context in which message queues preserve the order of messages.

We now comment on the testing theories developed for process calculi starting from the seminal work by De Nicola and Hennessy [DH84]. A careful comparison between the testing approach and our contract theory for synchronous communication can be found in [BZ07a] (where we resort to fair testing [RV07], a variant of De Nicola-Hennessy must testing for fair systems, to define an actual procedure to check contract refinement). The same comments apply also to the CSP failure refinement [Hoa85] as it is well known that the must testing pre-order and the CSP failure refinement coincide (at least for finitely branching processes without divergences) [DeN87]. As far as must testing for asynchronous communication is concerned, it has been investigated for asynchronous CCS in [CH98, BDP02]. An interesting law holding in that papers is that an input, immediately followed by the output of the same message, is equivalent to do nothing. This does not hold in our context. In fact, a receiver of a message cannot re-emit the read message because it is not possible for a service to introduce a message in its own message queue.

Finally, we would to report about related work on the study of services communicating via asynchronous mechanisms and their conversations. In particular, in [FuBS05] the authors present a technique to establish satisfaction of a given property on service conversations from the specifications of the involved services and in [FuBS04] the authors study, given a specification of possible conversations, whether there exists or not a set of services realizing them.

Acknowledgements. We thank the anonymous referees for their comments.

References

[ALM⁺07] van der Aalst, W.M.P., Lohmann, N., Massuthe, P., Stahl, C., Wolf, K.: From Public Views to Private Views - Correctness-by-Design for Services. In: Dumas, M., Heckel, R. (eds.) WS-FM 2007. LNCS, vol. 4937, pp. 139–153. Springer, Heidelberg (2008)

[BDP02] Boreale, M., De Nicola, R., Pugliese, R.: Trace and Testing Equivalence on Asynchronous Processes. Information and Computation 172(2), 139–164 (2002)

[BZ07a] Bravetti, M., Zavattaro, G.: Contract based Multi-party Service Composition. In: Arbab, F., Sirjani, M. (eds.) FSEN 2007. LNCS, vol. 4767, pp. 207–222. Springer, Heidelberg (2007)

[BZ07b] Bravetti, M., Zavattaro, G.: Towards a Unifying Theory for Choreography Conformance and Contract Compliance. In: Lumpe, M., Vanderperren, W. (eds.) SC 2007. LNCS, vol. 4829, pp. 34–50. Springer, Heidelberg (2007)

[BZ07c] Bravetti, M., Zavattaro, G.: A Theory for Strong Service Compliance. In: Murphy, A.L., Vitek, J. (eds.) COORDINATION 2007. LNCS, vol. 4467, pp. 96–112. Springer, Heidelberg (2007)

[BZ08]   Bravetti, M., Zavattaro, G.: Contract Compliance and Choreography
             Conformance in the Presence of Message Queues. Technical report,
             http://www.cs.unibo.it/~bravetti/html/techreports.html
[BGG+05]   Busi, N., Gorrieri, R., Guidi, C., Lucchi, R., Zavattaro, G.: Choreography
             and orchestration: A synergic approach for system design. In: Benatal-
             lah, B., Casati, F., Traverso, P. (eds.) ICSOC 2005. LNCS, vol. 3826,
             pp. 228–240. Springer, Heidelberg (2005)
[CHY07]   Carbone, M., Honda, K., Yoshida, N.: Structured Communication-
             Centred Programming for Web Services. In: De Nicola, R. (ed.) ESOP
             2007. LNCS, vol. 4421, pp. 2–17. Springer, Heidelberg (2007)
[CH98]   Castellani, I., Hennessy, M.: Testing Theories for Asynchronous Lan-
             guages. In: Arvind, V., Ramanujam, R. (eds.) FSTTCS 1998. LNCS,
             vol. 1530, pp. 90–101. Springer, Heidelberg (1998)
[CCL+06]   Carpineti, S., Castagna, G., Laneve, C., Padovani, L.: A Formal Account of
             Contracts for Web Services. In: Bravetti, M., Núñez, M., Zavattaro, G. (eds.)
             WS-FM 2006. LNCS, vol. 4184, pp. 148–162. Springer, Heidelberg (2006)
[CGP08]   Castagna, G., Gesbert, N., Padovani, L.: A Theory of Contracts for Web
             Services. In: POPL 2008, pp. 261–272. ACM Press, New York (2008)
[DKL+07]   Decker, G., Kopp, O., Leymann, F., Weske, M.: BPEL4Chor: Extend-
             ing BPEL for Modeling Choreographies. In: IEEE 2007 International
             Conference on Web Services (ICWS), Salt Lake City, Utah, USA. IEEE
             Copmuter Society, Los Alamitos (2007)
[DeN87]   De Nicola, R.: Extensional equivalences for transition systems. Acta In-
             formatica 24(2), 211–237 (1887)
[DH84]   De Nicola, R., Hennessy, M.: Testing Equivalences for Processes. Theo-
             retical Computer Science 34, 83–133 (1984)
[FHR+04]   Fournet, C., Hoare, C.A.R., Rajamani, S.K., Rehof, J.: Stuck-Free Con-
             formance. In: Alur, R., Peled, D.A. (eds.) CAV 2004. LNCS, vol. 3114,
             pp. 242–254. Springer, Heidelberg (2004)
[FuBS05]   Fu, X., Bultan, T., Su, J.: Synchronizability of Conversations among Web
             Services. IEEE Trans. Software Eng. 31(12), 1042–1055 (2005)
[FuBS04]   Fu, X., Bultan, T., Su, J.: Conversation protocols: a formalism for spec-
             ification and verification of reactive electronic services. Theor. Comput.
             Sci. 328(1-2), 19–37 (2004)
[Hoa85]   Hoare, T.: Communicating Sequential Processes. Prentice-Hall, Engle-
             wood Cliffs (1985)
[LP07]   Laneve, C., Padovani, L.: The must preorder revisited - An algebraic theory
             for web services contracts. In: Caires, L., Vasconcelos, V.T. (eds.) CON-
             CUR 2007. LNCS, vol. 4703, pp. 212–225. Springer, Heidelberg (2007)
[Mil89]   Milner, R.: Communication and Concurrency. Prentice-Hall, Englewood
             Cliffs (1989)
[RV07]   Rensink, A., Vogler, W.: Fair testing. Information and Computa-
             tion 205(2), 125–198 (2007)
[OAS]   OASIS. Web Services Business Process Execution Language Version 2.0
[RR02]   Rajamani, S.K., Rehof, J.: Conformance Checking for Models of Asyn-
             chronous Message Passing Software. In: Brinksma, E., Larsen, K.G. (eds.)
             CAV 2002. LNCS, vol. 2404, pp. 166–179. Springer, Heidelberg (2002)
[W3C]   W3C. Web Services Choreography Description Language,
             http://www.w3.org/TR/2004/WD-ws-cdl-10-20041217

Verification of Choreographies During Execution Using the Reactive Event Calculus

Federico Chesani, Paola Mello, Marco Montali, and Paolo Torroni

DEIS - University of Bologna, V.le Risorgimento 2, 40136 Bologna - Italy
{federico.chesani,paola.mello,marco.montali,paolo.torroni}@unibo.it

Abstract. This article presents a run-time verification method of web service behaviour with respect to choreographies. We start from DecSerFlow as a graphical choreography description language. We select a core set of DecSerFlow elements and formalize them using a reactive version of the Event Calculus, based on the computational logic SCIFF framework. Our choice enables us to enrich DecSerFlow and the Event Calculus with quantitative time constraints and to model compensation actions.

1 Introduction

Recent years have seen a wide adoption of the Service-Oriented Architecture (SOA) paradigm, both in the research field as well as in industrial settings, to enable distributed applications within intra- and inter-organizational scenarios. Such applications typically consist of a composition of heterogenous interacting services, each one providing a specific functionality. Complex business processes are realized by properly guiding and constraining service interactions. When collaboration is performed across different organizations, *service choreographies* come into play. A choreography models the interaction from a global viewpoint. As stated by the authors of WS-CDL [1], *"[a choreography] offers a means by which the rules of participation within a collaboration can be clearly defined and agreed to, jointly."*

Recent research has demonstrated a possible use of choreographies before service execution, either to establish an agreement among services [2,3], or to derive skeletons of local models [4,5] to be used for implementing the services. A different issue is to verify that a running service follows a given choreography. This is a task that has to be carried out during execution, when potential mismatches between a service's behavioural interface and its real implementation may lead to unexpected/undesired interactions. Therefore, monitoring and verifying the behaviour of services at execution time is a fundamental requirement.

Choreographies often involve the specification of complex constraints, such as conditions on the reached state or the possibility of violating certain prescriptions, at the expense of some compensating activity. Suitable, expressive formalisms are needed to model such constraints in an accurate way. Candidates could be temporal logic languages, such as linear temporal logic (LTL), branching time temporal logic (CTL) or CTL* [6], which can encode formulae such

R. Bruni and K. Wolf (Eds.): WS-FM 2008, LNCS 5387, pp. 55–72, 2009.
© Springer-Verlag Berlin Heidelberg 2009

as that a condition will eventually be true, or a condition must be true until another one becomes true, etc. However, these logics do not accommodate quantitative time, i.e, they enable reasoning about what happens "next" or "at some point in the future," but not "before 60 time ticks." Extensions to temporal logic languages, such as metric temporal logic [7], have been proposed to accommodate explicit time, but they can be hardly used for runtime verification because of their high computational complexity [8]. The well known "state-explosion" problem for temporal logics is even more critical when considering declarative specification languages such as DecSerFlow [9], where the system itself is specified as a conjunction of LTL formulae.

An alternative to temporal logics is the Event Calculus [10] ($\mathcal{EC}$ for short). Many authors believe the $\mathcal{EC}$ to be well suited for expressing the complex constraints of choreographies, especially because it enables the modeler to specify temporal requirements, in a declarative and easily understandable way. In fact, the $\mathcal{EC}$ has been (and is being) extensively applied in the SOA setting. However, little emphasis has been given so far to the possible adoption of the $\mathcal{EC}$ for performing compliance verification of service interaction during execution. We believe that this is mainly due to the lack of suitable underlying reasoning tools.

In this paper, we propose to adopt a reactive version of Event Calculus ($\mathcal{REC}$[11]) to perform run-time verification of the observed behaviour. $\mathcal{REC}$ is formalized as an axiom theory on top of the $\mathcal{S}$CIFF framework [12], a logic based formalism with a sound and complete proof procedure and an efficient implementation [13]. The literature is rich in languages proposed to specify service choreographies. WS-CDL [1] is one of the most prominent procedural ones. We have chosen to represent choreographies in DecSerFlow [9], a graphical representation language introduced by van der Aalst and Pesic to specify and constrain service flows in a declarative manner. This choice is motivated by the capability of DecSerFlow to capture in a flexible and concise way the "contractual nature" of choreographies. However, our approach based on $\mathcal{REC}$ is general and does not depend on a specific choreography specification language.

Besides providing a mapping from DecSerFlow to $\mathcal{REC}$, in this article we show how the approach can be easily extended (by adding new axioms) to support deadlines modeling and verification, and to reify the violations generated by the proof procedure during verification. This latter feature gives us two main advantages: *(i)* when a violation is detected, the proof does not terminate reporting the error, but continues the verification task; *(ii)* violations can be notied to the user, and even considered as rst-class objects during the modeling phase: hence compensation mechanisms related to the violation can be easily specified.

We show the benefits of our approach by way of a motivating example.

2   Background

In this section we briefly introduce the two components of our run-time verification framework, namely DecSerFlow as a specification language, and $\mathcal{REC}$ as its underlying reasoning mechanism.

2.1 DecSerFlow

DecSerFlow is a graphical language which specifies service flows by adopting a declarative style of modeling. Instead of defining rigid service flows, which may lead–especially with procedural languages like WS-CDL and BPEL–to over-specified and over-constrained models, DecSerFlow focuses on the minimal set of constraints which must be satisfied in order to correctly carry out the interaction. This makes DecSerFlow especially suited for representing the "contractual nature" of service choreographies. A DecSerFlow model is composed by a set of activities, which represent atomic units of work (such as message exchanges), and relations among activities, used to specify constraints on their execution. DecSerFlow provides constructs to define positive and negative constraints, that specify the desired and undesired courses of interaction while leaving undefined other possibilities of interaction that are neither desired nor undesired. Positive and negative constraints make the DecSerFlow approach *open*: services can interact freely unless when in the presence of constraints.

DecSerFlow constraints are grouped into three families (see Table 1, 2 and 3 for a complete description of all the basic constraints):

- *existence constraints*: unary cardinality constraints expressing how many times an activity can/should be executed;
- *relation constraints*: binary constraints which impose the presence of a certain activity when some other activity is performed;
- *negation constraints*: the negative version of relation constraints, used to explicitly forbid the execution of a certain activity when some other activity is performed.

Intuititely, a service composition is compliant with a DecSerFlow choreography if all positive constraints are eventually satisfied, and no activity forbidden by any negation constraint is performed. The DecSerFlow semantics is defined for finite execution traces.

Table 1. DecSerFlow existence constraints. In [9], `choice` used to be called `mutual substitution` and had a slightly different notation.

graphical	description	equivalent to
N..* a	`existence(N,a)`. a must be executed at least N times	basic
0..N+1 a	`absence(N+1,a)`. a cannot be executed more than N times	basic
N a	`exactly(N,a)`. a must be executed exactly N times	`existence(N,a)`$\wedge$ `absence(N+1,a)`
a ⊸ b	`choice(a,b)`. At least one activity among a and b must be executed	`existence(1,a`$\vee$`b)`

Table 2. An overview of DecSerFlow relation constraints

graphical	description	equivalent to
a •—— b	`responded existence(a,b)`. If a is executed, then b must be executed (before or after a)	basic
a •——• b	`coexistence(a,b)`. Either both a and b are executed, or none of them is executed	`resp. existence(a,b)`∧ `resp. existence(b,a)`
a •——▸ b	`response(a,b)`. If a is executed, then b must be executed afterwards	basic
a ——▸ b	`precedence(a,b)`. b can be executed only after a is executed	basic
a •——▸• b	`succession(a,b)`.	`response(a,b)`∧ `precedence(a,b)`
a ◀——▸ b	`alternate response(a,b)`. b is response of a and there has to be a b between two a	`response(a,b)`∧ `interposition(a,b,a)`
a ◀——▸ b	`alternate precedence(a,b)`. b is preceded by a and there has to be an a between two b	`precedence(a,b)`∧ `interposition(b,a,b)`
a ◀——▸• b	`alternate succession(a,b)`.	`alt. response(a,b)`∧ `alt. precedence(a,b)`
a ■——▸ b	`chain response(a,b)`. If a is executed then b is executed next (immediately after a)	`response(a,b)`∧ `interposition(a,b,X)` ∧X ≠ b
a ■——▸ b	`chain precedence(a,b)`. b can be executed only if a was the last executed activity	`precedence(a,b)`∧ `interposition(X,a,b)` ∧X ≠ a
a ■——▸ b	`chain succession(a,b)`. a and b are always executed next to each other	`chain response(a,b)`∧ `chain precedence(a,b)`

2.2 $\mathcal{REC}$: A Reactive Event Calculus in $\mathcal{SCIFF}$

The Event Calculus ($\mathcal{EC}$) is a framework, based on first-order logic, which enables reasoning about the effects of events [10,14]. The basic elements of the calculus are *events* which happen during the execution[1], and properties (called *fluents*) which describe a partial state of the world. To model a given event-based system, the user must simply provide a declarative description of how possible occurring events affect the corresponding fluents.

In the classical $\mathcal{EC}$ setting, given a description of the system and a set of desired temporal requirements, two main reasoning tasks can be carried out: *narrative verification*, exploiting $\mathcal{EC}$ in a deductive manner, to check whether a given execution trace of the system satisfies the requirements, and *planning*, using abduction to simulate narratives of the systems, trying to produce a possible execution which satisfies the requirements.

Such verifications are respectively carried out a posteriori (after execution), and a priori (before execution). The use of $\mathcal{EC}$ to monitor an ongoing execution, and to check if it complies with the requirements (run-time monitoring and verification), has been little exploited so far, mainly due to a lack of suitable

---

[1] We will consider only atomic events, i.e., events occur at a certain point in time.

Table 3. An overview of DecSerFlow negation constraints

graphical	description	equivalent to
a ●—++—□ b	responded absence(a,b). If a is executed, then b cannot be ever executed	not coexistence(a,b)
a ●—++—● b	not coexistence(a,b). a and b cannot be both executed	neg. response(a,b)∧ neg. response(b,a)
a ●—++▸— b	negation response(a,b). If a is executed, then b cannot be executed afterwards	basic
a —++▸● b	negation precedence(a,b). b cannot be executed if a was executed before	neg. response(a,b)
a ●—++▸● b	negation succession(a,b).	neg. response(a,b)
a ●═++▸— b	negation alternate response(a,b). b cannot be executed between two a	neg. interpos.(a,b,a)
a —++═● b	negation alternate precedence(a,b).a cannot be executed between two b	neg. interpos.(b,a,b)
a ●═++═● b	negation alternate succession(a,b).	neg. alt. resp.(a,b)∧ neg. alt. prec.(a,b)
a ■═++▸— b	negation chain response(a,b). b cannot be executed next to (i.e., immediately after) a	interposition(a,X,b) ∧X ≠ b
a —++═■ b	negation chain precedence(a,b). a cannot be last executed activity before b	n. chain response(a,b)
a ■═++═■ b	negation chain succession(a,b). a and b cannot be executed next to each other	n. chain response(a,b)

underlying reasoning tools. In a companion paper [11], we show how the computational logic-based $\mathcal{S}$CIFF framework [12] can be adopted to provide a reactive axiomatization of $\mathcal{EC}$ (called $\mathcal{REC}$), enabling reasoning about events and fluents at run-time. $\mathcal{S}$CIFF is a framework originally designed for the specification and run-time verification of global interaction protocols in open Multi-Agent Systems. Its usage for run-time verification of service choreographies has been presented at previous editions of this workshop series [15]. $\mathcal{S}$CIFF consists of a rule-based language with a declarative semantics for specifying what are the (un)desired courses of interaction as events occur. A corresponding execution model (the $\mathcal{S}$CIFF proof-procedure [12], implemented in the SOCS-SI tool [13]) enables run-time monitoring and compliance checking of the interacting entities' behavior. The $\mathcal{S}$CIFF proof-procedure is sound and complete w.r.t. its declarative semantics, and it natively provides the capability of reasoning upon dynamically occurring events, using constraint propagation to update the status of fluents. To represent time, $\mathcal{S}$CIFF uses variables that can range over finite domains or over real numbers, and that are associated to events. Therefore, while the procedure does not model itself the flow of time, the current time can be inferred, with some approximation, from the time of occurring events. For example, the expiration of a deadline can be made known to the reasoning engine by way of "tick" event, real or fictitious such as a "tick", which occurs at or after that time.

Table 4. The $\mathcal{REC}$ ontology

$happens(Ev, T)$	Event Ev happens at time T
$holds(F, T_i, T_f)$	Fluent F begins to hold from time T_i and persists to hold until time T_f
$holdsat(F, T)$	Fluent F holds at time T
$not\_holdsat(F, T)$	Fluent F does not hold at time T
$initially(F)$	Fluent F holds from the initial time
$initiates(Ev, F, T)$	Event Ev initiates fluent F at time T; this means that if F does not hold at time T, it is declipped by the happening of Ev at that time
$terminates(Ev, F, T)$	Event Ev terminates fluent F at time T; if F holds at time T, it is clipped by the happening of Ev at that time

The $\mathcal{REC}$ ontology is shown in Table 4; the main difference w.r.t. the classical $\mathcal{EC}$ ontology is that while $\mathcal{EC}$ focuses on time intervals inside which a fluent has been terminated or initiated, $\mathcal{REC}$ focuses on the maximum time intervals inside which the fluent uninterruptedly holds (represented by the holds/3 predicate).

$\mathcal{REC}$ integrates the advantages of $\mathcal{SCIFF}$ and $\mathcal{EC}$, by embedding the latter inside a framework that supports run-time reasoning, while extending $\mathcal{SCIFF}$ with fluents-based reasoning.

3   Mapping DecSerFlow to Event Calculus

We now present the mapping of DecSerFlow onto $\mathcal{EC}$. To this end, we follow a two-fold approach. We first show that all DecSerFlow constraints can be represented in terms of a small core set[2]. Then, we provide a fluent-based formalizations of such a set[3].

3.1   Expressing DecSerFlow with a Core Set of Constraints

Table 1, 2 and 3 respectively recall the basic existence, relation and negation DecSerFlow constraints, by also showing how constraints can be expressed by using a small set of core constraints. To this purpose, two further ternary constraints are used; they represent the concept of positive and negative interposition. In particular, interposition(a,b,c) states that between any execution of activity a and a future execution of activity c, b must be performed at least once. negation interposition(a,b,c) expresses the opposite constraint, specifying that the execution of a and a following c cannot be interleaved by b. X is sometimes used to represent an arbitrary activity (i.e., it is a variable matching with any activity).

---

[2] Some equivalences are already stated in [9].

[3] We will use the Prolog notation: variables starting by upper case, constants by lower case. To differentiate between formalisms, we use teletype for DecSerFlow formula names, and *italics* for Prolog terms and rules in the knowledge base.

All the 26 basic DecSerFlow constraints can be expressed in terms of eight core constraints:

- the two basic cardinality constraints (**existence** and **absence**);
- the three fundamental positive temporal orderings (**responded existence** for *any* ordering, **response** for the *after* ordering, **precedence** for the *before* ordering);
- the **negation response** constraint;
- the positive/negative **interposition** patterns.

For example, the **chain response** between **a** and **b** (see Table 2) can be expressed using a **response** formula and by stating that between each occurrence of activity **a** and another arbitrary activity different than **b**, there must exist at least an intermediate execution of **b** (hence **b** is necessarily next to **a**). The **not coexistence** constraint (Table 3) can instead be reduced to two opposite **negation responses**. In fact, expressing that two activities cannot coexist in a single execution is the same as stating that the *first* happening activity forbids future executions of the other one.

3.2   A Fluent-Based Formalization of DecSerFlow

The formalization of DecSerFlow in $\mathcal{REC}$ is composed by two parts (see Figure 1 for an overview):

- a general part, which describes how the different DecSerFlow constraints can be formalized as fluents in the $\mathcal{EC}$ setting;
- a specific part, whose purpose is to describe a specific DecSerFlow diagram.

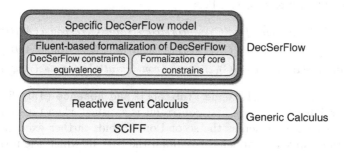

Fig. 1. Building parts of the DecSerFlow formalization in $\mathcal{REC}$

The specific part is a set of **constraint/2** facts. Each one of them corresponds to a DecSerFlow constraint in the diagram. For example, *constraint(c_1, response(order_item, ack))* states that the DecSerFlow choreography contains a constraint named c_1 which models a **response** between the **order_item** and **ack** activities.

The generic DecSerFlow formalization in $\mathcal{EC}$ splits itself in two sub-parts.

Formalization of constraints equivalence. The first part is a set of predicate definitions for `core_constraint/2`. They implement the reduction of the 26 basic DecSerFlow constraints to the set of eight core constraints listed above. In this way, we provide a full implementation of DecSerFlow (not only the core constraints). Examples of such definitions are those below, relating `alternate response` with `response` and `interposition`[4]:

$$core\_constraint(C, response(A, B)) \leftarrow constraint(C, alt\_response(A, B)).$$
$$core\_constraint(C, interposition(A, B, A)) \leftarrow constraint(C, alt\_response(A, B)).$$

Fluent-based formalization of the core constraints. The second part is a set of predicate definitions for `initially/1`, `initiates/3` and `terminates/3`. In other words, it is a knowledge base which formalizes constraints in terms of fluents, linking their initiation and termination to activities.

The fluents chosen to model DecSerFlow reflect the double nature of its constraints: some relations explicitly forbid the execution of a certain activity, whereas other ones express the necessity of performing some activity, becoming temporarily unsatisfied until such an activity indeed happens. More specifically, we exploit a $forbidden(C, A)$ fluent to model that an activity A is forbidden by a constraint C, and a $satisfied(C)$ fluent to model that a constraint C is satisfied.

Table 5 briefly indicates our usage of fluents in the formalization of the DecSerFlow core constraints. Some parts of the formalization are left implicit for ease of presentation. In particular, Table 5 omits the binding between each formalization and its corresponding `core_constraint`. For example, the complete formalization of `response` would be:

$$initially(satisfied(C)) \leftarrow core\_constraint(C, response(A, B)).$$
$$terminates(A, satisfied(C), \_) \leftarrow core\_constraint(C, response(A, B)).$$
$$initiates(B, satisfied(C), \_) \leftarrow core\_constraint(C, response(A, B)).$$

The formalization of `existence` (Tab. 5(1)) and `absence` (Tab. 5(2)) constraints is straightforward: the first constraint is satisfied when the n-th occurrence of a is executed, whereas the second one forbids further executions of a when its n-th occurrence happens. To obtain the time at which the n-th occurrence of activity a happens, we use a conjunction of n happened events involving a; then, we order such happened events by means of temporal constraints. The last happened event provides the desired time.

`responded existence` (Tab. 5(3)) is more complex to deal with, mainly due to the fact that it does not impose any ordering, whereas $\mathcal{EC}$, which considers the effects of events, reasons "forwards." To capture its semantics, we differentiate between two cases: the one in which b happens before any occurrence of a, and

---

[4] Note that the parameters of `core_constraint/2` have the same meaning of the parameters of `constraint/2`.

Table 5. A fluent-based formalization of DecSerFlow core constraints (f is used as constraint identifier); the last two constraints express the concepts of positive and negative interposition

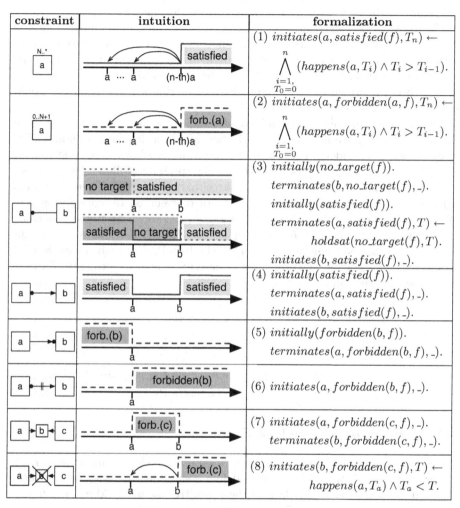

constraint	intuition	formalization
		(1) $initiates(a, satisfied(f), T_n) \leftarrow$ $$\bigwedge_{\substack{i=1, \\ T_0=0}}^{n} (happens(a, T_i) \wedge T_i > T_{i-1}).$$
		(2) $initiates(a, forbidden(a, f), T_n) \leftarrow$ $$\bigwedge_{\substack{i=1, \\ T_0=0}}^{n} (happens(a, T_i) \wedge T_i > T_{i-1}).$$
		(3) $initially(no\_target(f)).$ $terminates(b, no\_target(f), \_).$ $initially(satisfied(f)).$ $terminates(a, satisfied(f), T) \leftarrow$ $\qquad holdsat(no\_target(f), T).$ $initiates(b, satisfied(f), \_).$
		(4) $initially(satisfied(f)).$ $terminates(a, satisfied(f), \_).$ $initiates(b, satisfied(f), \_).$
		(5) $initially(forbidden(b, f)).$ $terminates(a, forbidden(b, f), \_).$
		(6) $initiates(a, forbidden(b, f), \_).$
		(7) $initiates(a, forbidden(c, f), \_).$ $terminates(b, forbidden(c, f), \_).$
		(8) $initiates(b, forbidden(c, f), T) \leftarrow$ $\qquad happens(a, T_a) \wedge T_a < T.$

the reverse. In the first case, the constraint is always satisfied: when a happens, b is already present in the execution trace, thus no further expectation is triggered. In the second case, instead, the occurrence of a switches the constraint to an unsatisfied state, waiting for activity b to be executed (as in the case of response, Tab. 5(4)). Since the happening of a concretely affects the status of the *satisfied* fluent only if no b was previously performed, we have to explicitly track the happening of b with another fluent (called *no_target* in Table 5).

precedence (Tab. 5(5)) is captured by observing that the backward constraint "b must be preceded by a" can be rephrased in a forward manner as "a enables the possibility of executing b". We formalize this by imposing that the constraint causes b to be initially forbidden, until the first execution of activity a happens.

The formalization of **negation response** (Tab. 5(6)) is straightforward: the happening of the source activity a causes b to be forbidden.

The **interposition** constraint (Tab. 5(7)) is captured by rephrasing "if c is performed after a, then at least one instance of activity b must be executed in between" as "when a is executed, c is forbidden until b is executed". Similarly, **negative interposition** (Tab. 5(8)) can be formalized by stating that when activity b is performed after a, then c becomes forbidden: its execution would lead to violate the constraint.

The proposed formalization can be easily adapted to deal also with branching constraints, which are interpreted in DecSerFlow in a disjunctive manner. For example, let us consider a **response** constraint, having both branching sources a and b and branching targets c and d. It is interpreted as follows: "when either a or b are executed, then c or d must be executed afterwards". To model such a behavior, we extend the way constraints are represented by considering lists of activities instead of individual activities (e.g., the above described branching **response** can be modeled as $formula(c_1, response([a, b], [c, d]))$). We then adapt the formalization shown in Table 5, using the built-in Prolog predicate **member/2**[5] to specify that each source (target resp.) activity is able to terminate (initiate resp.) the corresponding *satisfied* fluent:

$$initially(satisfied(C)) \leftarrow core\_constraint(C, response(As, Bs)).$$
$$terminates(A, satisfied(C), \_) \leftarrow core\_constraint(C, response(As, Bs))$$
$$\land member(A, As).$$
$$initiates(B, satisfied(C), \_) \leftarrow core\_constraint(C, response(As, Bs))$$
$$\land member(B, Bs).$$

3.3   Characterizing Compliant Executions

To effectively perform compliance verification of a service composition w.r.t. a DecSerFlow model, we finally have to define a suitable semantics for the *satisfied* and *forbidden* fluents, reflecting their intuitive meaning. More specifically, a correct execution must fulfill the following requirements:

– all constraints which involve a "positive" relation must eventually converge to a fulfilled state. This means that the satisfied fluent corresponding to the positive relation holds from a given point on and it is never declipped thereafter. We denote the set of "positive" constraints by $\mathcal{C}_{SAT}$. Since the "positive" behavior is formalized by means of a *satisfied* fluent, such a requirement can be expressed as a goal imposing that, for all contraints in $\mathcal{C}_{SAT}$, the corresponding *satisfied* fluent must hold when the interaction is completed. We model the completion of interaction as a special, last **complete** event,

---

[5] **member(E1, L)** is true if **E1** belongs to the list **L**.

happening at a time T_∞ (s.t. no further event will happen after T_∞). Thus, we have a goal:

$$\bigwedge_{\{c|c \in \mathcal{C}_{SAT}\}} holdsat(satisfied(c), T_\infty). \tag{1}$$

- the semantics of *forbidden* fluents is given as a *denial*, stating that if a certain activity A happens when it is forbidden by some negative constraint, then the execution is unsuccessful:

$$happens(A, T) \wedge holdsat(forbidden(\_, A), T) \rightarrow \bot.dov \tag{2}$$

In order to be compliant, services must eventually satisfy all the positive relations without undermining the negative ones.

4 Verification of Quantitative Time Constraints

We now discuss how it can be extended to model and verify quantitative temporal constraints, which are an important aspect when monitoring service interaction. In the context of DecSerFlow, temporal constraints can be used to extend positive relations with the concepts of delays and deadlines, i.e. minimum/maximum time intervals that should be respected between the execution of two activities[6].

To specify that "when an order is paid, a receipt must be delivered within 24 time units" the modeler may use a **response** constraint c_1, adding the information that c_1 cannot persist in a non-satisfied state for more than 24 time units. We suppose that, to describe this condition, the user simply uses a $deadline(satisfied(c_1), 24)$ declaration. In general, $deadline(F, D)$ states that fluent F can persist in a "not-holding" state at most D time units.

To capture and verify deadlines, we then add four new axioms. Let us suppose that fluent F is associated to a $deadline(F, D)$ condition. When F is terminated, a new fluent $d\_check(F, T_e)$ is initiated. This fluent represents that F is currently monitored, to check if the associated deadline will be met by the execution; T_e denotes the time at which the deadline will expire. Such a situation can be formalized by means of the following axiom:

$$initiates(A, d\_check(F, T_e), T) \leftarrow deadline(F, D), terminates(A, F, T),$$
$$T_e == T + D. \tag{3}$$

The fluent $d\_check(F, T_e)$ can be terminated in two cases. In the first case, an event capable to terminate F happens within the deadline (i.e., within T_e):

$$terminates(A, d\_check(F, T_e), T) \leftarrow deadline(F, \_), initiates(A, F, T), T < T_e. \tag{4}$$

---

[6] In the following, we will focus only on deadlines; delays can be handled in a similar way.

The second case deals with the expiration of the deadline. $\mathcal{SCIFF}$ has no notion of the flow of time: it becomes aware of the current time only when a new event occurs. Therefore, we can keep $\mathcal{SCIFF}$ up-to-date by generating special tick events. The deadline expiration is then detected and handled as soon as the first tick event after the deadline occurs:

$$terminates(tick, deadline\_check(F, T_e), T) \leftarrow deadline(F, \_), T \geq T_e. \tag{5}$$

A further axiom recognizes this abnormal situation, by evaluating whether the *deadline_check* has been terminated after the expiration time (and generating a violation if it is the case):

$$happens(tick, T) \wedge holdsat(deadline\_check(F, T_e), T) \wedge T \geq T_e \rightarrow \bot. \tag{6}$$

5   Extending the Calculus

In this section we show how violations can be captured and reified within the calculus itself. On the one hand, capturing violations prevents the termination of the proof procedure when an error is detected. On the other hand, reifying violations enable the possibility to consider them as first-class object during the modeling phase, supporting the possibility of specifying and verifying complex requirements such as compensating activities.

5.1   Reification of Violations

As described in Sections 3.3 and 4, two different kinds of non-compliance can be identified at run-time: violation of a negative constraint, by executing a forbidden activity, or violation of a positive constraint, if it is not satisfied when the execution terminates or, if a deadline is present, within the required expiration time.

In its basic form, $\mathcal{SCIFF}$ reacts to violations by terminating with answer "no": the observed happened events are evaluated as non compliant with the choreography. This is undesirable in a monitoring setting: we would like to continue the verification task even if some constraint has been violated.

To prevent termination of the proof, the underlying idea is to *reify* violations as occurrences of special events. In other words, we explicitly capture the possible run-time violations of a fluent F by generating a corresponding $violation(F)$ event upon violation of F. If we want to capture and handle violations, then we must remove axioms (1), (2) and (4), and substitute them with a corresponding "soft" version. In particular, a soft version of axiom (1) states that, for each constraint $C \in \mathcal{C}_{SAT}$, if the corresponding *satisfied* fluent does not hold at T_∞, then a corresponding $violation(satisfied(C))$ event must be generated:

$$happens(complete, T_\infty) \wedge$$
$$not\_holdsat(satisfied(C), T_\infty) \rightarrow happens(violation(satisfied(C)), T_\infty). \tag{7}$$

The same applies for axiom (4) (dealing with the deadline expiration), which becomes

$$happens(tick, T)\wedge$$
$$holdsat(deadline\_check(F, T_e), T) \wedge T \geq T_e \rightarrow happens(violation(F), T). \qquad (8)$$

A soft version of axiom (2) is the following axiom:

$$happens(A, T)\wedge$$
$$holdsat(forbidden(C, A), T) \rightarrow happens(violation(forbidden(C)), T). \qquad (9)$$

Reifying violations opens many possibilities. For example, we could associate an "importance degree" to each constraints, identifying and handling different levels of violation. In the next section we will briefly focus on another possibility, namely the specification of how to compensate for a violation.

5.2   Dealing with Compensations

Among the many possibilities offered by the reification of violations, an interesting option is to attach DecSerFlow constraints to such a generated event. This could be a way to specify how the interacting services must *compensate* for a violation, or to define a context for violations, i.e. to model constraints which become *soft* only in certain situations in the choreography.

Compensation can be modeled by e.g. inserting a **response** constraint having a violation event as source, and the compensation activity as target; **chain response** could be then used to handle critical violations: it states that when the violation is detected, the next immediate activity to be executed is the compensating one.

Contextualization of violations can be modeled using backward DecSerFlow constraints (e.g., **precedence**). For example, modeling a **precedence** constraint involving an activity A and the event *violation*(C) states that as soon as the event violation(C) is raised, the REC verify if previously an execution of the activity A has been performed (the activity A representing some how the idea of context). In such a case, the violation can be managed, otherwise a definitive, non compliant response is provided as a result.

6   Monitoring Example

We now briefly discuss a simple yet significant example of a choreography fragment, showing how the proposed approach can be fruitfully applied for run-time monitoring. Figure 2 shows the graphical DecSerFlow representation of the example, while Table 6 sketches its corresponding formalization.

The choreography involves a customer, who creates an order by choosing one or more items, and a seller, who collects the ordered items and finally gives a

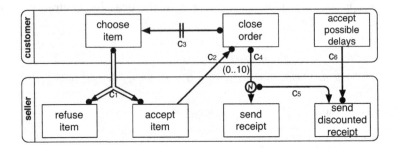

Fig. 2. A DecSerFlow choreography fragment, extended with a deadline and a compensation

Table 6. Formalization of the choreography fragment shown in Figure 2

ID	$\mathcal{REC}$ **Specification**
c_1	$formula(c_1, alternate\_succession([choose\_item], [refuse\_item, accept\_item])).$
c_2	$formula(c_2, precedence([accept\_item], [close\_order])).$
c_3	$formula(c_3, negation\_response([close\_order], [choose\_item])).$
c_4	$formula(c_4, response([close\_order], [send\_receipt])).$ $deadline(satisfied(c_4), 10).$
c_5	$formula(c_5, response([violation(c_4)], [send\_discounted\_receipt])).$
c_6	$formula(c_6, precedence([accept\_possible\_delays], [send\_discounted\_receipt])).$

receipt. The seller is committed to issue the final receipt within a pre-established deadline. Moreover, the seller offers the customer a fixed discount if he/she accepts some delays; in case of a delay, the seller also promises a further discount directly on the receipt.

In particular, the following rules of engagement must be fulfilled by the interacting services. It is worth noting that each constraint can be easily mapped by means of an (extended) DecSerFlow relation.

- Every **choose item** activity must be followed by an answer from the seller, either positive or negative; no further upload can be executed until the response is sent. Conversely, each positive/negative response must be preceded by a **choose item** activity, and no further response can be sent until a new item is chosen (constraint c_1).
- If at least one uploaded item has been accepted by the seller, then it is possible for the customer to close the order (constraint c_2).
- When an order has been closed, no further item can be choosen (constraint c_3); moreover, the seller is committed to send a corresponding receipt by at most 10 time units (constraint c_4).
- If the seller does not meet the deadline, it must deliver a discounted receipt (constraint c_5, modeled as a **response** constraint triggered by the violation of constraint c_4; the graphical representation of the violation is inspired by the BPMN *intermediate error* event).

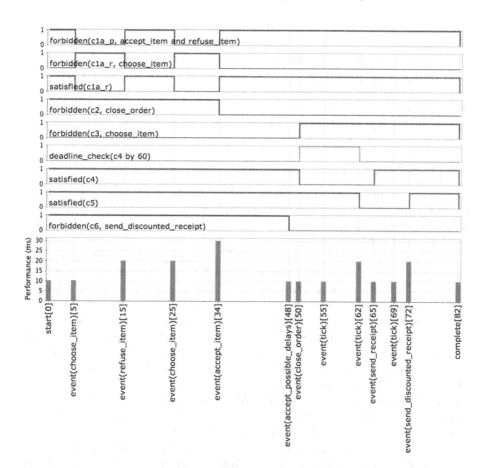

Fig. 3. Fluents trend generated by $\mathcal{REC}$ when monitoring a specific interaction, and using the diagram of Figure 2 as model. The verification time spent for reacting to each happened event is also reported.

— The possibility of sending a discounted receipt is enabled only if the customer has previously accepted the possibility of experiencing delays (constraint c_6).

Note that the obtained DecSerFlow diagram contains two constraints (c_4 and c_5) which are not envisaged by standard DecSerFlow, but are seamlessly supported by $\mathcal{REC}$ thanks to the extensions presented above.

Figure 3 illustrates how $\mathcal{REC}$ is able to reason upon a specific course of interaction w.r.t. the above described DecSerFlow model. Clipping and declipping of fluents are handled at run-time, thus giving a constantly updated snapshot of the reached interaction status. In the bottom part of the figure, verification performance is reported, showing the amount of time spent by $\mathcal{REC}$ in order to dynamically react to and reason upon occurring events.

The central part of the execution shows how $\mathcal{REC}$ deals with a deadline expiration. Indeed, as soon as the activity close_order is executed (at time 50), constraint c_4 becomes unsatisfied, and a corresponding deadline check is initiated, having 60 as expiration time. At time 62, a tick event makes the proof aware that the deadline related to the satisfaction of constraint $c4$ is expired. As a consequence, $\mathcal{SCIFF}$ reacts by terminating the *deadline_check* fluent and by installing the corresponding compensation; this is attested by the fact that constraint c_5 becomes unsatisfied.

7   Related Work

Event Calculus has been extensively applied to specify and verify event-based systems in many different settings. We will restrict our attention to the applications related to the SOA research field.

Rouached et al. propose a framework for engineering and verifying WS-BPEL processes is [16]. $\mathcal{EC}$ is used to provide an underlying semantics to WS-BPEL, enabling verification before and after execution. In particular, $\mathcal{EC}$ is exploited to verify consistency and safety of a service composition (i.e. to statically check if the specification always guarantees the desired requirements), and to check whether an already completed execution has deviated from the prescribed requirements. The authors rely on an inductive theorem prover for the verification task. Although our work adopts DecSerFlow as specification language, the mapping of WS-BPEL presented in [16] can be directly implemented on top of $\mathcal{REC}$. In [17], Aydın and colleagues use the Abductive Event Calculus to synthesize a web service composition starting from a goal. The composition process is a planning problem, where the functionality provided by individual services are (atomic) actions, requiring some inputs and producing certain outputs. Being $\mathcal{REC}$ based on an abductive proof-procedure, we will investigate the possibility of adopting $\mathcal{REC}$ to deal also with this issue.

Few authors have considered adopting the $\mathcal{EC}$ to perform run-time reasoning. Among those who have, Mahbub and Spanoudakis present a framework [18] for monitoring the compliance of a WS-BPEL service composition w.r.t. behavioral properties automatically extracted from the composition process, or assumptions/requirements expressed by the user. $\mathcal{EC}$ is exploited to monitor the actual behavior of interacting services and report different kinds of violation. The approach is extended in [19], where an extension of WS-Agreement is used to specify requirements. The monitoring framework relies on an ad hoc event processing algorithm, which fetches occurred events updating the status of involved fluents.

8   Conclusion

In this article we have presented a method for run-time verification of choreographies specified in DecSerFlow that makes use of a SCIFF implementation of the Event Calculus. The main features of our method are the presence of an *execution model*, which enables an efficient monitoring of the evolution of fluents and their verification; the coherence of an overall *declarative* framework, in which no information is lost when passing from DecSerFlow to SCIFF; and the *flexibility* of the language, which makes it possible to capture aspects of complex requirements, such as qualitative temporal conditions and violation handling by compensation, in a simple and intuitive way. We have chosen to start from DecSerFlow partly because it is well suited for representing the contractual nature of service choreographies, and to specify the desired and undesired courses of interaction while leaving undefined other possibilities of interaction that are neither desired nor undesired. We believe that this is a promising approach and in the future we plan to focus on other declarative and contractual aspects of choreographies. In particular, we intend to study the role of social commitments [20] in the choreographies and to investigate possible integrations of commitments into our framework.

Acknowledgments. This work has been partially supported by the FIRB project *TOCAI.IT*. The authors would like to thank the anonymous reviewers for their helpful comments.

References

1. Kavantzas, N., Burdett, D., Ritzinger, G., Fletcher, T., Lafon, Y.: Web services choreography description language. W3C Working Draft 17-12-04 (2004), http://www.w3.org/TR/ws-cdl-10/
2. Baldoni, M., Baroglio, C., Martelli, A., Patti, V.: A priori conformance verification for guaranteeing interoperability in open environments. In: Dan, A., Lamersdorf, W. (eds.) ICSOC 2006. LNCS, vol. 4294, pp. 339–351. Springer, Heidelberg (2006)
3. Li, J., Zhu, H., Pu, G.: Conformance validation between choreography and orchestration. In: First Joint IEEE/IFIP Symposium on Theoretical Aspects of Software Engineering, TASE 2007, Shanghai, China, pp. 473–482. IEEE Computer Society Press, Los Alamitos (2007)
4. Zaha, J., Dumas, M., Hofstede, A., Barros, A., Dekker, G.: Service Interaction Modeling: Bridging Global and Local Views. QUT ePrints 4032, Faculty of Information Technology, Queensland University of Technology (2006)
5. Decker, G., Weske, M.: Local enforceability in interaction petri nets. In: Alonso, G., Dadam, P., Rosemann, M. (eds.) BPM 2007. LNCS, vol. 4714, pp. 305–319. Springer, Heidelberg (2007)
6. Allen Emerson, E., Halpern, J.: "Sometimes" and "Not Never" revisited: On branching times versus linear time. Journal of the ACM 33, 151–178 (1986)
7. Alur, R., Henzinger, T.A.: Real-time logics: complexity and expressiveness. Information and Computation 104, 35–77 (1993)
8. Wang, F.: Formal verification of timed systems: A survey and perspective. Proceedings of the IEEE 92(8), 1283–1305 (2004)
9. van der Aalst, W.M.P., Pesic, M.: DecSerFlow: Towards a truly declarative service flow language. In: Bravetti, M., Núñez, M., Zavattaro, G. (eds.) WS-FM 2006. LNCS, vol. 4184, pp. 1–23. Springer, Heidelberg (2006)
10. Kowalski, R.A., Sergot, M.: A logic-based calculus of events. New Generation Computing 4(1), 67–95 (1986)

11. Chesani, F., Montali, M., Mello, P., Torroni, P.: An efficient SCIFF implementation of Reactive Event Calculus. Technical Report LIA-08-003, University of Bologna, Italy. LIA Series No. 89 (May 2008)
12. Alberti, M., Chesani, F., Gavanelli, M., Lamma, E., Mello, P., Torroni, P.: Verifiable agent interaction in abductive logic programming: the SCIFF framework. ACM Transactions on Computational Logic 9(4) (to appear, 2008)
13. Alberti, M., Chesani, F., Gavanelli, M., Lamma, E., Mello, P., Torroni, P.: Compliance verification of agent interaction: a logic-based software tool. Applied Artificial Intelligence 20(2-4), 133–157 (2006)
14. Shanahan, M.: The event calculus explained. In: Veloso, M.M., Wooldridge, M.J. (eds.) Artificial Intelligence Today. LNCS, vol. 1600, pp. 409–430. Springer, Heidelberg (1999)
15. Alberti, M., Chesani, F., Gavanelli, M., Lamma, E., Mello, P., Montali, M., Storari, S., Torroni, P.: Computational logic for run-time verification of web services choreographies: Exploiting the *socs-si* tool. In: Bravetti, M., Núñez, M., Zavattaro, G. (eds.) WS-FM 2006. LNCS, vol. 4184, pp. 58–72. Springer, Heidelberg (2006)
16. Rouached, M., Fdhila, W., Godart, C.: A semantic framework to engineering wsbpel processes. International Journal on Information Systems and e-business Management (2008)
17. Aydin, O., Cicekli, N.K., Cicekli, I.: Automated web services composition with event calculus. In: Proceedings of the 8th International Workshop in Engineering Societies in the Agents World (ESAW 2007) (2007)
18. Mahbub, K., Spanoudakis, G.: Run-time monitoring of requirements for systems composed of web-services: Initial implementation and evaluation experience. In: 2005 IEEE International Conference on Web Services (ICWS 2005), Orlando, FL, USA, pp. 257–265. IEEE Computer Society Press, Los Alamitos (2005)
19. Mahbub, K., Spanoudakis, G.: Monitoring ws-agreements: An event calculus-based approach. In: Baresi, L., Nitto, E.D. (eds.) Test and Analysis of Web Services, pp. 265–306. Springer, Heidelberg (2007)
20. Yolum, P., Singh, M.: Flexible protocol specification and execution: applying event calculus planning using commitments. In: The First International Joint Conference on Autonomous Agents & Multiagent Systems, AAMAS 2002, Bologna, Italy, Proceedings, pp. 527–534 (2002)

RESTful Petri Net Execution

Gero Decker, Alexander Lüders, Hagen Overdick,
Kai Schlichting, and Mathias Weske

Hasso-Plattner-Institute, University of Potsdam, Germany
{gero.decker,hagen.overdick,weske}@hpi.uni-potsdam.de,
{alexander.lueders,kai.schlichting}@student.hpi.uni-potsdam.de

Abstract. Representational State Transfer (REST) has received a lot
of attention recently as architectural style for distributed systems made
up of loosely coupled resources. While most research in process enactment focuses on BPEL and SOAP, most internet applications are based
on REST. To leverage this new architectural style also for process enactment, this paper introduces process enactment in REST environments.
The approach is based on Service Nets, a specific class of Petri nets
supporting value passing and link passing mobility. Implementation considerations of a prototype are presented. The approach is compared with
the traditional BPEL/SOAP approach to process enactment.

1 Introduction

The service-oriented architecture (SOA) is an architectural style for building
software systems based on services. Services are loosely coupled components
that can be discovered and composed [6]. Such composition is often realized
through process execution engines, interpreting business process models and invoking services accordingly. Using SOAP as communication protocol is a typical
option for realizing web services [8]. Furthermore, the Business Process Execution Language (BPEL [10]) is a widely used standard for implementing business
processes that are based on SOAP services.

SOAP services are a concrete implementation of a SOA, yet there are alternatives readily available. In [20], we characterized Representational State Transfer (REST [11]) as a restricted subset of SOA, hence RESTful usage of the Hyper
Text Transfer Protocol (HTTP [12]) qualifies as SOA just as well. The most important restrictions imposed by REST are globally unique identification of each
service instance (called resource) and identification of the interaction intention
at the protocol level. HTTP supports *resource reflection* (GET), *at-least once
delivery* (PUT/DELETE), and *at-most once delivery* (POST) directly, other intention can be represented by combining the former. In essence, SOAP-based
services merely use HTTP as a transfer protocol, REST advocates HTTP as
application protocol, enabling increased distributability, scalability and masha-
bility of service-based systems. A resource-oriented approach as demanded by
REST has proven strengths in environments of multiple autonomous peers [27],
the World Wide Web being the most prominent example of such a system.

R. Bruni and K. Wolf (Eds.): WS-FM 2008, LNCS 5387, pp. 73–87, 2009.
© Springer-Verlag Berlin Heidelberg 2009

Most research in the area of process-oriented service implementations focuses on BPEL and SOAP-based services, where machine-to-machine communication is at the center of attention. On the other hand, most successful internet applications (e.g., flickr.com, amazon.com, XING.com) are based on the REST architecture style. This paper introduces process enactment in REST environments, i.e., RESTful process enactment. The approach is conceptually based on Service nets, a specific class of high level Petri nets that include value passing, i.e. colored tokens and guard conditions. Dynamically evolving structures realized through URI passing is a core aspect in the REST world. Therefore, this notion of link passing mobility will also be captured in the formal model.

The remainder of this paper is structured as follows. The next section will present a motivating example and explain central REST concepts. Section 3 introduces the formal model specifying RESTful execution of processes specified by Service nets, before section 4 introduces implementation concepts of a prototypical engine that we have implemented. Section 5 reports on related work, especially focusing on the relationship of the presented approach to the BPEL/-SOAP approach to process enactment in web environments. Section 6 concludes and points to future work.

2   Motivating Example and Approach

Figure 1 shows the example we will use for illustration throughout this paper. The typical notation for Petri nets is used, where circles denote places, rectangles denote transitions and arrows flow connections between places and transitions. Read arcs as special kind of flow connection are represented by lines without arrowheads. The dashed rectangles denote different nets. The dashed arrows between transitions of different nets denote that the same transition appears in different nets.

Several participants are involved in the sample scenario: While browsing an online store, a customer creates a shopping cart where she selects items she is interested in. Before submitting the order, she is also allowed to already define the address where the goods should be delivered to. Once she is sure what to buy, she submits the order, triggering subsequent payment handling and delivery, which in turn can be done concurrently. Payment is handled through an external payment service. The customer is automatically forwarded to the respective web site. There are two alternatives for delivery: standard delivery and express delivery. For each alternative there is a respective service.

All interaction between two participants are carried out through HTTP requests/response cycles, represented as communication transitions in Figure 1. We mentioned before, that the HTTP reflects the intention of an interaction directly at the protocol level. REST calls this feature a uniform interface and HTTP provides the following verbs to express intentions:

GET. Messages labeled as GET have an empty service request and are guaranteed to have no effect within the receiver of such request, i.e. they are *safe* to call. GET responses are expected to be a description of the current state of the

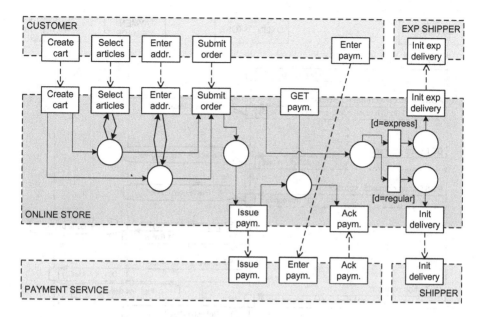

Fig. 1. Sample scenario

targeted resource. Also, as GET does not alter the state of the targeted resource, the response can be cached. This has great benefits to a distributed architecture and both aspects can be seized without prior semantic knowledge of the targeted resources.

PUT. Messages labeled as PUT do cause an effect in the targeted resource, but do so in an *idempotent* fashion. An idempotent interaction is defined as replayable, i.e. the effect of N identical messages is the same as that of 1. In a distributed system, where transactions may not be readily available, this is a great help to recover from situations where messages might have got lost. Here, it does not harm to simply resend a message. Again, this assumption can be made without any prior semantic knowledge of the resource involved.

DELETE. Messages labeled as DELETE do cause an effect in the targeted resource, where that effect has a negative connotation. Just as PUT, DELETE is defined as *idempotent.* However, as with all messages, the interpretation is solely the responsibility of the receiver, i.e. a DELETE has to be regarded as "please terminate".

POST. All other types of messages are labeled as POST, i.e. they cause an effect in the receiver and they are not safe to replay. This is a catch-all mechanism for all messages that can not be described by the prior verbs. Without a uniform interface, all messages would be treated like this, loosing context-free resource reflection, caching and replayability.

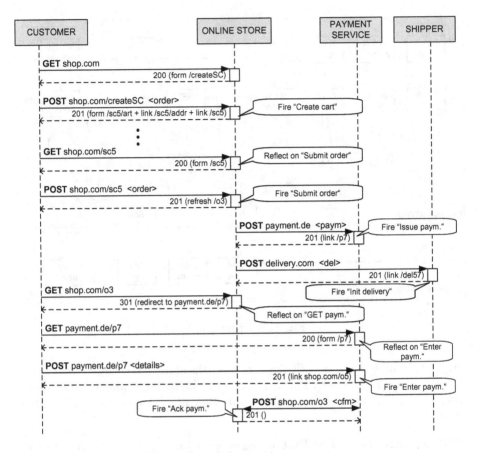

Fig. 2. Sample interaction sequence

The state of the online store service is represented by the marking of the Petri net. Most *GET* requests do not have any explicit representation in the net. The only exception in the example is the "GET paym." transition. As this transition only has a read arc, firing it does not affect the marking. Therefore, this communication is safe.

Unsafe communication corresponds to firing of the other transitions, in the context of the paper we resort to using *POST*. For instance selecting articles removes the token from the input place and produces a (possibly) different token to the same place. The internals of the payment and delivery services are not shown in Figure 1.

Figure 2 shows a sample sequence of message exchanges. Here, *GET* requests are also included. The first interaction happens between the customer's web browser and the online store. A *GET* request is issued for http://shop.com. As response, the HTTP code 200 (OK) is returned with an XHTML page as representation for http://shop.com. The intention of this interaction is to receive a representation of the targeted resource. This representation contains the reference to the shopping cart creation resource, namely `http://shop.com/createSC`. Invoking this service results in the creation of a new resource, identified by `http://shop.com/sc5`. Here, we already see how the topology dynamically evolves and navigation from one resource to another happens through URI passing.

Here comes in another vital feature of REST: hypermedia as the engine of application state. In a Petri net, application state is the position of all tokens in a net, the marking, at a given time. Calling a service is mapped to a transition with a certain set of input tokens in the underlying net. As we just learned, a new URI representing a transition (with input tokens), we can fire tokens in an at-most once fashion, therefore mapped to *POST*ing to the order service. The contained XML document is used as input to the service, the result is the creation of a new resource and returning a *201 created* response including the link to the newly created resource, here `http://shop.com/sc5` and a representation of the resource including references to the services `http://shop.com/sc5/art` and `http://shop.com/sc5/addr`. These services in turn return XHTML pages providing forms for selecting items and a delivery address respectively.

The remaining interactions correspond to submitting the order, triggering the payment service and triggering the delivery service. Upon *GET* request by the customer, the online store redirects her to the payment service.

GET requests are a resource reflection mechanism in the REST world. In our scenario, the returned representation of the identified resource describes how to interact with the resource and what data is being expected. In our scenario, all representations are optimized for rendering a human-readable web page in a browser. However, this information can also be used by a machine. An alternative representation could be a WSDL file also defining the data structure expected in a request for SOAP-legacy integration or more advanced techniques such as microformats [15] and RDFa [1]. If different representations are available, content negotiation realizes the selection of a desired representation.

Figure 1 contains several sample Universal Resource Identificators (URI [3]). The concept of web-wide unique identification of resources is at the center of REST. We can distinguish between at least two interesting types of resources to be identified:

- *Static ports* are entry points into process instances. *POST*ing data to such resources leads to the creation of activity instances or the data sent is routed to existing process instances. Static means that the URI is independent of any particular process instance. In our example, `http://shop.com/createSC` or `http://payment.de` identify static ports.
- *Dynamic ports* are also entry points into process instances, but here a dynamic port corresponds to exactly one activity instance. In our example, `http://shop.com/o3` or `http://payment.de/p7` identify dynamic ports.

The notion of dynamic ports or activity instances is not present in SOAP-based systems, where only static ports are available. Here, application-specific parameters are used for relating requests to process instances. This hampers the possibility of "bookmarking" activity instances, one of the driving features of the World Wide Web.

In the REST context it is crucial to avoid "URI guessing", i.e. all URIs that are actually addressed in a request must have been obtained somehow before. This implies that it should never be demanded that requesters know how to construct particular URIs, e.g. constructing the URI `http://shop.com/o3` from the store's URI and the store's internal Id of the shopping cart. This URI must have been passed to the customer previously. Again, the concept of *link passing mobility* [19] is of central importance for RESTful systems and taken even beyond by treating link passing mobility as the driver of the application flow, where the application is completely located within the client, the server side is simply providing services.

As all interactions with such services have explicit intention, exploiting edge conditions such as caching *GET* interaction possible without application knowledge on either side of the communication. The message itself is enough for any intermediary to optimize its own behavior and in turn optimize the operating cloud in total.

3   Formal Model

All message exchanges between the online store and its environment happen via HTTP request/response interactions. As already illustrated in Figure 1 such synchronous communication is modeled in the Petri net using communication transitions. This section will introduce *service nets* specifying the behavior of systems that implement processes in a RESTful manner.

The online store receives XML documents from the customer's browser and the payment service and sends XML documents to the payment and the delivery services. The tokens flowing within the online store also carry XML data. Branching decisions are based on such XML-tokens.

3.1   Basic Definitions

In the following definitions we will denote the (infinite) set of all XML documents as *XML* and the (infinite) set of all URIs as *URI*.

Definition 1 (Service Net). *A service net is a tuple* $S = (P, T, F, F_{read}, T_S, T_R, init, g, uri)$ *where*

- *P and T are disjoint sets of places and transitions,*
- *$F \subseteq (P \times T) \cup (T \times P)$ is the flow relation,*
- *$F_{read} \subseteq F \cap (P \times T)$ is a set of read arcs,*
- *$T_S, T_R \subseteq T$ are disjoint sets of send and receive transitions, collectively called communication transitions,*
- *$init : P \rightarrow \mathcal{MS}(XML)$ is the initial marking, a function assigning multi-sets of tokens to places,*

- *g is a function assigning guard conditions to transitions, where a condition $g(t) \subseteq (\bullet t \to XML)$ specifies combinations of input documents and*
- *uri is a function assigning URIs to tuples of communication transitions and combinations of input documents, i.e. $uri(t) : (\bullet t \to XML) \to URI$.*

The auxiliary function $\bullet t$ denotes all input places for a transition t, i.e. $\bullet t = \{p \in P \mid (p,t) \in F\}$, in analogy to this $t\bullet$ denotes all output places for a transition.

The definition of service nets shows how the distinction between static ports and dynamic ports is formally reflected: any receive transition t without input places is a static port. Here exists a URI *id*, such that $uri(t, \emptyset) = id$. Dynamic ports are characterized by a tuple (t, f_{in}) where $f_{in} : \bullet t \to XML$, i.e. by a receive transition with a set of input documents. Such a dynamic port's URI is given by $uri(t, f_{in})$.

The definition of function g allows for the same expressiveness as using boolean expressions that evaluate to true or false for given input documents. Imagine a transition t with one input place p. A sample guard condition could be $g(t) = \{\{(p, xml_p)\} \mid$ `<shippingType>express</shippingType>` *is part of xml_p*$\}$.

As seen in the motivating example, firing receive transitions might or might not result in state changes. In this context read arcs are a central feature. Firing transitions without outgoing arcs and only with read arcs as incoming arcs will not change the system's state and therefore is *safe*. Such transitions are solely used for resource reflection. However, this reflection is restricted to certain states of the system – defined by the read arcs.

Definition 2 (Transition Modes, Enablement and Firing). *Let $(P, T, F, F_{read}, T_S, T_R, init, g, uri)$ be a service net. A transition mode is a tuple $(\sigma_{in}, t, \sigma_{out})$ where $\sigma_{in} : \bullet t \to XML$ assigns documents to the input places of $t \in T$ and $\sigma_{out} : t\bullet \to XML$ documents to output places.*

A transition mode $tm = (\sigma_{in}, t, \sigma_{out})$ is enabled in marking m iff $\sigma_{in} \in g(t)$ and $\forall p \in \bullet t \ [\sigma_{in}(p) \in m(p)]$. The reached marking after firing of tm is m', where $m'(p) := m(p) - \{\sigma_{in}|_{q \in P|(q,t) \notin F_{read}}(p)\} + \{\sigma_{out}(p)\}$.

The firing semantics of service nets is similar to that of classical place / transition nets in the sense that a transition is enabled only if there is at least one token on each input place. Firing of a transition will lead to consuming one token from each input place (except in the case of read arcs) and producing one token onto each output place. Guard conditions further restrict the enablement of transitions. As tokens carry values, we speak of *transition modes*, i.e. bindings of values to input and output places of a transition.

We see that T_S, T_R and *uri* have no influence on the firing semantics of an individual service net. They are essential for the communication behavior, which is manifested in the composition of service nets.

3.2 Composition of Service Nets

The interaction behavior between multiple service nets is specified by the following definition of service net composition. We distinguish between *closed world*

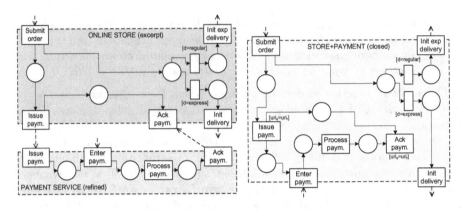

Fig. 3. Excerpt from the example   **Fig. 4.** Closed world composition

composition and *open world composition.* In a closed world, a communication transition is not available for communication any longer, once it is used in the composition. The definition of the open world is the more realistic one, where the same port can be used by different other services.

Definition 3 (Closed World Composition). *Let S_1 and S_2 be two service nets, where $P_1 \cap P_2 = \emptyset$ and $T_1 \cap T_2 \subseteq ((T_{S1} \cap T_{R2}) \cup (T_{S2} \cap T_{R1}))$. The closed world composition $S_1 \oplus_c S_2$ is the service net $(P', T', F', F'_{read}, T'_S, T'_R, init', g', uri')$ where*

- $P' = P_1 \cup P_2$, $T' = T_1 \cup T_2$, $F' = F_1 \cup F_2$, $F'_{read} = F_{read1} \cup F_{read2}$,
- $T'_S = (T_{S1} \cup T_{S2}) \setminus (T_1 \cap T_2)$,
- $T'_R = (T_{R1} \cup T_{R2}) \setminus (T_1 \cap T_2)$,
- $init' = init_1 \cup init_2$,
- $g'(t) = (g_1 \cup g_2)(t)$ *for all* $t \in (T_1 \cup T_2) \setminus (T_1 \cap T_2)$ *and else* $g'(t) = \{f_1 \cup f_2 \mid f_1 \in g_1(t) \wedge f_2 \in g_2(t) \wedge uri_1(t, f_1) = uri_2(t, f_2)\}$ *and*
- $uri' = (uri_1 \cup uri_2)|_{T'_S \cup T'_R}$.

The basic idea is to merge corresponding send and receive transitions when composing two service nets. As a transition might correspond to a number of ports, it is crucial to ensure that the URI addressed by the sender matches the URI offered by the receiver. This is manifested in the definition of $g'(t)$, where this matching of URIs is added as additional guard condition to the merged transitions. This URI matching realizes link passing mobility in service nets.

Figure 4 shows an example where parts of the online store's service net is composed with a service net describing the payment service. Here, the transitions "issue payment" and "ack. paym." are not communication transitions any longer.

Definition 4 (Open World Composition). *Let S_1 and S_2 be two service nets and $S_1 \oplus_c S_2 = (P, T, F, F_{read}, T_S, T_R, init, g, uri)$. Then the open world composition $S_1 \oplus_o S_2$ is the service net $(P, T', F', F'_{read}, T'_S, T'_R, init, g', uri')$, where*

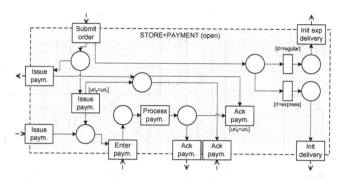

Fig. 5. Open world composition

- $T' = T \cup T_{new1} \cup T_{new2}$, where T_{new1} and T_{new2} are sets of new transitions where for each $x \in (T_1 \cap T_2)$ there is a transition t_{x1} in T_{new1} and a transition t_{x2} in T_{new2},
- $F' = F \cup \{(p, t_{x1}) \mid \exists p, x \ ((p, x) \in F_1)\} \cup \{(t_{x1}, p) \mid \exists p, x \ ((x, p) \in F_1)\} \cup \{(p, t_{x2}) \mid \exists p, x \ ((x, p) \in F_2)\} \cup \{(t_{x2}, p) \mid \exists p, x \ ((x, p) \in F_2)\}$,
- $F'_{read} = F_{read} \cup \{(p, t_{x1}) \mid \exists p, x \ ((p, x) \in F_{read1})\} \cup \{(p, t_{x2}) \mid \exists p, x \ ((p, x) \in F_{read2})\}$,
- $T'_S = (T_S \cup T_{new1} \cup T_{new2}) \cap (T_{S1} \cup T_{S2})$,
- $T'_R = (T_R \cup T_{new1} \cup T_{new2}) \cap (T_{R1} \cup T_{R2})$,
- $g'(t) = g(t)$ for all $t \in T$ and else $g'(t) = g_1(t)$ if $t \in T_{new1}$ and $g'(t) = g_2(t)$ if $t \in T_{new2}$ and
- $uri'(t) = uri(t)$ for all $t \in (T_S \cup T_R)$, $uri'(t) = uri_1(t)$ for all $t \in T_{new1}$ and $uri'(t) = uri_2(t)$ for all $t \in T_{new2}$.

Figure 5 illustrates the outcome of an open world composition for the same example. Here, payment might be issued to another service and other services might still issue payment. The same applies to the payment acknowledgment.

Regarding enablement and firing of service nets we assume that exactly one token is removed from every input place and exactly one token is placed onto every output place. That way, service nets can be simulated by corresponding place/transition nets. The only exception are read arcs, where corresponding tokens must be present on the place for a transition to be enabled. However, the token will not be consumed upon firing. For simulating this behavior in place/transition nets, read arcs could be seen as bi-flows. This works as long as the respective places that are read from are not output places at the same time.

We assume that there is no functional dependency between input token values and output token values, i.e. firing the same transition with the same input token values twice might yield different output token values.

4   Implementation Considerations

This section presents the service net execution engine we implemented. It behaves as specified in the previous section. Figure 6 provides an overview of the

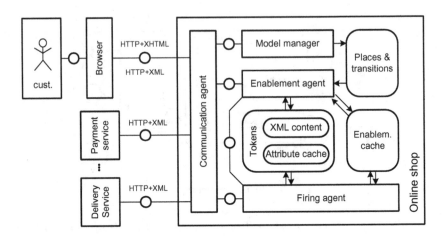

Fig. 6. Architecture of the service net execution engine

engine's overall architecture using the FMC block diagram notation [16]. Four main components can be distinguished within the engine:

- The *communication agent* handles incoming HTTP requests from the customer's web browser and the payment service and forwards them to the other agents. Furthermore, it issues HTTP requests to the payment service and the delivery services.
- The *model manager* deploys new Petri nets within the engine. The Petri Net Markup Language (PNML [4]) is used with engine-specific extensions. Internal representations of places and transitions are created.
- The *enablement agent* computes which transitions are currently enabled for what combinations of input tokens. This agent also evaluates guard conditions. If transitions are enabled and do not rely on an incoming HTTP request to be fired, the enablement agent triggers the firing agent.
- The *firing agent* is responsible for the firing of transitions. Firing leads to the deletion of tokens and the creation of new ones.

4.1 Concurrency

The engine runs within a web container and takes advantage of the multi-threading capabilities offered by the container. Parallel incoming HTTP requests are handled by different threads. The conflict between firing two transitions with the same input token is resolved on the database transaction level.

In the case of receive transitions, first the input tokens are consumed, then a response is returned to the requester, before output tokens are produced. This in turn immediately triggers the evaluation for enablement of subsequent transitions, which happens within the same thread. If such a subsequent transition is actually enabled, firing will occur immediately. Therefore, a certain sequentialization regarding internal transitions and send transitions applies. In case a send

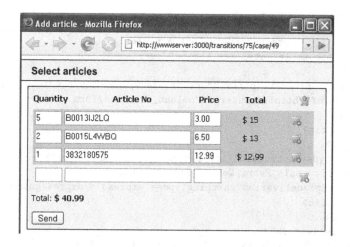

Fig. 7. Screenshot for "Select articles", realized using XForms

transition is enabled and the server handling requests for the corresponding URI does not respond or returns an error message, another outgoing HTTP request will be issued again later. A particular worker thread is assigned to realize such requests.

4.2 XForms Representations

In our case the web resources addressed are static and dynamic ports. Forms are the classical way for describing the data expected by a web resource. XForms [5] are a way for not only defining the syntax of expected XML documents but also prescribe how to render this XML information in an interactive web form. XForms is suited not only for interpretation by humans through web browser but also by machines, as the specification of the expected XML document can be given e.g. using an XML schema.

Figure 7 shows a screenshot of the form for the "select articles" transition from section 2. Upon submission of the form, the browser assembles an XML document as specified in the XForms model and sends it to the given URI as POST message.

4.3 Interchange Format

The Petri Net Markup Language (PNML [4]) is used as input format for the engine. While the concepts of places, transitions and arcs are already present in PNML, we added engine-specific extensions. Listing 1 shows a PNML code snippet for the example from section 2.

The listing shows two transitions and one place definition. The engine distinguishes four types of transitions: firing *receive* transitions is triggered through

Listing 1. PNML code snippet for the example

```
<transition type="receive" id="select_articles">...
  <toolspecific tool="Petri Net Engine" version="1.0">
    <output>
      <bindings href="http://wwwserver/select_articles/bindings.xml"/>
      <form href="http://wwwserver/select_articles/form.xml"/>
    </output>
  </toolspecific>
</transition>...
<transition type="automatic" id="forward_express_delivery">...
  <toolspecific tool="Petri Net Engine" version="1.0">
    <guard><expr>deliveries.shippingType=='express'</expr></guard>
  </toolspecific>
</transition>...
<place id="deliveries">...
  <toolspecific tool="Petri Net Engine" version="1.0">
    <locator>
      <name>shippingType</name><type>xsd:string</type>
      <expr>//shippingType/text()</expr>
    </locator>
  </toolspecific>
</place>...
```

incoming HTTP requests, firing *send* transitions results in outgoing HTTP requests, *automatic* transitions are internal transitions and *referer* transitions are used for GET messages only, referring the requester to another URI.

The definition of `select_articles` includes a reference to a XForms document. The *bindings* define how input token values are used as in the form. Transition `forward_express_delivery` includes the definition of a guard condition. `shippingType` is a so called *locator* for place `deliveries`. What part of the XML document is actually referenced by this locator is defined in the definition of place `deliveries`. This indirection mechanism allows caching of individual attributes that are relevant for guard conditions.

5   Related Work

This paper has used Petri nets as formal foundation for describing RESTful process execution. Petri nets are described in detail in [24] and colored Petri nets in [14]. The introduction of XML technology into Petri nets has already been done in [17] in the form of *XML nets*. Here, tokens carry XML documents that are consumed in and produced by transitions.

Petri nets have extensively been used for representing systems with interfaces to an outside world. In the case of *open workflow nets*, places serve as message channels that connect different systems. These nets can be used for deciding whether there are partners with which the system could interact successfully [25] and how such partners need to look like [18]. Using communication transitions for representing synchronous communication was already introduced in [28].

π-calculus is a process algebra that could be used as alternative to the service nets presented in this paper [19]. π-calculus directly supports link passing mobility. The distinction between static and dynamic ports made in this paper corresponds to free and bound names in π-calculus. The motivation for choosing Petri nets instead was driven by the need for using the Business Process Modeling Notation (BPMN) as high-level modeling language, and generating executable definitions out of it. Here, we could resort to existing implementations[1] doing BPMN to Petri net transformations, which are based on [9].

A first comparison between SOAP and REST as alternative technical grounding for service choreographies can be found in [29]. Although REST raises major interest among practitioners, it remains rather undiscussed in academia. Among the few academic papers concerning REST are [22,27].

RESTful process execution can be seen as alternative to service composition as proposed in Business Process Execution Language (BPEL [10]). A main difference is that BPEL only offers static ports. Relating messages to process instances is done by application-specific attributes, grouped into so called correlation sets. This hampers caching on the protocol level and does not allow for bookmarking of activity instances or process instances. Reflection is realized by event handlers in BPEL that do not alter the values of variables, resulting again in POST messages. Therefore, the communication intentions inherent in HTTP are largely ignored in BPEL. We have proposed an extension called RBPEL in [21], introducing dynamic ports through URI templates.

Bite [7] is a language for orchestrating REST services, using some of the constructs known from BPEL. With its scripting approach it does not require typing of variables nor the explicit definition of variables. However, the concept of dynamic ports as proposed in this paper is not present in this language. It still relies on correlation mechanisms similar to BPEL's.

Several process engines directly executing Petri nets have already been proposed [23,26]. Further engines use (colored) Petri nets as process definition language but translate the definition into an internal representation [2,13]. Our approach is different as it concentrates on RESTful communication with the environment, therefore allowing seamless integration into the World Wide Web.

6 Conclusion

This paper has discussed RESTful process execution on the basis of a special class of Petri nets. The main concepts of REST were introduced and related to the formal model. These include considering intentions on the protocol level and unique identification of resources. RESTful process execution as presented in this paper can be integrated with SOAP-based services. Before invoking such a service XML tokens would be wrapped into SOAP envelopes. In order to allow

---

[1] See http://oryx-editor.org for a running installation.

SOAP-based invocations by service requesters, a static port would be offered and the XML payload extracted from the SOAP message.

We have implemented a process engine that executes service nets. The engine is available under MIT license and a running installation including the example from section 2 can be accessed from the engine's homepage `http://code.google.com/p/pnengine/`.

Future work includes the introduction of further process execution aspects into service nets. As a major point, authorization needs to be considered, where static and dynamic ports are only accessible for certain users, e.g. only for those that where involved in the previous process steps. This requires extending guard conditions by the capability to refer to the requesting user. Other work centers around efficient execution of Petri nets. As BPMN serves as primary modeling language, the introduction of certain high-level Petri net constructs such as reset arcs and inhibitor arcs promises simplification of the nets and increased execution performance.

References

1. Adida, B., Birbeck, M.: RDFa Primer 1.0. Technical report, W3C (2006), `http://www.w3.org/TR/xhtml-rdfa-primer/`
2. Aversano, L., Cimitile, A., Gallucci, P., Villani, M.L.: FlowManager: A Workflow Management System Based on Petri Nets. In: COMPSAC 2002: Proceedings of the 26th International Computer Software and Applications Conference on Prolonging Software Life: Development and Redevelopment, Washington, DC, USA, pp. 1054–1059. IEEE Computer Society Press, Los Alamitos (2002)
3. Berners-Lee, T., Fielding, R., Masinter, L.: Uniform Resource Identifiers (URI): Generic Syntax. Technical report, The Internet Engineering Task Force (1998), `http://www.ietf.org/rfc/rfc2396.txt`
4. Billington, J., Christensen, S., van Hee, K.M., Kindler, E., Kummer, O., Petrucci, L., Post, R., Stehno, C., Weber, M.: The Petri Net Markup Language: Concepts, Technology, and Tools. In: van der Aalst, W.M.P., Best, E. (eds.) ICATPN 2003. LNCS, vol. 2679, pp. 483–505. Springer, Heidelberg (2003)
5. Boyer, J.M.: XForms 1.1. Technical report, W3C (November 2007), `http://www.w3.org/TR/xforms11/`
6. Burbeck, S.: The tao of e-business services: The evolution of web applications into service-oriented components with web services (October 2000), `www.ibm.com/developerworks/library/ws-tao/`
7. Curbera, F., Duftler, M.J., Khalaf, R., Lovell, D.: Bite: Workflow composition for the web. In: Krämer, B.J., Lin, K.-J., Narasimhan, P. (eds.) ICSOC 2007. LNCS, vol. 4749, pp. 94–106. Springer, Heidelberg (2007)
8. Curbera, F., Leymann, F., Storey, T., Ferguson, D., Weerawarana, S.: Web Services Platform Architecture: SOAP, WSDL, WS-Policy, WS-Addressing, WS-BPEL, WS-Reliable Messaging and More. Prentice Hall PTR, Englewood Cliffs (2005)
9. Dijkman, R.M., Dumas, M., Ouyang, C.: Semantics and Analysis of Business Process Models in BPMN. In: Information and Software Technology (IST) (2008)
10. Fallside, D.C., Walmsley, P.: Web Services Business Process Execution Language Version 2.0. Technical report (October 2005), `http://www.oasis-open.org/apps/org/workgroup/wsbpel/`

11. Fielding, R.: Architectural Styles and the Design of Network-based Software Architectures. PhD thesis, University of California, Irvine (2000)
12. Fielding, R., Gettys, J., Mogul, J., Frystyk, H., Masinter, L., Leach, P., Berners-Lee, T.: Hypertext Transfer Protocol – HTTP/1.1. Technical report, The Internet Engineering Task Force (1999), http://www.ietf.org/rfc/rfc2616
13. Guan, Z., Hernandez, F., Bangalore, P., Gray, J., Skjellum, A., Velusamy, V., Liu, Y.: Grid-Flow: a Grid-enabled scientific workflow system with a Petri-net-based interface. Concurr. Comput.: Pract. Exper. 18(10), 1115–1140 (2006)
14. Jensen, K.: Coloured Petri Nets: Basic Concepts, Analysis Methods and Practical Use, vol. 1. Springer, Heidelberg (1996)
15. Khare, R., Çelik, T.: Microformats: a Pragmatic Path to the Semantic Web. In: Proceedings of the 15th International World Wide Web Conference (2006)
16. Knopfel, A., Grone, B., Tabeling, P.: Fundamental Modeling Concepts: Effective Communication of IT Systems. Wiley, Chichester (2006)
17. Lenz, K., Oberweis, A.: Interorganizational Business Process Management with XML Nets. In: Ehrig, H., Reisig, W., Rozenberg, G., Weber, H. (eds.) Petri Net Technology for Communication-Based Systems. LNCS, vol. 2472, pp. 243–263. Springer, Heidelberg (2003)
18. Massuthe, P., Reisig, W., Schmidt, K.: An Operating Guideline Approach to the SOA. Annals of Mathematics, Computing & Teleinformatics 1(3), 35–43 (2005)
19. Milner, R., Parrow, J., Walker, D.: A Calculus of Mobile Processes. Information and Computation 100, 1–40 (1992)
20. Overdick, H.: The resource-oriented architecture. In: 2007 IEEE Congress on Services (Services 2007), pp. 340–347 (2007)
21. Overdick, H.: Towards Resource-Oriented BPEL. In: Proceedings of 2nd Workshop on Emerging Web Services Technology in Halle (Saale), German (2007)
22. Prescod, P.: Roots of the REST/SOAP Debate. In: Proceedings of the Extreme Markup Languages 2002 Conference, Montréal, Quebec, Canada (August 2002)
23. Purvis, M., Lemalu, S.: An adaptive distributed workflow system framework. In: APSEC 2000: Proceedings of the Seventh Asia-Pacific Software Engineering Conference, Washington, DC, USA, p. 311. IEEE Computer Society, Los Alamitos (2000)
24. Reisig, W.: Petri nets. Springer, Heidelberg (1985)
25. Schmidt, K.: Controllability of Open Workflow Nets. In: Enterprise Modelling and Information Systems Architectures, Bonn. Lecture Notes in Informatics (LNI), vol. P-75, pp. 236–249 (2005)
26. Verbeek, H.M.W.E., Hirnschall, A., van der Aalst, W.M.P.: XRL/Flower: Supporting Inter-organizational Workflows Using XML/Petri-Net Technology. In: Bussler, C.J., McIlraith, S.A., Orlowska, M.E., Pernici, B., Yang, J. (eds.) CAiSE 2002 and WES 2002. LNCS, vol. 2512, pp. 93–108. Springer, Heidelberg (2002)
27. Wilde, E.: What are you talking about? In: 2007 IEEE International Conference on Services Computing (SCC 2007), Salt Lake City, Utah, USA (July 2007)
28. Wolf, M.: Synchrone und asynchrone Kommunikation in offenen Workflownetzen. Studienarbeit, Humboldt-Universität zu Berlin (May 2007)
29. zur Muehlen, M., Nickerson, J.V., Swenson, K.D.: Developing web services choreography standards: the case of REST vs. SOAP. Decis. Support Syst. 40(1), 9–29 (2005)

Validation and Discovery of Non-deterministic Semantic e-Services

Luigi Dragone

CM Sistemi S.p.A. – via Simone Martini, 126 – Roma
luigi.dragone@gruppocm.it

Abstract. We present a logic-based framework that is able to model semantic e-services and to verify some of properties supporting the design and mainte-nance of cooperative information systems. This framework is based upon a formal foundation of the *Semantic Web*, as the Description Logic family, that provides an expressive specification language, allowing for complex application domains. We adopt the well-known IOPE (Input, Output, Preconditions, and Effects) par-adigm for the description of e-service contracts, providing a suitable operational semantics and we are able to reason about update effects also in case of under-specified e-services, using a repair-based approach. On this base, we firstly define some basic consistency and correctness properties, and then we characterize the adequacy of an e-service to achieve a user goal as foundational task in service discovery. We present decidable checking procedures for the devised properties using a reduction technique to First-Order Logic reasoning tasks, including an analysis in terms of computational complexity.

1 Introduction

The adoption of the service-oriented computing paradigm in the construction of Enter-prise and Cooperative Information Systems, given several issues concerning the level of autonomy and heterogeneity, has made manifest the requirement for a clear, flexi-ble and feasible way to denote the semantics of a generic e-service and to analyze its properties.

Indeed, given the emphasis on the strong encapsulation on the actual implementation of such cooperation units, the e-service interface specification is often the only avail-able way to formalize the *contract* between the provider and the requestor. So, several approaches integrating techniques stemming from different fields of Computer Science have been devised to address many foundational aspects in the design and maintenance of these complex systems as such: the specification of e-service contract semantics, the verification of consistency of such specifications w.r.t. a set of constraints regarding the surrounding environment, the specification of user requirements and the discovery of services that are able to achieve them. Roughly speaking, a semantically annotated e-service (or semantic e-service) adopts the formal base of the *Semantic Web*, enriched with the ability to deal with its intrinsic dynamic nature. Among different proposals, many of them rely on a family of knowledge representation languages, the Description Logics (DL), since they provide both a clear semantics and effective reasoning tools ([2]). While these languages are often very suitable to express the domain knowledge

R. Bruni and K. Wolf (Eds.): WS-FM 2008, LNCS 5387, pp. 88–106, 2009.
© Springer-Verlag Berlin Heidelberg 2009

and constraints about system states, given the fact that they are essentially devoted to the definition of static properties, they need an adequate enrichment in order to deal with dynamic features.

In our framework, we show how to address the mentioned topics using a logic-based approach that essentially relies on performing some computable reasoning tasks in First-Order Logic (FOL), even in case of incomplete specifications. In particular, in this paper we present the following main contributions: (1) an enriched knowledge-based system specification language allowing for non-deterministic and conditional behaviors; (2) the characterization of e-service consistency and correctness properties; (3) the characterization of semantic properties related to the e-service discovery problem; and (4) the corresponding verification algorithms including an analysis of the computational complexity.

The rest of the paper is organized as follows: we start presenting the service specification model, then we analyze correctness-related semantic properties and we introduce a model for the specification of user goals. On this foundation, we analyze the match-making problem between the service capabilities and user requirements, sketching the logic encoding approach, providing also a complexity analysis of devised problems. For the sake of brevity, we have omitted proofs of formal claims reported in this paper, the interested readers can refer to [5].

2 The Specification Model

In this section we introduce the syntax and the semantics of the specification model used in our framework. A first version of this model has been presented in [6]: we now extend it adopting a more expressive DL language. We also include in the model the ability to deal with complex service specifications, allowing conditional and non-deterministic behaviors.

2.1 Description Logics

The family of DLs ([2]) has been initially devised as a formal tool to support the specification of knowledge representation systems, providing a decidable, and preferably tractable, semantics.

Among a wide range of expressive languages, we adopt an extension of the well-known language $\mathcal{ALCQI}$ with enhanced role constructs. This language, denoted as $\mathcal{ALCQI}(\sqcup, \sqcap, \uparrow, \downarrow, \triangle)$, is defined in terms of concept and role expressions according to the following syntax:

$$C, C' \longrightarrow A \mid \neg C \mid C \sqcap C' \mid (\bowtie n\, R\, C)$$
$$R, R' \longrightarrow P \mid R^- \mid R \sqcup R' \mid R \sqcap R' \mid R \uparrow C \mid R \downarrow C \mid \triangle$$

where A and P denote, respectively, atomic concept and atomic role names, C and R denote, respectively, arbitrary concepts and roles, $n \in \mathbb{N}$ and $\bowtie \in \{=, <, >, \leq, \geq\}$ is a generic relational operator on natural numbers. The language $\mathcal{ALBO}$ ([11]) enriches

Table 1. Semantic of the $\mathcal{ALBO}$ description logic

$$A^{\mathcal{I}} \subseteq \Delta^{\mathcal{I}} \qquad\qquad P^{\mathcal{I}} \subseteq \Delta^{\mathcal{I}} \times \Delta^{\mathcal{I}}$$
$$(\neg C)^{\mathcal{I}} = \Delta^{\mathcal{I}} \setminus C^{\mathcal{I}} \qquad (\neg R)^{\mathcal{I}} = \Delta^{\mathcal{I}} \times \Delta^{\mathcal{I}} \setminus R^{\mathcal{I}}$$
$$(C \sqcap C')^{\mathcal{I}} = C^{\mathcal{I}} \cap C'^{\mathcal{I}} \qquad (R \sqcap R')^{\mathcal{I}} = R^{\mathcal{I}} \cap R'^{\mathcal{I}}$$
$$\{o\}^{\mathcal{I}} = \left\{ o^{\mathcal{I}} \right\} \qquad\qquad (R^-)^{\mathcal{I}} = \left\{ \langle o, o' \rangle \in \Delta^{\mathcal{I}} \times \Delta^{\mathcal{I}} | \langle o', o \rangle \in R^{\mathcal{I}} \right\}$$

$$(\bowtie n\, R\, C)^{\mathcal{I}} = \left\{ o \in \Delta^{\mathcal{I}} | \left\| \left\{ o' \in \Delta^{\mathcal{I}} | \langle o, o' \rangle \in R^{\mathcal{I}} \wedge o' \in C^{\mathcal{I}} \right\} \right\| \bowtie n \right\}$$
$$(R \upharpoonright C)^{\mathcal{I}} = \left\{ \langle o, o' \rangle \in \Delta^{\mathcal{I}} \times \Delta^{\mathcal{I}} | \langle o, o' \rangle \in R^{\mathcal{I}} \wedge o \in C^{\mathcal{I}} \right\}$$

the $\mathcal{ALCQI}(\sqcup, \sqcap, \upharpoonright, \downharpoonright, \triangle)$ expression language with nominals and arbitrary boolean role expressions:

$$C, C' \longrightarrow A \,|\, \neg C \,|\, C \sqcap C' \,|\, (\bowtie n\, R\, C) \,|\, \{o\}$$
$$R, R' \longrightarrow P \,|\, R^- \,|\, \neg R \,|\, R \sqcap R' \,|\, R \upharpoonright C$$

Other operators (e.g., $\sqcup, \forall, \exists, \top, \downharpoonright, \upharpoonright, \triangle$) can be defined in terms of primitive ones. The concepts $\top$ and $\bot$ denote resp. the interpretation universe and the empty set, while roles $\triangledown$ and $\triangle$ resp. the total symmetric and empty relations. The semantics of such a language is defined w.r.t. an interpretation structure $\mathcal{I}$ s.t. concept names are interpreted as subsets of the domain $\Delta^{\mathcal{I}}$ and roles and object names, respectively, as binary relations and elements over $\Delta^{\mathcal{I}}$, as reported in Tab. 1.

A *knowledge base* (KB) is a pair $\langle \mathcal{T}, \mathcal{A} \rangle$ formed of a *terminological box* or TBox $\mathcal{T}$ and an *assertional box* or ABox $\mathcal{A}$. The former is a set containing *concept inclusion axioms* in the form $C \sqsubseteq D$ (let C and D be arbitrary concept expressions) and *role inclusion axioms* $R \sqsubseteq S$ (let R and S be arbitrary role expressions). The latter is a set of object membership axioms or assertional sentences in the forms $o : C$ and $(o, o') : R$. An interpretation $\mathcal{I}$ satisfies, or is a *model* of, the knowledge base iff, for each $C \sqsubseteq D \in \mathcal{T}$, $C^{\mathcal{I}} \subseteq D^{\mathcal{I}}$, for each $R \sqsubseteq S \in \mathcal{T}$, $R^{\mathcal{I}} \subseteq S^{\mathcal{I}}$, for each $o : C \in \mathcal{A}$, $o^{\mathcal{I}} \in C^{\mathcal{I}}$ and for each $(o, o') : R \in \mathcal{A}$, $\langle o^{\mathcal{I}}, o'^{\mathcal{I}} \rangle \in R^{\mathcal{I}}$. Generally, the TBox is considered as the *intensional specification* of the knowledge base, while the ABox is the *extensional one*. The $\mathcal{ALBO}$ language allows also for another kind of axioms, i.e., *cardinality restrictions* that have the form $\sharp(C) \bowtie n$: an interpretation $\mathcal{I}$ is a model for the above axiom iff $\|C\|^{\mathcal{I}} \bowtie n$. Such a kind of DLs also have a *standard semantics* in terms of FOL fragment function-free with counting quantifiers $\mathcal{C}^2$ ([7]), that will be useful in the following. We point out that these languages are decidable in NEXP (both $\mathcal{ALBO}$ and $\mathcal{C}^2$ are NEXP-complete). It is worth noting that such languages are able to capture a large part of the underlaying formalization of concrete Semantic Web standards as DAML and OWL.

2.2 Syntax and Semantics

We now, briefly, introduce the specification language and its most relevant semantic definitions. In the following, we assume that an infinite countable universe $\mathfrak{U}$ is given and that the system is described using a *domain specification* $\langle A, P, O \rangle$ composed of three finite mutually disjoint sets: resp. the concept, the role and the object alphabets. The object names are constantly interpreted according to the *standard-names assumption* on a finite subset $\mathfrak{O} \subset \mathfrak{U}$ of the given universe, i.e., by a bijective function $\cdot^{\mathcal{I}} : \mathbf{O} \mapsto \mathfrak{O}$. A system state (or *world state*) is defined using an interpretation of these alphabets on a subset $\Delta^{\omega} \subseteq \mathfrak{U}$ of the whole interpretation domain (*active domain*), that includes all objects that are active at a given point.

Moreover, according to most applications of KR techniques, generally, not every interpretation can be considered to be a legal system state representation, so we introduce the ability to restrict the state space to the valid ones by means of a constraint set, expressed using a suitable language.

Definition 1 (World specification). *A world specification* $\mathcal{W} = \langle \mathcal{T}, \mathcal{A} \rangle$ *is a knowledge base expressed on the domain* $\langle A, P, O \rangle$ *using the DL* $\mathcal{ALCQI}(\sqcup, \sqcap, \uparrow, \downarrow, \triangle)$.

A world state ω is *legal* w.r.t. a specification $\mathcal{W}$ if it is a model of such a theory, while a specification is *consistent* if it admits at least a model. Considering the system axiomatized using such a KB, we can now introduce the language to specify the semantics of update operators that are able to realize system state transitions (i.e., e-services).

In the following, we basically distinguish between two kinds of such entities that are able to model resp. glass-box and black-box behaviors:

conditional e-services, which explicitly state how they select, among a set of declared behaviors, the enactment results;

non-deterministic e-services, which declare multiple possible alternative behaviors, keeping the decision protocol hidden.

While the first kind of e-service is more suitable to describe interfaces encapsulating components of conventional information management systems, which are implementing some kind of automated task (e.g., a database procedure), the latter is applicable to model (as an e-service) a complex business process that can possibly involve multiple autonomous actors (not necessarily a software component or application), interacting in order to select the enactment outcome. The following specification is able to catch both considered types, as well as any intermediate situations.

Definition 2 (e-service specification). *An e-service specification S, given a domain specification, is a quadruple formed by: (1) a (possibly empty) finite set of input variable names X; (2) a (possibly empty) finite set of output or instantiation variable names Y; (3) a (possibly empty) finite set of invocation precondition constraints* $\mathcal{P}$; *(4) a non-empty finite set* $\mathcal{E}$ *of conditional effect specifications.*

Informally, according to the IOPE (Input, Output, Preconditions, and Effects) paradigm, a service is defined specifying the values required for its execution, the values resulting from the execution itself, the conditions under which it can be requested by a client, and the updates performed. We point out that IOPE is a well-known approach widely adopted in many field of Software Engineering, not last to mention in reference standard languages for Semantic Web Services as OWL-S. The definition of the non-deterministic behavior can be obtained considering that the executing agent (the service provider) simply non-deterministically chooses a (conditional) effect and then realizes it. Generally speaking, a *precondition constraint* is a conjunction of positive (resp. negative) *atomic conditions*. An atomic condition is a pair $\langle s, Q(\mathbf{X}')\rangle$ where: (1) $s \in \{+, -\}$ is the sign of the precondition (positive or negative); (2) $Q(\mathbf{X}')$ is a *parametric query* over the domain specification in the variables $\mathbf{X}' \subseteq \mathbf{X}$. As query language we adopt both the concept and role expression languages of $\mathcal{ALBO}$, employed using an extended alphabet including also variable symbols as singleton concept names in the domain specification. A positive (resp. negative) condition is satisfied if the result of the query is not empty (resp. empty) given an input variable assignment and a world state[1].

A *conditional effect specification* is defined as a finite rooted labeled binary tree s.t. for each node n: (1) if n is a non-leaf node, then it is annotated with a set of branching conditions; (2) otherwise, it is annotated with a pair composed by an instantiation set and a simple effect. Intuitively, the labels corresponding to branching conditions are evaluated starting from the root node of the tree and using a pre-order visit strategy. If the current node n is a leaf one, the associated effect specification is kept as the execution outcome. For a non-leaf node, if the condition specified by the node label is satisfied, then the right child node is visited, otherwise the left one is visited, until a leaf node is reached. A *branching condition* is expressed, as precondition constraints, as a conjunction of signed atomic conditions. Given the tree-based structure of the condition specification model, we have that, given a world state ω and an input variable assignment $\sigma_{\mathbf{X}}$, exactly one effect is selected or, in other words, conditional e-services are always unambiguous and completely defined.

Let $\mathbf{Y}$ be the output variable set of a service S, an *instantiation set* $\mathbf{Y}'$ is any arbitrary (possibly empty) subset of $\mathbf{Y}$, denoting objects actually instantiated by the leaf effect, if selected. Finally, a *simple effect* E is an arbitrary set of atomic concept and role effects built according to its variable names and domain specification. An atomic concept (resp. role) effect is a triple $\langle s, A, a\rangle$ (resp., a quadruple $\langle s, P, l, r\rangle$ or a triple $\langle s, P, p\rangle$) s.t.: (1) $s \in \{+, -\}$ is the sign of the effect (insert or delete); (2) $A \in \mathbf{A}$ (resp. $P \in \mathbf{P}$) is the target concept (resp. role) name; (3) a (resp. l and r or p) is the argument of the update (positive or negative) according to the sign of the effect. A *positive effect argument* is any element $Y \in \mathbf{Y}'$ of the associated instantiation set or any parametric query $Q(\mathbf{X}')$ over the domain specification in the variables $\mathbf{X}' \subseteq \mathbf{X}$. A *negative effect argument* is defined as a parametric query $Q(\mathbf{X}')$. While a, l and r are concept expressions, p denotes a role expression. Roughly speaking, a simple effect specifies which elements (or pair of elements) are inserted or removed from a set (or a binary relation). Generally, each atomic effect can affect more elements since its application range is denoted using queries[2].

In order to introduce the semantics of dynamic features, we have to denote sets of elements (or element pairs) affected by an update. For example, a *concept insert set*

---

[1] Since we adopt a *conjunctive normal form* to express conditions, arbitrary boolean expressions whose atoms are parametric queries can be used ($F, F' \longrightarrow Q(\mathbf{X}) \mid \text{not } F \mid F \text{ and } F' \mid F \text{ or } F'$).

[2] Moreover, an atomic effect can be more concisely written also using the notation $+A(a), -A(a), +P(l, r), -P(l, r), +P(p), -P(p)$.

A^+ of concept $A \in \mathbf{A}$ denotes the extension of the model that is affected by the update as element that will be added to the interpretation of the name A. Analogously, we can define the set of removed elements and affected pairs of binary relations $P \in \mathbf{P}$ (denoted as A^-, P^+ and P^-). So, given the previous definitions, we can finally introduce dynamic aspects, defining the transition relation between system states resulting from the enactment of a service.

Definition 3 (Successor relation). *Given a pair of world states ω and ω', an input and output variable assignments σ_X and σ'_Y consistently defined w.r.t. ω, we say that ω' is a (potential) successor state of ω, resulting from the execution of an e-service S according to provided inputs, realizing the simple effect E^* and instantiating the set Y^*, iff: (1) there exists a conditional effect E of S s.t. the pair $\langle E^*, Y^* \rangle$ is associated to a leaf-node of E and it is selected according to ω and σ_X; (2) the output assignment is defined over Y^* or, in other words, that $dom(\sigma'_Y) = Y^*$; (3) the interpretation domain $\Delta^{\omega'}$ of the successor state is the smallest subset of $\mathfrak{U}$ s.t. $\Delta^\omega \cup cod(\sigma'_Y) \subseteq \Delta^{\omega'}$; (4) the interpretation of object names is preserved, i.e. $o^\omega = o^{\omega'}$; (5) for each concept or role name $N \in \mathbf{A} \cup \mathbf{P}$, the insert set is included in the successor state interpretation, i.e. $N^{\omega'} \supseteq N^+(\omega, \sigma_X, \sigma'_Y)$, and the delete set is excluded, i.e. $N^{\omega'} \cap N^-(\omega, \sigma_X) \subseteq \emptyset$.*

The set of possible successor states attainable from a state ω, applying the effect E of a service using the assignment σ_X and σ'_Y is denoted as $\Omega_E(\omega, \sigma_X, \sigma'_Y)$, where $\mathbf{Y}$ is the set of newly instantiated object names. Among the potential successor states resulting from the execution of a service that realizes its effects, we are interested in the states that minimally differ from the initial one according to a notion of *minimal-change semantics*. In particular, we adopt a structure-distance metric based on the number of elements whose interpretation (e.g., concept membership) changes from a structure to another based on the *set symmetric difference* ([10]), applied to concept and role alphabets $\mathbf{A}$ and $\mathbf{P}$ and denoted as $d(\cdot, \cdot)$.

Definition 4 (Transition relation). *Let ω and ω' be a pair of world states, s.t. the latter is resulting from the enactment of an e-service S in the state defined from the former, given an input and an output variable assignments σ_X and σ'_Y consistently defined, we say that there is a system state transition from ω to ω' using the specified e-service iff there exists an effect $E \in \mathcal{E}$ s.t.: (1) ω' is a (potential) successor state of ω w.r.t. the given assignments according to E; (2) and there does not exist any other potential successor state ω'' of ω, w.r.t. the same assignments and service effect, s.t. it is closer to ω than ω' according to the symmetric difference distance, that means that $d(\omega, \omega') \leq d(\omega, \omega'')$ for any $\omega'' \in \Omega_E(\omega, \sigma_X, \sigma'_Y)$.*

The *service enactment* $S(\omega, \sigma_X)$ for a state ω and a consistent input variable assignment σ_X is a set containing all the pairs $\langle \omega', \sigma'_Y \rangle$ s.t. there is a service effect $E \in \mathcal{E}$, σ'_Y is a consistent instantiation assignment of the selected effect in E w.r.t. ω and σ_X, and ω and ω' are in transition relation w.r.t. the assignment and the service effect. We notice that the number of possible enactments is infinite, due to the non-deterministic choice on the instantiation assignment, even in presence of a single conditional effect ($\|\mathcal{E}\| = 1$): however, it turns out that they are actually indistinguishable under as constraint language as $\mathcal{ALCQI}(\sqcup, \sqcap, \uparrow, \downarrow, \triangle)$, extending the conclusions of [9].

Table 2. An example world specification $\mathcal{W}$

$\exists \mathsf{resln}^-.\top \sqsubseteq \mathsf{Town}$	$\mathsf{Citizen} \sqcap \mathsf{Town} \sqsubseteq \bot$	$\exists \mathsf{own}^-.\top \sqsubseteq \mathsf{Citizen}$
$\exists \mathsf{resln}.\top \sqsubseteq \mathsf{Citizen}$	$\mathsf{Citizen} \sqcap \mathsf{Good} \sqsubseteq \bot$	$\mathsf{Shop} \sqsubseteq (\leq 1 \; \mathsf{own} \; \top)$
$\exists \mathsf{authFor}.\top \sqsubseteq \mathsf{Citizen}$	$\mathsf{Good} \sqcap \mathsf{Town} \sqsubseteq \bot$	$\mathsf{Good} \sqsubseteq (\leq 1 \; \mathsf{own} \; \top)$
$\mathsf{Citizen} \sqsubseteq (= 1 \; \mathsf{resln} \; \top)$	$\mathsf{Shop} \sqcap \mathsf{Town} \sqsubseteq \bot$	$\mathsf{Vehicle} \sqsubseteq \mathsf{Good}$
$\exists \mathsf{regln}^-.\top \sqsubseteq \mathsf{Town}$	$\mathsf{Shop} \sqcap \mathsf{Good} \sqsubseteq \bot$	$t_1 \; : \; \mathsf{Town}$
$\mathsf{Vehicle} \sqsubseteq (= 1 \; \mathsf{regln} \; \top)$	$\mathsf{Shop} \sqcap \mathsf{Citizen} \sqsubseteq \bot$	$t_2 \; : \; \mathsf{Town}$

Lemma 1. *Let ω be a world state, σ_X a consistent input variable assignment, and S an e-service. If $\langle \omega_1, \sigma'_1 \rangle$ and $\langle \omega_2, \sigma'_2 \rangle$ are two enactments in $S(\omega, \sigma_X)$ obtained by the same effect $E \in \mathcal{E}$, then they are isomorphic.*

Proof (sketch). In order to prove the claim we need to provide a bijective function, mapping the structures resulting from the enactment, $h : \Delta^{\omega_1} \mapsto \Delta^{\omega_2}$ s.t. the interpretation of concept, role and object names is preserved according to the morphism.

For instance, let p be a concept name, for any element $x \in \Delta^{\omega_1}$ we have that $x \in p^{\omega_1} \leftrightarrow h(x) \in p^{\omega_2}$. Similar conditions can be stated for role and object names. Such a function can be defined as:

$$h(x) = \begin{cases} x & x \in \Delta^\omega \\ \sigma'_2(Y) & \sigma'_1(Y) = x \end{cases}$$

This function is well-defined since it is total ($dom(h) = \Delta^{\omega_1} = \Delta^\omega \cup cod(\sigma'_1)$) and it maps each element of its domain to exactly one element of its codomain ($cod(h) = \Delta^{\omega_2} = \Delta^\omega \cup cod(\sigma'_2)$). Showing that h is bijective and it also satisfies conditions on the morphism w.r.t. the specification domain completes the proof.

Moreover, according to this claim, we need, at most, to keep into account, for a given starting condition, a successor state for each non-deterministic effect specification. This is a key property in order to ensure the decidability of the approach. As we show in following sections, we admit that service specifications can be only partial or, in other words, that they define only a subset of their effects (the most relevant to the designer), leaving the system to compute other side-effects required to preserve the global consistency. Moreover, the adopted repair-based strategy can deal with the minimal-change semantics also in case of side-effects, since we are able to select the smallest suitable repair among generated ones, in terms of number of affected elements or pairs.

Example 1. Let $\mathcal{W}$ be an axiomatization of a simple domain, where people interact with e-services provided by public administrations. $\mathcal{W}$ contains the assertions reported in Tab. 2, where concept and role names have the intuitive meaning. According to the given axiomatization, each good has an own, while vehicles must be registered in the local administrative department. Suppose, for example, that there exists a service S that allows a citizen to change its own residence and to specify the new one. It can be modeled considering the input parameters x_1 and x_2 denoting, resp., the citizen who is asking for the change and the new residence town, while output signature is void. The service preconditions can be expressed as $x_1 \sqcap$ Citizen and $x_2 \sqcap$ Town and not $x_2 \sqcap \exists\mathsf{resln}^-.x_1$, while the only effect is defined by the update $\{-\mathsf{resln}(x_1, \exists\mathsf{resln}^-.x_1), +\mathsf{resln}(x_1, x_2)\}$. This service is accessible by every citizen, and allows selecting any town as the new residence location. The town t_1 provides also an enhanced version to its inhabitants that ask for a residence change. Such enriched e-service S_1 is restricted only to citizens of t_1, but it is capable also to accordingly change the registration of vehicles belonging to the requestor, in the sense that the vehicles belonging to the requestor will be registered to the authority of the target town. The service preconditions are now $x_1 \sqcap \exists\mathsf{resln}.\{t_1\}$ and $x_2 \sqcap$ Town and not $x_2 \sqcap \{t_1\}$, while the only effect included in $\mathcal{E}$ is specified as:

$$E = \{-\mathsf{resln}(x_1, \exists\mathsf{resln}^-.x_1), +\mathsf{resln}(x_1, x_2), -\mathsf{regln}(\mathsf{Vehicle} \sqcap \exists\mathsf{own}.x_1, \{t_1\}))\}$$
$$\cup \{+\mathsf{regln}(\mathsf{Vehicle} \sqcap \exists\mathsf{own}.x_1, x_2)\}$$

3   Basic Semantic Properties

In the following we discuss about some basic properties of semantic e-services specified using the present framework. These properties are mainly related to the formal correctness of the system and are a typical application object of computer-aided validation techniques.

We have analyzed these properties in [6] considering the well-foundedness of simple e-services (essentially e-services allowing only for a single non-conditional effect). In this paper we extend the discussion even to non-deterministic conditional e-services, essentially showing that the same approach with some adequate technical adjustments is able to cope also with these new modeling primitives.

One of the first questions that we need to address during the analysis of the system is whether the service access preconditions are actually realizable in the world described by the constraint set. In other words, we are asking if a service is accessible from at least a system state that is compatible with $\mathcal{W}$. Since the set of precondition constraints $\mathcal{P}$, is interpreted as a disjunction of such constraints, a service is *accessible* if there exists a legal world state and an assignment s.t. it can be activated consistently with an element of such a set. Moreover, we can also require that an effect conditional branch is *non-redundant* or, in other words, that there exists some legal world state and admissible input assignment s.t. the leaf effect is selected (i.e., the formula obtained combining branching conditions from the root node is satisfied). A service is *well-founded* if there is no redundant effect.

In order to provide a consistent definition of service effects, we need also to verify that, for every concept or role, the insert and delete sets are always distinct. An effect is *consistent* if for each legal world state and for each consistent assignment, there is no element or element pair that belongs both to the insert set and the delete set of some concept or role.

This definition of consistency for service effects is a necessary but not sufficient condition in order to ensure the correctness of an e-service acting in a world subject to a constraint set represented by the specification $\mathcal{W}$. In fact, this is a kind of internal effect

consistency, since it simply assures that the enactment effects are *per se* not contradic-
tory. On the other hand, we are also interested in the property of a service that always
acts consistently with the specification of the system, and at the same time is able to fulfill its contract every time it is activated consistently. In other terms, given a legal state
where the service preconditions hold, the service invocation must result into a legal state
where the declared effects are realized. The service contract is defined presuming that
the invocation preconditions are sufficient in order to obtain the declared service effects
by an enactment. More specifically, we are interested in the analysis of consistency of
state transitions resulting from the enactment of a generic service: only transitions that
results into structures that are model of the world specification theory $\mathcal{W}$ are allowed.

Definition 5 (Valid e-service). *Let S be a consistent e-service, it is valid w.r.t. a world
specification $\mathcal{W}$, iff for each legal world state ω, for each consistent input assignment
σ_X, s.t. the service is accessible in ω using it, there exists at least a legal state ω' in the
enactment (i.e., $\omega \models \mathcal{W}$).*

The analysis of service validity is a useful tool, but in order to fully exploit the capabilities of a knowledge-based verification framework we need to address also the case of a
service incomplete specifications, where only primary effects are intentionally stated. In
other words, we remove the assumption that only declared effects are actually enforced,
allowing for some side-effects eventually realized in order to ensure a consistent behavior as an *update repair*. However, the problem of repairing even a simple update in
presence of a complex intensional knowledge base (or a complex constraint set) turns
out to be very hard, since, given the complexity of the axiom language, non-local repair
side-effects may arise. This means that, in order to enforce consistently an update, we
could have to retract a relevant part of the previous knowledge base. Some authors have
addressed the problem limiting the constraint language to a simpler form (e.g., acyclic
or definitorial TBox), but in the general case the problem is undecidable both in DL
([3]) and in relational database schemas ([1]). Indeed, according to [3], the problem is
undecidable in the general case allowing for unrestricted constraint set in expressive
DLs, but, we are interested to assess whether, if we renounce to the completeness of the
repair search, limiting to a restricted, and finite, set of possible repairs, we can regain
the decidability.

In particular, the devised approach relies on the syntactical generation of repairing
additional effects starting from singleton values (like variables and constants) mentioned in the problem setting, performing a kind of search in the space of candidate
interpretation structures locally w.r.t. the set symmetric distance. A *simple repair* R for
an e-service S is an arbitrary set of atomic concept and role repairs, possibly empty, s.t.
it does not contain any pair of conflicting atomic repairs (i.e., atomic repair differing
only by the sign). An *atomic repair* is a special kind of atomic effect, which arguments
range over any nominal introduced in the specification (i.e., object and input variable
names). Restricting our attention to simple repairs, we can assume, as repair search
space for a given e-service S, a set $\mathcal{R}$ s.t.: (1) it includes the null repair $\emptyset$; (2) given any
non-empty repair $R \in \mathcal{R}$, each subset $R' \subset R$ s.t. $\|R\| = \|R'\| + 1$ is also included in
$\mathcal{R}$. Such a set is also called *normal repair family*.

As discussed in [6], we can observe that the number of different repairs, or, in other
words, the size of the search space, is finite and exponentially bounded by the number

of alphabet elements (in terms of names). At the same time, the number of possible re-pairs is substantially independent of the number and size of world specification axioms and service effect statements. Given an e-service with such an update repair capabil-ity, we have to refine the definitions related to system dynamics, in order to keep into account also the repairing step that, intuitively, follows the instantiation and updating ones. Moreover, among multiple repaired successor states, the repairing strategy selects the one closest to the base successor state ω', in terms of symmetric difference between interpretation structures, in order to enforce a kind of minimal-change repair.

Definition 6 (Repairable e-service). *Let S be a consistent e-service, and $\mathcal{R}$ a set of repairs, S is repairable w.r.t. a world specification $\mathcal{W}$ iff for each legal world state ω, for each consistent input assignment σ_X, s.t. the service is accessible in ω using it, there exists a state ω' in the enactment and a repair $R \in \mathcal{R}$ s.t. the repaired state ω'_R is legal (i.e., $\omega'_R \models \mathcal{W}$).*

Example 2. The ability to deal with non-deterministic behaviors turns extremely useful to model a large class of e-government services: *authoritative services*. In fact, several services provided by public administration are concerning with allowing or disallowing a citizen to perform an action. Given the world specification introduced in the previous, the following e-service T allows owners of commercial activity (i.e., a shop) to ask for the authorization to start the business (i.e., such an activity it is regulated by some restrictive laws). Let x be the only input variable denoting the commercial activity, the service definition includes the preconditions $x \sqcap \mathsf{Shop} \sqcap \exists\mathsf{own}.\top$ and $\mathsf{not}\,(\exists\mathsf{own}^-.x) \sqcap (\exists\mathsf{authFor}.x)$ and two possible effects: the empty update if the authorization is denied (nothing changes) and the update $\{+\mathsf{authFor}(\exists\mathsf{own}^-.x, x)\}$ otherwise.

4 Semantic Service Discovery

Once introduced the foundational semantic properties, we now present the application of the proposed framework to the analysis of other semantic properties. In particular, a typical task in the construction of a service-oriented application is the lookup of a suitable, or preferably the most suitable, available service to achieve a user's goal. Gen-erally speaking, a goal is specified as a condition over the domain specification language stating the world desired properties as resulting from the execution of a service, from the user perspective (e.g., which conditions should be satisfied after a successful service enactment?) . Possibly, a goal can be enriched with a condition describing the properties that hold in the world before the enactment, as a sort of client commitment.

Definition 7 (Execution goal). *An execution goal G is defined as a triple formed by: (1) a (possibly empty) finite set U_G of goal instantiation parameter names; (2) a (possibly empty) finite set of simple conditions, expressed using the parameter names as variables, stating parameter properties and client commitment $\mathcal{H}_G$; (3) a non-empty finite set of simple conditions, expressed using the parameter names as variables, stat-ing the properties, in terms of the state of the world, that the client wants to achieve, as requirement conditions $\mathcal{R}_G$.*

The language adopted in the specification of goal constraints is the same employed in the specification of service conditions (e.g., preconditions or branching conditions). Generally speaking, in order to call a service, we need to accordingly assign its input parameters, so given a user goal (ground or not) we need to express a suitable way to bind service inputs. W.l.o.g. we can assume that a binding function is provided, which means that the adequacy of the service to the goal is analyzed w.r.t. such a kind of functions. In our framework, we restrict our attention to binding functions that are expressed by means of *access function queries* or, in other words, queries s.t., considering the world specification $\mathcal{W}$, given a suitable parameter assignment, are evaluated to singleton sets (i.e., they return at most a result element). So a *binding schema B* between two variable sets $\mathbf{V}_G$ and $\mathbf{V}_S$ is a function that assigns to each $V \in \mathbf{V}_S$ an access function, w.r.t. $\mathcal{W}$, parameterized over $\mathbf{V}_G$. We can, of course, impose some additional restrictions on allowable goals and binding schemas in order to ensure a more consistent behavior, we omit them here for the sake of brevity. Let G be an admissible execution goal, given a valid/repairable service S and a consistent binding schema B, we are interested in assessing the adequacy degree of the service to achieve a world state compatible with the goal requirement starting from a world state s.t. client commitments hold using the binding schema. According to the quantification on initial and resulting states from the service execution, we can distinguish different kinds of adequacy notions. For instance, if a service can always surely achieve a given goal, it can be declared as:

Definition 8 (Strong uniform adequacy). *A service S is strongly and uniformly adequate to a goal G iff, for each legal world state in which the service preconditions hold, and for each goal instantiation that is compliant to user commitments, every service enactment obtained applying the binding schema results in a state where the user requirements hold.*

Roughly speaking, the *strong adequacy* degree implies that the service can surely achieve the execution goal, provided that service and goal preconditions are satisfied. On the other hand, the *uniform adequacy* degree implies that, every time service and goal preconditions are satisfied, there exists a suitable service computation path that achieves the goal. In other words, the uniform adequacy is related to the quantification over initial states/input assignments, while the strong adequacy with the quantification over possible computation paths. We can combine strong/weak and uniform/non-uniform adequacy properties obtaining the other 3 following levels. They are summarized in Tab. 3.

Definition 9 (Weak uniform adequacy). *A service S is weakly and uniformly adequate to a goal G iff, for each legal world state in which preconditions hold and for each goal instantiation that is compliant to user commitments, there exists at least a service enactment obtained applying the binding schema resulting in a state where user requirements hold.*

Definition 10 (Strong non-uniform adequacy). *A service S is strongly and non-uniformly adequate to a goal G iff there exist a legal world state in which preconditions hold and a goal instantiation that is compliant to user commitments, s.t. every service enactment obtained applying the binding schema results in a state where user requirements hold.*

Table 3. Service/goal adequacy levels

Level	Description
Strong Uniform (SU)	The service always surely achieves the goal
Weak Uniform (WU)	The service can always possibly achieve the goal
Strong Non-Uniform (SNU)	The service sometime surely achieves the goal
Weak Non-Uniform (WNU)	The service can sometime possibly achieve the goal

Definition 11 (Weak non-uniform adequacy). *A service S is weakly and non-uniformly adequate to a goal G iff there exists a legal world state in which preconditions hold and a goal instantiation that is compliant to user commitments, s.t. there exists at least a service enactment obtained applying the binding schema resulting in a state where user requirements hold.*

Given the definitions of uniform/non-uniform adequacy properties, we can also conclude that is possible to induce on the adequacy level space $\mathcal{L} = \{\text{WNU}, \text{WU}, \text{SNU}, \text{SU}\}$ a partial order relation $\prec$ defined as depicted in Fig. 1. We have, indeed, that:

Proposition 1. *Let G be a goal and S be a service s.t. the adequacy level of the service w.r.t. G is $l \in \mathcal{L}$, then S is l'-adequate for each $l' \in \mathcal{L}$ s.t. $l' \prec l$.*

Fig. 1. The service/goal adequacy level order relation $\prec$

Example 3. Given the services defined in the previous, we consider the following simple parametric goal G, denoting a citizen that is attempting to change its own residence to town t_2, let $\mathbf{U} = \{u\}$, $\mathcal{H} = u \sqcap \text{Citizen and not } (\exists \text{resln}^-.u) \sqcap \{t_2\}$, and $\mathcal{R} = \{-\text{resln}(u, \exists \text{resln}^-.u), +\text{resln}(u, \{t_2\})\}$. The binding schema of input variable of the services is the same in both cases and it is defined as $B = \{x_1(u) = u, x_2(u) = t_2\}$. It is worth noting that, while the service S is strongly and uniformly adequate to accomplish the user goal, since its preconditions are always satisfied by user's commitment and its effects implies the user's requirements, the service S_1 is adequate but in a non-uniform way, since, if the requestor does not live in t_1, (s)he cannot access the service, even-through, once enacted, the service always accomplished the required effects.

5 The Encoding Strategy

In this section we briefly sketch the encoding strategy employed, summarizing some of more relevant computation complexity results obtained so far.

Table 4. The DL-expression translation function τ^*

$$\tau^*(A) \triangleq A$$
$$\tau^*(C \sqcap C') \triangleq \tau^*(C) \sqcap \tau^*(C')$$
$$\tau^*((\bowtie n\, R\, C)) \triangleq (\bowtie n\, \tau^*(R)\, \tau^*(C))$$
$$\tau^*(\{o\}) \triangleq \{o\}$$
$$\tau^*(\neg C) \triangleq \mathsf{Top} \sqcap \neg\tau^*(C)$$

$$\tau^*(P) \triangleq P$$
$$\tau^*(R^-) \triangleq \tau^*(R)^-$$
$$\tau^*(R \sqcap R') \triangleq \tau^*(R) \sqcap \tau^*(R')$$
$$\tau^*(\neg R) \triangleq (\mathsf{Top} \times \mathsf{Top}) \sqcap \neg\tau^*(R)$$
$$\tau^*(R \!\upharpoonright\! C) \triangleq \tau^*(R) \!\upharpoonright\! \tau^*(C)$$

In particular, we employ an encoding technique that, starting from a specification of a dynamic reasoning task about an evolving class-based system (or, in other words, a community of deployed semantic e-services), reduces it to a traditional inference task into a "slightly" more expressive logic. The adopted working logic is a function-free decidable fragment of FOL, denoted as $\mathcal{C}^2$: it restricts the first-order language allowing at most two variables, but it includes the support for counting-quantifiers and arbitrary boolean expressions, enabling us to effectively catch the semantics of the system.

The basic idea is to embed a system state transition, described in terms of initial and final states, parameter assignments, etc., into a single interpretation structure on which we solve some reasoning tasks (satisfiability or entailment) obtained by accordingly encoding the e-service checking problem into a suitable set of axioms. The link between original and "working" interpretation structures is caught by the following definition: it has to be extended in the following as we go along, in order to cope with various modeling refinements.

Definition 12 (Embedding relation). *Let $\omega = \langle \Delta^\omega, \cdot^\omega \rangle$ be an arbitrary world state defined on an interpretation domain $\Delta^\omega \subseteq \mathfrak{U}$, and let $\hat{\omega} = \langle \mathfrak{U}, \cdot^{\hat{\omega}} \rangle$ any interpretation over the alphabet $\langle \mathbf{A} \cup \{\mathsf{Top}\}, \mathbf{P}, \mathbf{O} \rangle$. The world state is embedded into the interpretation ($\omega \leadsto \hat{\omega}$) iff the following conditions hold: $\Delta^\omega = \mathsf{Top}^{\hat{\omega}}$, $N^\omega = N^{\hat{\omega}}$ and $o^\omega = o^{\hat{\omega}}$, for any $N \in \mathbf{A} \cup \mathbf{P}$ and for any $o \in \mathbf{O}$.*

We can easily generalize the provided definition introducing a name mapping function that embeds the structure using different concept or role names. We notice that using different mapping functions, which means having mutually disjoint co-domains (and possibly different embedded top names, which denotes corresponding active domains), distinct arbitrary world states can be embedded into an interpretation built over the union of mapped alphabets. Now, we inductively define a translation function τ^* over the concept/role expressions of the language $\mathcal{ALBO}$, from the alphabet $\langle \mathbf{A}, \mathbf{P}, \mathbf{O} \rangle$ to the alphabet $\langle \mathbf{A} \cup \{\mathsf{Top}\}, \mathbf{P}, \mathbf{O} \rangle$, as reported in Tab. 4. Let $KB = \langle \mathcal{T}, \mathcal{A} \rangle$ be an arbitrary knowledge base (i.e., a world specification), we define a new knowledge base $\tau^*(KB)$ over the extended alphabet s.t., for each general concept or role inclusion assertion $C \sqsubseteq D$ in the TBox $\mathcal{T}$, $\tau^*(KB)$ includes a new axiom of the form $\tau^*(C) \sqsubseteq \tau^*(D)$; and for each membership assertion $o : C$ or $(o, o') : R$ in the ABox $\mathcal{A}$, $\tau^*(KB)$ includes, resp., a new axiom $o : \tau^*(C)$ or $(o, o') : \tau^*(R)$. Given a domain specification, assuming, w.l.o.g., that Top and New are new concept names, we define

Table 5. Basic axiom schema $\tilde{K}B$

$\top \sqsubseteq \mathsf{Top} \sqcup \mathsf{New}$	$\top \sqsubseteq \forall P.\mathsf{Top}$	$A \sqsubseteq \mathsf{Top}$
$\mathsf{Top} \sqcap \mathsf{New} \sqsubseteq \bot$	$\top \sqsubseteq \forall P^-.\mathsf{Top}$	$o \;:\; \mathsf{Top}$

a knowledge base $\tilde{K}B$ composed by the instantiation of the axiom schema[3] reported in Tab. 5 for any concept name $A \in \mathbf{A}$, role name $P \in \mathbf{P}$ and object name $o \in \mathbf{O}$. Using the axiom schema $\tilde{K}B$ and the translation function τ^* we can show the following main properties of the embedding relation that enable us to rely on it in the rest of the paper.

Lemma 2. *Let be ω and $\hat{\omega}$ be respectively a world state and an arbitrary interpretation s.t. the world state is embedded into the interpretation ($\omega \rightsquigarrow \hat{\omega}$), then $E^\omega = [\tau^*(E)]^{\hat{\omega}}$ for any concept/role expression E of $\mathcal{ALBO}$ over the domain specification $\langle \mathbf{A}, \mathbf{P}, \mathbf{O} \rangle$.*

Theorem 1. *A $\mathcal{ALCQI}(\sqcup, \sqcap, \uparrow, \downarrow, \triangle)$ knowledge base KB is satisfiable on an arbitrary interpretation domain $\Delta \subseteq \mathfrak{U}$ iff the knowledge base $\tilde{K}B \wedge \tau^*(KB)$ is satisfiable on $\mathfrak{U}$.*

Such an approach can be extended to implement reasoning-based procedures that are able to check formal properties introduced in Sec. 3. Essentially we refine the definition of the embedding relation in order to cope with multiple world states at a time, leveraging on different name mapping functions and on the isomorphism property that finitely bounds the number of states to check for an enactment. In fact, the first property that we are interested to check is whether the world specification is itself consistently defined, or, if it admits at least a legal state. Given the complexity of reasoning in $\mathcal{C}^2$ we can easily show that the validation of an $\mathcal{ALCQI}(\sqcup, \sqcap, \uparrow, \downarrow, \triangle)$ world specification $\mathcal{W}$ is in NEXP.

In [6] we have addressed the analysis of these basic semantic properties in the case of simple e-services: in presence of non-deterministic/conditional behaviors most of the results can be extended, accordingly adjusting the formalization, in order to keep into account effect selection expressions and the multiple effect specifications. The analysis of accessibility is mainly unaffected and hence it is possible to encode the preconditions in a linearly bounded $\mathcal{C}^2$ sentence denoted as KB^P. The checking of effect consistency requires an adequate modification for branching conditions. In particular, given an effect $E \in \mathcal{E}$, for each leaf node n, we combine the label expressions on the path from the root to n in a conjunctive logical expression ϕ_n including label expressions with the corresponding logical sign. The resulting expression is satisfied only on interpretation structures corresponding to world state/assignment s.t. the leaf effect is selected.

Also the analysis of validity/repairability properties need some adjustments, since we are requiring that in each consistent service activation there exists at least a valid or repairable outcome. The most relevant enhancement to the encoding is the introduction of multiple renaming functions, since we need to keep into account multiple enactments at once.

---

[3] We use *axiom schemas* as an useful notation shorthands: given an alphabet, the instantiated theory is obtained by replacing name place-holders (e.g., A, P, o) with any compatible name.

Theorem 2. *A consistent and accessible non-deterministic e-service S is valid w.r.t. a world specification $\mathcal{W}$, iff the following implication holds:*

$$KB^P \wedge \tau^*(\mathcal{W}) \wedge \bigwedge_{E \in \mathcal{E}} \Delta KB^U_{E,m_E} \models \bigvee_{E \in \mathcal{E}} \tau^*_{m_E}(\mathcal{W})$$

where, for each effect $E \in \mathcal{E}$, we introduce: (1) a fresh name mapping function m_E for the domain and the instantiation variable names; (2) a $\mathcal{C}^2$ sentence $\Delta KB^U_{E,m_E}$, encoding instantiations and updates, whose length is polynomially bounded in the input size.

Theorem 3. *A consistent and accessible non-deterministic e-service S is repairable w.r.t. a world specification $\mathcal{W}$ using a normal family of repair $\mathcal{R}$, iff the following implication holds:*

$$KB^P \wedge \tau^*(\mathcal{W}) \wedge \bigwedge_{E \in \mathcal{E}} \left(\Delta KB^U_{E,m_E} \wedge \bigwedge_{R \in \mathcal{R}} \Delta KB^R_{R,m_E,n_{E,R}} \right) \models$$
$$\bigvee_{E \in \mathcal{E}} \bigvee_{R \in \mathcal{R}} \left(\tau^*_{n_{E,R}}(\mathcal{W}) \wedge \Delta KB^C_{R,m_E,n_{E,R}} \right)$$

where, for each effect E and for each repair R: (1) m_E and $n_{E,R}$ are the domain name mapping functions; (2) $\Delta KB^U_{E,m_E}$, $\Delta KB^R_{R,m_E,n_{E,R}}$ and $\Delta KB^C_{R,m_E,n_{E,R}}$ are $\mathcal{C}^2$ sentences, having length polynomially bounded in the problem size;

Informally, while $\Delta KB^U_{E,m_E}$ encodes the update resulting from effect E, the other two sentences are required in order to ensure that the repair $R \in \mathcal{R}$ does not interfere with the update effects. Considering the complexity of the entailment in $\mathcal{C}^2$ and the size of resulting encoded instance, we can conclude that checking the validity of a non-deterministic e-service is a problem in coNEXP, while, given a normal family of atomic repairs, the repairability checking problem is in coNEEXP. Considering results presented in [3], while we have approximated the repair search problem obtaining a decidable algorithm for arbitrary KB specifications, we have to pay a drawback in terms of complexity, since we are relying on a kind of extra-logic search.

Corollary 1. *Given a world specification $\mathcal{W}$ and a non-deterministic e-service S, the problem of checking if it is valid is in coNEXP. Given also a normal family of atomic repair, the problem of checking if it is repairable is in coNEEXP*

Now, we address the adequacy problem considering a non-deterministic e-service, but we initially ignore the effect repair, for the sake of simplicity. The case of partially specified services will be addressed in the rest.

Theorem 4. *An accessible, consistent, and valid non-deterministic e-service S is strongly and uniformly adequate to an admissible goal G given a (weakly) consistent binding schema B w.r.t. a world specification $\mathcal{W}$, iff the following implication holds:*

$$KB^P \wedge \tau^*(\mathcal{W}) \wedge KB^H \wedge \Delta KB^B \wedge \bigwedge_{E \in \mathcal{E}} \Delta KB^U_{E,m_E} \models \bigwedge_{E \in \mathcal{E}} \tau^*_{m_E}(\mathcal{W}) \rightarrow KB^T_{m_E} \quad (1)$$

where, for each effect $E \in \mathcal{E}$: (1) m_E is the name mapping function; (2) $KB_{m_E}^T$ is sentence expressing the user goal requirements; while KB^H are ΔKB^B two C^2 sentences encoding resp. the user goal commitment and the binding schema application.

Intuitively, we can observe that the implication in Eq. 1 finitely encodes the definition of strong uniform service adequacy. As for previous cases, the decidability of this problem essentially relies on the isomorphism property of successor states, which allow us to check the condition taking into account only a finite number of possible elements. We also point out that all newly introduced sentences have a length linearly bounded in the problem input size, so the reduction does not effect the overall computational complexity. Other adequacy levels can be checked in a similar way, adjusting: (1) the kind of reasoning task: entailment for the uniform adequacy, satisfiability otherwise; (2) the finite quantifications over successor states: universal for strong adequacy, existential otherwise ($\bigvee_{E \in \mathcal{E}} \tau_{m_E}^*(\mathcal{W}) \wedge KB_{m_E}^T$).

The problem becomes a bit trickier if also the repair strategy must be considered. In particular, in this scenario we do not only need to show that the service can accomplish the required task, but also that the repair does not interfere with its own side-effects. In order to show that such a property hold, we need to simulate the repair selection procedure that means that generally a goal is achieved iff its requirement constraints hold in the world state obtained by the minimal-change effective repair. Given a repair search space $\mathcal{R}$, we now introduce the expression $\theta_{\mathcal{E},\mathcal{R},\mathcal{W}}$ to denote the following material implication finitely quantified over service effects and repairs grouped by their size:

$$\theta_{\mathcal{E},\mathcal{R},\mathcal{W}} \triangleq \bigwedge_{E \in \mathcal{E}} \bigwedge_{k=0}^{s} \bigwedge_{R \in \mathbf{R}^k} \tau_{n_{E,R}}^*(\mathcal{W}) \wedge \Delta KB_{R,m_E,n_{E,R}}^C$$

$$\wedge \bigwedge_{R' \in \hat{\mathbf{R}}^k} \neg \left(\tau_{n_{E,R'}}(\mathcal{W}) \wedge \Delta KB_{R',m_E,n_{E,R'}}^C \right) \rightarrow KB_{n_{E,R}}^T$$

where $\mathbf{R}^k \triangleq \{R \in \mathcal{R} | \|R\| = k\}$ and $\hat{\mathbf{R}}^k \triangleq \bigcup_{j=0}^{j<k} \mathbf{R}^j$ denote resp. the set of repairs having size equal or less than k. We point out that the repair strategy, introduced in previous section, is completely unaware of user's goal since it keeps into account only service and domain specifications.

Theorem 5. *An accessible, consistent, and repairable non-deterministic e-service S is strongly and uniformly adequate to an admissible goal G given a consistent binding schema B w.r.t. a world specification $\mathcal{W}$ and a normal repair family $\mathcal{R}$, iff the following implication holds:*

$$KB^P \wedge \tau^*(\mathcal{W}) \wedge KB^H \wedge \Delta KB^B \wedge \bigwedge_{E \in \mathcal{E}} \left(\Delta KB_{E,m_E}^U \wedge \bigwedge_{R \in \mathcal{R}} \Delta KB_{R,m_E,n_{E,R}}^R \right) \models \theta_{\mathcal{E},\mathcal{R},\mathcal{W}}$$

Finally, we introduce a similar expression $\eta_{\mathcal{E},\mathcal{R},\mathcal{W}}$, which can be used instead of $\theta_{\mathcal{E},\mathcal{R},\mathcal{W}}$ in the encoding of weak adequacy verification problems, it finitely quantifies over service effects and repairs grouped by their size:

$$\eta_{\mathcal{E},\mathcal{R},\mathcal{W}} \triangleq \bigvee_{E\in\mathcal{E}} \bigvee_{k=0}^{s} \bigvee_{R\in\mathbf{R}^k} \tau^*_{n_{E,R}}(\mathcal{W}) \wedge \Delta KB^C_{R,m_E,n_{E,R}}$$

$$\wedge \bigwedge_{R'\in\hat{\mathbf{R}}^k} \neg\left(\tau_{n_{E,R'}}(\mathcal{W}) \wedge \Delta KB^C_{R',m_E,n_{E,R'}}\right) \wedge KB^T_{n_{E,R}}$$

The results about complexity of service/goal adequacy problems are summarized in Tab. 6, as for the correctness analysis, the introduction of a repair strategy, required to deal with partially-specified services, induces at most an exponential blow-up. Moreover, while uniform adequacy has to be checked solving an entailment inference problem instance, non-uniform adequacy can be assessed as a satisfiability task.

Table 6. Upper-bounds of service/goal adequacy property verification problems

	Non-Uniform (SNU/WNU)	Uniform (SU/WU)
Without repair	NEXP	coNEXP
With repair	NEEXP	coNEEXP

6   Related Works and Conclusions

In this paper, we have extended the specification model introduced in [6], allowing for: (1) the use of a more expressive DL ($\mathcal{ALBO}$ instead of $\mathcal{ALCQIO}$); (2) the ability to express also role-related constraints (GRI); and (3) the specification of non-deterministic conditional e-services. So we have applied such a model to the analysis of the adequacy level of a service to a user's goal. This is the formal foundation for providing the service community with a service discovery meta-service that is able to locate a suitable service provider given a goal. The ability of repairing service effects or, in other words, to compute some service side-effects, enable us also to deal with incomplete specifications. As consistency and correctness properties, also the analysis of goal/service adequacy can be considered as a foundational tool that can be employed in the study of other relevant semantic service properties on which our ongoing research is focused, as well as on the practicability issues involved with the computational complexity of devised problems.

Only from the theoretical perspective, the topics addressed in this paper have been extensively studied in the literature devoted to semantic aspects of service-oriented computing, in general, and applying knowledge representation tools as DLs, in particular. Among several approaches, we consider some proposals that are closer to the present one in the spirit and regarding the formal foundation, in order to emphasize the specificity of our one. For example, in [3] (and in its extensions as [12]) a general approach to the update of DL extensional knowledge bases is presented. Despite it is a general purpose action formalism, it has been applied to the analysis of properties of semantics e-services, in particular considering the role of the domain knowledge and incomplete specification. This approach, in fact, introduces an update repair mechanism that is able to complete the service effects with additional updates in order to obtain a resulting world state that is consistent with a set of constraints (i.e., a TBox). In presence of an expressive description logic language, the problem is decidable only restricting the specification to some special classes of TBoxes (i.e., acyclic or definitorial), while in our proposal we are able to deal with arbitrary specifications using a sound but incomplete approximation. In such a framework, the matchmaking problem can be formalized in terms of *projection* of action consequences. Moreover, given the limitation on the TBox language, such an approach lacks the ability to deal with unrestricted domain specifications, but it also shows some more tractable complexity bounds.

Another class of service analysis techniques based upon DLs is essentially oriented to address matchmaking problems (e.g., [4]): they are essentially *static approaches* since they are focused on the description of service entailments not on the world states (i.e., the interpretation structure is mapped upon possible actual instantiation of service activations), but they allow for a domain specific knowledge in the sense of the Semantic Web. In this respect, our proposal is, indeed, a truly dynamic approach that relies on reasoning on service update effects instead that on the declaration of the action. Regarding static DL-approaches, in [8] is introduced an interesting distinction between the service variety (i.e., the extension of service instance set) due to *incomplete knowledge* (i.e., multiple models of a given theory) and the variety due to *intended diversity* (i.e., multiple instances in a given model). While the latter is a goal of a service publisher (i.e, describing a service that is able to accept heterogeneous client requests), the former is generally a consequence of poorly defined domain specification. Stemming from these definitions, also service *availability* and *coverage* concept has been introduced to denote the applicability of a service to deal with a given class of requests. Matchmaking problems are reduced to various forms of reasoning tasks, but some kind of constraints/features are not addressable in a feasible and decidable way, since using only a DL or a two-variable fragment of FOL seems to be too restrictive. It is worth noting that static approaches, despite they are often adopted also in some standard service directory and lookup solutions, they generally ignore consistency-related issues.

References

1. Abiteboul, S., Hull, R., Vianu, V.: Foundations of Databases. Addison-Wesley, Reading (1995)
2. Baader, F., Calvanese, D., McGuinness, D.L., Nardi, D., Patel-Schneider, P.F. (eds.): The Description Logic Handbook: Theory, Implementation, and Applications. Cambridge University Press, Cambridge (2003)
3. Baader, F., Lutz, C., Milicic, M., Sattler, U., Wolter, F.: Integrating description logics and action formalisms: First results. In: Proc. of the 2005 National Conference on Artificial Intellingence (AAAI 2005) (2005)
4. Di Noia, T., Di Sciascio, E., Donini, F.M., Mongiello, M.: A system for principled matchmaking in an electronic marketplace. In: Proc. of the WWW 2003 Conference, Budapest, Hungary (2003)
5. Dragone, L.: Modeling and Resoning about e-services in Cooperative Information Systems. Ph.D thesis, Sapienza Università di Roma (2008)
6. Dragone, L., Rosati, R.: Checking e-service consistency using description logics. In: Proc. of the 2007 IEEE Service Computing Conference (SCC 2007) (2007)

7. Grädel, E., Otto, M., Rosen, E.: Two-variable logic with counting is decidable. In: Proc. of 12th IEEE Symposium on Logic in Computer Science, LICS 1997 (1997)
8. Grimm, S., Motik, B., Preist, C.: Variance in e-Business Service Discovery. In: Martin, D., Lara, R., Yamaguchi, T. (eds.) Proc. of the ISWC 2004 Workshop on Semantic Web Services (2004)
9. Immerman, N., Lander, E.: Describing graphs: A first-order approach to graph canonization. In: Complexity Theory Retrospective (1990)
10. Lin, J., Mendelzon, A.O.: Merging databases under constraints. International Journal of Co-operative Information Systems 7(1), 55–76 (1996)
11. Schmidt, R.A., Tishkovsky, D.: Using tableau to decide expressive description logics with role negation. In: Aberer, K., Choi, K.-S., Noy, N., Allemang, D., Lee, K.-I., Nixon, L., Golbeck, J., Mika, P., Maynard, D., Mizoguchi, R., Schreiber, G., Cudré-Mauroux, P. (eds.) ASWC 2007 and ISWC 2007. LNCS, vol. 4825, pp. 438–451. Springer, Heidelberg (2007)
12. Wang, H., Li, Z.: A semantic matchmaking method of web services based on $\mathcal{SHOIN}^+(\mathbf{D})^*$. In: Proc. of the Asia-Pacific Services Computing Conference, APSCC 2006 (2006)

Fault, Compensation and Termination in WS-BPEL 2.0 — A Comparative Analysis

Christian Eisentraut and David Spieler

Department of Computer Science, Saarland University,
Campus Saarbrücken, 66123 Saarbrücken, Germany
{eisentraut,spieler}@cs.uni-sb.de

Abstract. One of the most challenging aspects in Web Service composition is guaranteeing transactional integrity. This is usually achieved by
providing mechanisms for fault, compensation and termination (FCT)
handling. WS-BPEL 2.0, the de-facto standard language for Business Process Orchestration provides powerful scope-based FCT-handling
mechanisms. However, the lack of a formal semantics makes it difficult
to understand and implement these constructs, and renders rigid analysis impossible. The general concept of compensating long-running business transactions has been studied in different formal theories, such as
cCSP and Sagas, but none of them is specific to WS-BPEL 2.0. Other
approaches aim at providing formal semantics for FCT-handling in WS-
BPEL 2.0, but only concentrate on specific aspects. Therefore, they cannot be used for a comparative analysis of FCT-handling in WS-BPEL 2.0.
In this paper we discuss the BPEL approach to FCT-handling in the light
of recent research. We provide formal semantics for the WS-BPEL 2.0
FCT-handling mechanisms which aims at capturing the FCT-part of the
WS-BPEL 2.0 specification in full detail. We then compare the WS-
BPEL 2.0 approach to FCT-handling to existing formal theories.

1 Introduction

As a standard for Web Service Orchestration, the language WS-BPEL 2.0 [1]
(in the following BPEL) has gained wide acceptance over the past years. BPEL
provides primitives to specify the flow of execution and communication between
a process and its communication partners. Similar to the notion of transaction in
database systems, the successful completion of certain communication sequences
between processes must be ensured in order not to bring the course of business between the partners into an inconsistent state. Different to transactions
of database systems, transactions of orchestrations are inherently long running
(Long-Running-Transactions, LRT) with typical durations from hours to days,
for example because of sub-transactions that require human interaction or batch
processing, and may be subject to faults of various kinds. Therefore, the use
of the transaction paradigms as used in database systems, where resources are
locked for exclusive access, becomes infeasible in this context. Therefore BPEL
uses a concept called compensation in order to obtain a more relaxed notion

R. Bruni and K. Wolf (Eds.): WS-FM 2008, LNCS 5387, pp. 107–126, 2009.
© Springer-Verlag Berlin Heidelberg 2009

of undoing partial executions. Every activity within a transaction possesses an associated compensation that is (ideally) able to revert its effects. When a transaction fails, the effects of all activities executed within that transaction so far are undone by executing their respective compensations. This makes transactions behave atomically for an external observer: they always either complete successfully or they appear to have never been started at all. It seems appropriate to execute compensations in the reverse order relative to the execution of their respective activities. In BPEL this is the default order.

The compensation approach to LRTs is based on the seminal idea of Sagas [7]. [3] provides a formalization of Sagas together with several extensions to the basic calculus, such as nested transactions, programmable compensations and exception handling, which are vital ideas of modern Web Service composition languages like BPEL. A similar approach is pursued in cCSP [5] based on CSP [8]. Different approaches to and other aspects of LRTs, which we will not consider in our paper, have been studied in [4, 11, 12].

While the theory is thus reasonably well developed, the effective and reliable use of LRT concepts is of crucial importance for Web Services. Therefore LRT and compensation are an integral part of BPEL. However, it is difficult to analyze how LRTs are realized in BPEL, since the language does not come with formal semantics. While desirable formal properties of LRTs are known, they are uncheckable with the current BPEL specification.

Nested Sagas and cCSP are two recent formal approaches to the foundations of FCT-handling. However, due to the very different styles of giving semantics that are used for BPEL and Sagas and cCSP respectively, it seems almost impossible to faithfully validate to which extent the formal semantics of the calculi and the BPEL specification coincide without formal proofs.

In this paper, we provide an formalization of fault, compensation and termination handling in BPEL, following the BPEL documents as faithful as at all possible. The resulting operational small-step semantics describes BPEL in a step-wise fashion, which is small-grained enough to be validated as a formal translation of the specification. Since both our calculus and Sagas or cCSP are formulated in a process algebraic way, our calculus furthermore seems a natural choice for a formal comparison.

It turns out that an interesting fragment of BPEL corresponds to Sagas, as far as basic transaction handling without nesting is considered. This result is especially interesting since Sagas is designed in a syntactically and semantically slim and clean way, which makes it an appropriate choice for formal analysis. As shown in [2], the same subset also coincides with a subset of cCSP. We can therefore restrict our formal comparison to Sagas.

However, more advanced features of the languages like generalized exception handling, programmable compensations etc. seem incomparable.

To keep the calculus as simple as possible, we do not consider aspects of BPEL that are orthogonal to FCT-handling like correlation sets or the binding of partner links. Furthermore, we only consider control flow primitives that are also found in Sagas. Section 3 provides a more detailed discussion of our choice.

We furthermore abstract from time and data. For a formal treatment of these aspects we refer the reader for example to [13, 10, 18, 17, 14].

In summary, this paper makes the following contributions. It (i) provides a detailed, low-level semantics for BPEL's FCT-handling behavior and (ii) uses this semantics to place BPEL in the context of more abstract foundational work.

In Section 2 we give an overview of existing approaches to the formalization of BPEL. Syntax and semantics of our calculus $BPEL_{fct}$ are presented in Section 3. We also give a short introduction to the principle of *all-or-nothing* semantics in BPEL and how it is realized in our calculus. Section 4 formally compares $BPEL_{fct}$ to nested Sagas and discusses possible extensions and limitations of our comparative approach. Section 5 concludes our work.

2   Related Work

Several formalizations of BPEL and its FCT-handling mechanisms exist. For an overview see [6]. Most algebraic approaches either consider BPEL4WS, the predecessor of BPEL, or do not give full account to all features of FCT-handling in BPEL. [13] and [9] provide feature-complete semantics for BPEL. However, their graph-based semantics seem a less natural choice for the intended comparison with the algebraic calculus Sagas.

[15, 11, 12] show how compensation handling can be reduced to event handling in the webπ-calculus. However, their approach relies on statically specified compensation handlers. Thus BPELs default compensation and all-on-nothing semantics (cf. Section 3.2) are not represented in their model. In [14] a nearly complete encoding of the BPEL scope construct into the $web\pi_\infty$-calculus is given, although without termination handler. That calculus is derived from the $web\pi$-calculus and consequently suffers from the problems mentioned above.

In [19], Qiu et al. introduce the calculus $BPEL$ formalizing a subset of BPEL4WS. Our calculus was inspired by $BPEL$. However, as we will show in Section 3.2, their calculus cannot deal with *all-or-nothing semantics* to its full extent.

3   The $BPEL_{fct}$ Calculus

Being a real-word language, BPEL comes with a huge number of primitives needed to design business processes, for example partner links and correlation sets for communication purposes, many different control flow primitives and FCT-handling mechanisms, to only mention a few. It is in general not easy to decouple these mechanism and analyze them in isolation. For example, the FCT-handling mechanism we want to consider cannot be separated completely from the control flow primitives. When a faulted transaction needs to be compensated, this may be done in default compensation order, which means executing the compensations in reverse order relative to the execution order of their respective activities. This order is of course dependent of the control flow primitives provided. For example consider the flow construct with condition links. This construct can be easily encoded in a graph-based language such as Petri-nets, but is difficult to encode in algebraic languages like the one we use. Sagas, the calculus we will compare BPEL to in this paper only offers control flow primitives for sequential and parallel execution. Note that parallel execution as understood in Sagas, corresponds to the flow construct without using condition links. Therefore, we also restrict the set of control flow primitives to those supported in Sagas. However, if a control flow primitive as well as the resulting default compensations can be encoded with process algebraic operators, we are confident that our calculus can be extended to comprise this control flow primitive.

3.1   Syntax

$BPEL_{fct}$ is a formalization of BPEL focused only on fault, compensation and termination (FCT) handling. We assume an infinite set of basic activities Act. The language of $BPEL_{fct}$ is defined as follows

Syntax of $BPEL_{fct}$

$$S ::= 0 \mid A \mid \tau_A \mid \tau \mid exit \mid S \ ; \ S \mid S + S \mid S \parallel S \mid !_A \mid ! \mid \uparrow \mid \{S : S : S : S\}$$

$$P ::= \{\!| S : S |\!\} \qquad\qquad PT ::= \checkmark \mid \varnothing \mid \triangledown$$

$$C ::= S \mid P \qquad\qquad \alpha, \beta ::= (C, \alpha, \beta)^m \mid \alpha \ ; \ \beta \mid \alpha \parallel \beta$$

$$\text{where } A \in \mathsf{Act}, \ m \in \{n, f, n', f', c, t\}$$

Initial Terms ($BPEL^0_{fct}$):

$$S^0 ::= 0 \mid A \mid exit \mid S^0 \ ; \ S^0 \mid S^0 + S^0 \mid S^0 \parallel S^0 \mid !_A \mid ! \mid \uparrow \mid (\{S^0 : S^0 : S^0 : S^0\}, 0, 0)^n$$

$$P^0 ::= (\{\!| S^0 : S^0 |\!\}, 0, 0)^{n'}$$

S denotes a BPEL activity and P a process. PT, α and β are not part of BPEL and only needed for the semantics. The language $BPEL^0_{fct}$ is the subset of $BPEL_{fct}$ that can be directly translated to BPEL expressions and vice versa. It does not include the semantically necessary intermediate representations. All basic BPEL activities are abstracted to atomic activities A which are assumed to be taken from an arbitrary set of names Act. τ denotes an internal action, that is not part of BPEL, but is used in $BPEL_{fct}$ to denote the occurrence of some event that is not visible to an observer. In case this unobservable event originates from a named fault $!_A$, we write τ_A. Observable (named) faults are signalled by the action $!$ ($!_A$). For a external observer faults are never observable and always appear as τ or τ_A. We only need them for the inference rules. Unnamed faults $!$ (which appear simply as τ from an external observers perspective) and named silent actions τ_A are only introduced in the language to allow for a nice comparison of $BPEL_{fct}$ with Sagas. In order to model BPEL itself they are not needed. The set of all actions is denoted by

$\overline{\mathsf{Act}} = \mathsf{Act} \cup \{!, \tau, exit\} \cup \{!_A \mid A \in \mathsf{Act}\} \cup \{\tau_A \mid A \in \mathsf{Act}\}$. 0 can be considered the completed activity. Please note that completion/termination at process level is indicated by an element from PT. Activities can be executed in sequence (;) or in parallel ($\|$). The parallel construct corresponds to the *flow* activity of BPEL. Nondeterministic choice (+) allows us to abstract from orthogonal aspects such as data. All primitives so far are standard in process algebra. The other activities are introduced to model the FCT part of BPEL. We again abstract from details and use $!_A$ (!) in combination with nondeterministic choice to model faults communicated by partner Web Services as well as run-time errors. $\uparrow$ triggers the default compensation mechanisms. $\{S : S_F : S_C : S_T\}$ denotes a *scope*, consisting of four components: the main activity S, the fault handler S_F, the compensation handler S_C and the termination handler S_T, which are again arbitrary activities. When no compensation handler is specified, the default compensation handler $\uparrow$ is assumed. If no fault handler is specified, the default handler $\uparrow$;! is assumed, which first compensates all already executed activities enclosed by the scope and then rethrows the fault to the directly enclosing scope or process.

Compensation contexts are sequences and parallel constructs of *compensation closures* $(S, \alpha, \beta)^m$. They denote installed compensations of successfully completed scopes, where S is the compensation handler itself and β is the set of compensations that can be activated by $\uparrow$ inside of S. α is used to collect compensations of scopes that successfully terminated during the execution of S. These constructs allow for all-or-nothing semantics. (cf. Section 3.2). A BPEL process can be considered as a scope without compensation and termination handler. We use $\checkmark$ to denote successful termination of a process, $\varnothing$ to signal a process abortion due to the occurrence of a fault during fault handling. Forced termination of a process (using the *exit* activity) is denoted by $\triangledown$. The language can be extended to named fault and compensation handling as it is part of BPEL. However, the mechanisms behind BPEL-FCT handling are not influenced considerably by this extensions.

3.2   Semantics

Our semantics is given in SOS-style [16] together with a set of congruence rules, that allow for a more compact presentation of our rules. Analogous to [19], the state space of a BPEL-process consists of a term plus additional information about installed compensations. In contrast to [19] we use a pair (α, β) of such contexts. This is necessary in order to allow for repeated compensations [3], called *all-or-nothing semantics* in BPEL. This allows to compensate a failed compensation. In principle, it is also possible to compensate a failed compensation of a failed compensation, etc. Now, when a compensation is triggered by $\uparrow$, we have to make sure that we execute the right compensations. If, say, a compensation handler H of a successfully completed scope T is executed and it first performs a sequence of transaction S and then afterwards decides to start the default compensation $\uparrow$, then it is not supposed to compensate S, but to execute the installed compensations for T. However, if H fails while performing S, the partial execution of H has to be compensated. In this case, the installed compensations for S have to be executed, whereas those for T must remain untouched. We call the first component α of the compensation context *accumulated compensation context*. It contains all compensation handlers that have been installed by the currently executing transaction or handler (H in our example). The second component β is called *fixed compensation context*. It contains those compensation handlers that have been installed before the compensation handler (H) has been called and which are supposed to be activated, if the compensation does not fail. So in our example it contains the installed compensations for T.

In order to achieve all-or-nothing semantics it is necessary to enclose the activation of the compensation by a scope, since in case a fault occurs during the compensation, it is then intercepted by the fault handler of the scope, which might then activate the accumulated compensations of the compensations. Without an enclosing scope, the fault would abruptly abort the compensation handling procedure and thus rendering all-nothing semantics impossible, since this would require to revert the so far executed compensations. The use of only a single compensation context seems to inherently lead to a weaker notion of compensation semantics, where either all-or-nothing semantics are enabled at the cost of sacrificing the ability to call the default compensations as part of a user-specified compensation, as it is the case in [3], or the other way round, as in [19]. Our semantics allow for all-or-nothing semantics even in the case when the compensation is triggered directly inside a fault handler without an enclosing scope (generalized all-or-nothing semantics). We will now discuss the rules of our semantics.

Let in the following $x \in \mathsf{Act} \cup \{\tau, exit\} \cup \{\tau_A \mid A \in \mathsf{Act}\} \cup \{!_A \mid A \in \mathsf{Act}\}$.

BASIC

$$\frac{}{(\alpha, \beta) \vdash x \xrightarrow{x} (\alpha, \beta) \vdash 0}$$

CHOICE

$$\frac{(\alpha, \beta) \vdash S_1 \xrightarrow{x} (\alpha', \beta') \vdash S_1'}{(\alpha, \beta) \vdash S_1 + S_2 \xrightarrow{x} (\alpha', \beta') \vdash S_1'}$$

SEQ

$$\frac{(\alpha, \beta) \vdash S_1 \xrightarrow{x} (\alpha', \beta') \vdash S_1' \quad S_1' \not\equiv 0}{(\alpha, \beta) \vdash S_1 \, ; \, S_2 \xrightarrow{x} (\alpha', \beta') \vdash S_1' \, ; \, S_2}$$

SEQT

$$\frac{(\alpha, \beta) \vdash S_1 \xrightarrow{x} (\alpha', \beta') \vdash 0}{(\alpha, \beta) \vdash S_1 \, ; \, S_2 \xrightarrow{x} (0 \, ; \, \alpha', \beta') \vdash S_2}$$

PARL

$$\frac{(\alpha_1, \beta) \vdash S_1 \xrightarrow{x} (\alpha_1', \beta') \vdash S_1'}{((\alpha_1 \parallel \alpha_2) \, ; \, \alpha, \beta) \vdash S_1 \parallel S_2 \xrightarrow{x} ((\alpha_1' \parallel \alpha_2) \, ; \, \alpha, \beta') \vdash S_1' \parallel S_2}$$

PARR

$$\frac{(\alpha_2, \beta) \vdash S_2 \xrightarrow{x} (\alpha_2', \beta') \vdash S_2'}{((\alpha_1 \parallel \alpha_2) \, ; \, \alpha, \beta) \vdash S_1 \parallel S_2 \xrightarrow{x} ((\alpha_1 \parallel \alpha_2') \, ; \, \alpha, \beta') \vdash S_1 \parallel S_2'}$$

The inference rules so far are almost standard, except for SEQT, where we extend the accumulated compensation context by a leading 0. The reason is that in order to be applicable, rules PARL,PARR demand the structure $(\gamma_1 \parallel \gamma_2) \, ; \, \gamma_3$ of the accumulated compensation context. This is ensured by the following invariant: For every transition $(\gamma, \delta) \vdash T \xrightarrow{x} (\gamma', \delta') \vdash T'$ it holds that if the accumulated compensation context of the configuration on the left hand side is of the form $\gamma \equiv (\gamma_1 \parallel \gamma_2); \gamma_3$, then this will also be the case for the resulting context γ' on the right hand side (as long as $T' \not\equiv 0$). This invariant also holds for the accumulated compensation context α of closures $(C, \alpha, \beta)^m$. The invariant can be proven by induction on the term structure, i.e. by case analysis on the applicable inference rules. The execution of business processes described by $BPEL_{fct}$ starts in a configuration $(0,0) \vdash p$ with $p \in P^0$. Using rules CB1 and CB2, it is easy to see that the invariant holds at the beginning of an execution of a $BPEL_{fct}$ process. Using induction on the length of an execution, it can be shown that the invariant also holds during the whole execution (up to the last configuration). Therefore the rules PARR and PARL can always be applied if the term in execution is a parallel composition.

A scope S is always executed inside a closure $(S, \alpha_A, \beta_F)^m$, which stores information about the current compensation context (α_A, β_F). The effect of activities inside a scope may differ depending on the circumstances under which they are executed. The ! primitive, for instance, shows subtle differences in its effect depending on whether it is used inside a compensation handler or termination handler. Our semantics stores the information under which circumstances a term is executed in what we call the *mode* m of a closure. We refer to m as the mode of the scope or process that is directly enclosed by the closure. Possible modes are:

– normal mode n, i.e. the scope is executing its enclosed activity
– faulted mode f, i.e. a fault has happened while executing the enclosed activity
– compensating mode c, i.e. the scope is a compensation handler in execution
– terminating mode t, i.e. the scope is being terminated and is executing its termination handler

The primed variants are used when a process is in the corresponding mode instead of a scope. Let in the following $y \in \mathsf{Act} \cup \{\tau\} \cup \{\tau_A \mid A \in \mathsf{Act}\}$.

As long as no fault occurs, a scope executes its enclosed activity (cf. [1] 12.1, p. 116). Please note the use of β in SCOPE, which enables compensation handlers to have nested enclosed scopes that may trigger a compensation. This is needed in order to obtain correct *all-or-nothing* semantics of compensation handlers.

Exactly those scopes that complete successfully will install their compensation handler (cf. [1] 12.4.3 p. 122, 12.4.4.3 p.125, and 12.5 pp. 127). Those handlers are placed in front of the accumulated compensation context such that if the compensation is triggered later on, they will be executed in default compensation order.

SCOPE

$$\frac{(\alpha_A, \beta) \vdash S \xrightarrow{y} (\alpha'_A, \beta') \vdash S' \qquad S' \not\equiv 0}{(\alpha, \beta) \vdash (\{S : F : C : T\}, \alpha_A, 0)^n \xrightarrow{y} (\alpha, \beta') \vdash (\{S' : F : C : T\}, \alpha'_A, 0)^n}$$

SCOPE END

$$\frac{(\alpha_A, \beta) \vdash S \xrightarrow{y} (\alpha'_A, \beta') \vdash 0}{(\alpha, \beta) \vdash (\{S : F : C : T\}, \alpha_A, 0)^n \xrightarrow{y} ((C, 0, \alpha_A)^c \,;\, \alpha, \beta) \vdash 0}$$

SCOPE FCT
$$\frac{(\alpha_A, \beta_F) \vdash S \xrightarrow{y} (\alpha'_A, \beta'_F) \vdash S' \qquad S' \neq 0 \qquad m \in \{c, f, t\}}{(\alpha, \beta) \vdash (S, \alpha_A, \beta_F)^m \xrightarrow{y} (\alpha, \beta) \vdash (S', \alpha'_A, \beta'_F)^m}$$

SCOPE END FCT
$$\frac{(\alpha_A, \beta_F) \vdash S \xrightarrow{y} (\alpha'_A, \beta'_F) \vdash 0 \qquad m \in \{c, f, t\}}{(\alpha, \beta) \vdash (S, \alpha_A, \beta_F)^m \xrightarrow{y} (\alpha, \beta) \vdash 0}$$

If a scope throws a fault, it is intercepted by the fault handler. Before the fault handling activities are executed, the scope's remaining enclosed activity is forced to terminate (cf. [1] 12.5, p. 127 and pp. 131-132, and 12.6, p. 135). We discuss forced termination in detail later.

SCOPE FAULT
$$\frac{(\alpha_A, \beta) \vdash S \xrightarrow{!_A} (\alpha'_A, \beta) \vdash S'}{(\alpha, \beta) \vdash (\{S : F : C : T\}, \alpha_A, 0)^n \xrightarrow{\tau_A} (\alpha, \beta) \vdash ([S'] ; F, 0, \alpha'_A)^f}$$

In case that a fault handler faults itself, its activity will be terminated and the fault will be rethrown to the enclosing scope's or process' fault handler (cf. [1] 12.4.4.3, p. 126).

SCOPE FAULT F
$$\frac{(\alpha_A, \beta_F) \vdash S \xrightarrow{!_A} (\alpha'_A, \beta_F) \vdash S'}{(\alpha, \beta) \vdash (S, \alpha_A, \beta_F)^f \xrightarrow{\tau_A} (\alpha, \beta) \vdash [S'] ; !_A}$$

A faulting compensation handler will start the compensation of already executed compensation activities (enabling *generalized* all-or-nothing semantics) and then it will rethrow the fault to the initiator of the compensation (cf. [1] 12.4.4.3, p. 126).

SCOPE FAULT C
$$\frac{(\alpha_A, \beta_F) \vdash S \xrightarrow{!_A} (\alpha'_A, \beta_F) \vdash S'}{(\alpha, \beta) \vdash (S, \alpha_A, \beta_F)^c \xrightarrow{\tau_A} (\alpha, \beta) \vdash (\uparrow ; !_A, 0, \alpha'_A)^f}$$

A fault during termination handling leads to forced termination of the termination handler (cf. [1] 12.4.4.3, p. 127, and 12.6, p. 137).

SCOPE FAULT T
$$\frac{(\alpha_A, \beta_F) \vdash S \xrightarrow{!_A} (\alpha'_A, \beta_F) \vdash S'}{(\alpha, \beta) \vdash (S, \alpha_A, \beta_F)^t \xrightarrow{\tau_A} (\alpha, \beta) \vdash [S']}$$

Compensation is realized in $BPEL_{fct}$ by executing the fixed compensation context β of the current context, i.e. the compensation handlers of the child scopes enclosed by the original scope (cf. [1] 12.4.3.2, pp. 123-124).

COMP
$$(\alpha, \beta) \vdash \uparrow \xrightarrow{\tau} (\alpha, 0) \vdash \beta$$

The behavior of processes is quite similar to that of scopes. Because processes are top level terms, they are always executed in the empty context $(0,0)$.

PROCESS

$$\frac{(\alpha_A,0) \vdash S \xrightarrow{y} (\alpha'_A,0) \vdash S'}{(0,0) \vdash (\{\!|S:F|\!\},\alpha_A,0)^{n'} \xrightarrow{y} (0,0) \vdash (\{\!|S':F|\!\},\alpha'_A,0)^{n'}}$$

PROCESS F

$$\frac{(\alpha_A,\beta_F) \vdash S \xrightarrow{y} (\alpha'_A,\beta'_F) \vdash S'}{(0,0) \vdash (S,\alpha_A,\beta_F)^{f'} \xrightarrow{y} (0,0) \vdash (S',\alpha'_A,\beta'_F)^{f'}}$$

PROCESS FAULT

$$\frac{(\alpha_A,0) \vdash S \xrightarrow{!_A} (\alpha'_A,0) \vdash S'}{(0,0) \vdash (\{\!|S:F|\!\},\alpha_A,0)^{n'} \xrightarrow{\tau_A} (0,0) \vdash ([S'] \,;\, F,0,\alpha'_A)^{f'}}$$

Successful completion in either normal mode (no fault on process level happened so far) or faulted mode (a fault happened on process level and was handled successfully by the process' fault handler) will result in successful termination ($\checkmark$). If the execution of the fault handler failed the process will end up in a failed state $\varnothing$.

PROCESS FAULT F

$$\frac{(\alpha_A,\beta_F) \vdash S \xrightarrow{!_A} (\alpha'_A,\beta_F) \vdash S'}{(0,0) \vdash (S,\alpha_A,\beta_F)^{f'} \xrightarrow{\tau_A} (0,0) \vdash \varnothing}$$

PROCESS END

$$(0,0) \vdash (\{\!|0:F|\!\},\alpha_A,\beta_F)^{n'} \xrightarrow{\tau} (0,0) \vdash \checkmark$$

PROCESS END F

$$(0,0) \vdash (0,\alpha_A,\beta_F)^{f'} \xrightarrow{\tau} (0,0) \vdash \checkmark$$

The *exit* activity of BPEL forces a process to terminate immediately. The SOS rules for *exit* are straightforward. The *exit* signal is passed through until it reaches a process, where it leads to forced termination $\triangledown$. Due to space limitations we omit the rules and only present the rule for processes:

EXIT PROCESS

$$\frac{(\alpha_A,0) \vdash S \xrightarrow{exit} (\alpha'_A,0) \vdash 0}{(0,0) \vdash (\{\!|S:F|\!\},\alpha_A,0)^{n} \xrightarrow{exit} (0,0) \vdash \triangledown}$$

In the following we present the syntactical congruence rules. Since our representation of the compensation mechanism relies on a strong structural resemblance of the process term and its compensation contexts in the closure, we may not freely commute parallel terms. For the same reason associativity does not hold. As an example consider $((\alpha_1 \parallel \alpha_2); \alpha, \beta) \vdash S_1 \parallel S_2 \not\equiv ((\alpha_1 \parallel \alpha_2); \alpha, \beta) \vdash S_2 \parallel S_1$. This ensures that S_i stays associated with the accumulated compensation context α_i, where $i \in \{1,2\}$. In initial $BPEL_{fct}$ terms, however, parallel terms can by arbitrarily associated and commuted without changing the resulting semantics. So semantically, the parallel operator in $BPEL_{fct}$ is –as is the flow construct in BPEL– commutative and associative.

Rule CB1 has to be used to expand the leading 0 in front of the accumulated compensation context in case of the start of a new parallel flow inside the main activity of a scope or process. In detail e.g. $0; \alpha \equiv 0 \parallel 0; \alpha$. CB2 allows reduction of sequences of 0.

CB1	$0 \equiv 0 \parallel 0$	CB3	$S + (S' + S'') \equiv (S + S') + S''$	
CB2	$S ; 0 \equiv S$	CB4	$S + S' \equiv S' + S$	CB5 $\quad S + 0 \equiv S$

The last set of rules we consider deals with forced termination of terms mirroring section 12.6 of [1]. When in a parallel branch a fault occurs, then all other parallel branches have to be terminated. Forced termination has to happen as soon as possible, however, in order to allow for controllable terminations of scopes, BPEL introduces the concept of termination handlers, which are activated as soon as a scope is forced to terminate. The BPEL specification allows a fault that is about to occur either to happen or to be terminated without effect (CT9) (cf. Section 4). Note that the handling of a fault or termination are not affected by forced termination (CT12, CT13). This ensures that a transaction (scope), which has faulted before the forced termination occurred, is always able to complete its fault handler and any compensation activated there.

CT1 $[0] \equiv 0$

CT2 $[\tau] \equiv 0$

CT3 $[A] \equiv 0$

CT4 $[\uparrow] \equiv 0$

CT5 $[exit] \equiv 0$

CT6 $[S + S'] \equiv 0$

CT7 $[S ; S'] \equiv [S]$

CT8 $[S \parallel S'] \equiv [S] \parallel [S']$

CT9 $[!_A] \equiv !_A + \tau ; 0$

CT10 $[(\{S : F : C : T\}, \alpha_A, 0)^n] \equiv ([S] ; T, 0, \alpha_A)^t$

CT11 $[(S, \alpha_A, \beta_F)^c] \equiv [S]$

CT12 $[(S, \alpha_A, \beta_F)^f] \equiv (S, \alpha_A, \beta_F)^f$

CT13 $[(S, \alpha_A, \beta_F)^t] \equiv (S, \alpha_A, \beta_F)^t$

4   BPEL Is Sagas! Almost

$BPEL$'s FCT-handling mechanisms are –as stated in [1]– inspired by Sagas. However, there are several seemingly different concepts. Even if we prescind from constructs that are not at all represented in Sagas, like links inside a flow construct, some apparent differences remain. Before we will compare the two languages, we will shortly summarize Sagas syntax and semantics.

Sagas. Sagas is equipped with a big-step semantics [3] that distinguishes three different execution results for sagas (i.e. transactions): successful termination, faulted execution with successful compensation, faulted execution with unsuccessful compensation. During an execution a trace of observable basic activities is recorded up to partial order (partial order trace). A partial order trace induces a set of traces. Following [3], we assume that every basic activity that occurs in a Sagas term has a unique name. So the same action can never occur twice in a trace.

Definition 1 ((Partial-Order) Trace). *We call elements of $\overline{\mathsf{Act}}^{*}$ traces. A partial-order trace (pot) is a partial order (V, E) where $V \subseteq \overline{\mathsf{Act}}$. The set of all pots is denoted by* POT.

Note that every trace can be considered as a pot that is linear.
Notation: We write X_A to denote the component X of the tuple A, when $A = (\ldots, X, \ldots)$. For a partial order A we hence always assume $A = (V_A, E_A)$. We write singleton sets $\{x\}$ sometimes simply as x if no ambiguities arise. We define the following two operations on sets:
$A; B = \{(a, b) \mid a \in A, b \in B\}$, $C|_B = \{(a, b) \in C \mid a, b \in B\}$
It is sometimes useful to consider terms that are built from the operators $0, A, \|$ and ; as partial orders as follows:

- $0 = (\emptyset, \emptyset)$
- $A = (\{A\}, \emptyset)$
- $P; Q = (V_P \cup V_Q, E_P \cup E_Q \cup V_P; V_Q)$
- $P \parallel Q = (V_P \cup V_Q, E_P \cup E_Q)$

Definition 2 (Syntax of Sagas). *Sagas S are defined by the following grammar:*

$$X ::= 0 \mid A \mid A \div B \qquad\qquad (STEP)$$
$$P ::= X \mid P; P \mid P \parallel P \qquad\qquad (PROCESS)$$
$$S ::= \{\!| \, P \, |\!\} \qquad\qquad (SAGA)$$

We denote the set of all sagas terms by Sagas.

An atomic activity B can be attached to another atomic activity A as its compensation. Please note that different to $BPEL_{fct}$ compensations cannot be composite terms and cannot be attached to composite terms. A saga formalizes the idea of long-running transactions and corresponds to scopes in $BPEL_{fct}$. In Sagas there is no language primitive to signal a fault. The success or fault of an atomic activity is determined at run-time by an environment Γ mapping every activity either to success ($\square$) or fault ($\boxtimes$). The semantics of Sagas is given in terms of subsets of POT. For the complete semantic rules we refer the reader to [3]. In the original semantics faults cannot be observed and are not represented in the partial order traces. To allow for a decent comparison it is however necessary to make faults observable. This needs only a minor change to the original semantics where rule S-CMP is replaced by rule S-CMP'.

S-CMP
$$\frac{\Gamma \vdash \langle \beta, 0 \rangle \xrightarrow{\alpha} \langle \square, 0 \rangle}{A \mapsto \boxtimes, \Gamma \vdash \langle A \div B, \beta \rangle \xrightarrow{\alpha} \langle \boxtimes, 0 \rangle}$$

S-CMP'
$$\frac{\Gamma \vdash \langle \beta, 0 \rangle \xrightarrow{\alpha} \langle \square, 0 \rangle}{A \mapsto \boxtimes, \Gamma \vdash \langle A \div B, \beta \rangle \xrightarrow{\tau_{A;\alpha}} \langle \boxtimes, 0 \rangle}$$

4.1 Comparison

- In Sagas the main transaction and the sub-transactions are represented by one construct: a saga. In BPEL, the main transaction and subtransactions are represented by two different constructs: the process and scopes. However, for the language subsets that we compare, a process behaves identical to scopes (except that it cannot be terminated, since it always is top-level).
- BPEL's scope construct represents subtransactions and is at the same time used to associate compensations to forward activities. In Sagas, subtransactions are realized via nested *sagas*. In contrast to scopes, they do not have any explicit handlers. Furthermore, every forward activity is associated with its compensations immediately during its execution. In BPEL a compensation for an activity becomes available only after the surrounding scope has successfully finished. Despite the principles of transactions in Sagas seem rather different from those used by BPEL, we will see that it is rather straightforward to express them in BPEL.
- BPEL's and Sagas's compensation policy for concurrent processes forces all branches to compensating themselves in case of a fault in one of the branches. In Sagas, the compensation phases of all branches run independently of each other. This behavior is called *distributed interruption* in [2]. As we will see, BPEL follows the *coordinated interruption* policy (cf. [2]): as soon as a fault has occurred, all parallel branches have to be compensated immediately. BPEL has an additional termination phase, that is intermediary of forward flow phase and compensation phase. Hence every faulted BPEL (sub)transaction, can be divided into three phases that take place strictly in sequence: forward flow phase(F), termination phase(T) and compensation phase(C). Representing the fault with f, we can intuitively represent the execution of the faulted scope/process by $F; f; T; C$. As we will see this policy is an inherent part of BPEL FCT-handling mechanisms.
- Furthermore, the treatment of faults during compensation in both languages is different in principle and we cannot mimic Sagas behavior in BPEL. We will treat this in Section 4.2 in greater detail.

In order to formally compare the two languages we map every saga to a BPEL process and analyze their behaviors in terms of partial orders over actions. Since we want our mapping to be recursively defined over the term structure, we cannot map Sagas terms directly to $BPEL_{fct}$ processes, since processes are always top-level constructs. We therefore use a translation function that maps arbitrary Sagas term S to a $BPEL_{fct}$ term S' that is no process itself and in a final step S' is raised to a top-level process term by enclosing it with the process as follows: $(\{|S' : \uparrow|\}, 0, 0)^{n'}$. Since $BPEL$ to its full extent is very powerful, it is likely that in principle there exists some unobvious encoding of Sagas behavior even in $BPEL_{fct}$. However, by the choice of our translation mapping, we had in mind to investigated how the predefined structures for compensation handling in BPEL work compared to those of Sagas, so our mapping defines a translation as straightforward as possible. Please remember that we assume that compensations can never fault for reasons mentioned above. Furthermore, we do not allow two faults to occur at the same scope/process level. This restriction does not influence the principle results, but saves us some additional case distinction.

Definition 3 (Translation Function)

$$[\![\,]\!]_\Gamma : Sagas \rightarrow BPEL^0_{fct}$$
$$[\![A]\!]_\Gamma = A \ if \ \Gamma A = \square, \quad [\![A]\!]_\Gamma = \ ! \ if \ \Gamma A = \boxtimes,$$
$$[\![0]\!] = 0, \quad [\![P \parallel Q]\!] = [\![P]\!] \parallel [\![Q]\!], \quad [\![P \ ; \ Q]\!] = [\![P]\!] \ ; \ [\![Q]\!],$$
$$[\![A \div B]\!]_\Gamma = (\{[\![A]\!]_\Gamma : !_A : B : 0\}, 0, 0)^n, \quad [\![\{\!\!|\, P \,|\!\!\}]\!]_\Gamma = (\{[\![P]\!]_\Gamma : \uparrow : \uparrow : \uparrow\}, 0, 0)^n$$

We will sometimes write $[\![.]\!]$ instead of $[\![.]\!]_\Gamma$ if Γ is clear from the context.

The operators for sequential and parallel execution behave identical in $BPEL_{fct}$ and Sagas. Remember that parallel execution is a special case of the BPEL flow construct, which is however more powerful than the parallel operator and cannot be modelled in Sagas. If an action A fails in the environment Γ, we replace it by a nameless fault in $BPEL_{fct}$. An action/compensation pair $A \div B$ corresponds to a scope that executes A and has B as it compensation handler. When A fails, then the fault is simply rethrown by the fault handler $!_A$, which triggers already installed compensations at the level of the enclosing scope/process. The fact that faulting activities are themselves translated to a nameless fault !, while they are rethrown as a named fault in the respective fault handlers may be counterintuitive at first sight. Indeed, this is only done to allow for a nice comparison of the observable behavior and has no fundamental consequences or reasons. Nested sagas are translated into scope in a straightforward manner, where the default handlers are used where possible.

In order to compare the two calculi it is very helpful to note that the compensation handlers of both calculi can be translated bijectively into each other. Since $[\![\,]\!]_{cl}$ is bijective on the contexts of Sagas and the restricted variation of $BPEL_{fct}$, we will use α and $[\![\alpha]\!]_{cl}$ interchangeably when the meaning is clear from the context.

Definition 4 (Context Translation Function). *We translate Sagas contexts to $BPEL_{fct}$ contexts by the following function:*

$$[\![0]\!]_{cl} = 0, \quad [\![P; Q]\!]_{cl} = [\![P]\!]_{cl} \ ; [\![Q]\!]_{cl}, \quad [\![P \parallel Q]\!]_{cl} = [\![P]\!]_{cl} \parallel [\![Q]\!]_{cl},$$
$$[\![B]\!]_{cl} = (B, 0, 0)^c$$

In Sagas, the basic building blocks of a context are primitive compensation activities. In $BPEL_{fct}$, however, the basic building blocks are closures $(A, \alpha_C, \beta_F)^c$ signalling that the enclosed compensation activity is indeed a compensation (c). In Sagas and therefore in restricted BPEL the default compensation $(\uparrow)$ cannot be triggered explicitly, but only implicitly when a fault occurs. Since we assume no faults to occur during compensation, it is safe to arbitrarily let both contexts of the closure be 0.

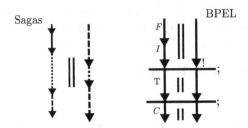

Fig. 1. Corresponding partial orders in Sagas and BPEL

BPEL$_{fct}$ Big-Step Semantics Let us in the following fix Γ and then let $BPEL'_{fct} = \{[\![S]\!]_\Gamma \mid S \in Sagas\}$. We present a big-step semantics for the subset $BPEL'_{fct}$ of our calculus that corresponds to Sagas following the translation function $[\![\;]\!]_\Gamma$. Our semantics will be for each term a set of structured partial-order traces as described below.

Definition 5 (Structured POT). *A structured pot (spot) is a tuple (V, E, P, D, t) where (V, E) is a pot and $P = (F, I, T, C, f) \in \mathcal{T}$ and $D \subseteq \mathcal{T}$, where $\mathcal{T} = (2^{Act})^4 \times \{\tau_A \mid A \in \mathsf{Act}\}$ and $t \in \{\boxdot, \boxtimes, \boxplus\}$. We call the set of all spots sPOT.*

To obtain a nifty comparison of the two languages, the semantics of each term will be represented by a of spots, which can be translated into partial-order traces. We can then compare the two languages by comparing partial-orders traces with identical underlying sets of activities. The partial order relation consists of two parts: One that exactly corresponds to the partial order for the corresponding term in Sagas (E) and one that represents the additional edges of the partial orders, that are induced by the more restricted termination/compensation policy of the top-level process (P) and of each (sub)scope (D). Furthermore V contains all observable activities of the represented execution, success or failure or forced termination of the execution of the (sub)transaction is expressed by t (where $\boxdot$ = successful termination, $\boxtimes$ = execution with compensation due to an internal fault, $\overline{\boxtimes}$ = execution with compensation due to external termination). Please remember that we will not consider faulted compensations. In case a fault occurred, the fault name is represented by f. P with its parts F, T and C represent the partition of the activities of the top-level transaction in forward, termination and compensation flow. The set I represents activities that can either occur before or after the fault f, i.e. during the termination phase, but before the compensation phase. Such activities arise when a subscope compensates itself due to a internal fault. Then this scope is not responsive to termination. D represents the activity partitions for non-successfully terminated subscopes. In Figure 1 the po traces of the same term are presented schematically in both calculi.

How the single parts of a spot exactly contribute to the pot that it represents is represented formally by the following transformation.

Definition 6. $\delta((V, E, (F, I, T, C, f), D, t)) = (V, E')$ *where*

$$E' = E \cup H \cup \bigcup_{(F,I,T,C,f) \in D} F; f; T; C \cup I; C$$

with $H = \begin{cases} \emptyset \ \text{if } t = \boxdot \\ F; f; T; C \cup I; C \ \text{otherwise} \end{cases}$

The *spots* for every term in $BPEL'_{fct}$ are constructed relative to an initial context compensation context $\beta = (V_\beta, E_\beta)$, which is itself a partial order trace. This intentionally strongly resembles the way the Sagas semantics is defined. We will now see how the big-steps semantics $\mathcal{S}(S, \beta)$ of a term $S \in BPEL'_{fct}$ and a context β is constructed recursively. Please note that for every $S \in BPELfct'$, the set $\mathcal{S}(S, \beta)$ contains the *spot* where $C = V_\beta$, $E = E_\beta$ and all other sets are empty and $t = \boxtimes$ and $f = 0$. We will not repeat this *spot* later. Intuitively, this *spot* describes the termination of S before starting its execution. It is the only element of $\mathcal{S}(0, \beta)$.

The following *spots* are in $\mathcal{S}(S, \beta)$:

Case $S = [\![A \div B]\!] = (\{[\![A]\!]_\Gamma : !_A : B : 0\}, 0, 0)^n$:
  - If $\Gamma A = \boxdot$: $(\{A\}, (E_\beta \cup A; B; V_\beta), (\{A\}, \emptyset, \emptyset, \emptyset, \{B\} \cup V_\beta, 0), \emptyset, \boxdot)$
  - If $\Gamma A = \boxtimes$: $(\{\tau_A\} \cup V_\beta, (E_\beta \cup \tau_A; V_\beta), (\emptyset, \emptyset, \emptyset, V_\beta, \tau_A), \emptyset, \boxtimes)$
  - If $\Gamma A = \overline{\boxtimes}$: $(\{A, B\} \cup V_\beta, E_\beta \cup A; B; V_\beta, (\{A\}, \emptyset, \emptyset, \{B\} \cup V_\beta, 0), \emptyset, \overline{\boxtimes})$

Case $S = [\![P; Q]\!]_\Gamma = [\![P]\!]_\Gamma ; [\![Q]\!]_\Gamma$:
  For all $p \in \mathcal{S}([\![P]\!]_\Gamma, \beta), q \in \mathcal{S}([\![Q]\!]_\Gamma, (C_p, E_P|_{C_P}))$:
  - If $t_P = \boxtimes \vee t_P = \overline{\boxtimes}$: p
  - If $t_P = \boxdot$: $(V_p \cup V_q, E_p \cup E_q \cup V_p; V_q, (F_p \cup F_q, I_q, T_q, C_q, f_q), D_p \cup D_q, t_q)$

Case $S = [\![P \parallel Q]\!]_\Gamma = [\![P]\!]_\Gamma \parallel [\![Q]\!]_\Gamma$: For all $p \in \mathcal{S}([\![P]\!]_\Gamma, 0), q \in \mathcal{S}([\![Q]\!]_\Gamma, 0)$:
  - If $t_p = t_q = \boxdot$: $(V_p \cup V_q, E_p \cup E_q \cup E_\beta \cup V_p; V_\beta \cup V_q; V_\beta, (F_p \cup F_q, I_p \cup I_q, T_p \cup T_q, C_p \cup C_q \cup V_\beta, f_p \star' f_q), D_p \cup D_q, t_p \star t_q)$
  - Otherwise: $(V_p \cup V_q \cup V_\beta, E_p \cup E_q \cup E_\beta \cup V_p; V_\beta \cup V_q; V_\beta, (F_p \cup F_q, I_p \cup I_q, T_p \cup T_q, C_p \cup C_q \cup V_\beta, f_p \star' f_q), D_p \cup D_q, t_p \star t_q)$

Case $S = [\![\{ P \}]\!]_\Gamma = (\{[\![P]\!]_\Gamma : \uparrow : \uparrow : \uparrow\}, 0, 0)^n$: For all $p \in \mathcal{S}([\![P]\!]_\Gamma, 0)$:
  - If $t_p = \boxdot$: $(V_p, E_p \cup E_\beta \cup V_p; V_\beta, (F_p, I_p, T_p, C_p \cup V_\beta, f_p), D_p, \boxdot)$
    and $(V_p \cup C_p \cup E_\beta, E_p \cup E_\beta \cup V_p; V_\beta, (F_p, I_p, T_p, C_p \cup V_\beta, f_p), D_p, \boxtimes)$
  - If $t_p = \boxtimes$: $(V_p, E_p, (F_p \cup f_p, I_p \cup T_p \cup C_p, \emptyset, \emptyset, 0), D_p \cup \{F_p, I_p, T_p, C_p, f_p\}, \boxdot)$
    and $(V_p \cup V_\beta, E_p \cup E_\beta \cup V_p; V_\beta, (F_p \cup f_p, I_p \cup T_p \cup C_p, \emptyset, V_\beta, 0), D_p \cup \{F_p, I_p, T_p, C_p, f_p\}, \overline{\boxtimes})$
  - If $t_p = \overline{\boxtimes}$: $(V_p \cup E_\beta, E_p \cup E_\beta \cup V_p; V_\beta, (F_p, I_p, T_p, C_p \cup V_\beta, f_p), D_p, \overline{\boxtimes})$

The operations $\star$ and $\star'$ are defined as follows:

$\star$	$\boxdot$	$\boxtimes$	$\overline{\boxtimes}$
$\boxdot$	$\boxdot$	$-$	$-$
$\boxtimes$	$-$	$-$	$\boxtimes$
$\overline{\boxtimes}$	$-$	$\boxtimes$	$\overline{\boxtimes}$

$\star'$	τ_A	0
τ_B	$-$	τ_B
0	τ_A	0

The following theorem relates the big-step semantics to the originally defined small-step semantics. Before, we need some additional definitions.

Definition 7 (Execution of a Trace). *When* $a_0 a_1 \ldots a_{n-1} = \alpha \in \overline{\mathsf{Act}}^*$ *is a trace, we let* $(\alpha, \beta) \vdash P \xrightarrow{\alpha} (\alpha', \beta') \vdash P'$ *mean that there are sequences of* P_i, α_i *and* β_i *with* $0 \le i \le n$, *such that* $(\alpha_i, \beta_i) \vdash P_i \xrightarrow{a_i} (\alpha_{i+1}, \beta_{i+1}) \vdash P_{i+1}$ *for* $0 \le i < n$ *and* $P_0 = P$, $\alpha_0 = \alpha$, $\beta_0 = \beta$ *and* $P_n = P'$, $\alpha_n = \alpha'$, $\beta_n = \beta'$.

Definition 8 (Induced Traces). *If* $(V_A, E_A) \in \mathsf{POT}$ *then* $\mathsf{Ind}(\alpha) \subseteq \overline{\mathsf{Act}}^*$ *denotes the set of induced traces, i.e. the set of linear orders* (V_A, E) *with* $(a, b) \in E \implies (b, a) \notin E_A$.

In the following we write $\overline{\alpha}$ to mean the result of removing all occurrences of (unnamed) τ in the trace $\alpha \in \overline{\mathsf{Act}}^*$.

Theorem 1 (Semantic Equivalence). *Let* $S \in BPEL'_{fct}$, *then*

1. *for every maximal execution trace* α *of a process with* $(0,0) \vdash (\{S : \uparrow\}, 0, 0)^{n'} \xrightarrow{\alpha} (0,0) \vdash \checkmark$ *there is a spot* $p \in \mathcal{S}(S, 0)$ *such that* $\overline{\alpha} \in \mathsf{Ind}(\delta(p))$ *and*
2. *for every* $p \in \mathcal{S}(S, 0)$ *and every trace* $\alpha' \in \mathsf{Ind}(\delta(p))$ *there is a trace* α *such that* $\overline{\alpha} = \alpha'$ *and* $(0,0) \vdash (\{S : \uparrow\}, 0, 0)^{n'} \xrightarrow{\alpha} (0,0) \vdash \checkmark$

The proof of this theorem is considerably large. In the following we only sketch some crucial observations for the proof. In the following, all terms are from $BPEL'_{fct}$ if not stated differently. We will now explain how all possible behaviors of a process (or a scope) are completely determined by the possible behaviors of its inner activity. The following statements apply to processes, but can be analogously transfered to scopes.

- By rule PROCESS we see that as long as α does not contain $!_A$ for some A and $(\beta, 0) \vdash S \xrightarrow{\alpha} (\beta', 0) \vdash S'$ then also $(0,0) \vdash (\{S : \uparrow\}, \beta, 0)^{n'} \xrightarrow{\alpha} (0,0) \vdash (\{S' : \uparrow\}, \beta', 0)^{n'}$. Furthermore PROCESS and PROCESS END are the only applicable rules. Exactly when $S' \equiv 0$ then together with PROCESS END as final step we can derive only the execution $(0,0) \vdash (\{S : \uparrow\}, \beta, 0)^{n'} \xrightarrow{\alpha} (0,0) \vdash \checkmark$.
- As soon as S throws a fault $!_A$, i.e. $(\beta', 0) \vdash S' \xrightarrow{!_A} (\beta', 0) \vdash S'_1$ after a faultless trace α, the process is bound to behave in the following way: $(0,0) \vdash (\{ [\![S]\!] : \uparrow\}, 0, 0)^n \xrightarrow{\alpha; !_A; \alpha'; \tau; \tau; \alpha''} (0,0) \vdash \checkmark$, where α' is an execution of $[\![S'_1]\!]$ and α'' is an execution of the compensation β'.

One can see this as follows: As above we infer that $(0,0) \vdash (\{\!|\ [\![S]\!]\ :$ $\uparrow\!|\!\},\beta,0)^n \xrightarrow{\alpha} (0,0) \vdash (\{\!|S' : \uparrow\!|\!\},\beta',0)^n$. By assumption furthermore $(\beta',0) \vdash S' \xrightarrow{!_A} (\beta',0) \vdash S'_1$. But then by rule PROCESS FAULT we get that $(0,0) \vdash (\{\!|S' : \uparrow\!|\!\},\beta',0)^n \xrightarrow{\tau_A} (0,0) \vdash ([S'_1];\uparrow,0,\beta')^f$. By our assumption about α' and repeated application of PROCESS F we get $(0,0) \vdash ([P'_1];\uparrow,0,\beta')^f \xrightarrow{\alpha'} (0,0) \vdash (0;\uparrow,\gamma,\beta')^f$ for some γ. By application of rule PROCESS F and rule SEQT and then by application of PROCESS F and rule COMP we obtain that $(0,0) \vdash (0;\uparrow,0,\beta')^f \xrightarrow{\tau\tau} (0,0) \vdash (\beta',\gamma,0)^f$. By assumption and repeated use of PROCESS F we can infer that $(0,0) \vdash (\beta',\gamma,0)^f \xrightarrow{\alpha''} (0,0) \vdash (0,\gamma,0)^f$. Finally using PROCESS END we obtain the desired result. In order to establish this we need additional lemmas stating that accumulated compensations are never changed during termination and compensation phases.

With this in mind we can represent processes/scope behavior by only looking at the forward activities of its inner activity and the behavior of the inner activity in case of termination at arbitrary intermediate states plus the behavior of its so far accumulated compensations. The following lemma is hence the missing link between the two semantics. The lemma uses this definition:

Definition 9 (Cut Set of a Partial Order). *A cut set X of a partial order (V,E) is a subset of V such that whenever $a \in X$ and $(b,a) \in E$ then also $b \in X$.*

Lemma 1. *Let $(\beta,0) \vdash S \xrightarrow{\alpha} (\beta',0) \vdash S'$. Let α contain no $!_A$. We now find exactly one $p \in \mathcal{S}(S,\beta)$ for each of the following cases*

1. *if $S' \equiv 0$ then $f_p = 0$ and $t_p = \boxdot$*
2. *if $(\beta,0) \vdash S' \xrightarrow{\tau_A} (\beta,0) \vdash S''$ then $f_p = \tau_A$ and $t_p = \boxtimes$ and for ρ' such that $(\beta',0) \vdash [S''] \xrightarrow{\rho'} (\beta',0) \vdash 0$ we have $\overline{\rho'} \in \mathsf{Ind}(\delta(p)|_{(I_p - I'_p) \cup T_p})$ where I'_p is a cut set of $(I_p, E_p|_{I_p})$*
3. *$f_p = 0$, $t_p = \boxtimes$ and for ρ' such that $(\beta',0) \vdash [S'] \xrightarrow{\rho'} (\beta',0) \vdash 0$ we have $\overline{\rho'} \in \mathsf{Ind}(\delta(p)|_{(I_p - I'_p) \cup T_p})$ where I'_p is a cut set of $(I_p, E_p|_{I_p})$.*

and in addition in each case $\overline{\alpha} \in \mathsf{Ind}(\delta(p)|_{F_p \cup I'_p})$ and for ρ such that $(0,0) \vdash \beta' \xrightarrow{\rho} (0,0) \vdash 0$ we have $\overline{\rho} \in \mathsf{Ind}(\delta(p)|_{C_p})$

Proof (Sketch). This lemma can be proven by induction over the term structure of the inner activity S of the process. The proof idea is to consider all states S' reachable from S by a faultless trace toghether with the compensation context accumulated so far and a distinction whether S' can fault in the next step. All statements about reachable states, traces, contexts and possible faults can always be determined recursively by corresponding statements for the direct subterms of S. Taking parallel composition as an example, i.e. $S = P \parallel Q$ for some P and Q, by induction we can find for each subterm P and Q, exactly one spot in $\mathcal{S}(P,0)$ and $\mathcal{S}(Q,0)$ that fits according to the lemma to all statements made. By the way $\mathcal{S}(P,\beta)$ is constructed out of the elements of $\mathcal{S}(P,0)$ and $\mathcal{S}(Q,0)$ we can conclude that there is again exactly one spot in $\mathcal{S}(P,0)$ that satisfies the lemma. Note that in the case of parallel composition we need to use the assumption that at most one fault can occur at the same level.

After we have related the two different semantics for $BPEL'_{fct}$, we are now ready to compare *Sagas* and $BPEL_{fct}$ in a formal way:

Theorem 2 (Correspondence Theorem)
For all sagas S and environments Γ: Whenever $\Gamma \vdash \langle \{\!|\, S\, |\!\}, \beta\rangle \xrightarrow{\alpha} \langle t', \beta'\rangle$ there is $(V, E, P, D, t, f) \in \mathcal{S}(\llbracket S \rrbracket_\Gamma, \llbracket \beta \rrbracket_{cl})$ (and vice versa) with $t = t'$ and $\alpha = (V, E|_V)$.

Intuitively, this means that the two languages behave identical (on the subsets considered) up to the more constrained behavior inside faulted and aborted transactions (scopes and the process itself) in BPEL that are imposed due to the more restrictive compensation policy. It is worth noting that if no (sub)transaction faults, the behaviors are completely identical.

Proof The proof is by structural induction over S along the recursive definition of $\mathcal{S}(.,.)$.

4.2 Relating Other Features to BPEL

Other more advanced features conceptually exist in different form in both languages. However, we found them hardly comparable in a reasonable manner. The most important difference is the way faults during compensation are handled. Consider the example of a transaction in BPEL where the inner activity is a parallel construct $P \parallel Q$. Assume that P faults. Then the transaction –which is either a scope or a process– will execute the fault handler and hence switch to faulted mode (f). The default fault handler will then trigger the compensation of P and Q. If now again a fault is caused by the compensation of, say, P, this will immediately cancel the whole compensation by rule SCOPE FAULT F, including the compensations for Q! In Sagas the same situation would be handled differently. By rule F-PAR we see that even if the compensation of P fails, Q's compensations will be completely executed and not aborted prematurely as in BPEL.

Another interesting aspect is that the principles of all-or-nothing semantics and programmable compensations are supported within Sagas via a generalization of the syntax which enables composite compensations and by adding the inference rule REPEATED-COMP. In BPEL the occurrence of a successful compensation of a failed compensation is communicated to a possible enclosing scope or to the process (cf. SCOPE FAULT C), whereas in Sagas such an occurrence remains hidden to an enclosing saga. Although the two languages do not differ fundamentally in this point, both realize different perceptions of all-or-nothing semantics.

In our comparison we used the fault handling mechanism of BPEL only to trigger compensations. Since fault handlers are fully-programmable, this mechanism can be used like the standard exception handling mechanism found in most modern programming languages. BPEL does not come with an explicit exception handling construct aside of scopes. Exception handling can be added to Sagas in form of a sagas/exception-handler pair **try** S **with** P [3], such that when an exception occurs in S, the execution continues with P. The compensations that are accumulated during the execution of both S and P are stored. In BPEL however, a fault handler is not allowed to install compensations at the same level as the activity it has been activated by, hence the two approaches to general exception handling are incompatible.

Other interesting differences and similarities may be found by a comparison to other important formal approaches to model FCT-handling like StAC [4] and cCSP [5]. StAC provides powerful compensation mechanisms similar to those of Sagas, so we also expect $BPEL_{fct}$ and StAC to share a non-trivial semantically equivalent subsets. However, we did not undertake formal investigations in this question and leave it to further research. In [2] it is shown that sequential Sagas without nesting and parallelism and cCSP coincide. The authors also show that cCSP can be changed such that both calculi behave equivalent in the presence of a parallel construct. Different to Sagas and $BPEL_{fct}$, the collected compensations of a successfully terminated subtransaction are dismissed and not stored for a possible later compensation of an enclosing transaction. This aspect and the result from [2] led us to only consider Sagas for a thorough formal comparison.

5   Conclusion

We have provided a fine-grained small-step semantics for BPEL. To the best of our knowledge this is the first process algebraic BPEL semantics that covers automated compensation handling including *all-or-nothing* semantics and compensation execution in default compensation order in its entirety. This makes it a natural choice for a comparison with recent process algebraic approaches to FCT-handling like Sagas. In this paper, we showed that Sagas coincides with a useful subset of BPEL apart from different compensation policies in the presence of parallelism. Sagas uses the concept of *distributed interruption*, which allows parallel branches to compensate their respective activities independently of each other when a fault has occurred in one branch. BPEL uses the *coordinated interruption* policy, where a fault forces all branches to start their compensations as soon as possible and at the same time. In BPEL an additional termination phase precedes the compensation phase where subtransactions are terminated in a safe manner. This phase is not distinguished as such in Sagas. Most notably, faulted compensations lead to evidently different behavior in the two compared calculi.

Our paper shows that FCT-handling in BPEL is rooted in firm formal grounds, and can be used in safe ways. However, the comparable common subsets of BPEL and Sagas seems to be rather small, although similar constructs are provided in both worlds. So in order to make FCT-handling still safer to use, more foundational analysis and comparative work has to be carried out.

References

1. Web services business process execution language version 2.0 - OASIS standard (April 2007),
   http://docs.oasis-open.org/wsbpel/2.0/OS/wsbpel-v2.0-OS.pdf
2. Bruni, R., Butler, M., Ferreira, C., Hoare, T., Melgratti, H., Montanari, U.: Comparing two approaches to compensable flow composition. In: Abadi, M., de Alfaro, L. (eds.) CONCUR 2005. LNCS, vol. 3653, pp. 383–397. Springer, Heidelberg (2005)
3. Bruni, R., Melgratti, H., Montanari, U.: Theoretical foundations for compensations in flow composition languages. SIGPLAN Not. 40(1), 209–220 (2005)
4. Butler, M., Ferreira, C.: An operational semantics for StAC, a language for modelling long-running business transactions. In: De Nicola, R., Ferrari, G.-L., Meredith, G. (eds.) COORDINATION 2004. LNCS, vol. 2949. Springer, Heidelberg (2004)
5. Butler, M., Hoare, C.A.R., Ferreira, C.: A trace semantics for long-running transactions. In: Abdallah, A.E., Jones, C.B., Sanders, J.W. (eds.) Communicating Sequential Processes. LNCS, vol. 3525, pp. 133–150. Springer, Heidelberg (2005)
6. Koshkina, M., van Breugel, F.: Models and verification of BPEL. Technical Report M3J 1P3, York University, Toronto, Canada (2006)
7. Garcia-Molina, H., Salem, K.: Sagas. SIGMOD Rec. 16(3), 249–259 (1987)
8. Hoare, C.A.R.: Communicating sequential processes. Prentice-Hall, Inc., Upper Saddle River (1985)
9. Khalaf, R.: Supporting Business Process Fragmentation While Maintaining Operational Semantics - A BPEL Perspective. Ph.D thesis, Universität Stuttgart (2008)
10. Koshkina, M.: Verification of business processes for web services. Master's thesis, York University, Toronto (2003)
11. Laneve, C., Zavattaro, G.: Foundations of web transactions. In: Sassone, V. (ed.) FOSSACS 2005. LNCS, vol. 3441, pp. 282–298. Springer, Heidelberg (2005)
12. Laneve, C., Zavattaro, G.: Web-Pi at work. In: De Nicola, R., Sangiorgi, D. (eds.) TGC 2005. LNCS, vol. 3705, pp. 182–194. Springer, Heidelberg (2005)
13. Lohmann, N.: A feature-complete petri net semantics for WS-BPEL 2.0. In: Dumas, M., Heckel, R. (eds.) WS-FM 2007. LNCS, vol. 4937, pp. 77–91. Springer, Heidelberg (2008)
14. Lucchi, R., Mazzara, M.: A pi-calculus based semantics for WS-BPEL. Journal of Logic and Algebraic Programming 70(1), 96–118 (2007)
15. Mazzara, M., Lucchi, R.: A framework for generic error handling in business processes. Electr. Notes Theor. Comput. Sci. 105, 133–145 (2004)
16. Plotkin, G.D.: A structural approach to operational semantics. Technical Report DAIMI FN-19, University of Aarhus (1981)
17. Pu, G., Zhao, X., Wang, S., Qiu, Z.: Towards the semantics and verification of BPEL4WS. Electr. Notes Theor. Comput. Sci. 151(2), 33–52 (2006)
18. Pu, G., Zhu, H., Qiu, Z., Wang, S., Zhao, X., He, J.: Theoretical Foundations of Scope-Based Compensable Flow Language for Web Service. Springer, Heidelberg (2006)
19. Qiu, Z., Wang, S., Pu, G., Zhao, X.: Semantics of BPEL4WS-Like Fault and Compensation Handling. Springer, Heidelberg (2005)

Refactoring Long Running Transactions*

Gian Luigi Ferrari[1], Roberto Guanciale[2], Daniele Strollo[1,2], and Emilio Tuosto[3]

[1] Università degli Studi di Pisa, Dipartimento di Informatica, Italy
{giangi,strollo}@di.unipi.it
[2] Institute for Advanced Studies IMT Lucca, Italy
{roberto.guanciale,daniele.strollo}@imtlucca.it
[3] University of Leicester, Computer Science Department, UK
et52@mcs.le.ac.uk

Abstract. Sagas calculi have been proposed to specify distributed Long Running Transactions (LRT) and, in previous work, a subset of naive sagas has been encoded in the Signal Calculus (SC) to enable their use in service-oriented systems. Here, we promote a formal approach to the refactoring of LRT represented in SC so that distributed LRT designed in the Business Process Modelling Notation (BPMN) can be faithfully represented. Firstly, we complete the initial encoding of naive sagas into SC. Secondly, on top of SC, we define a few refactoring transformations for distributed LRT. Finally, we prove that the given refactoring rules are sound by showing that they preserve (weak) bisimilarity.

1 Introduction

Service Oriented Computing (SOC) envisages systems as combination of basic computational activities, called *services*, whose interfaces can be dynamically published and bound. Typically, SOC systems are executed on *overlay networks* consisting of different inter-networked communication infrastructures (e.g., wired and wireless networks, telecommunication networks or their combination). Hence, high level mechanisms for composing and coordinating distributed activities of services are worthwhile.

The main methodologies for composing services are *orchestration* and *choreography*. Services are orchestrated when their execution workflow is described through an "external" process, called *orchestrator*. A *choreography* instead is a design that specifies how services should be connected and interact so that each service accomplishes its task within the given choreography. Roughly, choreographies yield an abstract global view of SOC systems that must eventually be "projected" on the distributed components.

Both orchestration and choreography can benefit from *model driven development* (MDD, for short) and *refactoring* [2] whereby (models of) systems are repeatedly transformed so that specific concerns are confined at different stages. In fact, MDD typically starts from a (semi)formal system specification that focuses on the core *business process* and neglects other aspects (e.g., communication mechanisms or distribution) tackled by subsequent transformations.

* Research supported by the EU FET-GC2 IST-2004-16004 Integrated Project SENSORIA and by the Italian FIRB Project TOCAI.IT.

An important concern of SOC is to enforce transactional behaviors. Classically transactions are thought of as a sequence of actions to be executed atomically. Namely, if some failure happens at any stage of the sequence, the computation must be reverted the previus stable state. Such kind of transactions are referred to as *ACID* (after atomicity, consistency, isolation and durability) [10] and are not suitable for SOC (see e.g. [14]). For instance, fully restoring the state in SOC is practically unfeasible (no atomicity). Being inherently loosely coupled, SOC systems require transactional behaviours possibly spanning over long temporal intervals. Therefore, ACID properties of classical transactions cannot be enforced.

The aim of this paper is to study the formal properties of some refactoring rules applied to *long running transactions* (LRTs). We adopt *sagas* calculi [9,3] as a formal framework into which semi-formal Business Process Modelling Notation (BPMN) [11] specifications can be precisely modelled. Sagas calculi feature *compensations* to deal with anomalous computations of LRT. Indeed, sagas specify transactional behaviours where the execution proceeds normally until one of its activities fails. Specifically, upon successful execution, an activity installs a *compensation* and invokes the next activities of the workflow. The compensation is executed on failure of subsequent activities: a failing activity signals to its invoker the anomalous execution triggering the invoker's compensation.

We use the *signal calculus* (SC) [6,7] to formally model LRT designed in BPMN. To this purpose, we exploit the encoding given in [4] that enables designers to specify LRTs in the familiar and semi-formal BPMN while leaving their precise specification to the mapping in SC. Moreover, SC processes can be automatically compiled into executable Java programs that can be distributively executed thanks to its implementation [6,1].

The refactoring rules presented here address some crucial issues of the deployment phase, that is the possible alterations that one would like (or has) to apply at the SC level where they can be more suitably tackled. Indeed, as a matter of fact, BPMN designs (*i*) neglect distribution aspects of the transactional activities, (*ii*) does not specify if activities are atomic or consisting of hidden sub-activities, (*iii*) delegate activities or compensations (e.g., according to patterns like farm).

Arguably, refactoring does not have to alter the intention of the designer, namely, refactoring rules must preserve the intended semantics. Our refactoring rules are proved sound by showing that they preserve (weak) bisimulation. The proofs are only sketched (the detailed proofs are in [5]) and rely on a bisimulation preserving mapping from SC to its choreographic view expressed in the NCP calculus, after Network Coordination Policy [4]. More precisely, we show that the NCP image $\hat{N}$ of an SC system N is weak bisimilar to a refactoring of $\hat{N}$ obtained by applying any of our rules. Albeit the proof could have been given directly at the SC level, we prefer to deviate through NCP for simplicity and, more importantly, because NCP provides a choreographic view of the SC system that is closer to the original BPMN design. Hence, NCP images of SC processes can help to change the BPMN design if problems spotted at the SC level require to modify the original BPMN design.

Structure of the paper. § 2 summarises background material. § 3 introduces our refactoring rules. § 4 drafts some final considerations.

2   Background

This section borrows a few concepts from previous work and aims to summarise the main ingredients of our framework by briefly recalling SC [7], the mapping from BPMN designs to SC [8], and NCP [4] (the similarities between NCP and the asynchronous π-calculus are omitted for space constraints and can be found in [4]).

Let T and C be two countable disjoint sets of *topic* and *component* names respectively. Topics (ranged over by $\tau, \tau', r, s, \ldots$) represent event types and session identifiers. Component names (ranged over by $a, b, c, \ldots$) identify services; we let $\mathbf{a}, \mathbf{b}, \ldots$ range over finite subsets of C.

2.1   A Walk through SC

In SC, systems are modelled as *components* reacting to *events*. A component $a\,[B]_F^R$ represents a service uniquely identified by $a \in C$, with internal behavior B, and whose interfaces are the *reactions* R and the *flows* F (both explained below). Event notifications (or *signals*) abstract messages typed by topics and issued in sessions. For simplicity, data carried by messages are neglected and messages are envisaged as pairs $\tau_{@}s$, where $\tau \in T$ is the message topic and $s \in T$ is the session identifier. *Subscribers* are notified and receive notifications for events raised by *publishers*.

A component subscribed to events of topic $\tau \in T$ installs either *lambda* or *check* reactions for τ; *lambda reactions*, written $\tau\,\lambda\,(s)B$ (with s bound in B), react to signals independently from their session while *check reactions*, written $\tau_{@}s \gg B$, respond to signals of specific sessions. Once a reaction is triggered, its behavior B is executed in parallel with the component's behavior. Reactions can be composed in parallel (written $R_1|\ldots|R_h$) or be the *empty reaction* 0, which does not respond to any signal.

The flow $F \subseteq T \times C$ of a component $a\,[B]_F^R$ yields the set of components subscribed to topics from a; intuitively, $(\tau, b) \in F$ states that component b is subscribed for signals of topic τ emitted by a. The flows of all components determine the network topology.

The behavior of $a\,[B]_F^R$ is a process B derived by the following grammar:

$$B ::= \mathtt{out}\langle \tau_{@}s \rangle.B \mid \mathtt{rupd}(R).B \mid \mathtt{fupd}(F).B \mid (\nu\tau)B \mid B\,|\,B' \mid X\langle \tau_1, \ldots, \tau_n \rangle \mid 0$$

Prefix $\mathtt{out}\langle \tau_{@}s \rangle.B$ emits a signal and then continues as B while interfaces can be updated by adding new reactions or elements in the set of flows by respectively using $\mathtt{rupd}(R)$ and $\mathtt{fupd}(F)$. As usual, behaviours can declare local topics (τ is bound in $(\nu\tau)B$), be composed in parallel, the recursive invocation[1], or be the empty process.

Example 1. The execution of a behaviour B after the collection of n signals $\tau_{@}s$ can be defined as

$$Sync_0^B(\tau, s) \stackrel{\text{def}}{=} B, \qquad Sync_{i+1}^B(\tau, s) \stackrel{\text{def}}{=} \mathtt{rupd}\left(\tau_{@}s \gg Sync_i^B(\tau_{@}s)(B) \right)$$

where i is a natural number.   ◇

---

[1] We assume given a set of identifiers for behaviours ranged over by X each with a unique definition $X(\tau_1, \ldots, \tau_n) \stackrel{\text{def}}{=} B$ where the free topics in B are all in $\{\tau_1, \ldots, \tau_n\}$.

Networks describe the component distribution and carry signals exchanged among components. Their syntax is defined as follows:

$$N ::= \mathbf{0} \mid a[B]_F^R \mid N \parallel N' \mid \langle \tau_{\copyright}s \rangle @a \mid (\nu n)N, \qquad n \text{ ranges over } \mathcal{T} \cup \mathcal{C}$$

where $\mathbf{0}$ is the empty network, $a[B]_F^R$ is a component, $N \parallel N'$ is the parallel composition of networks, $\langle \tau_{\copyright}s \rangle @a$ is called *envelope* and is a signal spawned for a, and $(\nu n)N$ is a network with a restricted name n. Networks can restrict both component and topic names, thus allowing to hide behavior of part of a network. Also, the usual structural congruence $\equiv$ relation is assumed on networks, behaviours and reactions and we say that N is *well-formed* if, for any $N_1 \parallel N_2 \equiv N$, $\mathrm{fn}(N_1) \cap \mathrm{bn}(N_2) = \emptyset$.

Example 2. As an example, we define an SC component that will be used in § 2.3 and § 3.2 and uses two distinguished topic names f and r; the component is defined as

$$Disp_{i,\mathbf{a},\mathbf{b}}^{f,r}(d) \overset{\text{def}}{=} d\,[0]_{\{f \leadsto \mathbf{a}, r \leadsto \mathbf{b}\}}^{f\ \lambda\ (s)(Sync_i^{\text{out}\langle r_{\copyright}s \rangle}(r,s)\ \mid\ \text{out}\langle f_{\copyright}s \rangle)}$$

representing a service d, a lambda reaction and, among others, flows for topic f towards a set of components $\mathbf{a} \subseteq \mathcal{C}$ (the behaviour $Sync_i^{\text{out}\langle r_{\copyright}s \rangle}(r,s)$ is defined in the Example 1).

The component $Disp_{i,\mathbf{a},\mathbf{b}}^{f,r}(d)$ responds to signals for topic f and, once triggered, s will be bound to session of the received message and the body will be executed so that i signals $r_{\copyright}s$ are collected before sending back a signa $r_{\copyright}s$. In parallel, the forward flow for sessioin s ($f_{\copyright}s$) is spawned to components in $\mathbf{a}$. Notice that the check reaction will collect exactly i messages of $r_{\copyright}s$ before propagating the r signal. ◇

The reduction semantics of SC is given in [7] as transitive closure of $\equiv \rightarrow \equiv$, where $\rightarrow$ is the smallest relation closed under the following rules:

$$a[\text{out}\langle \tau_{\copyright}s \rangle.B \mid B']_F^R \;\rightarrow\; a[B \mid B']_F^R \parallel \prod_{b \in F(\tau)} \langle \tau_{\copyright}s \rangle @b \quad (\text{emit})$$

$$\langle \tau_{\copyright}s \rangle @a \parallel a[B]_F^{\tau_{\copyright}s \triangleright B' \mid R} \;\rightarrow\; a[B\mid B']_F^R \quad (\text{check})$$

$$\langle \tau_{\copyright}s \rangle @a \parallel a[B]_F^{\tau\ \lambda\ (s')B' \mid R} \;\rightarrow\; a[B\mid \{s/s'\}B']_F^R \quad (\text{lam})$$

$$a[\text{rupd}(R').B]_F^R \rightarrow a[B]_F^{R\mid R'} \quad (\text{rupd}) \qquad\qquad a[\text{fupd}(F').B]_F^R \rightarrow a[B]_{F,F'}^R \quad (\text{fupd})$$

$$\frac{N \rightarrow N'}{N \parallel M \rightarrow N' \parallel M} \;(\text{npar}) \qquad\qquad \frac{N \rightarrow N_1}{(\nu n)N \rightarrow (\nu n)N_1} \;(\text{new})$$

Rule emit produces a new envelope for each component subscribed for the topic τ ($\prod$ stands for n-ary parallel composition and, for a flow F, $F(\tau) = \{b \in \mathcal{C} : (\tau, b) \in F\}$). Rule check (resp. lam) models the activation of check (resp. lambda) reactions, matching the session identifier (resp. receiving a session identifier as argument). Rules rupd and fupd update reactions and flows, respectively. Rules npar and new are the usual rules of process calculi.

2.2   From BPMN to SC (Informally)

This section shows how to encode in SC the subset of transactional primitives of BPMN [11], a graphical notation for modeling service coordination policies. BPMN permits to describe the workflow of a distributed system and its transactional properties by a global point of view. The software architect can abstract from the distribution of the processes, the communication mechanisms and the technologies that will implement each processes. We rely on the formal semantics of sagas [3] but only informally discuss the mapping from BPMN to SC (see [8] for details).

The basic units of BPMN are *transactional components*, namely pairs of main activities and compensations that can be composed sequentially or in parallel. Fig. 1 depicts the standard BPMN designs for sequential and parallel composition of transactional components.

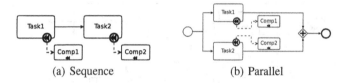

(a) Sequence   (b) Parallel

Fig. 1. Composition of BPMN transactional components

In BPMN main activities and compensations are represented as boxes linked by dashed arrows through a "compensation point", like `Task1` and `Comp1` in Fig. 1. The sequential composition of `Task1` and `Task2` is obtained by linking them together (cf. Fig. 1(a)), while their parallel composition requires to specify "fork" and "join" of the workflow. Fig.1(b) depicts the parallel composition of `Task1` and `Task2`; the circles represent the entry and exit points[2] of the whole process while the rhombus represents the joining of the two activities.

Transactional components of BPMN are mapped into SC components where fork and join entry points are respectively encoded as reactions and flows. For instance, the SC counterpart of the BPMN designs of Fig. 1 is graphically represented in Fig. 2 where $TC1$ (resp. $TC2$) embeds `Task1` and `Comp1` (resp. `Task2` and `Comp2`). Two distinguished event topics f and r are used (after sagas' terminology for forward and rollback flow, respectively) to signal successful termination of main activities (f topic) or their failure (r topic). In Fig. 2 the forward flows are represented by solid arrows while backward flows by dashed arrows.

Fig. 3 draws how transactional components are mapped into SC components. Initially, signals of type f trigger the execution of the main activity (hereafter referred as *Task*) and install the reactions to manage its continuation. The main activity *Task* eventually emits either an *ok* or an *ex* signal which are two distinguished topic used only by transactional components. An *ok* signal is emitted when *Task* terminate successfully, otherwise and *ex* signal is emitted. In the former case, the compensation is installed and the f signal is propagated outside the component, otherwise a r signal is emitted to the

---

[2] The BPMN terminology is *start* and *end events*.

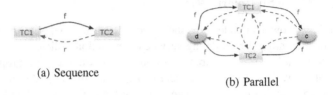

(a) Sequence

(b) Parallel

Fig. 2. Composition of SC transactional components

previous stages of the transaction. Notice that, as required by sagas, rollback signals can be consumed only by components that successfully executed their main activity (and therefore installed their compensation).

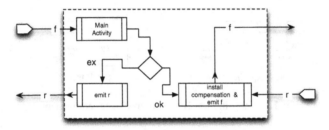

Fig. 3. SC Transactional Component

A transactional TC component is rendered as SC component as follows:

$$TC = (\nu\, ok, ex)\, a\, [0]_{\{ok \rightsquigarrow a, ex \rightsquigarrow a, f \rightsquigarrow c_1, r \rightsquigarrow c_2\}}^{f\, \lambda\, (s)\left(Task \mid \mathtt{rupd}\left(\begin{smallmatrix} ok@s \succ \mathtt{rupd}\,(r@s \succ Comp) \mid \mathtt{out}\langle f@s\rangle \\ \mid ex@s \succ \mathtt{out}\langle r@s\rangle \end{smallmatrix} \right) \right)} \tag{1}$$

where

- $Task = \iota.\mathtt{out}\langle ok@s\rangle + \iota.\mathtt{out}\langle ex@s\rangle$ represents the main activity[3];
- $Comp = \iota.\mathtt{out}\langle r@s\rangle$ represents the compensation of the transactional component;
- c_1 and c_2 represent the forward and the backward flows, respectively.

Parallel composition of components requires auxiliary components called *dispatcher* and *collector* to model the fork and join entry points. Dispatchers are responsible to collect notifications of the forward flow (signals of topic f) and redirect them to the parallel components. Symmetrically, dispatchers bounce rollback signals of topic r when the backward flow is executed. Analogously, collectors propagates forward and backward flows by sending the signals of topic f or r as appropriate. Fig. 2(b) yields a pictorial representation of how the forward and backward flows of the dispatcher d and collector c of parallel components a and b are coordinated using the f and r signals. Notice that

---

[3] Notice that SC is not directly equipped with non-deterministic choice. However non-determinism can be easily encoded exploiting the non-deterministic activation of reactions having the same signature.

a and *b* have rollback flows connecting each other; in fact, the semantics of saga prescribes that, when the main activity of a parallel component fails, the other components must be notified and start their compensations.

2.3 A Walk through the NCP Calculus

The NCP calculus takes inspiration by the asynchronous π-calculus for specifying coordination patterns that depend on a *network topology*, that is a structure $G = (V, E)$ where $V \subseteq C$ consists of the restricted component names of the network and $E \subseteq C \times T \times C$ are the flow connections among components; $(a, \tau, b) \in E$, meaning that component a has a flow towards b for signals of topic τ. Notice that, G induces a directed labelled graph whose vertexes are the names of the network components (the restricted ones of which are highlighted in V) and whose edges are the elements in E. Abusing notation, we will confuse G with its associated graph and a set of edges E sometimes will denote the network topology $(\emptyset, E)$.

Auxiliary notation will be useful. Let $|G|$ denote the set of vertexes of a graph G, $G = (V, E)$ be a network topology, and $a \in C$ and $\tau \in T$:

- $\mathrm{bn}(G) = V$ and $\mathrm{fn}(G) = |G| \setminus \mathrm{bn}(G)$;
- $G(a)$ are the *flows emanating from a in G*, namely $G(a) = \{(\tau, b) \mid (a, \tau, b) \in E\}$;
- $G(\tau)$ is the *topic graph of τ in G*, namely the unlabelled directed graph such that $|G(\tau)| = |G|$ and the edges are $\{(a, b) \in C \times C \mid (a, \tau, b) \in E\}$ (hereafter, we let T range on such graphs for which $\tau \square T = \{(a, \tau, b) \mid (a, b) \in T\}$);
- $G(a, \tau) = \{b \mid (\tau, b) \in G(a)\}$ is the *flow projection of τ for a in G*;
- $a \boxtimes F = \{(a, \tau, b) \mid (\tau, b) \in F\})$, for $F \subseteq T \times C$;
- if $G' = (V', E')$ is a network topology, $G \uplus G' = (V \cup V', E \cup E')$ and, if $|G| \cap |G'| = \emptyset$ then $G \setminus G' = (V, E \setminus E')$.

The NCP calculus supports multi-cast communication and multi-layered topologies with hidden layers that can be dynamically created and communicated among processes. A key feature of NCP is the interplay between restriction of topics and multi-cast communications. In fact, in NCP the extrusion of a topic τ transparently enriches the receiver, say a, with flows absent beforehand; hence, further emissions of signals on τ from a will generate envelopes on the inherited flows.

The syntax of NCP processes, called *coordination policies* is as follows:

$$P ::= \sum_{i \in I} p_i @ a_i.P_i \quad | \quad \overline{\tau}\, s @ a.P \quad | \quad \langle \tau_{@} s \rangle @ a$$
$$| \quad \mathtt{fupd}\,(F)\,@a.P \quad | \quad \iota.P \quad | \quad P \,\|\, P \qquad\qquad \text{where } p ::= \tau(s) \quad | \quad \tau\, s$$
$$| \quad (\nu\, \tau : T)P \quad | \quad (\nu\, a : G)P \quad | \quad Id\,\langle \mathbf{a} \rangle$$

where $\tau, s \in T$, $a \in C$, T is a topic graphs and I is a finite set. Non-deterministic (guarded) choice is denoted as $\sum$ (we let $\sum_{i \in I} p_i @ a_i.P_i = \mathbf{0}$ when $I = \emptyset$). A policy $p @ a.P$ represents an action p executed by the component a with continuation P; the prefix $\tau(s)$ corresponds to lambda reactions in SC (and therefore called *lambda input*) and it allows messages of topic τ to be received; $\tau\, s$ allows to receive signals having topic τ and session s and is therefore called *check input*. The policy $\overline{\tau}\, s$ emits an envelope on session s for those services that are listening on topic τ. The *envelope* $\langle \tau_{@} s \rangle @ a$

represents a pending message on the network and targeted to a. Notice that only the target of a signal is declared. The policy $\mathtt{fupd}\,(F)$ adds F to the flows departing from a. Prefix $\iota.P$ represents the execution of an internal activity before the execution of P. Coordination policies can be composed in parallel and have restricted names, namely $(\nu\,\tau:T)P$ and $(\nu\,a:G)P$ restrict τ and a in P. Finally, $Id\,\langle\langle\mathbf{a}\rangle\rangle$ is the recursive invocation[4]. Noteworthy, graph T permits to extend the topology with the connections among components for the fresh topic τ, while the network topology G yields the flows from/to a. (Free names $\mathrm{fn}(P)$ and bound names $\mathrm{bn}(P)$ are defined as expected.)

The semantics[5] of NCP [4] is specified by a labelled transition system (LTS) whose states $\langle G\,;P\rangle$ are pairs of network topologies and coordination policies; $\langle G\,;P\rangle \xrightarrow{\alpha} \langle G'\,;P'\rangle$ states that the coordination policy P, plugged in the topology G, can perform the action α, evolving $\langle G'\,;P'\rangle$. Labels α are defined by the following grammar:

$$\alpha ::= \varepsilon \mid \tau\,s@a \mid (\tau\,s@a) \mid \langle\tau_{\odot}s\rangle@a \mid \langle\tau_{\odot}(s:T)\rangle@a$$

where ε is the silent action; $\tau\,s@a$ is a free reaction activation; $(\tau\,s@a)$ represents the reception of a message that is put in parallel with the current process (this action is observable in any system, including the empty policy); $\langle\tau_{\odot}s\rangle@a$ is the *free* event notification to a for τ in session s while $\langle\tau_{\odot}(s:T)\rangle@a$ is a *bound* event notification on τ of a topic with network graph T. Hereafter, $n(\alpha)$ will denote the names of α.

The semantics of NCP is given by the transitive closure of $\equiv\xrightarrow{\alpha}\equiv$ where $\xrightarrow{\alpha}$ is the smallest relation closed under the rules in Fig. 4. which use a dynamic network topology (namely the evaluation of a coordination policy depends from the dynamic network topology) and rely on the congruence rule

$$\langle(\mathbf{a},E)\,;(\nu\,a:G)P\parallel Q\rangle \equiv \langle(\mathbf{a}\cup\{a\},E)\uplus G\,;P\parallel Q\rangle, \qquad \text{if } a\notin |(\mathbf{a},E)|\cup\mathrm{fn}(Q)$$

that casts in NCP the scope rule of π-calculus.

We now comment on the rules of Fig. 4. Rule $\mathtt{skip}$ trivially fires the silent action. Rule $\mathtt{fupd}$ appends the sub network $a\boxtimes F$ to the environment G (newly added flows departs from a). Rule $\mathtt{emit}$ spawns an envelope for each subscriber in $G(\tau)(a)$; the continuation policy P is executed regardless the reception of envelopes as typical in asynchronous communications. Notification of envelopes is ruled by $\mathtt{notify}$ as much like as the output in the asynchronous π-calculus. Rule $\mathtt{async}$ permits any system to perform an input as the rule in_0 in [12]. Rules $\mathtt{lambda}$ and $\mathtt{check}$ model input actions: in the former, the selected input p_j reads any signal with topic τ and binds s' to s in an early-style semantics; when a check input is selected, only envelopes of topic τ in session s can be consumed. Rules $\mathtt{open}$ and $\mathtt{close}$ govern scope extrusion of topics. Rule $\mathtt{new}$ permits to extend the topology with a freshly generated topic provided that it is not communicated outside the scope ($\tau\notin n(\alpha)$) and hides the changes to the

---

[4] We assume given a set of identifiers for networks ranged over by Id each with a unique definition $Id(\mathbf{a}) \stackrel{\mathrm{def}}{=} P$ where $\mathrm{fn}(P)\subseteq\mathbf{a}$.

[5] Though NCP is reminiscent of the asynchronous π-calculus, its semantics is centred on network topologies, that is on the environment of the computation. This enables the modelling in a natural way multi-cast communication: for example, in order to receive $\bar{\tau}\,s$, it is necessary "to listen on τ" and have "τ-connection" between listener and emitter.

$$\text{skip}\quad \langle G\,;\, \iota.P\rangle \xrightarrow{\varepsilon} \langle G\,;\, P\rangle \qquad\qquad \text{fupd}\quad \langle G\,;\, \mathtt{fupd}(F)\,@a.P\rangle \xrightarrow{\varepsilon} \langle G \uplus (a \boxtimes F)\,;\, P\rangle$$

$$\text{emit}\quad \langle G\,;\, \bar{\tau}\, s@a.P\rangle \xrightarrow{\varepsilon} \left\langle G\,;\, P \parallel \textstyle\prod_{b \in G(\tau,a)} \langle \tau_{\copyright} s\rangle @b\right\rangle$$

$$\text{notify}\quad \langle G\,;\, \langle \tau_{\copyright} s\rangle @a\rangle \xrightarrow{\langle \tau_{\copyright} s\rangle @a} \langle G\,;\, \mathbf{0}\rangle \qquad \text{async}\quad \langle G\,;\, P\rangle \xrightarrow{(\tau\, s@a)} \langle G\,;\, P \parallel \langle \tau_{\copyright} s\rangle @a\rangle$$

$$\frac{j \in I \qquad p_j = \tau(s')}{\left\langle G\,;\, \sum_{i \in I} p_i @a_i.P_i\right\rangle \xrightarrow{\tau\, s@a_j} \langle G\,;\, \{^s/_{s'}\}P_j\rangle}\quad \text{lambda}$$

$$\frac{j \in I \qquad p_j = \tau\, s}{\left\langle G\,;\, \sum_{i \in I} p_i @a_i.P_i\right\rangle \xrightarrow{p_j @a_j} \langle G\,;\, P_j\rangle}\quad \text{check}$$

$$\frac{\langle G \uplus (s \boxdot T)\,;\, P\rangle \xrightarrow{\langle \tau_{\copyright} s\rangle @a} \langle G'\,;\, P'\rangle \quad T' = G'(s)}{\langle G\,;\, (\nu\, s:T)P\rangle \xrightarrow{\langle \tau_{\copyright}(s:T')\rangle @a} \langle G' \setminus (s \boxtimes T')\,;\, P'\rangle}\quad \text{open}$$

$$\frac{\langle G\,;\, P_1\rangle \xrightarrow{\tau\, s@a} \langle G\,;\, P_1'\rangle \quad \langle G\,;\, P_2\rangle \xrightarrow{\langle \tau_{\copyright}(s:T)\rangle @a} \langle G\,;\, P_2'\rangle}{\langle G\,;\, P_1 \parallel P_2\rangle \xrightarrow{\varepsilon} \langle G\,;\, (\nu\, s:T)(P_1' \parallel P_2')\rangle}\quad \text{close}$$

$$\frac{\langle G \uplus (\tau \boxtimes T)\,;\, P\rangle \xrightarrow{\alpha} \langle G'\,;\, P'\rangle \quad \tau \notin n(\alpha) \quad T' = G'(\tau)}{\langle G\,;\, (\nu\, \tau:T)P\rangle \xrightarrow{\alpha} \langle G' \setminus (\tau \boxdot T')\,;\, (\nu\, \tau:T')P'\rangle}\quad \text{new}$$

$$\frac{\langle G\,;\, P_1\rangle \xrightarrow{\tau\, s@a} \langle G\,;\, P_1'\rangle \quad \langle G\,;\, P_2\rangle \xrightarrow{\langle \tau_{\copyright} s\rangle @a} \langle G\,;\, P_2'\rangle}{\langle G\,;\, P_1 \parallel P_2\rangle \xrightarrow{\varepsilon} \langle G\,;\, P_1' \parallel P_2'\rangle}\quad \text{com}$$

$$\frac{\langle G\,;\, P\rangle \xrightarrow{\alpha} \langle G'\,;\, P'\rangle}{\langle G\,;\, P \parallel P_1\rangle \xrightarrow{\alpha} \langle G'\,;\, P' \parallel P_1\rangle}\quad \text{par} \qquad \frac{\langle G\,;\, P\rangle \xrightarrow{\alpha} \langle G'\,;\, P'\rangle}{\langle G\,;\, Id\langle \mathbf{a}\rangle\rangle \xrightarrow{\alpha} \langle G'\,;\, P'\rangle}\quad Id(\mathbf{b}) \stackrel{\text{def}}{=} \{^\mathbf{a}/_\mathbf{b}\}P \quad \text{rec}$$

Fig. 4. Rules for the semantics of NCP

environment that involve the name outside the scope $G' \setminus (\tau \boxdot T')$. Rule com allows the communication of a free session name s. Rule par and rec have are standard.

The LTS semantics yields the following definition of bisimulation which is obtained by confining the NCP bisimulation in [4] to public names of components.

Definition 1. *A symmetric binary relation $\mathcal{B}$ over NCP states is a* bisimulation *if whenever $\langle G_1 ; P_1 \rangle \mathcal{B} \langle G_2 ; P_2 \rangle$ and $\langle G_1 ; P_1 \rangle \xrightarrow{\alpha} \langle G_1' ; P_1' \rangle$*

- *if $\alpha \in \{\varepsilon, \langle \tau_{\circledcirc} \tau' \rangle @a, (\tau \tau' @a)\}$ and $a \notin \mathrm{bn}(G_1)$, there is $\langle G_2 ; P_2 \rangle \xrightarrow{\alpha} \langle G_2' ; P_2' \rangle$ and $\langle G_1' ; P_1' \rangle \mathcal{B} \langle G_2' ; P_2' \rangle$*
- *if $\alpha = \langle \tau_{\circledcirc} (\tau' : T) \rangle @a$ with $\tau' \notin \mathrm{fn}(G_2, P_2)$ and $a \notin bnG_1$, there is*
  $$\langle G_2 ; P_2 \rangle \xrightarrow{\langle \tau_{\circledcirc} (\tau':T') \rangle @a} \langle G_2' ; P_2' \rangle \text{ and } \langle G_1' ; P_1' \rangle \mathcal{B} \langle G_2' ; P_2' \rangle.$$

The bisimilarity *relation is defined as usual and denoted by $\sim$. The definition of weak bisimulation is defined in the standard way by considering the* weak transition relation *defined as the union of $\Longrightarrow$ and $\bigcup_{\alpha \neq \varepsilon} \Longrightarrow \xrightarrow{\alpha} \Longrightarrow$, where $\Longrightarrow$ is the reflexive and transitive closure of ε. We define $\approx$ as the largest weak bisimulation.*

In [4] it is given a mapping taking an SC network N to the NCP state $[\![N]\!]$ so that the topology of $[\![N]\!]$ is determined by the flows of all components of N and its policy is obtained by the reactions and behaviors of components of N. The correctness of the mapping is proved in [4].

Example 3. The translation of the SC dispatcher in Example 2 with 2 rollback messages to synchronise is the NCP state

$$[\![Disp_{2,\mathbf{a},\mathbf{b}}^{f,r}(d)]\!] = \left\langle (\emptyset, \bigcup_{a \in \mathbf{a}, b \in \mathbf{b}} \{(d,f,a), (d,r,b)\}) ; P \right\rangle$$

where P is the policy $f(s) @d.(\iota.r\, s@d.\iota.r\, s@d.\bar{r}\, s@d \parallel \bar{f}\, s@d)$ and initially there are no restricted vertexes. $\diamond$

3   Refactoring LRT

The need for refactoring rules emerges because some crucial aspects of SOC systems are neglected during the design phase but concern other specification or implementation levels. In fact, either such aspects do not pertain to designs or, more pragmatically, they can more suitably considered at later stages of the development. For example, BPMN designs sketches how the overall transaction among transactional components should proceed regardless how services implement such components (or where they are located); these concerns can be considered in SC.

We argue that the translation of BPMN transactions into SC networks provides a suitable level of abstraction to which refactoring steps can be applied. For example, deployment of distributed components or rearrangement of points of control can be automatically transformed at the SC level preserving the original semantics of automatically translated designs.

In the following, we presents useful refactoring rules that transform SC networks without altering their semantics. In fact, our refactoring rules preserve bisimulation for SC networks that are images of BPMN designs.

3.1   Refactoring Transactional Components

Our first refactoring rule can be applied to any SC component obtained by translating a transactional component as shown in the equation (1), § 2.2.

As said, both the main activity and the compensation of a transactional component are embedded into a single SC component that manages ok and ex signals so to propagate forward/backward flows. However, it might be useful to assign the compensation task to a different component. For example, the compensation $Comp1$ in Figure 1(a) should run on a different host than $Task1$, because it involve a remote service. Instead, when the business process is mapped in an SC network, it is possible to allocate $Comp1$ on a different host by taking advantage of the implementation of JSCL [6] that permits to distributed deployment orthogonally to how the network is generated. This cannot be specified in BPMN.

The delegation of the compensation of a transactional component a to a component b produces the following SC network:

$$TC_{Delegated} = (\nu b, ok, ex)\left(a\,[0]^{f\,\lambda\,(s)\left(\begin{smallmatrix}\texttt{rupd}\,(ok@s\,\gg\,Ok_a\,|\,\texttt{out}\langle f@s\rangle)\\ |\;Task\end{smallmatrix}\right)}_{\{ok\rightsquigarrow a,ex\rightsquigarrow b,f\rightsquigarrow c_1,r\rightsquigarrow b\}} \quad\|\quad b\,[0]^{R_b}_{\{r\rightsquigarrow c_2\}} \right) \quad (2)$$

where $Ok_a = \texttt{rupd}\,(r@s \gg \texttt{out}\langle r@s\rangle)$ and $R_b = ex\,\lambda\,(s)\texttt{out}\langle r@s\rangle \mid r\,\lambda\,(s)Comp$. The refactoring rule uses a restricted component b (where $b \in C$ is fresh) that handles the compensation and the backward flow. For this reason, the compensation of a is moved to b towards which a directs r and ex signals as specified in the flows of the refactored a in (2) which only checks for the successful termination of $Task$. In fact, the check reaction of a in (2) propagates the forward flow and activates Ok_a, a listener for the rollback of signals possibly raised by subsequent transactional components. Notice that Ok_a delegates the execution of the compensation $Comp$ to b which captures ex signals emitted from $Task$ or r signals from subsequent components.

The initial reactions of b are given by R_b. Intuitively, b waits the notification of an exception from $Task$ or a rollback signal from subsequent components. In the former case, b simply activates the backward flow (e.g. the reaction migrated from a) while, in the latter case, b executes $Comp$ that, upon termination, starts the backward flow.

This refactoring rule is safe as it preserves weak bisimulation.

Theorem 1. $[\![TC]\!] \approx [\![TC_{Delegated}]\!]$

Proof outline. The theorem can be proved verifing that each transition of TC is (weakly) matched by a transition of $TC_{Delegated}$, and viceversa. Notice that each step of the first process is mimicked by the corresponding step on the second one with the exception of the action $r\,(s)\,@b$ that is unobservable because b is restricted. $\square$

3.2   Refactoring Parallel Composition

Let N_1 and N_2 be two SC networks images of two BPMN designs. The parallel composition of N_1 and N_2 uses two components, $Disp^{f,r}_{i,\mathbf{a},\mathbf{b}}(d)$ and $Coll_{f,r,s}(c)$, act that as the entry and exit point of the whole composition.

$$N = (\nu\, d,c) \left(N_1 \underset{d}{\overset{c}{\bowtie}} N_2 \ \| \ Disp^{f,r}_{i,\mathbf{a},\mathbf{b}}(d) \ \| \ Coll_{f,r,s}(c) \right) \tag{3}$$

where the operator $\underset{d}{\overset{c}{\bowtie}}$ is described later and

- $Disp^{f,r}_{i,\mathbf{a},\mathbf{b}}(d)$ (cf. Example 2) activates the forward flow of subsequent components (**c**), and synchronizes their backward flows
- $Coll_{f,r,s}(c) \overset{def}{=} c\,[0]^{f©s \triangleright \mathrm{rupd}(f©s \triangleright \mathrm{out}\langle f©s\rangle.\mathrm{rupd}(r©s \triangleright \mathrm{out}\langle r©s\rangle))}_{\{r \rightsquigarrow \mathbf{b}\}}$ propagates the forward flow when all components of N_1 and N_2 terminate correctly and notifies rollback signals when subsequent components fail.

Fig. 5(a) illustrates the mapping when N_1 is the parallel composition of the transactional components TC_1 and TC_2, and N_2 is just the components TC_3 (d and c being the dispatcher and collector, respectively).

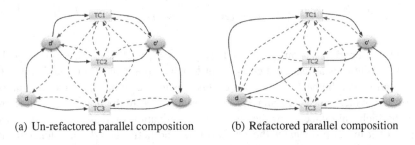

(a) Un-refactored parallel composition   (b) Refactored parallel composition

Fig. 5. Parallel composition and its refactoring

Upon reaction to a forward signal say $f©s$, d propagates the event $\mathrm{out}\langle f©s\rangle$ to TC_3 and (through d′) to TC_1 and TC_2. Concurrently, the dispatcher activates installs two nested reactions for the topic r and the workflow session s ($\mathrm{rupd}(\triangleright r©s\mathrm{rupd}(r©s \triangleright ...))$) in order to send back possible rollback signals $\mathrm{out}\langle r©s\rangle$. The operator $\underset{d}{\overset{c}{\bowtie}}$ configures the flows of parallel transactional components, e.g., those in N_1 and N_2 in (3). For the forward flow f, d is connected to all entry points while each exit point is attached to c. For the backward flow r, viceversa, c is connected to all exit points, and all entry points are connected to d, to propagate the backward flow. Finally, the parallel branches are interconnected for the rollback flow. These connections permit to start the compensations of the concurrent activities whenever one of the branches fails.

The mapping in (3) introduces two distinct dispatchers/collectors for the transactional compensations in N_1 and N_2. Though necessary when mapping BPMN designs in SC, dispatchers and collectors do not exhibit an observable behaviour; in fact, they silently route forward and backward signals. Notice that in some cases it is desirable to have different dispatchers (or collectors). For instance, if the components in N_2 (e.g., TC_1 and TC_2 in Fig. 5) reside on the same host, the generated dispatcher (e.g., d′) reduces the communications across sites for the forward and backward flow; indeed, it receives only one remote envelope and then generates two intra-site envelopes to the components TC_1 and TC_2.

In other cases on the contrary, it would be desirable to have a single dispatcher and/or collector in order to simplify the system. For instance, if the transactional components of N_1 and N_2 are all distributed on different sites, merging dispatchers/collectors would simplify the system so to improve its maintainability, for instance.

We propose a "two-way" transformation that can (i) merge dispatchers/collectors (simplifying the SC design) or (ii) split them (refining communications as needed). For lack of space, we consider only dispatchers, the case of collectors being dual.

Consider the SC network $N_{d,d'} = (v\ d, d')(N \parallel Disp^{f,r}_{i, \mathbf{a} \cup \{d'\}, \mathbf{b}}(d)) \parallel Disp^{f,r}_{i', \mathbf{a'}, \{d\}}(d'))$. We can merge the two parallel dispatcher, moving the flows of d' to d and adding to d the reactions of d':

$$N'_{d,d'} = (v\ d)\left(\{^d/_{d'}\}N \parallel Disp^{f,r}_{i+i'-1, \mathbf{a} \cup \mathbf{a'}, \mathbf{b}}(d)\right) \qquad (4)$$

We start by characterizing the behavior of the two systems $N_{d,d'}$ and $N'_{d,d'}$. Our refactoring changes only the flows of N by migrating all flows towards d onto d'. The resulting network $\{^d/_{d'}\}N$ performs the same actions as the original one, but for the notifications to d', that are delivered to d. In this case, we say that for the policy corresponding to N the name d' can be *fused* with d.

Definition 2. *Given $a, b \in C$ and an NCP state $\langle G\ ; P \rangle$, we say that b can be* fused *with a in $\langle G\ ; P \rangle$, in symbols $\delta_{a,b}(\langle G\ ; P \rangle)$, if for any transition $\langle G\ ; P \rangle \xrightarrow{\alpha} \langle G'\ ; P' \rangle$:*

1. if $a, b \in n(\alpha)$ then α is an output action
2. $\{^a/_b\}\langle G\ ; P \rangle \xrightarrow{\{^a/_b\}\alpha} \{^a/_b\}\langle G'\ ; P' \rangle$ and $\delta_{a,b}(\langle G'\ ; P' \rangle)$

In Definition 2, (1) simply avoids inputs for a and b, but leaves their behavior unconstrained otherwise.

The network D should be refactored according to the changes applied to the network N. Since the N refactoring will notify the same events respect to the starting network, the D refactoring should be able to consume the same events of the starting dispatcher network. However, all events that in $Disp^{f,r}_{i, \mathbf{a} \cup \{d'\}, \mathbf{b}}(d)) \parallel Disp^{f,r}_{i', \mathbf{a'}, \{d'\}}(d'))$ where consumed by the component d or d' will be consumed in the refactoring only by the component a. Moreover, the refactored network must deliver the same envelopes to the network N. If the refactoring is correct, we say that it merges of the behavior of the two dispatcher.

Definition 3. *Given an NCP state $\langle G\ ; P \rangle$ containing (among others) two components, say $a, b \in C$, a state $\langle G'\ ; P' \rangle$ merges a and b, written $\rho_{a,b}(\langle G\ ; P \rangle, \langle G'\ ; P' \rangle)$, if the following conditions hold:*

- *$\langle G\ ; P \rangle \xRightarrow{\alpha} \langle \hat{G}\ ; \hat{P} \rangle$ and $a, b \notin n(\alpha)$ implies $\langle G'\ ; P' \rangle \xRightarrow{\alpha} \langle \hat{G'}\ ; \hat{P'} \rangle$ and $\rho_{a,b}(\langle \hat{G}\ ; \hat{P} \rangle, \langle \hat{G'}\ ; \hat{P'} \rangle)$*

- *$\langle G\ ; P \rangle \xRightarrow{\tau\ s@c} \langle \hat{G}\ ; \hat{P} \rangle$ and $c \in \{a, b\}$ implies*

- $\langle G' ; P' \rangle \overset{\tau s@a}{\Longrightarrow} \langle \hat{G}' ; \hat{P}' \rangle$ and $\rho_{a,b}(\langle \hat{G} ; \hat{P} \rangle, \langle \hat{G}' ; \hat{P}' \rangle)$

- otherwise $\langle G' ; P' \rangle \overset{\varepsilon}{\Longrightarrow} \langle \hat{G}' ; \hat{P}' \rangle$ and $\langle \hat{G} ; \hat{P} \rangle \overset{\langle \tau©s \rangle @c}{\Longrightarrow} \langle \hat{G} ; \hat{P} \rangle$ and $\rho_{a,b}(\langle \hat{\hat{G}} ; \hat{N} \rangle, \langle \hat{G}' ; \hat{P}' \rangle)$

Informally, this relation characterize two policies, the second policy is obtained by the first by merging two components (b with a). The first constraint requires that the two networks must perform the same actions for all components that are not merged. The second constraint requires that all input actions of a and b are performed by the new network, with the exception of the input actions that where consumed by internal communications (i.e. event notification from the component b to the component a).

An NCP state that involves two internal components (in the following a and b) can be decomposed into two sub-policies; one describing the usage of the two component ($\langle G' ; P' \rangle$) and the other one describing their behavior ($\langle G ; P \rangle$). If the component b can be *fused* with a in the first policy ($\delta_{a,b}(\langle G' ; P' \rangle)$) then we can substitute the second policy with any other that *merges* the behavior of the two components. This substitution does not change the external behavior of the whole NCP state.

Theorem 2. *Given $a,b \in C$ and three SC networks N, N' and N_1, if $\delta_{a,b}([\![N_1]\!])$ and $\rho_{a,b}([\![N]\!], [\![N']\!])$ then $[\![(va,b)(N_1 \parallel N)]\!] \approx [\![(va)(\{^a/_b\}N_1 \parallel N')]\!]$.*

Proof outline. By double induction over transition rules and over the syntactic structure of SC terms that implement the transactional behaviors. □

Lemma 1. *Let $D \overset{\text{def}}{=} Disp^{f,r}_{i,\mathbf{a}\cup\{d'\},\mathbf{b}}(d) \parallel Disp^{f,r}_{i',\mathbf{a}',\{d\}}(d')$. If $N_{d,d'} = (v\,d,d')(N \parallel D)$ is an SC network with dispatcher d triggering the dispatcher d', then*

- $\delta_{d,d'}([\![N]\!])$ *holds*
- *if $\hat{D} \overset{\text{def}}{=} Disp^{f,r}_{i+i'-1,\mathbf{a}\cup\mathbf{a}',\mathbf{b}}(d)$ (cf. (4)) then $\rho_{d,d'}([\![D]\!], [\![\hat{D}]\!])$ holds.*

Theorem 3. *Let $N_{d,d'}$ be as in Lemma 1 and $N'_{d,d'}$ as in (4) then $[\![N_{d,d'}]\!] \approx [\![N'_{d,d'}]\!]$*

Proof outline.
If $N_{d,d'}$ the network is as in Lemma 1, it can be decomposed as $N_{d,d'} = (v\,d,d')(N \parallel D)$, where $D \overset{\text{def}}{=} Disp^{f,r}_{i,\mathbf{a}\cup\{d'\},\mathbf{b}}(d) \parallel Disp^{f,r}_{i',\mathbf{a}',\{d\}}(d')$, while the network in (4) is $N'_{d,d'} = (v\,d)(\{^d/_{d'}\}N \parallel \hat{D})$.
The Lemma 1 ensures that $\delta_{d,d'}([\![N]\!])$ and $\rho_{d,d'}([\![D]\!], [\![\hat{D}]\!])$ hold. Then the hypothesis of the Theorem 2 are guaranteed and the weak bisimulation verified. □

4 Concluding Remarks

We have presented a framework for refactoring long running transactions that relies on the (formal semantics of) BPMN [11] designs emerging from their mapping on SC calculus [8], amenable to model and implement sagas calculi [3].

The paper contains two main contributions. Firstly, we define several refactoring rules of the SC realisation of long running transactions designed in BPMN. Secondly, the proof that the proposed rules are sound as they preserve weak bisimilarity.

Also, the refactoring framework presented here, far from being complete, shows how long running transaction can be implemented in a model-driven approach highlighting the level of abstractions at which some transformations can be suitably applied. Remarkably, the proposed rules may be applied either for efficiency or architectural reasons so that BPMN designs of LRT can actually be refined and deployed automatically.

An interesting line of research is to extend our framework with other bisimulation-preserving refactoring rules and consider a larger part of BPMN. Very likely, many of our rules can scale to more general designs than LRT.

We also plan to extend the current JSCL implementation with the refactoring rules introduced here so that LRTs can be designed in BPMN and then automatically refactored transparently to the designer.

Other specification languages have been proposed for LRT [15,13]. Albeit, based on BPMN, we conjecture that our proposal can be easily applied to other specification languages for LRTs.

Acknowledgements. We thank the reviewers for the useful comments and suggestions.

References

1. Tao4WS website, http://www.tao4ws.net
2. Batory, D.: Program refactoring, program synthesis, and model-driven development. In: Goos, G., Harmanis, J., Leeuwen, J. (eds.) CC 2007. LNCS, vol. 4420, pp. 156–171. Springer, Heidelberg (2007)
3. Bruni, R., Melgratti, H., Montanari, U.: Theoretical foundations for compensations in flow composition languages. In: POPL 2005 ACM SIGPLAN-SIGACT symposium on Principles of programming languages, pp. 209–220. ACM Press, New York (2005)
4. Ciancia, V., Ferrari, G., Strollo, D., Guanciale, R.: Global coordination policies for services. In: FACS 2008 International Workshop on Formal Aspects of Component Software. ENTCS. Elsevier, Amsterdam (2008) (in print)
5. Ferrari, G., Guanciale, R., Strollo, D., Tuosto, E.: Refactoring Long Running Transactions – Full Version,
   http://wsfm08full.tao4ws.net
6. Ferrari, G., Strollo, D., Guanciale, R.: JSCL: A middleware for service coordination. In: Bochmann, G.V., Bolognesi, T., Derrick, J., Turner, K. (eds.) FORTE 2006. LNCS, vol. 4229, pp. 46–60. Springer, Heidelberg (2006)
7. Ferrari, G., Strollo, D., Guanciale, R., Tuosto, E.: Coordination Via Types in an Event-Based Framework. In: Derrick, J., Vain, J. (eds.) FORTE 2007. LNCS, vol. 4574, pp. 66–80. Springer, Heidelberg (2007)
8. Ferrari, G., Strollo, D., Guanciale, R., Tuosto, E.: Event-based Service Coordination. In: Degano, P., De Nicola, R., Meseguer, J. (eds.) Concurrency, Graphs and Models. LNCS, vol. 5065, pp. 312–329. Springer, Heidelberg (2008)
9. Garcia-Molina, H., Salem, K.: Sagas. In: SIGMOD Conference, pp. 249–259 (1987)
10. Gray, J.: The transaction concept: virtues and limitations (invited paper). In: VLDB 1981: Proceedings of the seventh international conference on Very Large Data Bases, pp. 144–154. VLDB Endowment (1981)

11. Group, O.: Business Process Modeling Notation (2002), http://www.bpmn.org
12. Honda, K., Tokoro, M.: An object calculus for asynchronous communication. In: America, P. (ed.) ECOOP 1991. LNCS, vol. 512, pp. 133–147. Springer, Heidelberg (1991)
13. IBM. Business Process Execution Language (BPEL). Technical report (2005)
14. Little, M.: Transactions and web services. Commun. ACM 46(10), 49–54 (2003)
15. W3C. Web Services Choreography Description Language (v.1.0). Technical report

On-The-Fly Model-Based Testing of Web Services with Jambition

Lars Frantzen[1,2], Maria de las Nieves Huerta[3], Zsolt Gere Kiss[4],
and Thomas Wallet[3]

[1] Istituto di Scienza e Tecnologia della Informazione "Alessandro Faedo"
Consiglio Nazionale delle Ricerche, Pisa – Italy
[2] Institute for Computing and Information Sciences
Radboud University Nijmegen – The Netherlands
lf@cs.ru.nl
[3] Pragma Consultores – Argentina
{mhuerta,twallet}@pragmaconsultores.com
[4] 4D Soft – Hungary
zsolt.kiss@4dsoft.hu

Abstract. Increasing complexity and massive use of current web services raise multiple issues for achieving adequate service validation while sticking to time-to-market imperatives. For instance: How to automate test case generation and execution for stateful web services? How to realistically simulate web service related operation calls? How to ensure conformance to specifications? The PLASTIC validation framework tackles some of these issues by providing specific tools for automated model-based functional testing. Based on the Symbolic Transition System model, test cases can be generated and executed on-the-fly. This testing approach was applied for validating the ALARM DISPATCHER eHealth service, aimed at providing health attention through mobile devices in B3G networks. In this paper we report how this modeling and testing approach helped to detect failures, support conformance, and reduce drastically the testing effort spent usually in designing test cases, validating test coverage, and executing test cases in traditional testing approaches.

1 Motivation

The usage of Web Services has been strongly growing during the last decade [3,26], uncovering new business possibilities and reaching a very broad public. Moreover Third Generation (3G) and Beyond Third Generation (B3G) mobile devices proliferation [1] reinforces such growth and leads to new massive business taking into account user mobility and connectivity [23]. As a consequence, the Web Service paradigm had to evolve to cope with emerging issues such as:

- More users directly connected and directly interacting with Web Services
- Users potentially connected from any place at any moment
- More complexity required to support new business possibilities

R. Bruni and K. Wolf (Eds.): WS-FM 2008, LNCS 5387, pp. 143–157, 2009.
© Springer-Verlag Berlin Heidelberg 2009

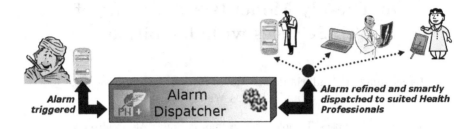

Fig. 1. PLASTIC eHealth ALARM DISPATCHER Service

Such issues require complex Web Services, which may for instance be stateful and carry on related operations according to a complex logic, or interact directly with users through mobile devices.

The eHealth ALARM DISPATCHER *Web Service Example*
We will now introduce the eHealth ALARM DISPATCHER Web Service, which illustrates some of the issues mentioned above and will serve as a running example for the remainder of the paper. The ALARM DISPATCHER Web Service is part of the PLASTIC eHealth services, aimed at providing medical attention through mobile devices over B3G networks. PLASTIC [25] is a European research project aimed at providing a service-oriented platform for adaptable and lightweight services in B3G networks. The ALARM DISPATCHER is a passive robot which receives medical alarms triggered by patients from their mobile device (see Fig. 1). Its main goal is to interact with each patient in order to characterize and refine the alarm kind, so as to be able to forward it to suited health professionals according to the situation. For instance, the ALARM DISPATCHER will ask to the patient the emergency type; get some patient information, etc. The ALARM DISPATCHER finally broadcasts the refined alarm to the best suited health professionals. Based on this broadcast, some other PLASTIC eHealth Web Services enable the patient to select an available health professional who will start a remote diagnosis. The medical attention finishes with the professional sending his diagnosis or forwarding the alarm to other specific medical services (see [25] and [27] for technical details on PLASTIC eHealth Services Development).

Emerging Web Services Validation Issues
The validation of Web Services of the kind of the ALARM DISPATCHER reveals some specific issues where new testing solutions must be provided in order to deal with the emerging complexity. For instance, the ALARM DISPATCHER Web Service involves logical dependencies between its different operations, which cannot be invoked independently or in any order. Another aspect that increases validation complexity is that the ALARM DISPATCHER is a stateful service, which means that some operation results depend on data from previously executed operations of the service. Moreover, most of the ALARM DISPATCHER operations receive some inputs from the patient and an important part of the service logic is based on those inputs.

Validating Web Services like the ALARM DISPATCHER requires dealing with these issues and should lead to the design and execution of numerous and complex test cases. Moreover, these test cases should take into account the operation dependencies, the service states, and the data to simulate user inputs. Test automation can drastically limit the testing effort due to such complexity, but should rely on detailed behavior specification models in order to ensure adequate validation coverage.

Overview In this paper we will present how a model-based testing approach with the JAMBITION and MINERVA tools of the PLASTIC validation framework was applied for testing the ALARM DISPATCHER Web Service. We will enumerate the benefits found in the light of the experiment. Section 2 briefly introduces the PLASTIC validation framework which provides the model-based testing tools JAMBITION and MINERVA, which are explained in more detail in Section 3. Section 4 presents the results and benefits of applying this approach for the validation of the ALARM DISPATCHER Web Service, while presenting conclusions, related- and future work in Section 5.

2   Plastic and Its Validation Framework

The PLASTIC project [25] adopts and revisits service-oriented computing for B3G networks, in particular assisting the development of services targeted at mobile devices. The resulting PLASTIC platform enables robust distributed lightweight services in the B3G networking environment through:

- A development environment leveraging model-driven engineering for the thorough development of Service Level Agreement and resource-aware services, which may be deployed on various networked nodes, including handheld devices
- A service-oriented middleware leveraging multi-radio devices and multi-network environments for applications and services run on mobile devices, further enabling context-aware and secure discovery and access to such services
- A validation framework enabling off-line and on-line validation of networked services regarding functional and extra-functional properties

The PLASTIC development process is evolutionary and comprehensive, i.e., it encompasses the full service lifecycle, from development to validation, and exploits as much as possible model-to-model and model-to-code transformations, as well as model-based testing. To support such a comprehensive design approach we have defined the PLASTIC UML2 profile, which allows designers to create service models conforming to the PLASTIC domain. This PLASTIC UML2 profile includes *Symbolic Transition System* (STS) diagrams (explained in Section 3.1), which are used for specifying the functional behavior and for model-based testing of Web Services. The PLASTIC UML2 profile additionally provides five views of service models and their corresponding diagrams for other purposes outside the scope of this paper.

The PLASTIC *validation framework* provides different tools for *off-line* and *on-line* validation of Web Services. Off-line validation activities are performed while no user ("paying customer") is using the service. Hence, off-line validation of a system implies that it will be tested in one or more artificially evolving environments that simulate possible real interacting situations. On-line approaches concern a set of techniques, methodologies and tools to monitor the system after its deployment in one of its real working contexts.

This paper deals with the JAMBITION [31] and MINERVA [31] tools, which enable functional off-line validation of Web Services, based on a model-based testing approach. In this approach, the STS model is used for the automatic generation and execution of black-box test cases for a given Web Service, as explained in the next Section.

3   Modeling and Testing Services

As mentioned above, the functional behavior of a service is modeled using an automata model called *Symbolic Transition System*. STSs are a well studied formalism in modeling and testing of reactive systems [11]. STSs can be seen as a formal semantics for a variant of UML 2.0 state machines [24]. We have developed the MINERVA library, which transforms state machines modeled with MAGICDRAW [19] – a commercial UML modeling tool – into an STS representation understood by the STS-based testing tool JAMBITION. Firstly, we introduce the STS model in Section 3.1. Next, we summarize MINERVA in Section 3.2. Finally, we present JAMBITION in Section 3.3.

3.1   Symbolic Transition Systems

In our setting, STSs specify the functional aspects of a service interface. The ALARM DISPATCHER service from Fig. 1 has two interfaces - one to the patient and one to the health professionals. We focus here on specifying the interface to the patient.

Firstly, there are the static STS-constituents like types, messages, parameters, and operations. This information is commonly denoted in the *Web Services Description Language* (WSDL) [8]. Secondly, there are the dynamic constituents like states, and transitions between the states. STSs can be seen as a dynamic extension of a WSDL. They specify the legal ordering of the message flow at a service interface, together with constraints on the data exchanged via message parameters (called *parts* in the WSDL).

An STS can store information in STS-specific variables. Every STS transition corresponds to either a message sent to the service (input), or a message sent from the service (output). Furthermore, a transition can be guarded by a logical expression. After a transition has fired, the values of the variables can be updated. A special kind of transition is an *unobservable* transition, which does not specify a message, but represents an internal step the STS performs. Such a transition fires without any external trigger, and may update the variables. In the underlying theories such a transition is also referred to as a τ-transition.

Due to its extent and generality we do not give here the formal definition of STSs, which can be found in [11]. Instead, we exemplify the concepts in a setting relevant for this paper.

Let us consider a WSDL operation `receiveAlarm`. The input message has a part `patient` of type `Patient`; the output message has a part `return` of type `String`. The `Patient` type is a complex type sequence with the element `age` of type `Integer`. This operation could for instance correspond to a Java method `String receiveAlarm(Patient patient)`, together with the `Patient` class. A message in an STS corresponds to a message in the WSDL. Hence, we model the call of the `receiveAlarm` operation in the STS by two consecutive transitions. The first one with input message `receiveAlarm(patient:Patient)` represents the operation invocation, the second one represents the returned value via the `receiveAlarm(return:String)` output message.

Regarding the ALARM DISPATCHER service, the `receiveAlarm` operation is one of the five operations offered in the interface specification. They are summarized in the following table:

Operation	Input Parameters	Output Parameters
receiveAlarm	*patient* : Patient	*return* : String
cancelAlarm	—	—
confirmAlarm	*lifeRisk* : Boolean	*return* : String
emergencyType	*type* : TypeOfEmergency	*return* : String
consciousness	*con* : Boolean	*return* : String

The `TypeOfEmergency` is an enumeration having the values `fatal`, `heart`, `car`, `pregnancy`, `fire`, `home`, `pediatric`, `digestion`, and `other`. Figure 2 shows an STS specifying the ALARM DISPATCHER[1]. Initially, the STS is in state 1. Now a user of the service (in our case study the patient's service) can invoke the `receiveAlarm` operation by sending a `Patient` object identifying the sender. This corresponds to the transition from state 1 to state 2. The guard of the transition restricts the attribute `age` of parameter `patient` to be greater than 0, and less than 120. Next, the ALARM DISPATCHER has to return a `String` via the return parameter `return`. The string is interpreted as being displayed on the patient's mobile device. This string is determined by the guard to be `"Confirm Alarm!"` (transition from state 2 to state 3). Next, two things can happen. Either, the patient cancels the alarm by sending the `cancelAlarm` message. This returns the STS to the initial state. Or the patient confirms the alarm via the `confirmAlarm` message, which additionally indicates if the life of the patient is at risk via the `lifeRisk` parameter, which is stored in the variable `risk` via the update statement `update = "risk = lifeRisk;"` (transition from state 3 to state 4). If the life is at risk, the alarm is immediately forwarded to the emergency service (state 4 to state 9), and the STS returns to its initial state via an unobservable transition. Otherwise the patient is queried for the type of

---

[1] In the picture you find the acronym SSM, which stands for *Service State Machine*, which is just another term for STS.

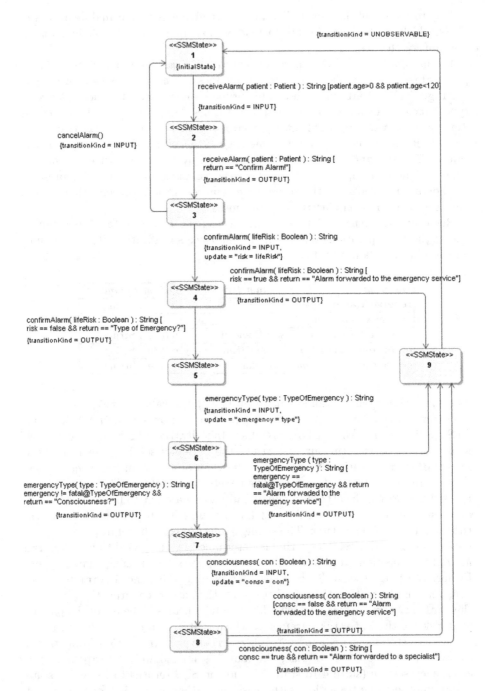

Fig. 2. An STS-Specification of the Alarm Dispatcher

emergency (state 4 to state 5), which must be subsequently transmitted by the patient via the `emergencyType` operation (state 5 to state 6). The type is saved in the `emergency` variable by the update statement. If the emergency type is `fatal`, the alarm is forwarded to the emergency service (state 6 to state 9). For other types of emergencies, the state of consciousness is determined before either the emergency service or a specialist is contacted (state 6 to state 9 via states 7 and 8).

Formal Testing
Semantically, STSs map to Labeled Transition Systems (LTSs). A rich set of formal testing theories has been defined on LTSs, see for instance [6]. A *testing relation* precisely defines when a System Under Test (SUT) conforms to its specification by relating the formal models representing SUTs with formal models representing the specifications. The gain of this effort is that one can unambiguously express what a testing algorithm is testing for, since the notions of *passing* or *failing* a test case are formally defined. Furthermore, the testing algorithm itself can be proven to be sound and complete for a given testing relation.

A well-accepted testing relation for LTSs is ioco [32]. The testing relation implemented in the JAMBITION tool is called sioco [11], a sound and complete adaption of ioco for STSs. These relations originate from the domain of reactive systems, which are inherently more complex than services. The main difference is, that a reactive system can actively send a message whenever it likes to, whereas a service sends a message only as a response to a previous request. Even though the WSDL allows in principle to specify *active* services via *solicit-response* and *notification* operations, such services are not in common use since they do not easily map to current programming paradigms and service deployment infrastructures. Due to the restriction to *passive* services the testing relations simplify, concepts like *quiescence* [32] are not relevant here. sioco simplifies to the requirement: *If the service produces a response message x after some specified trace σ, then the STS specification can also produce response message x after σ.* In other words, each observed response message must be allowed by the STS specification.

3.2 Minerva - Service Modeling

The MAGICDRAW modeling tool and the MINERVA PLASTIC tool facilitate the graphical development of services by designing and drawing the corresponding artifacts in UML diagrams, conforming to the PLASTIC UML2 Profile. By using this profile for all objects (classes, diagrams, etc.) one can ensure that the resulting product will comply with the PLASTIC conceptual model. A service in the PLASTIC concept is specified by two subviews: a *Structural View* and a *Behavioral View*. A Structural View is given by means of *Service Description diagrams* that describe the services which will constitute the final application. They provide the service interfaces and data structures. The Behavioral View specifies the dynamic service capabilities, modeled with STS diagrams.

Structural View: Defining the Data Types and Service Descriptions
The data structures supported are a commonly used subset of the XML Schema

types. There are the simple types `Integer`, `Boolean`, and `String`, and the so called complex types: literal enumerations and classes. Class types represent a sequence of types, either simple or complex. But defining recursive types like *lists* in this manner is not supported by the current framework.

Having the data types specified, the service interface can be modeled via a Service Description Diagram. Once the service description is ready, WSDL files, and the corresponding service stubs, can be generated by further tools from the PLASTIC toolchain.

Behavioral View: Creating the Symbolic Transition System
To define the dynamic behavior of a service, an `STS Diagram` is modeled, which specifies a conversation between a service interface and another actor. Figure 2 already showed an `STS Diagram` as it appears in MAGICDRAW. An STS transition has the following properties:

- **Operation** – This is the operation which triggered the transition
- **TransitionKind** – It can be:
  - `INPUT`, corresponding to an input transition (request)
  - `OUTPUT`, denoting an output transition (response)
  - `UNOBSERVABLE`, denoting an unobservable transition

- **Guard** – The guard is a boolean expression which has to hold for the transition to fire (like `patient.age>0 && patient.age<120`). To express a guard a simple language is used which offers most common operators known from programming languages. For details please refer to the JAMBITION [31] manual.
- **Update** – Variables of the STS are updated here, after the transition has fired. Such variables usually serve for recording state information, global to the conversation session.

After having created the model, the next step is creating the service implementation. Empty service stubs can be created automatically, as mentioned above. Next they have to be implemented, keeping in mind the conditions defined in the STS transition guards. Having the services in place, the STS model can be used by JAMBITION to automatically test the service. For this, it has to be exported, using the `Export to XMI feature`.

3.3 Jambition

JAMBITION is a Java tool we have developed to automatically test Web Services based on STS specifications. As said above, the underlying testing relation is sioco. Furthermore the testing approach of JAMBITION is *random* and *on-the-fly*. This basically means that out of the set of specified input actions one input is chosen randomly, and then given to the service (i.e., an operation is invoked). Next, the returned message (if any) is received from the service. If that output message is not allowed by the STS, a failure is reported. Otherwise the next input is chosen – and so on.

For the ALARM DISPATCHER service, as being specified by the STS from Fig. 2, this means that JAMBITION plays the role of a patient's service. Initially, being in state 1, the only specified input message is the `receiveAlarm` invocation. JAMBITION has to construct here a `Patient` object, with the guard-requirement that the `age` attribute must be greater 0 and less than 120. To respect such requirements, the constraint solver of GNU Prolog [18] is queried via a Socket connection. Four heuristics can be applied:

- **min**: choose the smallest solution
- **max**: choose the greatest solution
- **middle**: choose the solution in the middle
- **random**: choose a random solution

If we decide to choose the smallest solution, we get `age` = 1. Since always choosing 1 might not be sufficient for achieving a desired coverage, a random solution is commonly good practice. Having the parameter object constructed, the `receiveAlarm` operation in invoked. JAMBITION moves the STS into state 2 and receives next the string the `receiveAlarm` operation returns. If this string does not equal `"Confirm Alarm!"`, a failure is reported. Otherwise state 3 is reached. Here, again randomly, JAMBITION chooses either to cancel the alarm (back to state 1), or to invoke the `confirmAlarm` operation. In the latter case the `lifeRisk` parameter is not constrained, a random value (`true` or `false`) is chosen. Being in state 4 the returned string is received. Assuming a `lifeRisk` of value `true` had been generated, that string must equal `"Alarm forwarded to the emergency service"`. If the chosen risk was `false`, the string must instead be `"Type of Emergency?"`, and JAMBITION moves to state 5, where an emergency type must be constructed to invoke the `emergencyType` operation. This process continues in this manner until either a failure is spotted, or the user halts the testing.

The *on-the-fly* approach differs from more classical testing techniques by not firstly generating a set of test cases, which are subsequently executed on the system. Instead, the test case generation, -execution, and -assessment happen in lockstep. So doing has, inter alia, the advantage of allaying the state space explosion problem faced by several conventional model-based testing techniques. The rationale here is that a test case developed beforehand has to consider all possible outputs the system might return, whereas the *on-the-fly* tester directly observes the specific output, and can guide the testing accordingly. Another cause of state space explosion is the transformation of symbolic models like STSs into semantical models like LTSs. Several tools do this step to apply test algorithms which are defined on the semantical model. JAMBITION also solves this issue by skipping this transformation step. Instead, its test algorithm directly deals with the STS, see [10] for details.

To visualize the ongoing testing process, and to understand a reported failure, JAMBITION can display the messages exchanged with the service while being tested in real-time via the QUICK SEQUENCE DIAGRAM EDITOR [21], an external open-source visualizer for UML sequence diagrams. Furthermore, Jambition

displays the achieved state- and transition coverage of the STS. We will show
these features of JAMBITION in more detail in the next section.

4 Results

The STS-based modeling and testing approach presented in the preceding chapter was used to specify, develop, and validate the functional behavior of the
ALARM DISPATCHER service. In this section we present the experiences and
benefits that the approach brought to the project.

eHealth ALARM DISPATCHER *Experiment Setup*
Starting from the requirements addressed by the ALARM DISPATCHER service,
the experiment began with the modeling of the corresponding STS with the
PLASTIC UML2 Profile in the MAGICDRAW tool. The resulting diagrams of this
activity were a diagram of the ALARM DISPATCHER Web Service and operations,
a diagram of the involved data types and a diagram of the STS. As depicted
in Fig. 2 the ALARM DISPATCHER STS consists of 9 states and 13 transitions,
specifying how the dispatcher must deal with different kinds of emergencies and
other emergency attributes like life risk and consciousness. Based on these specifications, the Alarm Dispatcher Web Service was implemented via the Netbeans
IDE [20] and deployed on the GlassFish Application Server [17]. At this point we
finished the setup of the experiment. The experiment steps were the following:

1. *STS model exportation*: from MAGICDRAW we exported automatically the
   ALARM DISPATCHER STS.
2. JAMBITION *STS importation*: we loaded the STS file into JAMBITION. The
   importation includes checking the deployment of the corresponding service.
   During this step, the following types of errors where detected:
   (a) Consistency errors in the models (for instance, a data type was wrongly
       referenced in the STS).
   (b) Consistency errors between the models and the deployed service (for
       instance, a parameter of a service operation was declared with different
       types in the deployed service and in the model).
   (c) Service uncompleted deployment problems (for instance, the service deployment process could not be completed).
3. ALARM DISPATCHER *Validation*: we started the JAMBITION validation process that cycles continuously the STS till errors are found. During this step,
   the following types of errors where detected:
   (a) Transition guards violated (for instance, the emergency was not considered fatal in a case where the STS specified that it should be treated as
       fatal).
   (b) Never ending operations (for instance, an operation was not returning a
       result or had some bugs that stopped the operation).
   (c) States or transitions never reached (for instance, the validation coverage
       was never completed since some states or transitions were never reached
       due to missing features, or faults in the model itself, like non-reachable
       states).

Table 1. ALARM DISPATCHER Experiment Steps

Step	Duration	Details
STS model exportation	25 sec	This is a MAGICDRAW feature
JAMBITION STS importation	3 sec	For successful importations
ALARM DISPATCHER Validation	8 sec	Reaching full STS coverage without errors

Errors found in steps two and three were corrected, and the experiment was repeated until all the failures disappeared, and a full coverage of states and transitions was reached. To achieve this, an average of 191 input and output messages were automatically processed by the random exploration of the STS. Table 1 presents average durations of the experiment steps[2].

JAMBITION *Added Value*
Benefits of well applied testing automation and model-based testing approaches such as testing effort saving, coverage assurance, test reuse, regression reliability and testing duration compression have been extensively discussed in literature (for instance, see [16],[2],[7]). In addition to these generic benefits of test automation, JAMBITION brought some specific added value when validating Web Services as in the ALARM DISPATCHER experiment. Next we give a list of the JAMBITION benefits that were of particular interest for our ALARM DISPATCHER experiment:

- Automatic and on-the-fly generation, execution and assessment of numerous test cases
- Real-time visualization of test cases execution coverage (percentage of STS states and transitions visited, as shown in Fig. 3)
- Test cases generation and execution time is very quick
- Debugging visualization facilities for tracking operations and data (with the QUICK SEQUENCE DIAGRAM EDITOR, as shown in Fig. 4)
- JAMBITION and MINERVA are released under the open source GPLv3 license

Testing Effort Reduction
A specific benefit of JAMBITION comes from the testing effort reduction provided by the tool automation. We will now give some considerations indicating the order of magnitude of this reduction by referring again to the ALARM DISPATCHER example. For this purpose we are comparing only the test activities automated by Jambition, i.e., test case generation, -execution, and -assessment. We are not taking into account other activities usually involved in testing such as test planning, defect reporting, code debugging and correction, testing environment preparation, etc. Indeed we do consider that such activities, as well as the STS modeling, remain unchanged when testing with or without Jambition.

Comparing with traditional, manual testing techniques is not straightforward, since JAMBITION does not generate a set of test cases. To still have a metric at

---

[2] Experiment conduced on a standard Intel Core Duo CPU T2350 1,86GHz, 1GB RAM.

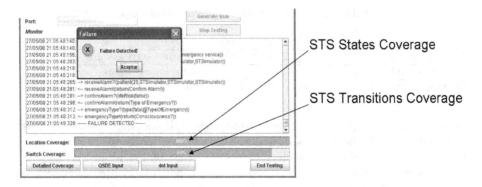

Fig. 3. JAMBITION Test Coverage Indicators

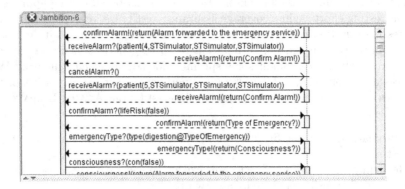

Fig. 4. Quick Sequence Diagram Editor

hand we first define what we mean by a test case, namely a path in the STS which starts and ends at the initial state 1. Such a path basically corresponds to a scenario, or transaction, like *receiving an alarm having fatal emergency*. To achieve full transition coverage, 5 such test cases are needed, see table 2.

In a traditional testing approach, these test cases must be designed and executed manually. We have said before that on average JAMBITION processed 191 messages to achieve the same coverage, which corresponds to ca. 37 test cases. Table 1 has shown that less than 8sec are needed to generate and execute these test cases. No matter how precisely you measure, this small example already shows how JAMBITION is an order of magnitude faster than the manual way. And, that JAMBITION executes more test cases to achieve the same coverage is another advantage, since more test cases simply can find more failures. For instance, to achieve full transition coverage, it is sufficient to make a test case with a fatal emergency type, and one with a non-fatal type. Since JAMBITIONexecutes on average 37 test cases, it is very likely, that it tests for more than just these two emergency types.

Table 2. Full Transition Coverage with Five Scenarios

Scenario	State Sequence
Cancelled Alarm	$1 \rightarrow 2 \rightarrow 3 \rightarrow 1$
Risk of Life	$1 \rightarrow 2 \rightarrow 3 \rightarrow 4 \rightarrow 9 \rightarrow 1$
Fatal Emergency	$1 \rightarrow 2 \rightarrow 3 \rightarrow 4 \rightarrow 5 \rightarrow 6 \rightarrow 9 \rightarrow 1$
Consciousness	$1 \rightarrow 2 \rightarrow 3 \rightarrow 4 \rightarrow 5 \rightarrow 6 \rightarrow 7 \rightarrow 8 \rightarrow 9 \rightarrow 1$
No Consciousness	$1 \rightarrow 2 \rightarrow 3 \rightarrow 4 \rightarrow 5 \rightarrow 6 \rightarrow 7 \rightarrow 8 \rightarrow 9 \rightarrow 1$

But there is also a drawback if coverage depends on mere random decisions, since they may simply not be sufficient to reach each state and transition. We will point to that in the next and concluding Section.

5 Conclusions, Related- and Future Work

To the best of our knowledge, JAMBITION is the only current testing tool which allows for automatic and on-the-fly model-based testing based on symbolic models. Other testing approaches which are also based on (variants of) the STS model are [9,14]. Instead of on-the-fly testing, they use *test purposes* to deal with the state-space explosion problem. The specific value of random and on-the-fly testing has been demonstrated for instance in [4].

Several approaches exist to test Web Services based on other models than state machines. To name just a few, in [15] the authors propose to include graph transformation rules that enable the automatic derivation of meaningful test cases. To apply the approach they require that a service implements interfaces that increase its testability. A somewhat similar model than STSs is the *Business Process Execution Language* (BPEL) [29]. Since BPEL is an implementation language for service orchestration, its focus is different than ours. Several interesting testing and verification issues can be formulated on BPEL specifications, see for instance [5,12,13].

Despite its smallness the ALARM DISPATCHER validation experiment gave very promising results, satisfying the expectations raised by using test automation tools in a real development project. PLASTIC tools adoption for service modeling and testing was straightforward and resulted in an important reduction of the testing effort, which can scale up to very important savings for more complex services, representing an important productivity gain over conventional manual testing approaches. These conclusions settled the foundation for further experiments with JAMBITION in more complex Web Services development case studies.

The JAMBITION tool is based on a Java library which allows to model and simulate STSs, called STSIMULATOR [22]. One current limitation of the library is the lack of recursive data types like *lists*. Several web services use lists (via XML Schema unbounded sequences) to transmit data objects of variable length. We are currently investigating how to deal best with such recursive types.

We have already indicated that a mere random approach for test data selection is not necessarily sufficient to reach a full state- and transition coverage. It is even less appropriate for more sophisticated coverage criteria like condition coverage of the guards. Several approaches based on symbolic execution exist to guide the test case generation in a way that coverage becomes a search problem, see for instance [28,30]. Combining JAMBITION with such approaches is a major future goal. Also, techniques like equivalence partitioning and boundary value analysis can be a very fruitful combination with the random approach. For example, in its current version JAMBITION does not test for invalid equivalence class boundaries (like a patient at the age of 120). Also the combination of measuring model-coverage and code coverage can give further insight in the test efficiency.

STSs can in principle also be used to model the communication between several Web Services. To do so they have to embrace the message flow at several interfaces, like BPEL does. For instance, an STS could be modeled which also deals with the ALARM DISPATCHER interface to the health professionals. Testing based on such multi-interface STSs would allow to test more complex scenarios like coordinated and composed Web Services.

Acknowledgments. The PLASTIC Project is funded under FP6 STREP contract number 26955 by the Information Society Technologies (IST). Special thanks to Lorenzo Jorquera and Daniel Yankelevich for their detailed review of early versions of this paper. Lars Frantzen is further supported by the Marie Curie Network TAROT (MRTN-CT-2004-505121) and by the Netherlands Organization for Scientific Research (NWO) under project STRESS.

References

1. 3G Americas. 2.5 Billion GSM Subscribers Worldwide - More than a Million New Users Daily (press release), http://www.3gamericas.org/English/News_Room/DisplayPressRelease.cfm?id=2982&s=ENG, June 5 (2007)
2. Apfelbaum, L.: Automated Functional Test Generation. In: Proceedings of the Autotestcon 1995 Conference. IEEE, Los Alamitos (1995)
3. Business Wire Article. SOA Software Products Drive More Than 10 Billion Web Service Transactions, http://findarticles.com/p/articles/mi_m0EIN/is_2006_Sept_18/ai_n16728778, September 18 (2006)
4. Belinfante, A., Feenstra, J., de Vries, R.G., Tretmans, J., Goga, N., Feijs, L., Mauw, S., Heerink, L.: Formal test automation: A simple experiment. In: Csopaki, G., Dibuz, S., Tarnay, K. (eds.) TestCom 1999, pp. 179–196. Kluwer Academic Publishers, Dordrecht (1999)
5. Bianculli, D., Ghezzi, C., Spoletini, P.: A model checking approach to verify BPEL4WS workflows. In: IEEE SOCA 2007, pp. 13–20. IEEE Computer Society Press, Los Alamitos (2007)
6. Brinksma, E., Tretmans, J.: Testing transition systems: an annotated bibliography. In: Cassez, F., Jard, C., Rozoy, B., Dermot, M. (eds.) MOVEP 2000. LNCS, vol. 2067, pp. 187–195. Springer, Heidelberg (2001)
7. Bruno, G., Varani, M., Vico, V., Offerman, C.: Benefits of using model-based testing tools. In: Nesi, P. (ed.) Objective Quality 1995. LNCS, vol. 926, pp. 224–235. Springer, Heidelberg (1995)

8. Christensen, E., et al.: Web Service Definition Language (WSDL) ver. 1.1 (2001), http://www.w3.org/TR/wsdl
9. Clarke, D., Jéron, T., Rusu, V., Zinovieva, E.: STG: a Symbolic Test Generation tool. In: Katoen, J.-P., Stevens, P. (eds.) TACAS 2002. LNCS, vol. 2280, p. 470. Springer, Heidelberg (2002)
10. Frantzen, L., Tretmans, J., Willemse, T.A.C.: Test generation based on symbolic specifications. In: Grabowski, J., Nielsen, B. (eds.) FATES 2004. LNCS, vol. 3395, pp. 1–15. Springer, Heidelberg (2005)
11. Frantzen, L., Tretmans, J., Willemse, T.A.C.: A symbolic framework for model-based testing. In: Havelund, K., Núñez, M., Rosu, G., Wolff, B. (eds.) FATES 2006 and RV 2006. LNCS, vol. 4262, pp. 40–54. Springer, Heidelberg (2006)
12. Fu, X., Bultan, T., Su, J.: Analysis of interacting BPEL web services. In: Proc. of WWW 2004, New York, USA, May 17-22, pp. 17–22 (2004)
13. García-Fanjul, J., Tuya, J., de la Riva, C.: Generating test cases specifications for compositions of web services. In: Bertolino, A., Polini, A. (eds.) WS-MaTe2006, pp. 83–94 (2006)
14. Gaston, C., Le Gall, P., Rapin, N., Touil, A.: Symbolic execution techniques for test purpose definition. In: Uyar, M.Ü., Duale, A.Y., Fecko, M.A. (eds.) TestCom 2006. LNCS, vol. 3964, pp. 1–18. Springer, Heidelberg (2006)
15. Heckel, R., Mariani, L.: Automatic conformance testing of web services. In: Cerioli, M. (ed.) FASE 2005. LNCS, vol. 3442, pp. 34–48. Springer, Heidelberg (2005)
16. Hoffman, D.: Cost Benefits for Test Automation. In: STAR West 1999 (1999)
17. GlassFish Application Server homepage, https://glassfish.dev.java.net
18. GNU Prolog homepage, http://www.gprolog.org/
19. MagicDraw homepage, http://www.magicdraw.com
20. Netbeans IDE homepage, www.netbeans.org
21. Quick Sequence Diagram Editor homepage, http://sdedit.sourceforge.net/
22. STSimulator homepage, http://www.cs.ru.nl/~lf/tools/stsimulator/
23. Lau, J.: The State of European Enterprise Mobility in 2006, October 13, 2006. Forrester Research (2006)
24. Object Management Group. UML 2.0 Superstructure Specification, ptc/03-08-02 edition. Adopted Specification
25. PLASTIC project homepage, http://www-c.inria.fr/plastic
26. Web Host Industry Review. Web Services to Reach $21 Billion by 2007: IDC, http://www.thewhir.com/marketwatch/idc020503.cfm
27. Rong, L., Wallet, T., Fredj, M., Georgantas, N.: Mobile Medical Diagnosis: An m-Health Initiative through Service Continuity in B3G. In: Middleware 2007 Demos - ACM/IFIP/USENIX Middleware Conference (November 2007)
28. Sen, K., Agha, G.: CUTE and jCUTE: Concolic Unit Testing and Explicit Path Model-Checking Tools. In: Ball, T., Jones, R.B. (eds.) CAV 2006. LNCS, vol. 4144, pp. 419–423. Springer, Heidelberg (2006)
29. Business Process Execution Language for Web Services version 1.1 specification, http://www-128.ibm.com/developerworks/library/specification/ws-bpel/
30. Tillmann, N., de Halleux, J.: Pex - White Box Test Generation for.NET. In: Beckert, B., Hähnle, R. (eds.) TAP 2008. LNCS, vol. 4966, pp. 134–153. Springer, Heidelberg (2008)
31. PLASTIC tools homepage, http://plastic.isti.cnr.it/wiki/tools
32. Tretmans, J.: Test generation with inputs, outputs and repetitive quiescence. Software—Concepts and Tools 17(3), 103–120 (1996)

Towards a Formal Framework for Workflow Interoperability

Sarah D. Induruwa Fernando and Andrew C. Simpson

Oxford University Computing Laboratory
Parks Road, Oxford OX1 3QD, UK
{Sarah.Fernando,Andrew.Simpson}@comlab.ox.ac.uk

Abstract. As the importance of workflow languages increases in both commercial and scientific application domains, requirements to verify properties of workflows, and compositions thereof, will start to emerge. A lack of formal foundations for workflow languages means that constructing and reasoning about such compositions is currently an impossible task, thereby limiting the potential for their assured execution within service-oriented contexts. To this end, we present a language with formal foundations to act as an intermediary in facilitating build-time interoperability by the transformation of legacy workflows.

1 Introduction

The lack of a standard process interchange format between workflow definition languages (WDLs) makes the provision of interoperability between these languages difficult. In [1] we highlighted the importance of enabling workflow interoperability during the build-time of a workflow to promote re-use and collaboration between end-users; we distinguished between interoperability when the workflow is built and when it is run. The advantage of build-time interoperability is that users can also modify workflows according to their needs before submitting them for execution. Furthermore, they do not need to reproduce (or have access to) the other WDL's infrastructure to be able to reuse workflows. In this paper we take initial steps towards the provision of such interoperability by introducing an Intermediate Workflow Representation Language (IWRL).

Workflow design involves defining the structure of a workflow by connecting different activities to produce a workflow definition. Using basic constructs, such as sequence, parallelism, choice, and, in some cases, iteration, it is possible to capture complex patterns. While business-oriented WDLs typically support a rich set of control flow constructs with control flow defined implicitly within a model, scientific workflows tend to be data-driven with the need to handle complex data structures, which may need manipulation during design stage.

We define an IWRL workflow to include a collection of coordinated activities, consisting of 'atomic activities', which represent a single step within a workflow, and 'control activities', which form the workflow execution model. One of the key features of the execution model is that control activities can be combined and nested within each other to make complex arbitrary flow patterns.

R. Bruni and K. Wolf (Eds.): WS-FM 2008, LNCS 5387, pp. 158–174, 2009.
© Springer-Verlag Berlin Heidelberg 2009

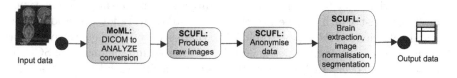

Fig. 1. A composite workflow

In Section 2 we discuss the motivation for our work. In Section 3 we introduce the syntax and the semantics of the IWRL. In Section 4 we illustrate how the IWRL can facilitate interoperability. Finally, in Section 5 we summarise our contribution and outline potential areas of future work.

2   Motivation

The primary motivation for our work is enabling the reuse and composition of pre-existing workflows. Consider, for example, Figure 2, which illustrates a composite workflow. Here, a user wishes to analyse a set of MRI images, consisting of a combination of DICOM[1] and ANALYZE[2] file formats. The workflow systems interoperating in this scenario are Taverna [2] and Kepler [3], which are the engines for the SCUFL[3] and MoML [4] WDLs respectively. The user aims to segment the brain and calculate the volumes of the white, grey and cerebrospinal fluid (CSF) matter. Each step is achieved using the service implementations of image processing algorithms, either used directly or as activities of partial workflows that make up the overall workflow, with each component being defined in one of MoML or SCUFL. Assuming that the user is on the Kepler system with a library of existing workflows, the workflow consists of the following steps:

1. Ensure that all images are in ANALYZE format (MoML workflow fragment).
2. Produce raw images by checking for correct orientation settings and image attributes, and applying inhomogeneity corrections on images to correct site-specific image distortions (SCUFL workflow fragment).
3. Anonymise data by header stripping, face and ear stripping and removing unwanted attributes from data sets (SCUFL workflow fragment).
4. Separate out the brain and skull tissue from images, using the Brain Extraction Tool (BET) [5] (SCUFL workflow fragment). In parallel to brain extraction, brain normalisation is done.
5. Segment the brain and calculate each segment's volume (SCUFL workflow fragment).

While SCUFL and MoML are both data-driven WDLs, they vary considerably in terms of expressive power. In MoML, the semantics of the interactions

---

[1] See http://medical.nema.org/
[2] See http://www.mayo.edu/bir/PDF/ANALYZE75.pdf
[3] See http://www.ebi.ac.uk/t̃mo/mygrid/XScuflSpecification.html

between services can be specified using a 'director' component: different types of directors exist which can be attached to a MoML workflow to produce the required behaviour of the model. In SCUFL, there is only one semantic model for the behaviour of activities, which is built into the programming model of SCUFL processors. Moreover, MoML allows the user to specify workflows with a finer granularity than SCUFL does (such as expressive conditional statements) where the user has more control over specifying complex data flow and control flow constraints between workflow components. In general, SCUFL and MoML workflows follow a similar structural pattern, and include: *environmental information* (e.g. URIs pointing to external services and applications required); *task-based information* that make up activities in a workflow; and *link definitions* forming a high level view of the topology of a workflow. Unlike in scientific workflows, there is limited desire for re-using business workflows due to privacy issues. Nevertheless, there is an increasing need for integrated approaches for modelling business processes, as businesses take part in virtual enterprises collaborating with one another by sharing data and exchanging process models. As such, although our work is being driven by examples from the scientific community, we would argue that it has applicability in other contexts.

During the composition of workflow fragments that have been transformed to the target WDL, we need to ensure that no redundancies and other unwanted anomalies have been introduced to the resulting model. For example, mismatched datatypes of the workflow fragments that are being composed will cause problems in the overall composition and it has to be ensured that inputs and outputs of the activities being plugged are directly compatible. Using formal constraints, there is the potential for possible discrepancies to be detected in advance. Furthermore, we need to check for equivalence once a workflow has been translated to the target WDL, which may be achieved by checking for equivalent post-conditions. While consideration of issues such as these is a key concern of our work, our focus in this paper is exclusively on the design of the intermediate WDL.

3   The IWRL

The basic structure of the IWRL is divided such that there is a separation between computation and coordination, with the following elements being included in a workflow definition: a set of atomic activities that perform computations and are to be coordinated, e.g. external software components such as web services or local applications such as Java programs; a set of control activities that define the coordination and interdependencies between activities, specifying the overall execution model of the workflow; and a data layer that captures the flow of data between workflow activities and workflow inputs and outputs.

Capturing this information, an IWRL workflow is a combination of: imported elements that may include external activity definitions and existing workflow definitions, inputs and outputs comprising its interface definition, an execution model, and an optional set of properties.

⟨workflow⟩ ::= "workflow" ⟨id⟩ "{" ⟨imports-list⟩$^?$
                              ⟨interface-definition⟩
                              ⟨execution-model⟩
                              ⟨properties-list⟩$^?$ "}"

3.1   The Computational Model

The computation component of an IWRL workflow consists of a set of specifications of atomic activities and an optional set of sub-workflows. A number of
basic elements assist in defining the main workflow components, including: identifiers, which are used to uniquely identify each component (within the context
of a single namespace); datatypes, which may be primitive (integers, etc.) or
structured (lists, etc.); and properties, which describe attributes of components.
Furthermore we provide a datatype-name description to name primitive datatypes
literally, to define the binding datatype of inputs/outputs and ports.

⟨datatype-name⟩ ::= "integer" | "real" | "boolean" | "string"

A workflow and an activity interact with external entities via interface definitions, which consist of ports and parameters. Ports act as data containers and
only bind to data values during run-time, whereas parameters give an activity context-specific information and are used to configure the operation of an
activity. Their values are fixed at build-time.

⟨interface-definition⟩ ::= "interface" "{" ⟨ports-list⟩$^+$ ⟨parameters-list⟩* "}"

The need to operate on large sets of data in scientific workflows is addressed
in the IWRL by allowing the passing of data by reference using file identifiers,
where the file type is given by its extension. Small data sets are passed by value,
which can be in one of the supported datatypes.

⟨transfer-strategy⟩ ::= "transfer" ⟨by-value⟩ | ⟨file-path⟩
⟨by-value⟩ ::= "type" "=" "byvalue" "(" ⟨datatype-name⟩ ")" ;
⟨file-path⟩ ::= "type" "=" "file" "(" ⟨extension⟩ ")" ;

Ports act as the external interface of workflows and activities. The two vari-
eties of port—input and output— both have associated globally unique identifiers. Input port values can be specified by the data-source attribute which refers
to either an output port of an activity, a data set, or a reference to a data
file; output ports of control activities and workflows have a data-source attribute,
while those of atomic activities do not. As such, we include the port-type element
to determine which type of entity a port belongs to. In addition, a port may
contain an optional set of properties.

We model a data source as an expression, as, for certain control activities (such
as if-conditions with a conditional set of activities), it cannot be determined at
build-time which port of which activity will be the actual data source.

⟨data-source⟩ ::= ⟨expr⟩
⟨port-type⟩ ::= "activity-port" | "workflow-port" | "control-activity-port"

A data source, called the iterating-value, is defined for iterating values; this represents the data made available during an iteration, and is transferred to the input port of the iterative activity. The iterating value is given by an identifier that refers to an activity port; this is an optional element of an input port.

⟨iterating-value⟩ ::= "iterating-value" "{" ⟨id⟩$^?$ ";" "}"

The complete port description takes the following form:

⟨input-port⟩ ::= "input" ⟨id⟩ "{" ⟨port-type⟩ ";"
                    ⟨transfer-strategy⟩ ";"
                    ⟨data-source⟩ ";"
                    ⟨iterating-value⟩$^?$ ";"
                    ⟨properties-list⟩$^?$ ";" "}"
⟨output-port⟩ ::= "output" ⟨id⟩ "{" ⟨port-type⟩ ";"
                    ⟨transfer-strategy⟩ ";"
                    ⟨data-source⟩$^?$ ";"
                    ⟨properties-list⟩$^?$ ";" "}"
⟨ports-list⟩ ::= "ports" "{" ⟨input-port⟩$^+$ ⟨output-port⟩$^+$ "}"

Parameters give a workflow or an activity context-specific information, and are used to configure their operation. Their values are configured at workflow build-time, and do not change during the workflow's execution.

⟨parameter⟩ ::= ⟨id⟩ "{" "type" "=" ⟨datatype-name⟩ ";"
                    "value" "=" ⟨value⟩ ";"
                    ⟨properties-list⟩ ";" "}"
⟨parameters-list⟩ ::= "parameters" "{" ⟨parameter⟩$^+$ "}"

We define two types of activities: 'atomic activities', which represent a single step of execution within a workflow, and 'control activities', which are constructs used to create the control flow model of a workflow.

⟨activity⟩ ::= ⟨atomic-activity⟩ | ⟨control-activity⟩

There are different types of atomic activities, depending on the functionality they model. An activity has a globally unique identifier, an activity type, a set of input and output ports, and optional sets of parameters and properties.

⟨activity-type⟩ ::= "data-transformation" | "web-service" | "local-app" | "user-action"
⟨atomic-activity⟩ ::= "activity" ⟨id⟩ "{" "type" "=" ⟨activity-type⟩ ";"
                    ⟨interface-definition⟩
                    ⟨properties-list⟩$^?$ "}"

3.2   The Execution Model

The execution model consists of a set of control activities:

⟨execution-model⟩ ::= "{" ⟨control-activity⟩⁺ "}"

When defining control flows, control activities make use of expressions in order to specify conditional statements, make comparisons, etc. (We omit the definition of expressions for reasons of brevity.)

Control activities are used to coordinate the execution of activities. Each defines a unique control construct as shown below.

⟨command-name⟩ ::= "seq" | "par" | "if" | "while"

The interface definition and the optional set of properties follow the same pattern as those of atomic activities and workflows. In addition, a control activity contains a body which describes its behaviour and coordination capabilities. One of the key features of the execution model is that control activities can be combined and nested within each other to make complex arbitrary flow patterns.

The sequence activity indicates the sequential execution of a set of atomic or control activities. While the linked data input/output ports of the different activities define the data flows, the list of activities within the sequence activity specifies their sequential execution.

⟨activity-list⟩ ::= "activities" "{" ⟨activity⟩⁺ "}"
⟨sequence⟩ ::= "seq" ⟨id⟩ "{" ⟨interface-definition⟩ ⟨activity-list⟩ "}"

The parallel activity indicates the parallel execution of two or more workflow paths, where a path consists of a list of activities ordered by the execution sequence.

⟨path⟩ ::= "path" "{" ⟨activity-list⟩ "}"
⟨parallel-paths⟩ ::= ⟨path⟩ ⟨path⟩ ⟨path⟩*
⟨parallel⟩ ::= "par" ⟨id⟩ "{" ⟨interface-definition⟩ ⟨parallel-paths⟩ "}"

Conditional workflow paths can be defined using the if-condition activity. The conditions are represented as expressions and the possible execution paths are given similarly to those of a parallel activity, with the difference being that only paths that satisfy the condition will be executed.

⟨if-condition⟩ ::= "if" ⟨id⟩ "{" ⟨interface-definition⟩
                "condition" "{" ⟨expr⟩ "}" "{" ⟨path⟩ ";" "}"
                ("else-if" "{" "condition" "{" ⟨expr⟩ "}" "{" ⟨path⟩ ";" "}" "}") *
                "else" "condition" "{" ⟨expr⟩ "}" "{" ⟨path⟩ ";" "}"

The while–do activity enables the repeated execution of a specified activity or a sub-workflow zero or more times.

⟨while-do⟩ ::= "while" ⟨id⟩ "{"
                ⟨interface-definition⟩
                "condition" "{" ⟨expr⟩ "}" "{" ⟨path⟩ ";" "}"

3.3   Formalisation

We now give formal definitions of the language components, to ensure that work-flows are well-formed and consistent, using the Z formal description language (see, for example, [6] and [7]). In the short term, the intention is that our formal semantics will give confidence in transformations; in the longer term, the intention is that our formal semantics will allow us to reason about properties of workflow compositions. Throughout the paper, we present schema definitions in the following format:

$$Name \mathrel{\widehat{=}} [declaration \mid predicate]$$

We treat identifiers and datatypes as opaque objects via the use of basic types.

$$[Identifier, Char, String, Integer, Real]$$
$$String == \operatorname{seq} Char$$
$$DataType ::= IntegerType \mid StringType \mid BooleanType \mid RealType$$
$$Boolean ::= true \mid false$$

Properties map identifiers to values:

$$Value ::= IntegerValue \mid StringValue \mid BooleanValue \mid RealValue \mid IdentifierValue$$
$$Properties == Identifier \nrightarrow Value$$

Ports and parameters are modelled as follows:

$$Port \mathrel{\widehat{=}} [name : Identifier;\ dataSource : Identifier;$$
$$dataType : DataType;\ properties : Properties]$$
$$Parameter \mathrel{\widehat{=}} [name : Identifier;\ dataType : DataType;$$
$$value : Value;\ properties : Properties]$$

With these definitions in place, we can now define a schema to represent an interface definition of a component, with constraints to ensure that inputs and outputs of a component are mutually exclusive, and that the name of each input, output and parameter matches its key.

$$InterfaceDef \mathrel{\widehat{=}}$$
$$[inputs, outputs : Identifier \nrightarrow Port;\ parameters : Identifier \nrightarrow Parameter \mid$$
$$\operatorname{dom} inputs \cap \operatorname{dom} outputs = \emptyset \wedge$$
$$\forall id : \operatorname{dom} parameters \bullet (parameters\ id).name = id \wedge$$
$$\forall id : \operatorname{dom} inputs \bullet (inputs\ id).name = id \wedge$$
$$\forall id : \operatorname{dom} outputs \bullet (outputs\ id).name = id]$$

A data link denotes the connection between a workflow input/activity output port and a workflow output/activity input port, resembling the flow of data through the workflow. It has a name, a source and a target. Since the IWRL allows iteration of activities we do not impose the restriction of a link connecting an activity to itself.

$$DataLink \mathrel{\widehat{=}} [name, source, target : Identifier \mid name \neq source \wedge name \neq target]$$

An atomic activity is modelled as follows.

$AtomicActivity \cong [name : Identifier;\ type : ActivityType;\ InterfaceDef\,]$

Here the type of an activity can be a web service, a local application or another type of supported type.

$ActivityType ::= \mathsf{webservice} \mid \mathsf{localapp} \mid \ldots$

The body of a workflow consists of the coordination of activities, defined using combinations of the four basic control activity types. First, a definition for an execution path is given as a sequence of identifiers; as a path cannot contain multiple instances of a the same activity, the sequences are injective.

$Path == \mathrm{iseq}\ Identifier$

Sequential execution of activities ensures that the source activity of a data flow link completes execution prior to the start of the target activity; parallel execution of activities with synchronisation includes a set of activities that represent the parallel paths of execution.

$Sequence \cong$
$\quad [InterfaceDef;\ name : Identifier;\ executions : Path;\ dlinks : \mathbb{P}\,DataLink \mid$
$\qquad \forall\, dl : dlinks \bullet executions^{\sim}(dl.target) = executions^{\sim}(dl.source) + 1]$
$ParallelWithSync \cong [InterfaceDef;\ name : Identifier;\ activities : \mathbb{P}\,Identifier]$

In a conditional execution, the *trueActivity* executes if the conditional expression evaluates to true, the *falseActivity* otherwise. These identifiers may represent atomic or control activities. Nested if-statements can be supported by referring to further if-condition structures from the conditional paths.

$IfCondition \cong [InterfaceDef;\ condition : Expression;$
$\qquad\qquad\qquad name, trueActivity, falseActivity : Identifier]$

The while–do loop takes the form of a structured iteration, where if the *loopCondition* holds, the *loopBody* is executed iteratively until the condition fails to hold.

$Loop \cong [InterfaceDef;\ name, loopBody : Identifier;\ loopCondition : Expression]$

Using the above definitions, an activity can be defined as a free type:

$Activity ::= atomic\langle\!\langle AtomicActivity \rangle\!\rangle \mid seq\langle\!\langle Sequence \rangle\!\rangle$
$\qquad\quad \mid par\langle\!\langle ParallelWithSync \rangle\!\rangle \mid \mathsf{if\text{-}condition}\langle\!\langle IfCondition \rangle\!\rangle \mid \mathsf{while}\langle\!\langle Loop \rangle\!\rangle$

Taken together, the structure of an IWRL workflow contains the following:

1. A set of inputs and outputs, defined within the *InterfaceDef* schema.
2. A sequence of identifiers that represent the executions of the workflow (these are the top level control activities). This order of execution is sequential, with control activities hiding the complex control flows. An execution is an instance of one of the workflow's activities which is executed atmost once.

3. A set of dataflow links that form connections between activity elements.
4. The entire set of activities that the workflow graph is made up of (this includes the activities inside top level control activities).

To ensure that a workflow is valid, we impose several structural constraints upon it. In *ValidLinkSources*, we specify that if a dataflow link starts at a workflow input, and ends at a top level workflow activity, then the connecting ports' datatypes should match (for reasons of space, we omit the constraint part of the schema). A *ValidLinkTargets* schema is defined similarly.

$ValidLinkSources \mathrel{\widehat{=}}$
$\quad [InterfaceDef;\ executions : \text{seq } Identifier;\ dataLinks : \mathbb{P}\, DataLink \mid \ldots]$

Finally, an IWRL workflow can be defined as follows.

$IWRLWflow \mathrel{\widehat{=}}$
$\quad [InterfaceDef;\ executions : \text{seq } Identifier;\ dataLinks : \mathbb{P}\, DataLink;$
$\qquad activities : Identifier \nrightarrow Activity;\ properties : Properties \mid$
$\qquad\quad \text{ran } executions \subset \text{dom } activities\ \wedge$
$\qquad\qquad ValidLinkSources\ \wedge\ ValidLinkTargets]$

3.4 Dynamic Semantics

We model the execution semantics of the IWRL as a chain of states that a workflow goes through. At each transition, the overall state of the workflow consists of sets of activities that are in different states. The next state is decided from the possible state changes that are offered to the system. The state of a workflow at a particular point in time can be expressed as a combination of a set of activities that are ready to execute, a set of activities that are already executing, and a set of activities that have completed execution.

$WflowState \mathrel{\widehat{=}}$
$\quad [ready,\ running,\ completed : \mathbb{P}\, Identifier \mid$
$\qquad \forall\, x, y : \{ready,\ running,\ completed\} \mid x \neq y \wedge x \cap y = \emptyset]$

We regard atomic activities as black boxes whose internal structures are not visible. Therefore we consider only the conditions that govern the start of activities, and do not model their intermediate execution states.[4]

$ActivityState ::= \text{ready} \mid \text{running} \mid \text{completed}$

Both atomic and control activities go through state changes during the workflow life cycle, and each time such a change in state occurs, the overall workflow state is updated accordingly. The *StateChange* function captures this behaviour, by updating the relevant sets in the new workflow state. For instance, the change of state from *running* to *complete* is achieved by removing the activity from the

---

[4] It is also possible, although we do not do so in this presentation, to consider failed and cancelled activity states.

running set and adding it to the *complete* set of the new workflow state. An activity is initially in the *ready* state, and changes to the *running* state only when data becomes available. Due to space limitations, we present only the signature of this function.

$$StateChange : (Identifier \times ActivityState \times WflowState) \rightarrow WflowState$$

As an example, a workflow with a current state ws_0, with activity A running will give state ws_1 at the completion of activity A, as a result of applying the *StateChange* function.

$ws_0 = \langle ready\{B, C\}, running \rightsquigarrow \{A\}, complete \rightsquigarrow \emptyset \rangle$

$StateChange(A, \mathsf{running}, ws_0))$

$ws_1 = \langle ready\{B, C\}, running \rightsquigarrow \emptyset, complete \rightsquigarrow \{A\} \rangle$

Given a workflow definition in the IWRL and the initial state of a workflow, the *IWRLSem* function describes how the workflow proceeds to execute when presented with a sequence of control activities. Initially, all activities within the workflow are in the *ready* state. The workflow execution model consists of a sequence of control activity identifiers, and the execution would start at the head of the sequence. This function calls *ExecSem* (defined below), which recursively calls itself when activities change state.

$$IWRLSem : (IWRLWflow \times WflowState) \rightarrow WflowState$$

$\forall w : IWRLWflow;\ s : WflowState \bullet$
$\quad IWRLSem(w, s) =$
$\quad\quad ExecSem(w.executions, w, StateChange(head\ w.executions, \mathsf{ready}, s))$

As a simple example, consider a sequential workflow consisting of two atomic activities, A and B, which are in the *ready* state at the beginning of the workflow execution. The *executions* attribute of the workflow contains a single element, $sq01$, which is in the *ready* state initially. The initial workflow state that is fed into the *IWRLSem* function is ws_0, shown below:

$ws_0 = \langle ready\{sq01, A, B\}, running \rightsquigarrow \emptyset, complete \rightsquigarrow \emptyset \rangle$
$IWRLSem(iw, ws_0) = ExecSem(\langle sq01 \rangle, iw, StateChange(sq01, \mathsf{ready}, ws_0))$

As a result of the *StateChange* function being applied to the $sq01$ activity, it is changed to the *running* state. *ExecSem* operates on this new workflow state. *ExecSem* is recursively called when traversing the *executions* sequence, and each subsequent state of the workflow is calculated upon the current state of the workflow. The function *ActivitySem* performs the changes in state for each activity by calling the *StateChange* function, in such a way that resembles the execution of a workflow in terms of state transitions.

$ExecSem : (\text{seq } Identifier \times IWRLWflow \times WflowState) \rightarrow WflowState$

$\forall exec : \text{seq } Identifier; \ iw : IWRLWflow; \ ws, ws' : WflowState \bullet$
$\quad ExecSem(exec, iw, ws) = \textbf{if } exec = \langle\rangle \textbf{ then } ws$
$\qquad \textbf{else (if } head \ exec \in ws.completed \textbf{ then } ExecSem(tail \ exec, iw, ws)$
$\qquad\quad \textbf{else (if } head \ exec \in ws.running \textbf{ then}$
$\qquad\qquad ExecSem(tail \ exec, iw,$
$\qquad\qquad ActivitySem(iw.activities \ (head \ exec), \textsf{running}, iw, ws))$
$\qquad\qquad \textbf{else (if } head \ exec \in ws.ready \textbf{ then}$
$\qquad\qquad\quad ExecSem(exec, iw,$
$\qquad\qquad\quad ActivitySem(iw.activities \ (head \ exec), \textsf{ready}, iw, ws))$
$\qquad\qquad \textbf{else } ws)))$

$ActivitySem : (Activity \times ActivityState \times IWRLWflow \times WflowState) \rightarrow$
$\qquad\qquad\qquad WflowState$

$\forall a : AtomicActivity; \ s : ActivityState; \ iw : IWRLWflow; \ ws : WflowState \bullet$
$\quad ActivitySem(\textsf{atomic}(a), s, iw, ws) = StateChange(a.name, s, ws)$
$\forall sq : Sequence; \ s : ActivityState; \ iw : IWRLWflow; \ ws : WflowState \bullet$
$\quad ActivitySem(\textsf{seq}(sq), s, iw, ws) =$
$\qquad \textbf{if } s = \textsf{ready then } StateChange(sq.name, s, ws)$
$\qquad \textbf{else (if } s = \textsf{running then } StateChange(sq.name, s,$
$\qquad\quad ExecSem(sq.activities, iw, ws)) \textbf{ else } ws)$
$\forall p : ParallelWithSync; \ s : ActivityState; \ iw : IWRLWflow;$
$\quad ws, ws' : WflowState \bullet ActivitySem(\textsf{par}(p), s, iw, ws) =$
$\qquad \textbf{if } s = \textsf{ready then } StateChange(p.name, s, ws)$
$\qquad \textbf{else (if } s = \textsf{running then } StateChange(p.name, s,$
$\qquad\quad ParSync(p, iw, ParStart(p.activities, iw, ws))) \textbf{ else } ws)$
$\forall if : IfCondition; \ s : ActivityState; \ iw : IWRLWflow; \ ws : WflowState \bullet$
$\quad ActivitySem(\textsf{if-condition}(if), s, iw, ws) =$
$\qquad \textbf{if } s = \textsf{ready then } StateChange(if.name, s, ws)$
$\qquad \textbf{else (if } s = \textsf{running then } StateChange(if.name, s,$
$\qquad\quad IfEval(if, iw, ws)) \textbf{ else } ws)$
$\forall lp : Loop; \ s : ActivityState; \ iw : IWRLWflow; \ ws : WflowState \bullet$
$\quad ActivitySem(\textsf{while}(lp), s, iw, ws) =$
$\qquad \textbf{if } s = \textsf{ready then } StateChange(lp.name, s, ws)$
$\qquad \textbf{else (if } s = \textsf{running then } StateChange(lp.name, s,$
$\qquad\quad LoopEval(lp, iw, ws)) \textbf{ else } ws)$

ActivitySem is the core function that defines the semantics of different types of activities, and is called recursively from within control activities. For an atomic activity, given its current state, the subsequent state is derived using the *StateChange* function. All control activities are in the *ready* state when they receive execution control; they then change to the *running* state.

A sequence activity starts simulating the execution of the sequence of activities it contains, one after the other. Once the last activity in the sequence has completed, the control activity changes state from *running* to *complete*, and returns the workflow state on completion. Once a parallel activity starts execution, the set of activities that are to be executed in parallel are input to the *ParStart* function, which ensures that all activities in the *ready* state are now being executed simultaneously. As the parallel construct requires synchronisation of activities, the *ParSync* function is called, which operates on the resulting state of the workflow that is returned by the *ParStart* function. Once all of the activities have completed, the control activity changes state from *running* to *complete*, and returns the workflow state on completion. We give the signatures of *ParStart* and *ParSync* below.

$$ParStart : (\mathbb{P}\ Identifier \times IWRLWflow \times WflowState) \rightarrow WflowState$$
$$ParSync : (ParallelWithSync \times IWRLWflow \times WflowState) \rightarrow WflowState$$

A conditional expression is evaluated using the *IfEval* function, where the corresponding activities are executed depending of the result; the *ActivitySem* function is called to process the conditional activities.

$$IfEval : (IfCondition \times IWRLWflow \times WflowState) \rightarrow WflowState$$

The *LoopEval* function is called (recursively) from a *Loop* activity that is in the running state until the *loopCondition* evaluates to false. Again, we present only the signature of this function.

$$LoopEval : (Loop \times IWRLWflow \times WflowState) \rightarrow WflowState$$

4   Achieving Interoperability via the IWRL

Achieving interoperability via the IWRL consists of two parts, the first being the transformation of the computational model of a workflow by mapping activity descriptions. While direct mappings may not exist at all times, we show how the IWRL can be utilised to help identify and match semantic correspondences between workflow concepts. The second part of the transformation process involves mapping the workflow topology from the source to the target model. Unless the transformations are between two control-driven WDLs, perfoming a direct transformation becomes more complex when dealing with a dataflow-based language and a control-flow based language. SCUFL and MoML are examples of predominantly dataflow-oriented WDLs, where the order of execution of activities depends on the availability of data. For such WDLs to be interoperable with control-flow based WDLs such as WS-BPEL, their workflows need to be adapted such that they include explicit control-flow structure embedded into their definitions.

4.1   Transformation of the Computational Model

Figure 2 illustrates the transformation of a web service activity definition in SCUFL to the corresponding actor in MoML via the IWRL. The direct translations are mostly syntactic, and it shows how the WSDL URL of the web service and the operation name are transported across to the target language.

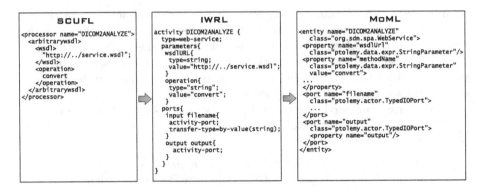

Fig. 2. Translation from a SCUFL processor to a MoML actor

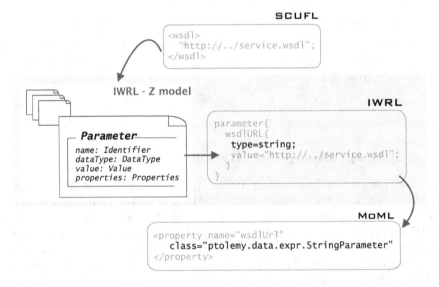

Fig. 3. IWRL allows to capture implicit information within candidate WDLs

In general, not every concept pertaining to a workflow is explicitly modelled as a first-class citizen by every workflow language. Certain concepts may be hidden or merged to be used in combination with other elements. Therefore, it is necessary to capture such implicit information from the candidate WDLs to ensure the completness and correctness of transformations between two WDLs. The example in Figure 3 shows how the formal specifiation of the IWRL in Z can be utilised to capture information that is hidden within the source workflow elements, to be transported across to the target workflow. The goal in this example is to map the WSDL location of a web service activity in SCUFL to the corresponding element in MoML. The transformation via the IWRL captures the WSDL location as a parameter of the web service activity, with its

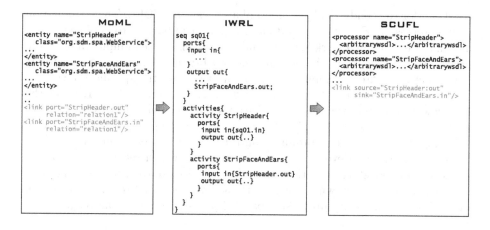

Fig. 4. Translation of sequential execution from MoML to SCUFL

datatype being assigned to 'string'. While this piece of information is not explicitly given in the SCUFL definition, it is required by MoML. The transformation from SCUFL to MoML via the IWRL will introduce this piece of data, enabling a simple transformation from the type attribute in the IWRL parameter and class attribute in a MoML <property> element.

In order to carry out transformations between languages, we need to identify and match semantic correspondences. Using Z, it is possible to formally define the elements of the IWRL such that when performing transformations, it allows one to clearly distinguish and reason about corresponding features between a candidate WDL and the IWRL. In the example given in Figure 3, it is shown how the WSDL location in SCUFL is categorised as a parameter by the IWRL during the transformation. This makes it possible to apply a direct transformation from the IWRL to MoML by mapping the parameter element in the IWRL to a <property> element in MoML, as they represent the same concept.

4.2   Transformation of the Workflow Topology

While there have been a number of developments in achieving interoperability between control flow oriented WDLs, no focus has been given to the transformation between dataflow-based WDLs and control flow based WDLs. We intend to fill this gap by utilising the IWRL.

Step 3 of our scenario was concerned with anonymising the data, and consisted of a sequential execution of two activities that perform the stripping of image headers, followed by the stripping of face and ear parts of an image. Figure 4 presents the corresponding *Sequence* activity in the IWRL, which is created after having identified this sequential connection using the data links in the MoML script, and the result of converting the IWRL script to its SCUFL version to produce the two sequentially connected processors. A conditional execution can be mapped to the 'if-condition' control activity of the IWRL; there is no direct construct for the conditional execution of activities in SCUFL. The combination of two processors, *Fail_if_true* and *Fail_if_false*, can be used to implement conditional branching in a workflow. Depending on their Boolean input value, these processes fail or succeed, whereby the relevant branch is enabled for execution.

Currently, we are developing an algorithm to create the specific IWRL constructs while traversing the source workflow graph. For each activity in the workflow we compute the set of predecessors that each activity is connected to by either data links or control links. Then, we now look at how, by detecting such dependencies, we can produce control flow structures within a workflow. For example, the top-level activities of a workflow which return empty predecessor sets denote start activities. The existence of more than one start activity represents concurrency, where each starts an independent thread of execution. In the IWRL, this is captured using parallel paths in a parallel activity.

5   Discussion

Various efforts have been made to model workflows and workflow languages formally, with [8], [9], [10] and [11] being prime examples; our focus here, though, is interoperability. The Wf-XML specification[5] recommends the establishment of an 'interoperability contract' between participating workflow systems, which states the communication protocol and details of the interoperating scenario. Here, interoperability is achieved at run-time using a set of API calls to invoke external tasks on the remote workflow system, such as creating, modifying or querying a workflow instance; our focus, though, is on build-time interoperability—with a view to providing assurances to users and designers prior to execution. Other efforts at achieving build-time interoperability include that of [12], which attempts to derive a consolidated schema that encompasses a superset of concepts present in existing WDLs, and [13], which translates workflows with aribitrary topologies written into WS-BPEL.[6]

Our approach for facilitating build-time interoperability involves the development of an intermediate language—the IWRL—to allow for translation and (in the longer term) analysis of compositions. The main benefit of our approach is that it enables users to compose a variety of existing workflows, regardless of their underlying WDL, without a need to learn a new WDL or use a new tool. This paper implements a majority of the functional requirements listed in our previous work [1], including control flow, data flow and support for web services. The level of expressibility of the IWRL will be determined later, by analysing its control flow support based on the 20 workflow patterns.

Despite various attempts to standardise WDLs, achieving interoperability among existing ones has proven to be a significant research challenge. The 20 workflow patterns described in [14] are widely accepted as the benchmark for comparing different workflow languages' control flow aspects. In our approach, a set of primitive control flow constructs with a mechanism to define new, more

---

[5] See www.wfmc.org/standards/docs/WfXML20-200410c.pdf

[6] See http://www.oasis-open.org/committees/tc_home.php?wg_abbrev=wsbpel

complex constructs for user-defined compositions is provided, rather than building these patterns into the IWRL itself. This is in contrast to the YAWL language [15], which has been created to specifically support the workflow patterns. Using Z, we have given formal definitions of language components to ensure that workflows are well-formed and consistent. While process algebraic notations have the potential to provide the ability to model the actual behaviour of a workflow and allow the formal verification of the behavioural aspects of a workflow, it is the consideration of the complex structural aspects that underpin WDLs that is our concern here: hence the utilisation of Z. The dynamic semantics of the IWRL are modelled as a chain of state transitions that a workflow goes through. Functions define the outcome of a given control flow construct within a workflow as a chain of possible state changes in the activities contained within it.

Having defined an intermediate format, we have given brief examples of transformations between certain constructs of two WDLs. This has been undertaken a proof of concept to validate the initial version of the IWRL. Immediate future work will focus on the creation of algorithms to translate the workflow topology in an automated manner.

Acknowledgments. The work described in this paper is being funded by the NeuroGrid project. We thank Dominic Job for his suggestion of the example in Section 2.

References

1. Induruwa-Fernando, S.D., Creager, D.A., Simpson, A.C.: Towards build-time interoperability of workflow definition languages. In: Proc. of the 9th Int'l Symposium on Symbolic and Numeric Algorithms for Scientific Computing (2007)
2. Oinn, T.M., Addis, M., Ferris, J., Marvin, D., Greenwood, R.M., Carver, T., Pocock, M.R., Wipat, A., Li, P.: Taverna: a tool for the composition and enactment of bioinformatics workflows. Bioinformatics 20(17), 3045–3054 (2004)
3. Ludäscher, B., Altintas, I., Berkley, C., Higgins, D., Jaeger-Frank, E., Jones, M., Lee, E., Tao, J., Zhao, Y.: Scientific workflow management and the Kepler system: Research articles. Conc. & Comp'n: Practice & Experience 18, 1039–1065 (2006)
4. Lee, E.A., Neuendorffer, S.: MoML: A Modeling Markup Language in XML, Version 0.4. Technical report, University of California at Berkeley (March 2000)
5. Smith, S.M.: Fast robust automated brain extraction. Human Brain Mapping 17(3), 143–155 (2002)
6. Spivey, J.M.: The Z Notation: A Reference Manual. Prentice-Hall Int'l, Englewood Cliffs (1992)
7. Woodcock, J.C.P., Davies, J.W.M.: Using Z: Specification, Refinement, and Proof. Prentice-Hall, Englewood Cliffs (1996)
8. Eshuis, R., Wieringa, R.: A formal semantics for UML activity diagrams - formalising workflow models. Technical report, University of Twente (2001)
9. Stefansen, C.: SMAWL: A Small Workflow Language based on CCS. In: CAiSE Short Paper Proc. (2005)
10. Wong, P.Y.H., Gibbons, J.: A Process-Algebraic Approach to W'flow Specification & Refinement. In: Lumpe, M., Vanderperren, W. (eds.) SC 2007. LNCS, vol. 4829, pp. 51–65. Springer, Heidelberg (2007)

11. Farrell, A., Sergot, M., Bartolini, C.: Formalising workflow: A CCS-inspired characterisation of the yawl workflow patterns. Group Decision and Negotiation 16(3), 213–254 (2007)
12. Mendling, J.: Towards an integrated BPM schema. In: Proceedings of the 12th CAiSE Doctoral Consortium (CAiSE DC), pp. 126–133 (2005)
13. Ouyang, C., Dumas, M., Breutel, S., ter Hofstede, A.: Translating Standard Process Models to BPEL. In: CAiSE, pp. 417–432 (2006)
14. van der Aalst, W., ter Hofstede, A., Kiepuszewski, B., Barros, A.: Workflow patterns. Distributed and Parallel Databases 14(1), 5–51 (2003)
15. van der Aalst, W., ter Hofstede, A.: YAWL: Yet Another Workflow Language. Inf. Systems 30(4), 245–275 (2005)

Security Types for Sessions and Pipelines

Marija Kolundžija

Dipartimento di Informatica, Università di Torino, Italy

Abstract. The growing importance of service-oriented computing has triggered development of formal computational models for service description and orchestration. Several versions of the Service Centered Calculus (SCC) and its successor, the Calculus of Services with Pipelines and Sessions (CaSPiS) have emerged as outcome of those studies, and are based on the notion of interaction patterns called sessions between the service and the client who invokes it. We propose a security oriented extension of Bruni and Mezzina's typed variant of CaSPiS, where security levels have been assigned to service definitions, clients and data. In order to invoke a service, a client must be endowed with an appropriate clearance, and once the service and client agree on the security level, the data exchanged in the initiated session will not exceed this level. We study a type system that statically ensures these security properties.

1 Introduction

Popularity of communication centered applications distributed over the web (*web services*) has provoked urgent interest in the development of automatic tools to assure safe uses of these applications. *Service Oriented Computing* (SOC) has emerged as a new computational paradigm and various process calculi have been designed to model service behaviour (see for example the references in [6]).

An interesting proposal is the *Calculus of Services with Pipelines and Sessions* (CaSPiS) [6], which is a dataflow–oriented successor of the Service Centered Calculus (SCC) [5]. In both these calculi communications can either follow fixed protocols (*session*) or be disciplined data flows (*pipelines*).

The pipeline constructor of CaSPiS was first introduced in [15]. In [14], the authors have proposed the session as a language construct for communication based programming.

There are also various type disciplines for calculi originated from SCC [16,17] and in particular for minor modifications of CaSPiS [1,8]. In both typed versions of CaSPiS the communications between parallel processes are controlled by *session types*, which are lightweight descriptions of protocols first used in [14]. The typed versions of CaSPiS have safe communications, since they enjoy the subject reduction and the progress property (formalized in [11,10]). Surprisingly, little work has been done to address security issues in the session–type setting. The authors of [4] have proposed correspondence assertions as means of control of data propagation over multiple parties. However, to the best of our knowledge, no notion of secrecy has been considered so far, and therefore no assurance that private data will never become visible to unauthorized bodies can be given.

R. Bruni and K. Wolf (Eds.): WS-FM 2008, LNCS 5387, pp. 175–190, 2009.
© Springer-Verlag Berlin Heidelberg 2009

The present paper tries to fill this gap by building on well-known typing techniques for controlling *access rights* [2,7,12,18,19,20]. To this aim we have considered session types decorated by security levels and designed a type system that guarantees both safe communications and data security.

Consider, for example, a service which keeps track of grades of a University course. The name of the service is $UnivRec$, and it offers two possibilities of record manipulation. A student (code guarded with level student) is allowed to access his grade for a given course by sending the service his file–number (the $StudentId$) and the number of the course (the $CourseId$), to which the service responds by outputting his grade as a result of a function grade. Only a teacher (code guarded with level teacher) can be allowed to update the grades by calling a service *update*, which changes the grade records for the given student and course ID.

$$UnivRec. \text{ (student} \ltimes \text{ ((check)}.(StudentId).(CourseId).\langle \text{grade}(CourseId)\rangle$$
$$+(\text{update}).(StudentId).(CourseId).(grade).\langle\text{fail}\rangle)\uplus$$
$$\text{teacher} \ltimes \text{ ((check)}.(StudentId).(CourseId).\langle\text{grade}(CourseId)\rangle$$
$$+(\text{update}).(StudentId).(CourseId).(grade).\langle\text{success}\rangle.$$
$$\overline{update}.\langle CourseId\rangle.\langle grade\rangle)$$
$$)$$

Assuming that the privileges of a student are less than those of a teacher, this service should provide both the interface for a student and a teacher, rejecting student's attempt to update the grades (and in this example, informing him of the failure), while when activated by the teacher, the update operation is allowed, and the *update* service is activated on teacher's behalf.

This paper is organized as follows: Sections 2 and 3 present the syntax, operational semantics and the type system of the language, illustrated by the example given in Section 4. The properties of the language are stated with proof sketch in Section 5. Then we briefly conclude.

2   Syntax and Operational Semantics

The present calculus is essentially the calculus of [8] enriched with security levels. As usual [3,9] we assume a lattice of security levels: we use $\ell, \imath, \kappa$ to range over security levels and $\sqsubseteq, \sqcup, \sqcap$ to denote partial order, join and meet, respectively.

The syntactical constructs are listed in order of non-increasing precedence [1] in Figure 1. The nil process and the process constructors input, output, parallel composition and matching have the standard meanings. Values (ranged over by u, v, w) can be either basic values, variables, function calls, services or session names. In well-typed processes only the first two kinds of values can be

---

[1] More precisely the prefixes in lines 2-7 have the precedence over the constructors on lines 8-11 and the remaining constructors have decreasing precedence, but for the restrictions which have the same precedence.

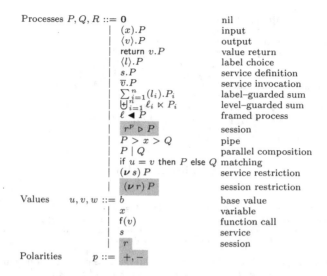

Processes	$P, Q, R ::=$	$\mathbf{0}$	nil
	$\mid$	$(x).P$	input
	$\mid$	$\langle v \rangle.P$	output
	$\mid$	return $v.P$	value return
	$\mid$	$\langle l \rangle.P$	label choice
	$\mid$	$s.P$	service definition
	$\mid$	$\overline{v}.P$	service invocation
	$\mid$	$\sum_{i=1}^{n} (l_i).P_i$	label–guarded sum
	$\mid$	$\biguplus_{i=1}^{n} \ell_i \ltimes P_i$	level–guarded sum
	$\mid$	$\ell \blacktriangleleft P$	framed process
	$\mid$	$r^p \triangleright P$	session
	$\mid$	$P > x > Q$	pipe
	$\mid$	$P \mid Q$	parallel composition
	$\mid$	if $u = v$ then P else Q	matching
	$\mid$	$(\boldsymbol{\nu} s) P$	service restriction
	$\mid$	$(\boldsymbol{\nu} r) P$	session restriction
Values	$u, v, w ::=$	b	base value
	$\mid$	x	variable
	$\mid$	$f(v)$	function call
	$\mid$	s	service
	$\mid$	r	session
Polarities	$p ::=$	$+, -$	

Fig. 1. Syntax, where syntax occurring only at runtime appears shaded

exchanged, while all kinds of values can appear in the conditions of pattern matching.

A label choice selects one of the labels offered by a label-guarded sum. The pipe constructor $P > x > Q$ is inspired by [15]: a value from P replaces the variable x in a freshly spawned copy of Q.

Service definitions are permanent: a new occurrence of the session body is created when the service is called.

Characteristic of our approach to security are *framed processes* [7,12,18]: in $\ell \blacktriangleleft P$ the process P can exercise rights of security level not exceeding ℓ. So a service invocation $\ell \blacktriangleleft \overline{s}.P$ is well typed only if the security level ℓ is not lower than the security level of s. Framed processes are also necessary in order to reduce level-guarded sums: an arbitrary branch whose level is less than or equal to that of the current frame can be arbitrary chosen.

Service calls can be nested and the value return prefix allows to send a value to the upper nesting level.

A session name has two polarized session ends, the client side − and the service side +, one being dual to the other. At runtime fresh session names with opposite polarities are generated and restricted. All communications of values and labels are executed inside the scopes of the same session names with opposite polarities.

We give the operational semantics by means of reduction rules (listed in Figure 2), as proposed in the appendix of the technical report of the original paper [8], instead of a labelled transition system as in the final version of [8]. In this way we get less rules. We let m range over service and session names.

We use evaluation contexts with either one or two holes. The evaluation contexts with two holes are necessary in order to model the interaction between two

$$
\begin{array}{ll}
(\text{Inv}) & \mathbb{D}[\![\ell \blacktriangleleft \overline{s}.P, s.Q]\!] \to (\nu\, r)\, \mathbb{D}[\![r^- \rhd \ell \blacktriangleleft P, r^+ \rhd \ell \blacktriangleleft Q \mid s.Q]\!] \\
& r \notin \mathsf{fn}(\mathbb{D}[\![\overline{s}.P, s.Q]\!]) \\
(\text{Com}) & \mathbb{D}_r[\![(x).P, \langle v \rangle.Q]\!] \to \mathbb{D}_r[\![P[^v\!/x], Q]\!] \\
(\text{Lcom}) & \mathbb{D}_r[\![\sum_{i=1}^n (l_i).P_i, \langle l_k \rangle.Q]\!] \to \mathbb{D}_r[\![P_k, Q]\!] \\
(\text{Ret}) & \mathbb{D}_{r_1}[\![(x).P, \mathbb{C}_{r^p}[\![\text{return } v.Q]\!]]\!] \to \mathbb{D}_{r_1}[\![P[^v\!/x], \mathbb{C}_{r^p}[\![Q]\!]]\!] \\
(\text{Pipe}) & \mathbb{C}[\![\langle v \rangle.P > x > Q]\!] \to \mathbb{C}[\![P > x > Q \mid Q[^v\!/x]]\!] \\
(\text{PipeRet}) & \mathbb{C}[\![\mathbb{C}_{r^p}[\![\text{return } v.P]\!] > x > Q]\!] \to \mathbb{C}[\![\mathbb{C}_{r^p}[\![P]\!] > x > Q \mid Q[^v\!/x]]\!] \\
(\text{IfT}) & \mathbb{C}[\![\text{if } u = v \text{ then } P \text{ else } Q]\!] \to \mathbb{C}[\![P]\!] \quad (u = v) \downarrow \text{true} \\
(\text{IfF}) & \mathbb{C}[\![\text{if } u = v \text{ then } P \text{ else } Q]\!] \to \mathbb{C}[\![Q]\!] \quad (u = v) \downarrow \text{false} \\
(\text{LevSel}) & \mathbb{C}[\![\ell \blacktriangleleft \biguplus_{i=1}^n \ell_i \ltimes P_i]\!] \to \mathbb{C}[\![\ell \blacktriangleleft P_i]\!] \quad \text{if } \ell_i \sqsubseteq \ell \\
(\text{Scop}) & P \to P' \;\Rightarrow\; (\nu\, m)\, P \to (\nu\, m)\, P' \\
(\text{Str}) & P \equiv P' \,\wedge\, P' \to Q' \,\wedge\, Q' \equiv Q \;\Rightarrow\; P \to Q
\end{array}
$$

Fig. 2. Reduction Rules

$$
\begin{array}{ccc}
P \mid 0 \equiv P & P \mid Q \equiv Q \mid P & (P \mid Q) \mid R \equiv P \mid (Q \mid R) \qquad \ell \blacktriangleleft 0 \equiv 0 \\
\end{array}
$$

$$
(\nu\, m)\,(\nu\, m')\, P \equiv (\nu\, m')\,(\nu\, m)\, P \qquad ((\nu\, m)\, P) \mid Q \equiv (\nu\, m)\,(P \mid Q) \text{ if } m \notin \mathsf{fn}(Q)
$$

$$
((\nu\, m)\, P) > x > Q \equiv (\nu\, m)\,(P > x > Q) \text{ if } m \notin \mathsf{fn}(Q) \qquad 0 > x > Q \equiv 0
$$

$$
(P \mid R) > x > Q \equiv (P > x > Q) \mid (R > x > Q)
$$

$$
\ell \blacktriangleleft (P > x > Q) \equiv (\ell \blacktriangleleft P) > x > (\ell \blacktriangleleft Q)
$$

$$
r^p \rhd \ell \blacktriangleleft 0 > x > Q \equiv r^p \rhd \ell \blacktriangleleft 0 \qquad (\nu\, r)\,(r^+ \rhd \ell \blacktriangleleft 0 \mid r^- \rhd \ell \blacktriangleleft 0) \equiv 0
$$

$$
r^p \rhd \ell \blacktriangleleft (P \mid r_1^q \rhd \ell' \blacktriangleleft 0) \equiv r^p \rhd \ell \blacktriangleleft P \mid r_1^q \rhd \ell' \blacktriangleleft 0
$$

Fig. 3. Structural Equivalence

processes. Moreover we express through contexts the condition that a process is in the scope of some session name with a given polarity. More precisely we define the following four kinds of evaluation contexts:

$$
\begin{array}{ll}
\mathbb{C} & ::= [\,\cdot\,] \mid \mathbb{C} \mid P \mid r^p \rhd \mathbb{C} \mid \mathbb{C} > x > P \mid \ell \blacktriangleleft [\,\cdot\,] \\
\mathbb{C}_{r^p} & ::= r^p \rhd \ell \blacktriangleleft [\,\cdot\,] \mid P \\
\mathbb{D} & ::= \mathbb{C}[\![\mathbb{C}' \mid \mathbb{C}'']\!] \\
\mathbb{D}_r & ::= \mathbb{D}[\![\mathbb{C}'_{r^p}, \mathbb{C}''_{r^{\overline{p}}}]\!] \quad r \notin \mathsf{fn}(\mathbb{D})
\end{array}
$$

In rule (Inv) a client of level ℓ calls a service: the body of the client and a copy of the body of the service are framed by the client level ℓ and prefixed by two occurrences of the freshly generated and private session name r with opposite polarities.

In rules (Com) and (Lcom) two processes in the scopes of the same session name with opposite polarities exchange values and labels, respectively. When a label is received, the execution of the label-guarded sum continues with the corresponding process.

Rule (Ret) allows the inner session (named r) to communicate the value v to the outer session (named r_1).

In rules (Pipe) and (PipeRet) a new parallel copy of Q is created: in this copy the value v replaces the variable x. The difference between these rules is that in the first one the value v is sent by an output prefix, while in the second one the value v is sent by a return prefix that occurs in an inner session (named r).

Finally rule (LevSel) non deterministically chooses a process whose security level is less than or equal to the level of the current frame.

$$
\begin{aligned}
T, U ::=\ &\text{end} &&\text{(no action)}\\
\mid\ &?(S_\ell).T &&\text{(input of a value)}\\
\mid\ &!(S_\ell).T &&\text{(output of a value)}\\
\mid\ &\&\{l_1\ :\ T_1,\ldots,l_n\ :\ T_n\} &&\text{(external choice)}\\
\mid\ &\oplus\{l_1\ :\ T_1,\ldots,l_n\ :\ T_n\} &&\text{(internal choice)}\\
\mid\ &\uplus\{\ell_1 \propto T,\ldots,\ell_n \propto T\} &&\text{(level choice)}
\end{aligned}
$$

$$
\begin{aligned}
S_\ell ::=\ &[T]_\ell &&\text{(session type)}\\
\mid\ &\mathcal{B}_\ell &&\text{(basic type)}
\end{aligned}
$$

Fig. 4. Syntax of Types

$$
\begin{gathered}
\overline{\text{end} \backsim \text{end}}\\[2pt]
\overline{?(S_\ell).T \backsim !(S_\ell).\overline{T}}\\[2pt]
\overline{!(S_\ell).T' \backsim ?(S_\ell).\overline{T'}}\\[2pt]
\overline{\oplus\{l_1\ :\ T_1,\ldots,l_n\ :\ T_n\} \backsim \&\{l_1\ :\ \overline{T}_1,\ldots,l_n\ :\ \overline{T}_n\}}\\[2pt]
\overline{\&\{l_1\ :\ T_1,\ldots,l_n\ :\ T_n\} \backsim \oplus\{l_1\ :\ \overline{T}_1,\ldots,l_n\ :\ \overline{T}_n\}}\\[2pt]
\overline{\uplus\{\ell_1 \propto T,\ldots,\ell_n \propto T\} \backsim \overline{T}}
\end{gathered}
$$

Fig. 5. Duality Relation

$$
\begin{gathered}
I \subseteq \{1,\ldots,n\}\\
\&\{l_1\ :\ T_1,\ldots,l_n\ :\ T_n\} \leq \&\{l_i\ :\ T_i\}_{i\in I}\\
\oplus\{l_i\ :\ T_i\}_{i\in I} \leq \oplus\{l_1\ :\ T_1,\ldots,l_n\ :\ T_n\}\\
\uplus\{\ell_1 \propto T,\ldots,\ell_n \propto T\} \leq \uplus\{\ell_i \propto T\}_{i\in I} \text{ if } \exists j \in I.\ell_j = \textstyle\bigsqcap_{i\in I}\ell_i\\
(1 \leq i \leq n)\quad T_i \leq T_i' \Rightarrow
\begin{cases}
\&\{l_1\ :\ T_1,\ldots,l_n\ :\ T_n\} \leq \&\{l_1\ :\ T_1',\ldots,l_n\ :\ T_n'\}\\
\oplus\{l_1\ :\ T_1,\ldots,l_n\ :\ T_n\} \leq \oplus\{l_1\ :\ T_1',\ldots,l_n\ :\ T_n'\}
\end{cases}\\
T \leq T' \Rightarrow
\begin{cases}
!(S_\ell).T \leq !(S_\ell).T'\\
?(S_\ell).T \leq ?(S_\ell).T'\\
\uplus\{\ell_1 \propto T,\ldots,\ell_n \propto T\} \leq \uplus\{\ell_1 \propto T',\ldots,\ell_n \propto T'\}
\end{cases}
\end{gathered}
$$

Fig. 6. Subtyping Relation $\leq$

The remaining rules are standard. The structural equivalence is as usual, but for the rules dealing with security levels and sessions. The last three rules are, respectively, garbage collection of pipes of exhausted code, garbage collection of exhausted sessions and pushing the exhausted nested session outside of the scope of the parent session.

It is interesting to notice that CaSPiS mixes linear communication inside and between sessions with non–linear communication due to the pipe construct.

3   Type System

The type system is a security annotated variant of the type system in [8], consisting of sorts and session types.

$$\Gamma, s : S_\ell \vdash s : S_\ell \;(\mathsf{Service}) \qquad \Gamma, x : S_\ell \vdash x : S_\ell \;(\mathsf{Var}) \qquad \frac{\tau^b \in \mathcal{B}_\ell}{\Gamma \vdash b : \tau^b_\ell}\;(\mathsf{BasVal})$$

$$\frac{\Gamma \vdash v^{(1)} : S^{(1)}_{\ell_1} \ldots, \Gamma \vdash v^{(n)} : S^{(n)}_{\ell_n} \quad \tau^b_\imath \in \mathcal{B} \quad \ell_1 \sqcup \ldots \sqcup \ell_n \sqsubseteq \imath}{\Gamma, \mathsf{f} : S^{(1)}_{\ell_1} \times \cdots \times S^{(n)}_{\ell_n} \to \tau^b_\imath \vdash \mathsf{f}(v^{(1)}, \ldots, v^{(n)}) : \tau^b_\imath}\;(\mathsf{Fun})$$

$$\Gamma \vdash \mathbf{0} : \mathsf{end} \therefore^{\perp} [\mathsf{end}]_\perp \;(\mathsf{Nil}) \qquad \frac{\Gamma \vdash P : U \therefore^{\imath} [T]_\kappa \quad \Gamma \vdash v : [\overline{T'}]_\ell \quad T' \leq T}{\Gamma \vdash \overline{v}.P : \mathsf{end} \therefore^{\perp} [U]_{\kappa \sqcup \ell \sqcup \imath}}\;(\mathsf{Inv})$$

$$\frac{\Gamma, x : S_\ell \vdash P : U \therefore^{\imath} [T]_\kappa}{\Gamma \vdash (x).P : U \therefore^{\imath} [?(S_\ell).T]_{\kappa \sqcup \ell}}\;(\mathsf{Inp}) \qquad \frac{\Gamma \vdash P : U \therefore^{\imath} [T]_\kappa \quad \Gamma \vdash v : S_\ell}{\Gamma \vdash \langle v \rangle.P : U \therefore^{\imath} [!(S_\ell).T]_{\kappa \sqcup \ell}}\;(\mathsf{Out})$$

$$\frac{\Gamma \vdash P : U \therefore^{\imath} [T]_\kappa \quad \Gamma \vdash v : S_\ell}{\Gamma \vdash \mathsf{return}\ v.P :!(S_\ell).U \therefore^{\imath \sqcup \ell} [T]_\kappa}\;(\mathsf{Ret})$$

$$\frac{\Gamma \vdash P_i : U \therefore^{\imath} [T_i]_{\kappa_i} \quad (1 \leq i \leq n)}{\Gamma \vdash \sum_{i=1}^{n} (l_i).P_i : U \therefore^{\imath} [\&\{l_1 : T_1, \ldots, l_n : T_n\}]_{\kappa_1 \sqcup \ldots \sqcup \kappa_n}}\;(\mathsf{Branch})$$

$$\frac{l = l_i \quad i \in \{1, \ldots, n\} \quad \Gamma \vdash P_i : U \therefore^{\imath} [T_i]_{\kappa_i}}{\Gamma \vdash \langle l \rangle.P : U \therefore^{\imath} [\oplus\{l_1 : T_1, \ldots, l_n : T_n\}]_{\kappa_1 \sqcup \ldots \sqcup \kappa_n}}\;(\mathsf{Choice})$$

$$\frac{\begin{array}{c}\Gamma \vdash P : U \therefore^{\imath} [T]_\kappa \quad \Gamma, x : S_\ell \vdash Q : U' \therefore^{\imath'} [T']_{\kappa'} \\ \mathsf{pipe}(U \therefore^{\imath} [T]_\kappa, U' \therefore^{\imath'} [T']_{\kappa'}, S_\ell) = U'' \therefore^{\imath''} [T'']_{\kappa''}\end{array}}{\Gamma \vdash P > x > Q : U'' \therefore^{\imath''} [T'']_{\kappa''}}\;(\mathsf{Pipe})$$

$$\frac{\Gamma \vdash v_i : S_{\ell_i} \quad \Gamma \vdash P : U \therefore^{\imath} [T]_\jmath \quad \Gamma \vdash Q : U \therefore^{\imath} [T]_\kappa \quad \ell_i \sqsubseteq \jmath \sqcap \kappa \quad i = 1, 2}{\Gamma \vdash \mathsf{if}\ v_1 = v_2\ \mathsf{then}\ P\ \mathsf{else}\ Q : U \therefore^{\imath} [T]_{\jmath \sqcup \kappa}}\;(\mathsf{If})$$

$$\frac{\Gamma \vdash P_i : U \therefore^{\imath} [T]_{\kappa_i} \quad \kappa_i \sqsubseteq \ell_i \quad (1 \leq i \leq n) \quad \exists j (1 \leq j \leq n).\ell_1 \sqcap \ldots \sqcap \ell_n = \ell_j}{\Gamma \vdash \biguplus_{i=1}^{n} \ell_i \ltimes P_i : U \therefore^{\imath} [\uplus\{\ell_1 \propto T, \ldots, \ell_n \propto T\}]_{\ell_j}}\;(\mathsf{LevSel})$$

$$\frac{\Gamma \vdash P : U \therefore^{\imath_1} [T_1]_{\kappa_1} \quad \Gamma \vdash Q : U' \therefore^{\imath_2} [T_2]_{\kappa_2}}{\Gamma \vdash P \mid Q : U \circ U' \therefore^{\imath_1 \sqcup \imath_2} [T_1 \bowtie T_2]_{\kappa_1 \sqcup \kappa_2}}\;(\mathsf{Par})$$

Fig. 7. Typing Rules for Inner Processes

$$\text{pipe}(U \therefore^{\imath}[\text{end}]_\kappa, U' \therefore^{\imath'}[T']_{\kappa'}, S_\ell) = U \therefore^{\imath}[\text{end}]_\kappa$$
$$\text{pipe}(U \therefore^{\imath}[!(S_\ell).\text{end}]_\kappa, U' \therefore^{\imath'}[T]_{\kappa'}, S_\ell) = U \circ U' \therefore^{\imath \sqcup \imath'}[T]_{\kappa \sqcup \kappa'}$$
$$\text{pipe}(U \therefore^{\imath}[!(S_\ell)^h.\text{end}]_\kappa, U' \therefore^{\imath'}[\text{end}]_{\kappa'}, S_\ell) = U \circ U'^h \therefore^{\imath \sqcup \imath'}[\text{end}]_{\kappa \sqcup \kappa'} \quad h > 1$$

Fig. 8. Function pipe

$$\frac{\Gamma \vdash P : \text{end} \therefore^{\perp}[T]_\kappa \quad \Gamma \vdash s : [T]_\ell \quad \kappa \sqsubseteq \ell}{\Gamma \vdash_{\{s\}} s.P : \text{end} \therefore^{\perp}[\text{end}]_\kappa} \text{ (ServDef)}$$

$$\frac{\Gamma \vdash_{S_1} P : \text{end} \therefore^{\perp}[\text{end}]_{\kappa_1} \quad \Gamma \vdash_{S_2} Q : \text{end} \therefore^{\perp}[\text{end}]_{\kappa_2}}{\Gamma \vdash_{S_1 \cup S_2} P \mid Q : \text{end} \therefore^{\perp}[\text{end}]_{\kappa_1 \sqcup \kappa_2}} \text{ (TopPar)}$$

$$\frac{\Gamma \vdash P : \text{end} \therefore^{\perp}[\text{end}]_\kappa \quad \kappa \sqsubseteq \ell}{\Gamma \vdash_\emptyset \ell \blacktriangleleft P : \text{end} \therefore^{\perp}[\text{end}]_\ell} \text{ (LevSign)}$$

$$\frac{\Gamma, s : S \vdash_{S,s} P : \text{end} \therefore^{\perp}[\text{end}]_\kappa}{\Gamma \vdash_S (\nu s) P : \text{end} \therefore^{\perp}[\text{end}]_\kappa} \text{ (ServRestr)}$$

Fig. 9. Typing Rules for Top Level Processes

$$\frac{\Gamma \vdash P : U \therefore^{\imath}[T]_\kappa \quad \kappa \sqcup \imath \sqsubseteq \ell}{\Gamma, r : [T]_\ell \vdash r^+ \triangleright \ell \blacktriangleleft P : \text{end} \therefore^{\perp}[U]_\ell} \text{ (Sess)} \qquad \frac{\Gamma \vdash P : U \therefore^{\imath}[T]_\kappa \quad \kappa \sqcup \imath \sqsubseteq \ell \quad T' \leq T}{\Gamma, r : [\overline{T'}]_\ell \vdash r^- \triangleright \ell \blacktriangleleft P : \text{end} \therefore^{\perp}[U]_\ell} \text{ (SessI)}$$

$$\frac{\Gamma, r : S_\ell \vdash P : U \therefore^{\imath}[T]_\kappa}{\Gamma \vdash (\nu r) P : U \therefore^{\imath}[T]_\kappa} \text{ (SessRestr)}$$

Fig. 10. Typing Rules for Runtime Processes

Basic data types are decorated with their security levels (cf. [21]), and the security levels appearing in annotation of sessions represent the join of the levels of data manipulated inside the session by communication and activation.

A *typing environment* Γ is a finite partial mapping from variables, services and sessions to sorts (i.e. session types and basic types) and function types. The empty environment is denoted by $\emptyset$, and if u is a variable, a service or a session name, then $\Gamma, u : S_\ell$ is the extension with the binding of u to S_ℓ, if $u \notin \text{dom}(\Gamma)$. The extension for a function name with a function type is defined similarly.

The typing judgments have the form $\Gamma \vdash v : S_\ell$ for the values, and $\Gamma \vdash P : U \therefore^{\imath}[T]_\kappa$ for processes, where U is the output (sequence of outputs) of the process P to the parent session with the level $\imath$, and T is the type of P's activities in the current session, and κ is the level of values communicated in the current session and in all of the nested sessions.

The rules (Service), (Var), (BasVal) and (Fun) are standard typing rules for values. The rule (Fun) inserts an external function in the typing environment while ensuring that the level of the function output is not less than the level of its arguments.

The type end $\therefore \,^\perp[\text{end}]_\perp$ of $\mathbf{0}$ (rule (Nil)) means that no action is performed neither in the current nor in the parent session.

Rules for input and output of a value ((Inp), (Out)) add the performed action to the current session type, and increase the level assigned to the current session by the level of the communicated value. Rule (Ret) adds the output of a value to the return sequence U, updating its level in a similar way.

Rules (Branch) and (Choice) for internal and external choice take the join of levels of all the branches as the current session level. Rule (If) is the standard conditional branching on the result of the comparison of two values, which does not allow low–level branches to depend on high–level values in the choice.

Two parallel processes can both offer outputs to the parent session when there is no way of distinguishing the outputs at the type system level. The composition of outputs used in rule rule (Par) is defined as $U \circ U' = !(S_\ell)^{h+k}.\text{end}$ if $U = !(S_\ell)^h.\text{end}$ and $U' = !(S_\ell)^k.\text{end}$, i.e. U and U' are sequences of the same output, and undefined otherwise. Rule (Par) parallelly composes two processes if at least one of them does not have any action in the current session, i.e. the operator $\bowtie$ is defined only when one of the types is end:

$$T \bowtie T' = \begin{cases} T', \text{ if } T = \text{end} \\ T, \text{ if } T' = \text{end} \\ \text{undefined otherwise} \end{cases}$$

Rule (Pipe) derives the type of pipe using the function pipe, given in Figure 8. If P outputs a single value (and has no other action in the current session), the pipe Q consumes the value, and may have other actions in the current session. If the current session activity of P consists of a sequence of h outputs where $h > 1$, h instances of Q will be activated to consume the outputs and put in parallel with P, but Q will only be allowed to produce values upwards to the parent session. If Q will be activated, the outputs of P and Q will be composed as in parallel composition.

The innovation with respect to the type system in [8] is rule (LevSel). It is similar to the test–rule in access control typing systems [18,12,7]. Each branch of the choice is guarded with a security level greater than or equal to the one necessary for its activation. The level of the session type is increased to take into account only the least of the branch–levels. Since all the branches have the same type, differing only in the security annotation, the process is required to have at least the privilege to activate the lowest one, but depending on the process privileges, one of the higher branches may be selected. This rule permits a better modularity of service definitions, allowing the same service to offer both high and low–level response, depending on the clearance of the client who activated it.

Rule (Inv) for session invocation allows a process to invoke a session if its body matches the defined session w.r.t the duality relation, defined in Figure 5. The type of the defined session is required to be a *subtype* of the client's dual (in the sense of the relation inspired by [13], defined in Figure 6). This is justified by reasoning that the service can offer more choices than required by the client (with label and level branching), and that different clients may make different choices. After the process has been prefixed with service invocation, the return sequence U becomes the current session usage, and its level, together with the level of the invoked session is added to the level of the current session.

A *top level process* is a process of type end $\therefore^{\perp}[\text{end}]_\kappa$, which means that it has no activity in the current session, and produces no value upwards. The typing of the top level processes is given in Figure 9. The typing judgments of the top level processes have the form $\Gamma \vdash_S P : \text{end} \therefore^{\perp}[\text{end}]_\kappa$, where S is the set of defined services.

An *initial configuration* consists of parallel compositions of service definitions and framed top level client processes.

Rule (ServDef) defines a service with as body the process P. Each time a service is defined, the turnstile is decorated with its name, and when processes are parallelly composed (rule (TopPar)), the sets of defined services are joined. When we want to restrict a service name (rule (ServRestr)), it is required that this name is already defined (i.e. present in S), and after restricting it, we remove it from the set S. In this way we prevent calls of nonexistent services.

Rule (LevSign) promotes an inner process P to the top level process $\ell \blacktriangleleft P$ by assignment of a security clearance ℓ only if the intended activity of P (reflected in the level κ) agrees with ℓ.

By requiring that the initial configuration consists only of top level processes, we avoid stuck configurations of dangling communications outside of sessions waiting for synchronization.

The typing of the processes that appear only at runtime is given in Figure 10. Rules (Sess) and (SessI), similarly to the rules for service invocation and definition, require a session matching the type of the session body process P in the typing environment, signed with the level ℓ with which the session was invoked. The difference between these pairs of rules is that the assumptions for sessions are added in the conclusions of the typing rules, while the assumptions for the services must be always present in the premises of the typing rules. The reason is that we want to allow nested calls of the same service name, but not nested usages of the same session name.

Rule (SessRestr) restricts the session name and removes it from the environment.

4   Example

We give an example of an e–commerce service, such as **e–bay**. Three levels of users are assumed – guests, with level 1, which do not have an account with the service, and who are allowed only to browse through the items in the catalogue. The registered users have a level 2, and they are additionally allowed to bid for an item, or buy an item that is for direct sale, but are allowed to pay for it only by sending a personal cheque. The VIP–users with the level 3 can also pay with credit card or PayPal account. We assume that $1 \sqsubseteq 2 \sqsubseteq 3$. By letting

$P = \langle catalogue_1 \rangle (itemNo_1) \langle \mathtt{price}_1 (itemNo_1) \rangle$,

$Q = \overline{pay}.\langle bid_1 \rangle.\langle cheque \rangle.\langle personalId_2 \rangle$,

$R = \overline{pay}.\langle bid_1 \rangle.$if $(\mathtt{payMeth}_3(personalId_2) = 1)$ then $\langle cheque \rangle.\langle personalId_2 \rangle$
else if $(\mathtt{payMeth}_3(personalId_2) = 2)$ then $\langle card \rangle.\langle \mathtt{cardNb}_3(PersonalId_2) \rangle$ else
$\langle paypal \rangle.\langle \mathtt{accPars}_3(PersonalId_2) \rangle$

we can define the services *ebay*, *pay*, *card* and *paypal* as follows:

$ebay_1.\ (1 \ltimes ((\mathsf{browse}).P + (\mathsf{bid}).(itemNo_1).(bid_1).(pId_1)$
$\qquad + (\mathsf{buy}).(itemNo_1).(pId_1))$

$\qquad \uplus\ 2 \ltimes ((\mathsf{browse}).P + (\mathsf{bid}).(itemNo_1).(bid_1).(personalId_2).$

$\qquad\qquad$ if $\mathtt{highestBid}_1(itemNo_1) = bid_1$ then Q else $\mathbf{0}$
$\qquad\qquad + (\mathsf{buy}).(itemNo_1).Q)$

$\qquad \uplus\ 3 \ltimes ((\mathsf{browse}).P + (\mathsf{bid}).(itemNo_1).(bid_1).(personalId_2).$

$\qquad\qquad$ if $\mathtt{highestBid}_1(itemNo_1) = bid_1$ then R else $\mathbf{0}$
$\qquad\qquad + (\mathsf{buy}).(itemNo_1).(personalId_2).R))$

$pay_2.(amount_1).\ (2 \ltimes ((\mathsf{cheque}).(personalId_2)$
$\qquad\qquad\qquad + (\mathsf{card})(cardPar_2) + (\mathsf{paypal})(accountPar_2))$
$\qquad \uplus\ \ 3 \ltimes ((\mathsf{cheque}).(personalId_2)$
$\qquad\qquad\qquad + (\mathsf{card}).(cardNo_3).\overline{card}.\langle amount_1 \rangle.\langle cardNo_3 \rangle$
$\qquad\qquad\qquad + (\mathsf{paypal}).(accountPars_3).$
$\qquad\qquad\qquad\ \ \overline{paypal}.\langle amount_1 \rangle.\langle accountPars_3 \rangle))$

$card_3.(amount_1).(cardNo_3)$

$paypal_3.(amount_1).(accountPars_3)$

The service *ebay* offers essentially three kinds of services: browsing through the item catalogue, biding for an item (with obligatory purchase of the customer who won the bid) and buying an item that is put for direct sale. Options for bidding and buying are different for users and VIP–users, since the VIP–users are allowed different payment methods based on their preference (retrieved by the function $\mathtt{payMeth}$), while the ordinary users automatically have to pay by sending a personal cheque.

The payment is done by activating a service *pay*, which for a received amount triggers a payment method branch, which, in turn, might activate services that handle card and PayPal payments (services *card* and *paypal*, respectively).

The more interesting assumptions in the environment for typing *ebay* are (we omit the end terminators):

$paypal : [?(int_1).?(string_3)]_3,\quad card : [?(int_1).?(int_3)]_3,$

$pay : [?(int_1).\uplus\{2 \propto \&\{(\mathsf{cheque}):?(string_2), (\mathsf{card}):?(int_2), (\mathsf{paypal}):?(string_2)\},$
$3 \propto \&\{(\mathsf{cheque}):?(string_2), (\mathsf{card}):?(int_3), (\mathsf{paypal}):?(string_3)\}\}]_2,$

$$\begin{array}{ll} \text{end} \, \lessdot \, T & T \, \lessdot \, T \\ T \, \lessdot \, ?(S_\ell).T & T \, \lessdot \, !(S_\ell).T \\ T_i \, \lessdot \, \&\{l_1 \, : \, T_1, \ldots, l_n \, : \, T_n\} \, T_i \, \lessdot \, \oplus\{l_1 \, : \, T_1, \ldots, l_n \, : \, T_n\} \\ T \, \lessdot \, \uplus\{\ell_1 \propto T, \ldots, \ell_n \propto T\} \end{array}$$

Fig. 11. Subtyping Relation $\lessdot$

$ebay : [\uplus\{1 \propto T(1), 2 \propto T(2), 3 \propto T(3)\}]_1,$
where $T(\ell) = \&\{(\text{browse}) \quad :?(string_1).!(int_1).?(int_1), (\text{bid}) \quad :$
$?(int_1).?(int_1).?(string_\ell),$
$(\text{buy}) :?(int_1).?(string_\ell)\}.$

Notice that although some options reserved for high users are formally (in name) present among the lower level choices, the actual activation of high–level services and communication of high–level data is reserved for high users.

5   Properties

Firstly, we will discuss the Subject Reduction property, namely that typability of expressions is preserved by the reduction relation. Due to space limitations, the auxiliary properties, such as strengthening, weakening and substitution will be omitted, as they are quite standard. In Figure 11 we introduce the relation $\lessdot$ in order to express the consumption of the session types by reduction.

Lemma (Replacement $\mathbb{C}$) 4.1. If $\Gamma \vdash \mathbb{C}[P] : U \therefore {}^{\imath_1}[T]_{\kappa_1}$, then there exist some $U', \imath', T', \kappa'$ such that $\Gamma \vdash P : U' \therefore {}^{\imath'}[T']_{\kappa'}$, and if there exists Q such that $\Gamma \vdash Q : U' \therefore {}^{\imath''}[T']_{\kappa''}$, $\imath'' \sqsubseteq \imath'$, $\kappa'' \sqsubseteq \kappa'$ then $\Gamma \vdash \mathbb{C}[Q] : U \therefore {}^{\imath_2}[T]_{\kappa_2}$ for some $\imath_2, \kappa_2$ such that $\imath_2 \sqsubseteq \imath_1$, $\kappa_2 \sqsubseteq \kappa_1$.

Proof. by induction on the structure of $\mathbb{C}$ and by compositionality of the type system. □

Lemma (Replacement $\mathbb{D}$) 4.2. If $\Gamma \vdash \mathbb{D}[P, Q] : U \therefore {}^{\imath}[T]_{\kappa}$, then there exist some $U_1, \imath_1, T_1, \kappa_1$ and $U_2, \imath_2, T_2, \kappa_2$ such that $\Gamma \vdash P : U_1 \therefore {}^{\imath_1}[T_1]_{\kappa_1}$ and $\Gamma \vdash Q : U_2 \therefore {}^{\imath_2}[T_2]_{\kappa_2}$ and if there exist P', Q' such that $\Gamma \vdash P' : U_1 \therefore {}^{\imath_3}[T_1]_{\kappa_3}$, and $\Gamma \vdash Q' : U_2 \therefore {}^{\imath_4}[T_2]_{\kappa_4}$ and $\imath_3 \sqsubseteq \imath_1$, $\kappa_3 \sqsubseteq \kappa_1$, $\imath_4 \sqsubseteq \imath_2$, $\kappa_4 \sqsubseteq \kappa_2$, then $\Gamma \vdash \mathbb{D}[P', Q'] : U \therefore {}^{\imath'}[T]_{\kappa'}$ for some $\imath', \kappa'$ such that $\imath' \sqsubseteq \imath$, $\kappa' \sqsubseteq \kappa$.

Proof. by induction on the structure of $\mathbb{D}$ and by compositionality of the type system. □

Lemma (Replacement $\mathbb{D}_r$) 4.3. If $\Gamma \vdash \mathbb{D}_r[P, Q] : U \therefore {}^{\imath}[T]_{\kappa}$, then there exist some $U_1, \imath_1, T_1, \kappa_1$ and $U_2, \imath_2, T_2, \kappa_2$ such that $\Gamma \vdash P : U_1 \therefore {}^{\imath_1}[T_1]_{\kappa_1}$ and $\Gamma \vdash Q : U_2 \therefore {}^{\imath_2}[T_2]_{\kappa_2}$ and, depending on the polarity, either $T_1 \leq \overline{T_2}$ or $T_2 \leq \overline{T_1}$ and if there exist P', Q' such that $\Gamma \vdash P' : U_3 \therefore {}^{\imath_3}[T_3]_{\kappa_3}$, and $\Gamma \vdash Q' : U_4 \therefore {}^{\imath_4}[T_4]_{\kappa_4}$ and $U_3 \lessdot U_1$, $T_3 \lessdot T_1$, $\imath_3 \sqsubseteq \imath_1$, $\kappa_3 \sqsubseteq \kappa_1$, $U_4 \lessdot U_2$, $T_4 \lessdot T_2$, $\imath_4 \sqsubseteq \imath_2$, $\kappa_4 \sqsubseteq \kappa_2$ and $T_3 \leq \overline{T_4}$ (if $T_1 \leq \overline{T_2}$) or $T_4 \leq \overline{T_3}$ (if $T_2 \leq \overline{T_1}$), then

(INV) $\mathbb{D}[\![\ell \blacktriangleleft \overline{s_{\ell'}}.P, s_{\ell'}.Q]\!] \to (\nu\, r_\ell)\, \mathbb{D}[\![r_\ell^- \rhd \ell \blacktriangleleft P, r_\ell^+ \rhd \ell \blacktriangleleft Q \mid s_{\ell'}.Q]\!] \quad \ell' \sqsubseteq \ell$
          $r_\ell \notin \mathrm{fn}(\mathbb{D}[\![\overline{s_{\ell'}}.P, s_{\ell'}.Q]\!])$

(COM) $\mathbb{D}_{r_\ell}[\![\ell \blacktriangleleft (x_\imath).P, \ell \blacktriangleleft \langle v_\imath\rangle.Q]\!] \to \mathbb{D}_{r_\ell}[\![\ell \blacktriangleleft P[^{v_\imath}/x_\imath], \ell \blacktriangleleft Q]\!] \quad \imath \sqsubseteq \ell$

(LCOM) $\mathbb{D}_{r_\ell}[\![\ell \blacktriangleleft \sum_{i=1}^n (l_i).P_i, \ell \blacktriangleleft \langle l_k\rangle.Q]\!] \to \mathbb{D}_{r_\ell}[\![\ell \blacktriangleleft P_k, \ell \blacktriangleleft Q]\!]$

(RET) $\mathbb{D}_{r_{1\ell}}[\![\ell \blacktriangleleft (x_\imath).P, \mathbb{C}_{r_\ell^p}[\![\ell \blacktriangleleft \text{return } v_\imath.Q]\!]]\!] \to \mathbb{D}_{r_{1\ell}}[\![\ell \blacktriangleleft P[^{v_\imath}/x_\imath], \mathbb{C}_{r_\ell^p}[\![\ell \blacktriangleleft Q]\!]]\!] \quad \imath \sqsubseteq \ell \sqcap \ell'$

(PIPE) $\mathbb{C}[\![\ell \blacktriangleleft \langle v_\imath\rangle.P > x_\imath > Q]\!] \to \mathbb{C}[\![\ell \blacktriangleleft P > x_\imath > Q \mid \ell \blacktriangleleft Q[^{v_\imath}/x_\imath]]\!] \quad \imath \sqsubseteq \ell$

(PIPERET) $\mathbb{C}[\![\ell \blacktriangleleft \mathbb{C}_{r_\ell^p}[\![\ell \blacktriangleleft \text{return } v_\imath.P]\!] > x_\imath > Q]\!]$
                   $\to \mathbb{C}[\![\ell \blacktriangleleft \mathbb{C}_{r_\ell^p}[\![\ell \blacktriangleleft P]\!] > x_\imath > Q \mid \ell \blacktriangleleft Q[^{v_\imath}/x_\imath]]\!] \quad \imath \sqsubseteq \ell \sqcap \ell'$

(IFT) $\mathbb{C}[\![\ell \blacktriangleleft \text{if } u_\imath = v_\jmath \text{ then } P \text{ else } Q]\!] \to \mathbb{C}[\![\ell \blacktriangleleft P]\!] \quad (u_\imath = v_\jmath) \downarrow \text{true}$

(IFF) $\mathbb{C}[\![\ell \blacktriangleleft \text{if } u_\imath = v_\jmath \text{ then } P \text{ else } Q]\!] \to \mathbb{C}[\![\ell \blacktriangleleft Q]\!] \quad (u_\imath = v_\jmath) \downarrow \text{false}$

(LEVSEL) $\mathbb{C}[\![\ell \blacktriangleleft \biguplus_{i=1}^n \ell_i \ltimes P_i]\!] \to \mathbb{C}[\![\ell \blacktriangleleft P_i]\!] \quad \text{if } \ell_i \sqsubseteq \ell$

(SCOP) $P \to P' \Rightarrow (\nu\, m)\, P \to (\nu\, m)\, P'$

(STR) $P \equiv P' \wedge P' \to Q' \wedge Q' \equiv Q \Rightarrow P \to Q$

Fig. 12. Labeled Operational Semantic Rules

(INVERR) $\mathbb{D}[\![\ell \blacktriangleleft \overline{s_{\ell'}}.P, s_{\ell'}.Q]\!] \xrightarrow{\text{error}} \quad\quad\quad\quad \ell' \not\sqsubseteq \ell$

(COMERR) $\mathbb{D}_{r_\ell}[\![\ell \blacktriangleleft (x_\imath).P, \ell \blacktriangleleft \langle v_\imath\rangle.Q]\!] \xrightarrow{\text{error}} \quad\quad \imath \not\sqsubseteq \ell$

(RETERR) $\mathbb{D}_{\tilde{r}_{\ell'}}[\![\ell' \blacktriangleleft (x_\imath).P, \mathbb{C}_{r_\ell^p}[\![\ell \blacktriangleleft \text{return } v_\imath.Q]\!]]\!] \xrightarrow{\text{error}} \imath \not\sqsubseteq \ell \sqcap \ell'$

(PIPEERR) $\mathbb{C}[\![\ell \blacktriangleleft \langle v_\imath\rangle.P > x_\imath > Q]\!] \xrightarrow{\text{error}} \quad\quad\quad \imath \not\sqsubseteq \ell$

(PIPERETERR) $\mathbb{C}[\![\ell' \blacktriangleleft \mathbb{C}_{r_\ell^p}[\![\ell \blacktriangleleft \text{return } v_\imath.P]\!] > x_\imath > Q]\!] \xrightarrow{\text{error}} \imath \not\sqsubseteq \ell \sqcap \ell'$

(IFERR) $\mathbb{C}[\![\ell \blacktriangleleft \text{if } u_\imath = v_\jmath \text{ then } P \text{ else } Q]\!] \xrightarrow{\text{error}} \quad \imath \sqcup \jmath \not\sqsubseteq \ell$

(LEVSELERR) $\mathbb{C}[\![\ell \blacktriangleleft \biguplus_{i=1}^n \ell_i \ltimes P_i]\!] \xrightarrow{\text{error}} \quad\quad\quad \forall i (1 \leq i \leq n).\ell_i \not\sqsubseteq \ell$

Fig. 13. Security Errors

$\Gamma \vdash \mathbb{D}_r[\![P', Q']\!] : U' \mathrel{\therefore}^{\imath'} [T']_{\kappa'}$ for some $U' \mathrel{\therefore}^{\imath'} [T']_{\kappa'}$ such that $U' \lessdot U, T' \lessdot T$, $\imath' \sqsubseteq \imath, \kappa' \sqsubseteq \kappa$.

Proof. by induction on the structure of $\mathbb{D}_r$ and by compositionality of the type system.   □

Proposition (Subject Reduction) 4.4. If $\Gamma \vdash_S P : U \mathrel{\therefore}^{\imath} [T]_{\kappa}$, and $P \to P'$ then there exist $U', \imath', T', \kappa'$ such that $U' \lessdot U, T' \lessdot T, \imath' \sqsubseteq \imath, \kappa' \sqsubseteq \kappa$ and $\Gamma \vdash_S P' : U' \mathrel{\therefore}^{\imath'} [T']_{\kappa'}$.

Proof. by case analysis of the reduction rules given in Figure 2, using Lemmas 4.1, 4.2 and 4.3. For illustration purpose, we give the proof for the case (LEVSEL).

Case (LevSel): From the typing of the l.h.s.:

$$\cfrac{\cfrac{\Gamma \vdash P_i : \text{end} \mathrel{\therefore}^{\perp} [T]_{\kappa_i} \quad \kappa_i \sqsubseteq \ell_i \quad (1 \leq i \leq n) \quad \exists j (1 \leq j \leq n).\ell_1 \sqcap \ldots \sqcap \ell_n = \ell_j}{\Gamma \vdash \biguplus_{i=1}^n \ell_i \ltimes P_i : \text{end} \mathrel{\therefore}^{\perp} [\uplus\{\ell_1 \propto T, \ldots, \ell_n \propto T\}]_{\ell_1 \sqcap \ldots \sqcap \ell_n}} \text{(LevSel)} \quad \ell_j \sqsubseteq \ell}{\Gamma \vdash_{\emptyset} \ell \blacktriangleleft \biguplus_{i=1}^n \ell_i \ltimes P_i : \text{end} \mathrel{\therefore}^{\perp} [\text{end}]_\ell} \text{(LevSign)}$$

and the condition $\ell_i \sqsubseteq \ell$ we get $\kappa_i \sqsubseteq \ell$ and then we can type the r.h.s. as follows:

$$\cfrac{\Gamma \vdash P_i : \text{end} \mathrel{\therefore}^{\perp} [T]_{\kappa_i} \quad \kappa_i \sqsubseteq \ell}{\Gamma \vdash_{\emptyset} \ell \blacktriangleleft P_i : \text{end} \mathrel{\therefore}^{\perp} [\text{end}]_\ell} \text{(LevSign)}$$

                                                                         □

From an access control point of view, clients are regarded as "subjects", and services and basic values as "objects". Therefore, a client is required to possess an appropriate clearance to activate a service or to communicate a value. On the other hand, services are regarded as trusted entities, and they are allowed to act on behalf of the client who invoked them (this is reflected in the operational semantics, where the body process of the service definition "inherits" the clearance from the client after the activation).

A process can be active (or running) only in the scope of a security framing. In fact, the reduction rules from Figure 2 can be redefined with explicit notion of reduction under the security frame, and decorating the values with their security levels. This reduction relation is given in Figure 12.

This allows a straightforward definition of *security error*, given in Figure 13. A process runs in a security error in the following cases:

1. when it tries to activate a service with a level not below its clearance;
2. when it tries to communicate a value with a level not below its clearance in the current session;
3. when it tries to return a value with a level not below its clearance toward the parent session;
4. when it tries to communicate a value with a level not below its clearance to a pipe;
5. when it uses values with a level not below its clearance in the control expression of conditional branching;
6. when it enters into the level branching where all the levels are not below its clearance.

This allows us to express the main result of this paper as a type safety property in the following theorem.

Theorem 4.5. Typable processes do not run into security errors.

Proof. by contradiction and case analysis of the reduction rules given in Figure 13. In each case we show the subdeductions which assure the required order between security levels.

Case (InvErr)

$$\dfrac{\dfrac{\Gamma \vdash P : \text{end} \therefore {}^{\perp}[T]_\kappa \quad \Gamma \vdash v_{\ell'} : [\overline{T'}]_{\ell'} \quad T' \leq T}{\Gamma \vdash \overline{v}.P : \text{end} \therefore {}^{\perp}[\text{end}]_{\kappa \sqcup \ell' \sqcup \imath} \quad (\text{Inv}) \quad \kappa \sqcup \ell' \sqcup \imath \sqsubseteq \ell}{\Gamma \vdash_{\emptyset} \ell \blacktriangleleft \overline{v_{\ell'}}.P : \text{end} \therefore {}^{\perp}[\text{end}]_\ell} \quad (\text{LevSign})$$

As it can be seen, the typing rule ensures that $\ell' \sqsubseteq \kappa \sqcup \ell' \sqcup \imath \sqsubseteq \ell$.

Case (ComErr)

$$\dfrac{\dfrac{\Gamma, x_\imath : S_\imath \vdash P : U \therefore {}^{\jmath}[T]_\kappa}{\Gamma \vdash (x_\imath).P : U \therefore {}^{\jmath}[?(S_\imath).T]_{\kappa \sqcup \imath}} \quad (\text{Inp}) \quad \kappa \sqcup \jmath \sqcup \imath \sqsubseteq \ell}{\Gamma, r : [T']_\ell \vdash r^p \triangleright \ell \blacktriangleleft (x_\imath).P : \text{end} \therefore {}^{\perp}[U]_\ell} \quad (\text{Sess})$$

where $T' = \begin{cases} T, & \text{if } p = + \\ T', \ T' \leq T, & \text{if } p = - \end{cases}$. We get $\imath \sqsubseteq \kappa \sqcup \jmath \sqcup \imath \sqsubseteq \ell$.

Case (RetErr): As in previous case the typing of $\tilde{r}^{p_1}_{\ell'} \triangleright \ell' \blacktriangleleft (x_\imath).P$ assures $\imath \sqsubseteq \ell'$. Moreover we have:

$$\frac{\dfrac{\Gamma \vdash Q : U \therefore {}^{\jmath}[T]_\kappa \quad \Gamma \vdash v_\imath : S_\imath}{\Gamma \vdash \text{return } v_\imath.Q :\,!(S_\imath).U \therefore {}^{\imath \sqcup \jmath}[T]_\kappa} \text{ (Ret)} \quad \imath \sqcup \jmath \sqcup \kappa \sqsubseteq \ell}{\Gamma, r : [T']_\ell \vdash r^p \triangleright \ell \blacktriangleleft \text{return } v_\imath.Q : \text{end} \therefore {}^{\perp}[!(S_\imath).U]_\ell} \text{ (Sess)}$$

where $T' = \begin{cases} T, & \text{if } p = + \\ T', \ T' \leq T, & \text{if } p = - \end{cases}$, which implies $\imath \sqsubseteq \imath \sqcup \jmath \sqcup \kappa \sqsubseteq \ell$.

Case (PipeErr)

$$\frac{\dfrac{\Gamma \vdash P : \text{end} \therefore {}^{\perp}[!(S_\imath)^{n-1}.\text{end}]_\kappa \quad \Gamma \vdash v : S_\imath}{\Gamma \vdash \langle v_\imath \rangle.P : \text{end} \therefore {}^{\perp}[!(S_\imath)^{n}.\text{end}]_{\kappa \sqcup \imath}} \text{ (Out)} \quad \Gamma, v_\imath : S_\imath \vdash Q : \text{end} \therefore {}^{\perp}[T']_{\kappa'}}{\dfrac{\Gamma \vdash \langle v_\imath \rangle.P > x > Q : \text{end} \therefore {}^{\perp}[T']_{\kappa \sqcup \imath \sqcup \kappa'}}{\Gamma \vdash_{\emptyset} \ell \blacktriangleleft \langle v_\imath \rangle.P > x_\imath > Q : \text{end} \therefore {}^{\perp}[U]_\ell}} \text{ (Pipe)} \quad \kappa \sqcup \imath \sqcup \kappa' \sqsubseteq \ell$$

(LevSign)

which implies $\imath \sqsubseteq \kappa \sqcup \imath \sqcup \kappa' \sqsubseteq \ell$.

Case (PipeRetErr): The reasoning is similar to that of cases (RetErr) and (PipeErr).

Case (IfErr)

$$\frac{\dfrac{\Gamma \vdash v_i : S_{\ell_i} \quad \Gamma \vdash P : \text{end} \therefore {}^{\perp}[\text{end}]_\jmath \quad \Gamma \vdash Q : \text{end} \therefore {}^{\perp}[\text{end}]_\kappa \quad \ell_i \sqsubseteq \jmath \sqcap \kappa \quad i = 1, 2}{\Gamma \vdash \text{if } v_1 = v_2 \text{ then } P \text{ else } Q : \text{end} \therefore {}^{\perp}[\text{end}]_{\jmath \sqcup \kappa}} \text{ (If)} \quad \jmath \sqcup \kappa \sqsubseteq \ell}{\Gamma \vdash_{\emptyset} \ell \blacktriangleleft \text{if } v_1 = v_2 \text{ then } P \text{ else } Q : \text{end} \therefore {}^{\perp}[\text{end}]_\ell} \text{ (LevSign)}$$

Note that $\ell_i \sqsubseteq \jmath \sqcap \kappa \sqsubseteq \jmath \sqcup \kappa \sqsubseteq \ell$.

Case (LevSelErr)

$$\frac{\dfrac{\Gamma \vdash P_i : \text{end} \therefore {}^{\perp}[T]_{\kappa_i} \quad \kappa_i \sqsubseteq \ell_i \quad (1 \leq i \leq n) \quad \exists j(1 \leq j \leq n).\ell_1 \sqcap \ldots \sqcap \ell_n = \ell_j}{\Gamma \vdash \uplus^n_{i=1} \ell_i \ltimes P_i : \text{end} \therefore {}^{\perp}[\uplus\{\ell_1 \propto T, \ldots, \ell_n \propto T\}]_{\ell_j}} \text{ (LevSel)} \quad \ell_j \sqsubseteq \ell}{\Gamma \vdash_{\emptyset} \ell \blacktriangleleft \uplus^n_{i=1} \ell_i \ltimes P_i : \text{end} \therefore {}^{\perp}[\text{end}]_\ell} \text{ (LevSign)}$$

$\square$

We conclude by stating the progress property. The proof of this property is similar to the one given in [8], taking into account that the security constructs and annotations do not lead to stuck states by Theorem 4.5.

Definition (Normal Form) 4.6. A process P is in *normal form* if $P \equiv (\nu\, s_1) \ldots (\nu\, s_n) \prod^n_{i=1}(s_i.Q_i)$.

Theorem (Progress) 4.7. If P is a top level process s.t. $\emptyset \vdash_{\emptyset} P : \text{end} \therefore {}^{\perp}[\text{end}]_\kappa$, then for each Q s.t. $P \to^* Q$, either Q is reducible or Q is in normal form.

6   Conclusion

This paper addresses security issues in a calculus for services and pipelines (CaSPiS) by employing static analysis access control methodology, and by offering increased modularity of the services with options of different behaviours of a service depending on the privileges of the client who activated it. The type system ensures at compile time that a service can be activated only by clients with appropriate clearance, while preserving the safety and progress properties of previous versions of CaSPiS.

The approach in this paper was to consider mandatory access control, with no mechanisms of access right elevation or demotion. A next step might be to consider discretionary access control with a possibility of permission passing among subjects.

Acknowledgments. I would like to thank Mariangiola Dezani for her invaluable advice, directions and assistance throughout the genesis of this work. The present version of this paper strongly improved with respect to the submitted one thanks to referee suggestions.

References

1. Acciai, L., Boreale, M.: A Type System for Client Progress in a Service-Oriented Calculus. In: Degano, P., De Nicola, R., Meseguer, J. (eds.) Concurrency, Graphs and Models. LNCS, vol. 5065, pp. 642–658. Springer, Heidelberg (2008)
2. Banerjee, A., Naumann, D.A.: A Simple Semantics and Static Analysis for Java Security. Technical Report 2001-1, Stevens Institute of Technology (2001)
3. Bell, D.E., LaPadula, L.J.: Secure Computer Systems: Mathematical Foundations. Technical Report MTR-2547, Vol. 1, MITRE Corp., Bedford, MA (1973)
4. Bonelli, E., Compagnoni, A., Gunter, E.: Correspondence assertions for process synchronization in concurrent communications. J. Funct. Program. 15(2), 219–247 (2005)
5. Boreale, M., Bruni, R., Nicola, R.D., Lanese, I., Loreti, M., Montanari, U., Sangiorgi, D., Zavattaro, G.: SCC: a Service Centered Calculus. In: ACSAC 2006. LNCS, vol. 4186, pp. 38–57. Springer, Heidelberg (2006)
6. Boreale, M., Bruni, R., Nicola, R.D., Loreti, M.: Sessions and Pipelines for Structured Service Programming. In: Barthe, G., de Boer, F.S. (eds.) FMOODS 2008. LNCS, vol. 5051, pp. 19–38. Springer, Heidelberg (2008)
7. Boudol, G., Kolundzija, M.: Access Control and Declassification. In: Computer Network Security. CCIS, vol. 1, pp. 85–98. Springer, Heidelberg (2007)
8. Bruni, R., Mezzina, L.G.: Types and Deadlock Freedom in a Calculus of Services, Sessions and Pipelines. In: Meseguer, J., Roşu, G. (eds.) AMAST 2008. LNCS, vol. 5140, pp. 100–115. Springer, Heidelberg (2008)
9. Denning, D.E.: A lattice model of secure information flow. Comm. of the ACM 19(5), 236–243 (1976)
10. Dezani-Ciancaglini, M., de' Liguoro, U., Yoshida, N.: On Progress for Structured Communications. In: Barthe, G., Fournet, C. (eds.) TGC 2007 and FODO 2008. LNCS, vol. 4912, pp. 257–275. Springer, Heidelberg (2008)

11. Dezani-Ciancaglini, M., Mostrous, D., Yoshida, N., Drossopoulou, S.: Session Types for Object-Oriented Languages. In: Thomas, D. (ed.) ECOOP 2006. LNCS, vol. 4067, pp. 328–352. Springer, Heidelberg (2006)
12. Fournet, C., Gordon, A.D.: Stack Inspection: Theory and Variants. In: POPL 2002, pp. 307–318 (2002)
13. Gay, S., Hole, M.: Subtyping for Session Types in the pi Calculus. Acta Inf. 42(2), 191–225 (2005)
14. Honda, K., Vasconcelos, V.T., Kubo, M.: Language Primitives and Type Disciplines for Structured Communication-based Programming. In: Hankin, C. (ed.) ESOP 1998. LNCS, vol. 1381, pp. 122–138. Springer, Heidelberg (1998)
15. Kitchin, D., Cook, W.R., Misra, J.: A Language for Task Orchestration and Its Semantic Properties. In: Baier, C., Hermanns, H. (eds.) CONCUR 2006. LNCS, vol. 4137, pp. 477–491. Springer, Heidelberg (2006)
16. Lanese, I., Vasconcelos, V.T., Martins, F., Ravara, A.: Disciplining Orchestration and Conversation in Service-Oriented Computing. In: SEFM 2007, pp. 305–314. IEEE Computer Society Press, Los Alamitos (2007)
17. Lapadula, A., Pugliese, R., Tiezzi, F.: A Calculus for Orchestration of Web Services. In: De Nicola, R. (ed.) ESOP 2007. LNCS, vol. 4421, pp. 33–47. Springer, Heidelberg (2007)
18. Pottier, F., Skalka, C., Smith, S.: A Systematic Approach to Static Access Control. ACM TOPLAS 27(2) (2005)
19. Skalka, C., Smith, S.: Static Enforcement of Security with Types. ACM SIGPLAN Notices 35(9), 34–45 (2000)
20. Volpano, D., Smith, G., Irvine, C.: A Sound Type System for Secure Flow Analysis. J. Computer Security 4(3), 167–187 (1996)
21. Zdancewic, S.: Programming Languages for Information Security. PhD thesis, Cornell University (2002)

Why Does My Service Have No Partners?

Niels Lohmann

Universität Rostock, Institut für Informatik, 18051 Rostock, Germany
niels.lohmann@uni-rostock.de

Abstract. Controllability is a fundamental correctness criterion for interacting service models. A service model is controllable if there exists a partner service such that their composition is free of deadlocks and livelocks. Whereas controllability can be automatically decided, the existing decision algorithm gives no information about the reasons of why a service model is uncontrollable. This paper introduces a diagnosis framework to find these reasons which can help to fix uncontrollable service models.

Keywords: Controllability, diagnosis, partner synthesis, verification.

1 Introduction

In the paradigm of service-oriented computing [1,2], a *service* is an component that offers a functionality over a well-defined interface and is discoverable and accessible via a unique identifier. By composing several services, complex tasks (e. g., inter-organizational business processes) can be realized. Thereby, the correct interplay of distributed services is crucial to achieve a common goal.

A fundamental correctness criterion for a service model is *controllability* [3]: A service S is controllable if there exists a partner service S' such that their composition is free of deadlocks and livelocks; that is, a desired final state is always reachable. The algorithm proposed to decide controllability [3] is constructive: If a partner service for S exists, it can be synthesized and serves as a witness for the controllability of S. If, however, S is uncontrollable, such a partner service does not exist and the decision algorithm returns no service. Obviously, this does not give any information about the reasons of *why* S is uncontrollable. Nevertheless, diagnosis information are important to support the modeller to correct the ill-designed service (see [4] for first results on service correction).

Controllability of a service model has a close relationship to soundness in the area of workflow models [5]. Intuitively, for a controllable service exists another service that their composition is a sound workflow. However, existing diagnosis techniques for unsound workflow models [6] are not applicable to diagnose uncontrollability, because the service's environment has to be taken into account.

In this paper, we study the reasons of uncontrollability and define a diagnosis algorithm that calculates a counterexample why a service model is uncontrollable. This counterexample can be used to repair the service model towards controllability. The paper employs *open nets* [7], a class of Petri nets [8], as formal model. With translations [9,10] from and to WS-BPEL [11], the results can be directly applied to industrial service specification languages.

R. Bruni and K. Wolf (Eds.): WS-FM 2008, LNCS 5387, pp. 191–206, 2009.

The rest of this paper is organized as follows. The next section recalls the required definitions on open nets, controllability and its decision algorithm. These definitions are crucial to understand the diagnosis framework and therefore are quite detailed. Reasons that can make a net uncontrollable are described in Section 3. The main contribution of this paper is a diagnosis algorithm for uncontrollable nets which is described in Section 4. Section 5 concludes the paper and gives directions for future research.

2   Formal Models for Services

2.1   Open Nets

Open nets [7] extend classical Petri nets [8] with an interface for asynchronous message exchange. We assume the standard firing rule and denote the set of all markings of a net N that are reachable from m with $\mathcal{R}_N(m) = \{m' \mid m \xrightarrow{*}_N m'\}$. $m \xrightarrow{t}_N$ denotes that in N, the marking m enables the transition t, and $m \not\rightarrow_N$ denotes that m does not activate any transition (i.e., m is a deadlock).

Definition 1 (Open Net, inner structure). *An* open net *is a Petri net* $N = [P, T, F, m_0]$, *together with an* interface $I = P_{in} \cup P_{out}$ *such that* $P_{in}, P_{out} \subseteq P$, $P_{in} \cap P_{out} = \emptyset$, *and* $p \in P_{in}$ *(resp.* $p \in P_{out}$*) implies* $^\bullet p = \emptyset$ *(resp.* $p^\bullet = \emptyset$*); and a set* Ω *of* final markings. P_{in} *(resp.* P_{out}*) is called the set of* input *(resp.* output*) places. We further require that* $m(p) = 0$ *for all* $p \in I$ *and* $m \in \Omega \cup \{m_0\}$, *and that no marking* $m_f \in \Omega$ *enables a transition.* N *is called* closed *iff* $|I| = \emptyset$. N *is called* normal *iff every transition of* N *is connected to at most one interface place. For a normal net* N, *define the mapping* $\ell : T \rightarrow I \cup \{\tau\}$ *such that* $\ell(t)$ *is the interface place connected to* t *if one exists, and* $\ell(t) = \tau$ *otherwise. The* inner structure *of* N *is the closed net* $Inner(N) = [P \setminus I, T, F \setminus ((I \times T) \cup (T \times I)), m_{0|P \setminus I}, \emptyset, \emptyset, \Omega_{|P \setminus I}]$.

The interface places are unidirectional: messages sent to N or received from N cannot be "unsent" or "unreceived", respectively. The inner structure of N models the control flow of N and can be compared to a classical workflow net [5].[1] In the rest of this paper, we only consider normal open nets. This restriction is rather technical, because every open net can be transformed [12] into a normal open net, and nets translated [9] from WS-BPEL processes are normal by construction.

Figure 1(a) depicts an open net N_1. We follow the standard graphical notation for Petri nets. The initial marking $m_0 = [\alpha]$ is depicted by a token on place α. We further assume $\Omega = \{[\omega]\}$ to be the set of final markings. Interface places $(I = \{a, b, c, d\})$ are located on the dashed frame, and the transition label $\ell(t)$ is written inside the respective transition t.

An open net N is *bounded* iff $\mathcal{R}_{Inner(N)}(m_{0|Inner(N)})$ is finite. Throughout this paper, we only consider bounded open nets, because for unbounded nets,

---

[1] Open nets do not share the structural constraints of workflow nets and allow arbitrary initial and final markings.

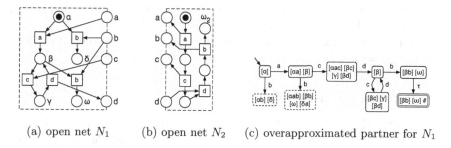

(a) open net N_1 (b) open net N_2 (c) overapproximated partner for N_1

Fig. 1. Two open nets and an overapproximated partner

controllability is undecidable [13]. Boundedness can be verified using standard state space verification techniques [14]. Again, open nets translated from WS-BPEL processes are bounded by construction. See [9] for details.

Open nets can be composed by connecting the interfaces appropriately:

Definition 2 (Composition). *Two open nets N_1 and N_2 are composable iff $P_{in1} = P_{out2}$, $P_{out1} = P_{in2}$, $P_1 \cap P_2 = I_1 \cup I_2 \neq \emptyset$, and $T_1 \cap T_2 = \emptyset$. The composition of two composable open nets N_1 and N_2, denoted $N_1 \oplus N_2$, is the closed net with the following constituents: $P = P_1 \cup P_2$, $T = T_1 \cup T_2$, $F = F_1 \cup F_2$, $m_0 = m_{01} \oplus m_{02}$, $P_{in} = P_{out} = \emptyset$, and $\Omega = \{m_{f1} \oplus m_{f2} \mid m_{f1} \in \Omega_1, m_{f2} \in \Omega_2\}$. The composition of markings is defined as $m_1 \oplus m_2(p) = m_1(p)$ if $p \in P_1$, and $m_1 \oplus m_2(p) = m_2(p)$, otherwise.*

Definition 3 (Trapped marking). *Let N be a normal open net. A strongly connected component (SCC) is a maximal set of markings $\mathcal{M}$ of N such that $m, m' \in \mathcal{M}$ implies $m \xrightarrow{*}_N m'$. A terminal SCC (TSCC) is a SCC from which no other SCC is reachable. A marking m of N is a trapped marking if $m \in \mathcal{M}$ for a TSCC $\mathcal{M}$ and $\mathcal{M} \cap \Omega_N = \emptyset$. If additionally $m_{|Inner(N)} \xrightarrow{t}_{Inner(N)}$, $m \not\xrightarrow{t}_N$, and $\ell(t) \cap P_{in} \neq \emptyset$ then m is a resolvable trapped marking and $\ell(t)$ resolves m. If no such t exists and $m_{|Inner(N)} \in \Omega_{Inner(N)}$, m is a covered final marking. If no such t exists and $m_{|Inner(N)} \notin \Omega_{Inner(N)}$, m is an unresolvable trapped marking.*

Resolvable trapped markings model situations the net can only leave with communication (i. e., message receipt). In contrast, unresolvable trapped markings can never be left. Covered final markings model situations in which the inner of an open net reached a final marking, but messages are still pending on some input places. Note that by definition of Ω, the TSCC of a covered final marking is a singleton; that is, a covered final marking is a deadlock.

Definition 4 (Weak termination, k-controllability, message bound). *A closed net N weakly terminates iff, for every marking $m \in \mathcal{R}_N(m_0)$, a final marking $m_f \in \Omega$ is reachable. A normal, bounded open net N is k-controllable for $k \in \mathbb{N}^+$ (called message bound) iff there exists a normal, bounded open net M such that N and M are composable, $N \oplus M$ weakly terminates, and for all $m \in \mathcal{R}_{N \oplus M}(m_{0N} \oplus m_{0M})$ holds that $m(p) \leq k$ for all $p \in I$.*

It is easy to check that the open nets N_1 and N_2 (see Fig. 1(a) and Fig. 1(b)) are bounded and composable. With $\Omega_{N_2} = \{[\omega_2]\}$, we have $\Omega_{N_1 \oplus N_2} = \{[\omega, \omega_2]\}$. The composition weakly terminates, and for all reachable markings m, it holds $m(p) \leq 1$ for all $p \in I_{N_1}$. Thus, the open net N_1 is 1-controllable.

2.2 Deciding Controllability

For the rest of this section, let N be a normal, bounded open net, and let $k \in \mathbb{N}^+$. In the following, we sketch the decision algorithm for controllability presented in [15] which extends the one of [3]. The next definition synthesizes a transition system as first overapproximation of a partner of N. Thereby, each state consists of a set of markings N can reach after each communication step. The element "#" is a special symbol to denote final states.

Definition 5 (Partner overapproximation TS_0). *For a set of markings $\mathcal{M}$ of N, define $closure(\mathcal{M}) = \bigcup_{m \in \mathcal{M}} \mathcal{R}_N(m)$. Let $TS_0 = [Q, E, q_0, Q_F]$ be a transition system (consisting of a set Q of states, a set $E \subseteq Q \times (I \cup \{\tau\}) \times Q$ of labeled edges, an initial state $q_0 \in Q$, and a set $Q_F \subseteq Q$ of final states) inductively defined as follows:*

1. *$q_0 = closure(\{m_0\})$; $q_0 \in Q$;*
2. *If $q \in Q$, then*
    (a) *if $\# \notin q$ and $q \cap \Omega \neq \emptyset$, then $q' = q \cup \{\#\} \in Q$, $q' \in Q_F$, and $[q, \tau, q'] \in E$;*
    (b) *if $m^* \in q$ is a resolvable trapped marking that can be resolved by x, $\# \notin q$, then $q' = closure(\{m + [x] \mid m \in q\}) \in Q$ and $[q, x, q'] \in E$;*
    (c) *if $m^* \in q$ with $m^*(x) > 0$ for an $x \in P_{out}$, then $q' = \{m - [x] \mid m \in q, m(x) > 0\} \setminus \{\#\} \in Q$ and $[q, x, q'] \in E$.*

Thereby, $[x]$ denotes the marking with $[x](x) = 1$ and $[x](y) = 0$ for $y \neq x$. The operations $+$ and $-$ on markings are defined pointwise.

A transition system TS can be composed with an open net N in a canonic way (see [12] for details). In particular, we identify states of $N \oplus TS$ with $[m, q]$ where m is a marking of N and $q \in Q$ is a state of TS. Thereby, a path σ in the transition system TS can be extended to the composition $N \oplus TS$. As each state of TS can contain multiple markings, this resulting path may not be unique.

The following definition removes all states from the overapproximation TS_0 that jeopardize weak termination of the composition $N \oplus TS_0$.

Definition 6 (Interaction graph TS^*). *Let TS_1 be the graph that is obtained from TS_0 by removing all states q that contain a marking m with $m(p) > k$ for a $p \in I_N$. Given TS_i $(i > 0)$, the graph TS_{i+1} is obtained by removing each state q from TS_i that contains a marking m where no state $[m_f, q_f]$ is reachable in $N \oplus TS_i$ from $[m, q]$ where $q_f \in Q_{F_{TS_i}}$ and $m_f \in \Omega$.*

Thereby, removal of a state includes removal of its adjacent arcs and all states that become unreachable from q_0. Let TS^* be TS_j for the smallest j with $TS_j = TS_{j+1}$. TS^* is the interaction graph *of N.*

Theorem 1. N is k-controllable iff $Q_{\mathcal{TS}^*} \neq \emptyset$.

A proof to a similar theorem can be found in [15]. Intuitively, each state that is removed in Def. 6 cannot be part of a controlling partner. Thereby, the step from $\mathcal{TS}_0$ to $\mathcal{TS}_1$ assert that the message bound is respected and all future state removals assert weak termination. Note that τ-edges are a necessary technicality to assure livelock freedom. The interested reader is referred to [15].

Figure 1(c) depicts $\mathcal{TS}_0$ for the open net N_1. This graph coincides with $\mathcal{TS}_1$, because no marking exceeds the message bound of $k = 1$. From $\mathcal{TS}_1$, the dashed states are removed, because they contain the unresolvable trapped markings $[\delta]$ and $[\delta a]$, respectively, from which the final marking is unreachable. The resulting graph without dashed states is the interaction graph $\mathcal{TS}^*$ of N_1. From this graph, we can conclude that a partner may only send a b-message after having received a d-message, because only then the partner can be sure that N_1 has left its initial marking. The open net N_2 (cf. Fig. 1(b)) models one possible partner of N_1.

3   Reasons for Uncontrollability

Obviously, the empty interaction graph (i. e., a graph with an empty set of states) calculated in case of uncontrollability gives no information why N has no partners and how N can be fixed. Before we examine uncontrollable nets, we study a related diagnosis approach.

3.1   Relationship to Soundness

For a controllable open net N exists an open net M such that $N \oplus M$ weakly terminates. Weak termination is closely related to soundness [5]. For soundness, an elaborate diagnosis algorithm exists [6] which exploits several properties of the soundness criterion to avoid a complex state space exploration where possible. For example, soundness can be expressed in terms of two simpler properties, namely liveness and boundedness. An unsound workflow net fails one of these tests. This result can be used to give detailed diagnosis information. In addition, several simple necessary or sufficient criteria for soundness can be checked prior to liveness and boundedness checks. For example, certain net classes such as free choice Petri nets [16] allow for efficient analysis algorithms.

However, this diagnosis approach cannot be adapted to diagnose the reasons of why an open net is uncontrollable. Firstly, a sound control flow is not related to controllability: the inner structure of the controllable net in Fig. 1(a) is not sound, and the uncontrollable net in Fig. 4(a) has a sound inner structure. Similarly, weaker criteria such as *relaxed soundness* or *non-controllable choice robustness* [17] are not applicable. The latter, for example, assumes that the environment (i. e., a partner) can completely observe the net's state, whereas the internal state of an open net can only be guessed from observations on the interface (a state of the interaction graph is a *set* of markings of the open net). Secondly, controllability is not a local, but a global criterion: controllability is now known to be decomposable. Therefore, only trivial necessary or sufficient

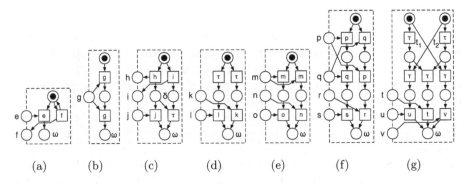

Fig. 2. Uncontrollable open nets ($k = 1$)

criteria for (un)controllability exists. Thirdly, structural results like the invariant calculus [18] are not applicable, because an open net usually deadlocks when considered in isolation.

3.2 Classifying Harmful Markings

During the construction of the interaction graph of N, states that contain a marking m^* that is considered harmful are iteratively removed. The nature of m^* can be mapped back to the open net under consideration to understand the reasons that led to uncontrollability:

Inappropriate Message Bound. The message bound k influences the removal of states of $\mathcal{TS}_0$ when constructing $\mathcal{TS}_1$. This removal can make states containing a final marking unreachable. There are two situations to consider:

Unbounded communication. If a message channel is unbounded (e. g., due to a loop of the open net in which it sends messages without waiting for acknowledgements), then obviously no partner can exist such that the composition is k-bounded. Figure 2(a) shows an example where the output place f is unbounded.

Exceeded message bound. If a net is k-controllable for some bound $k \in \mathbb{N}^+$, it is also l-controllable for any $l > k$. However, the converse does not hold: Figure 2(b) shows a net that is 2-controllable, but not 1-controllable, because the receipt of the first g-message cannot be enforced before sending a second g-message. Thus, even if a message bound exists for a net, it might be considered k-uncontrollable if the message bound k chosen for analysis is too small.

Unreachable Final Marking. Definition 6 removes all states of the composition from which a final marking is unreachable. This can be due to a deadlock or a livelock in the composition. From the nature of a trapped marking, we can derive different diagnosis information. Hence, we classify different kinds of trapped markings of N that can be reached while communicating with a partner (cf. Def. 3).

Unresolvable trapped markings. If the inner of the net reaches a deadlock (called an *internal deadlock*), it cannot be left by communication with a partner. There are different reasons the control flow can contain deadlocks:

- *Design flaws.* The reason of an internal deadlock can be a classical design flaw as known from unsound workflow nets. For example, the deadlock [δ] of the open net in Fig. 2(c) is caused by mismatching splits and joins and cannot be avoided by communication, because the net internally decides whether to send an h-message or an i-message.
- *Service choreographies.* Internal deadlocks need not stem from modeling errors. One source of internal deadlocks can also be the composition of several services[2] in a service choreography. There, it is possible that the behavior of two participants A and B is mutually exclusive which leads to an internal deadlock. This deadlock, however, might be avoided by the message exchange with another participant C. Then C is a controlling partner for $A \oplus B$.
- *Behavioral constraints.* Another reason for internal deadlocks that are no design flaws can be behavioral constraints [19]. Such a constraint C influences the control flow and the final markings of an open net N such that some final markings of N are considered as internal deadlocks in the constrained net N_C.

Covered final markings. A covered final marking models a situation in which the control flow of N reached a final marking, but a message sent to N is still pending on a channel and will never be received. This might be negligible for generic acknowledgement messages, but in general, an unreceived message models an undesired situation (e. g., if the message contains private or payment information). Again, there are numerous reasons for this problem:

- *Hidden choices.* The net can make an internal decision (e. g., with WS-BPEL's <if> activity) that is not communicated to the partner (thus hidden), but requires different reactions of the partner depending on the outcome of the decision. Consider for example the net in Fig. 2(d) which either chooses the left or the right branch. Depending on this choice, a partner has to send a k-message or an l-message. The final marking is only reached, if the partner's "guess" was right. Otherwise, the "wrong" message keeps pending.
- *Conflicting receives.* If the net can reach a marking in which more than one transition is activated that can receive the same message (e. g., the initial marking of the net in Fig. 2(e)), these transitions are "conflicting receives". The decision which of these transitions fires can neither be influenced nor observed by a partner yielding a "hidden choice" situation. Note that conflicting receives are treated as runtime faults in execution languages like WS-BPEL. Like internal deadlocks, we do not want to forbid such situations in the first place, but check whether these problems are actually the reason why a service is uncontrollable.
- *Pending messages.* Open nets model asynchronous message exchange: messages can keep pending on a channel, and overtake each other. Therefore, a

---

[2] Composition as defined in Def. 2 is restricted to exactly two services, but can be canonically extended to allow for composition of an arbitrary number of open nets.

partner has only limited control over the net, because after sending a message to N, a partner cannot be sure that N actually received that message. Again, this can result in a "hidden choice" situation, see the net in Fig. 2(f) for an example. For either branch, a p-message and a q-message message has to be sent eventually. After sending these messages, the environment has to guess whether to continue with sending an r-message or an s-message.

– *Confusion.* In a Petri net model, confusion [8] is a situation in which concurrency and conflicts coexist. Two concurrent transitions can influence each other without being in conflict; that is, whichever transition fires first can constrain the markings reachable by firing the other transition. Consider the net in Fig. 2(g) for an example: The transitions t_1 and t_2 are not in conflict, but whichever transition fires first, confines the choices reachable by firing the other transition. For example, firing first t_1 makes the firing of the transition receiving the v-message impossible. Now a partner has to guess whether to send a t-message or a u-message.

Livelocks. A livelock in the communication between N and a partner M is a situation in which in $N \oplus M$ transitions are fired continuously, but a final marking can never be reached. While this might be acceptable for technical systems where the concept of a "final state" is not applicable or irrelevant, services that implement business processes are usually required to reach a state in which a business instance is properly finished.

Note that the characterization of harmful markings as well as the definition of soundness is a behavioral and not a structural criterion. The nets depicted in Fig. 2 cannot be used as "anti-patters". If an open net contains one of these nets as a subnet, it might still be controllable. For example, prior communication might exclude the harmful subnet (e. g., using a deferred choice) or a concurrent or subsequent subnet "fixes" the communication of the net (e. g., by receiving pending message).

In the following section, we will present an algorithm to diagnose the problems described above except the problem of "unbounded communication". In the rest of this paper, we do not consider open nets without a fixed message bound. We assume that the message bound k is known prior to the controllability analysis. The value of k may be chosen by considerations on the physical message channels, by a static analysis that delivers a "sufficiently high" value, etc.

4   Diagnosing Reasons for Uncontrollability

4.1   Counterexamples for Controllability

In the area of computer-aided verification, model checking techniques [14] usually provide a *counterexample* if a model does not meet a specification. This counterexample is a useful artifact (e. g., a deadlock trace) to understand the reasons why the model contains an error. To find a counterexample for controllability is hard due to the criterion's nature. Controllability is "proven" by constructing a witness: N is k-controllable iff there *exists* some open net M such that the composition $N \oplus M$ is k-message bounded and weakly terminates. In other words, M can be seen as a counterexample for N's *uncontrollability*. If N is not controllable, we can only conclude that *no* such open net exists, and hence cannot provide a counterexample which can be used to find out which of the various problems we described in the last section rendered the net uncontrollable.

The algorithm to decide controllability (see Def. 5–6) overapproximates a partner for N and then iteratively removes states of this overapproximation that will not be part of any partner of N. If N is uncontrollable, all states will be eventually deleted. In this section, we define an algorithm to use information why states are deleted from TS_0 to give diagnosis information for an uncontrollable net N.

As a motivation for the desired style of diagnosis information, consider again the open net in Fig. 2(e). We already described the reason why this net is uncontrollable: after sending an m-message, a partner has to either send an n-message or an o-message to the net. Depending on the net's choice, a sent message might keep pending on its channel. This eventually yields a covered final marking. Let's analyze this informal description of why the net is uncontrollable: it contains of:

(I) an indisputable initial part ("after sending an m-message"),
(C) a description of continuations ("a partner has to either send an n-message or an o-message"), and
(P) the problem that hinders a partner to control the net to a final marking ("Depending on the net's choice, a sent message might keep pending on its channel. This eventually yields a covered final marking.").

The initial part (I) consists of communication steps that are necessary to resolve a resolvable trapped marking and that would also be taken by partner who *knows* the outcome of the net's decision in advance. Sending m is not source of the problem, because m *will* be received by the net. In contrast, after sending m, any continuation (C) *can* lead to a situation where reaching a final marking is not any more guaranteed. Finally, the possible problem that can occur if after sending either message is described (P).

In the following, we generalize this approach and define an algorithm that automatically derives such diagnosis results for an uncontrollable net N consisting of these three parts:

(I) From TS_0, we find a maximal subgraph TS_0^* such that the composition $N \oplus TS_0^*$ is free of markings from which markings with exceeded message bound (EMB), deadlocks/livelocks (DLL), or covered final markings (CFM) cannot be avoided any more. We use TS_0 as a starting point in order to consider all possible markings of N that can be reached with communication.
(C) The subgraph TS_0^* is not a partner of N, because its nodes contain resolvable trapped marking that are not resolved in TS_0^* (because the respective edge to a successor is missing). When these resolvable trapped markings are resolved by sending messages to N, the composition might reach a state from which EMB, DLL, or CFM cannot be avoided any more. Therefore, in the second part of the diagnosis result, each unresolved resolvable trapped marking is described including a communication trace from q_0 to the state containing this resolvable trapped marking.

(P) Finally, we give detailed information how the resolution of the resolvable trapped marking can reach EMB, DLL, or CFM in the composition. For each problem, witness paths to the problematic situation and/or pointers to the structure of N are given to locate the problem.

To derive these diagnosis information — our counterexample for controllability —, we first need a criterion to decide for each state of TS_0 whether it is a state of the subgraph TS_0^*, too. We already motivated that TS_0^* should only contain those states which only contain markings from which it is still possible to avoid EMB, DLL, and CFM problems. For each problem, it is possible to characterize situations in which the problem either already occurred (e. g., an unresolvable trapped marking is reached) or cannot be avoided any more (e. g., only one transition is activated whose firing results in an an unresolvable trapped marking). If such a situation is found in a state of TS_0, this state is obviously problematic. Thus, we define a blacklist for each problem that contains such problematic states. With these blacklists, we then can define the subgraph TS_0^*.

In addition, for each problem, we define a witness. A witness is an artifact that can help to visualize the problem (e. g., a trace to an internal deadlock that can be simulated) or to locate the parts of the uncontrollable net that cause the problem (e. g., the transitions modeling a hidden choice). In the next three subsections, we define a blacklist and a witness for each problem (EMB, DLL, or CFM). Finally, we sketch an algorithm that applies the blacklists to TS_0, analyzes the resulting subgraph TS_0^*, and provides diagnosis information.

4.2   Blacklist for Deadlocking and Livelocking Control Flow

Unresolvable trapped markings and covered final markings have the same property: once the composition $N \oplus TS_0$ reaches such a situation, a final marking becomes unreachable. Therefore, Def. 6 removes such states, because they jeopardize weak termination. However, the nature of these problems differ.

Unresolvable trapped markings model problems related to the control flow of N (modeled by $Inner(N)$). Therefore, detection and diagnosis of such control flow-related problems should differ from problems where the control flow of N already reached a final state, but an unreceived message is still pending on a channel. Hence, we differentiate unresolvable trapped markings from covered final markings.

We use the inner structure of N to detect markings from which a final marking is already unreachable. Any state of TS_0 is blacklisted if it contains a marking from which, when restricted to the inner of N, a final marking is unreachable:

Definition 7 (DLL-blacklist, DLL-witness). *Define the* blacklist *for a control flow deadlocks and livelocks as* $blacklist_{DLL} = \{q \in Q_0 \mid \exists m \in q : m$ *is an unresolvable trapped marking*$\}$.

For each state $q^* \in blacklist_{DLL}$, *define* $\sigma_{DLL}(q^*)$ *to be a witness path* $N \oplus TS_0$ *with* $[m_0, q_0] \xrightarrow{\sigma_{DLL}(q^*)} [m^*, q^*]$ *where* $m^* \in q^*$ *is an unresolvable trapped marking.*

In case m^* is a deadlock, the path $\sigma_{DLL}(q^*)$ is a witness path from the initial state of the composition to this deadlock. In case m^* is part of a livelock, any

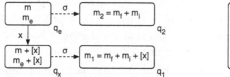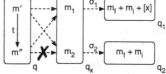

Fig. 3. Illustration of Lemma 1 (left) and a hidden choice transition of Def. 9 (right)

marking reachable from m^* is part of the same TSCC on which a final marking is unreachable and $\sigma_{DLL}(q^*)$ is a witness path for this TSCC.

4.3 Blacklist for Exceeded Message Bound

Markings that exceed the message bound k can be easily detected by analyzing the markings occurring in states of TS_0. The blacklist as well as the witness can be defined straightforwardly:

Definition 8 (EMB-blacklist, EMB-witness). *Define the* blacklist *for exceeded message bound as* $blacklist_{EMB} = \{q \in Q_0 \mid \exists m \in q : \exists p \in I : m(p) > k\}$. *For each state* $q^* \in blacklist_{EMB}$, *define* $\sigma_{EMB}(q^*)$ *to be a witness path in* $N \oplus TS_0$ *such that* $[m_0, q_0] \xrightarrow{\sigma_{EMB}(q^*)} [m^*, q^*]$ *with* $m^* \in q^*$ *with* $m^*(p) > k$.

The witness consists of a path in the composition that shows how the message bound of a place can be exceeded.

4.4 Blacklist for Covered Final Markings

In a covered final marking m_c reachable in $N \oplus TS_0$, the control flow (the inner structure of N) has reached a final marking, but a message is pending on an input channel. Due to the construction of TS_0 (cf. Def. 5(b)), this message was originally sent to N in order to resolve an resolvable trapped marking.

The following observation is needed to justify the later definition of a blacklist for covered final markings.

Lemma 1 (For each covered final marking there exists a final marking). *Let N be an open net and TS_0 as defined in Def. 5. Let q_1 be a state of TS_0 with a covered final marking $m_1 \in q_1$ with $m_1 = m_f + m_i + [x]$ such that $m_f \in \Omega$ is a final marking, m_i is a marking such that $m_i(p) > 0$ implies $p \in P_{in}$, and $[x]$ is a marking that marks an input place $x \in P_{in}$. Then exists a state q_2 of TS_0 containing a marking $m_2 \in q_2$ with $m_2 = m_f + m_i$.*

Proof. Let q_e and q_x be states of TS_0, let $[q_e, x, q_x]$ be an edge of TS_0, and let σ be a path from q_x to q_1 that does not contain an x-labeled edge. Let $m_1 = m_f + m_i + [x]$ be as above. The x-message is only sent to N in order to resolve an resolvable trapped marking (cf. Def. 5). Let $m_e \in q_e$ be such a resolvable trapped marking.

Let $m \in q_e$. Then $(m + [x]) \in q_x$. Let σ^* be an extension of σ to the composition $N \oplus TS_0$ such that $[(m + [x]), q_x] \xrightarrow{\sigma^*} [(m_f + m_i + [x]), q_1]$. This transition sequence σ^* does not contain a transition producing a token on x, because $\sigma^*_{|TS_0} = \sigma$ does not contain an x-labeled edge. Therefore, σ^* is realizable independently from the submarking $[x]$ of N; that is, σ^* is realizable *without* the submarking $[x]$. In particular, there exists a state q_2 of TS_0 such that $[m, q_e] \xrightarrow{\sigma^*} [(m_f + m_i), q_2]$.   □

Lemma 1 states that, for each covered final marking with a pending x-message occurring in a state of TS_0, there exists a state that contains a covered final marking (or a final marking if $m_i = []$) *without* that pending message. After iteratively applying Lemma 1, we can conclude that with each covered final marking occurring in TS_0, also a respective "uncovered" final marking is present in a state of TS_0.

Each application of Lemma 1 identifies an x-labeled edge from q_e to state q_x from which a state q_1 is reached that contains a covered final marking with a pending x-message. For state q_e, an alternative continuation to q_2 without an x-edge is possible. Figure 3(a) illustrates this.

Hence, such a state q_x should be considered critical which yields the following definition of a blacklist for covered final markings:

Definition 9 (CFM-blacklist, CFM-witness). *Define the* blacklist *for covered final markings,* $blacklist_{CFM}$, *to contain all states* $q_x \in Q_0$ *such that:*

– *there exists a state* q_1 *and a path* σ *in* TS_0 *with* $q_x \xrightarrow{\sigma} q_1$,
– $m_c \in q_1$ *is a covered final marking with* $m_c(x) > 0$ *for an input place* $x \in P_{in}$
– σ *does not contain an* x-labeled edge
– q_e *is a predecessor of* q_x *with an edge* $[q_e, x, q_x]$

For each state $q_x \in blacklist_{CFM}$, *define* $\sigma_{CFM}(q_x) = [\sigma_1, \sigma_2, T^*]$ *to be a witness where:*

– σ_1 *is a path in* $N \oplus TS_0$ *with* $[m_1, q_x] \xrightarrow{\sigma_1} [(m_f + m_i + [x]), q_1]$ *where* $m_1 \in q_x$,
– σ_2 *is a path in* $N \oplus TS_0$ *with* $[m_2, q_x] \xrightarrow{\sigma_2} [(m_f + m_i), q_2]$ *where* $m_2 \in q_x$ *such that* $\sigma_{1|N} = \sigma_{2|N}$, *and*
– *the set* T^* *containing all transitions* $t \in T$ *of* N *such that:*

  • *there exists a state* q *in* TS_0 *with* $m', m'' \in q$,
  • $[m', q] \xrightarrow{*} [m_1, q_x]$, $[m', q] \xrightarrow{*} [m_2, q_x]$, $[m', q] \xrightarrow{t} [m'', q]$,
  • $[m'', q] \xrightarrow{*} [m_1, q_x]$, *and* $[m'', q] \xrightarrow{\ast} \!\!\!\!\!/ \; [m_2, q_x]$.

A covered final marking is a situation that occurs when N is composed to a partner. With the help of Lemma 1, the blacklist for covered final markings can be defined only by checking markings of nodes of TS_0 and paths in TS_0. This can be easily done while building TS_0 instead of analyzing paths in $N \oplus TS_0$. Lemma 1 also allows for finding a set T^* of *hidden choice transitions* (see Fig. 3(b)) which model a hidden decision as described in Section 3.2. These transitions can be the starting point to repair the net to avoid the covered final marking.

Algorithm 1. Blacklist-based diagnosis for uncontrollable open nets

---

Input: uncontrollable, normal, and bounded open net N; message bound $k \in \mathbb{N}^+$
Output: diagnosis information why N is uncontrollable; subgraph TS_0^* of TS_0

1: calculate TS_0 from N
2: calculate $blacklist_{DLL}$ from $Inner(N)$
3: calculate $blacklist_{EMB}$ from TS_0
4: calculate $blacklist_{CFM}$ from TS_0

5: **if** q_0 is blacklisted **then**

6:   **if** $q_0 \in blacklist_{DL}$ **then**
7:     **print** "control flow deadlock or livelock reachable without interaction"
8:     **print** DL-witness $\sigma_{DL}(q_0)$

9:   **if** $q_0 \in blacklist_{EMB}$ **then**
10:     **print** "message bound of communication place p exceeded without interaction"
11:     **print** EMB-witness $\sigma_{EMB}(q_0)$

12: **else**

13:   **for all** states q reachable from q_0 by a sequence σ without visiting blacklisted states **do**
14:     **if** (state q is not blacklisted **and** no resolvable trapped marking in q is resolved) **then**
15:       **for all** resolvable trapped markings $m_e \in q$ where
           ($m_{e|Inner(N)}$ activates a transition t with $\ell(t) = x$ **and**
           state q_x reachable by edge $[q, x, q_x]$ is blacklisted) **do**

16:         **print** path σ from q_0 to q

17:         **if** $q_x \in blacklist_{DLL}$ **then**
18:           **print** "sending message x to N to resolve an resolvable trapped marking in q_e
               reachable by σ from q_0 can reach a control flow deadlock or livelock"
19:           **print** DLL-witness $\sigma_{DLL}(q_x)$

20:         **if** $q_x \in blacklist_{EMB}$ **then**
21:           **print** "sending message x to N to resolve an resolvable trapped marking in q_e
               reachable by σ from q_0 can exceed the message bound"
22:           **print** EMB-witness $\sigma_{EMB}(q_x)$

23:         **if** $q_x \in blacklist_{CFM}$ **then**
24:           **print** "message x necessary to resolve an resolvable trapped marking in q_e
               reachable by σ from q_0 might be left unreceived due to a hidden choice"
25:           **print** CFM-witness $\sigma_{EMB}(q_x)$

26:   **print** subgraph TS_0^* of TS_0 where all blacklisted states are removed

---

4.5   Blacklist-Based Diagnosis

With the definitions of the blacklists for deadlocks/livelocks, exceeded message bound, and covered final markings, we are able to define the subgraph (i. e., the counterexample for controllability of N) TS_0^* of TS_0 which only contains states that are not contained in any of the three blacklists.

Algorithm 1 combines the defined blacklists together with their witnesses, and gives information for each detected problem. After a preprocessing phase (line 1–4) in which TS_0 as well as the blacklists are calculated, the states of TS_0 are analyzed. Thereby, two cases are differentiated: if already the initial state of q_0 is blacklisted, then the open net reaches a problem independently of a partner. Covered final markings cannot occur in this setting. As a diagnosis information, the initial state q_0 and the respective problem(s) are printed (line 5–11). The rest of the algorithm (line 12–26) treats situations in which TS_0^* is nonempty.

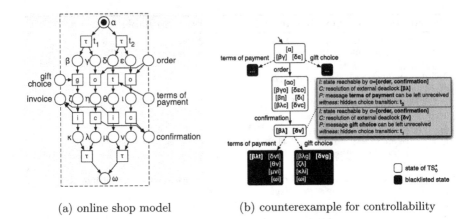

(a) online shop model   (b) counterexample for controllability

Fig. 4. Example for the application of Algorithm 1

The diagnosis messages can be classified into the three categories (initial part I, possible continuation C, and occurring problem P) as follows:

(I) line 26 prints the non-blacklisted subgraph TS_0^*,
(C) line 16 prints, for each resolvable trapped marking that is not resolved in TS_0^*, a communication trace from q_0 to the state containing the resolvable trapped marking,
(P) line 7–8, 10–11, 18–19, 21–22, and 24–25 print information about the problem that might be unavoidable after resolving the respective deadlock, including witnesses.

It is worth mentioning that the algorithm lists all problems that can occur if TS_0^* is "left" by resolving a deadlock. If, for example, sending an x-message in some state can result in a message bound violation *and* yield an internal deadlock, then both problems are reported.

4.6   Diagnosis Example

To demonstrate the proposed diagnosis framework, we applied Algorithm 1 to an uncontrollable net we presented and discussed in [20]. This net which is depicted in Fig. 4(a) is a model of a WS-BPEL online shop which after receiving a login message from a customer (not depicted in Fig. 4), internally decides whether to treat the customer as premium customer (t_1) or standard customer (t_2). As the customer is not informed about the outcome of the decision, the shop is uncontrollable, because either a message gift choice or terms of payment might be left unreceived. Experiments showed that even experienced Web service designers would consider the online shop as correct even when it is presented in other formalisms such as WS-BPEL or BPMN. This underlines the need for a diagnosis framework for such incorrect models, because concurrent control flow combined with asynchronous message flow is hard to oversee.

Figure 4(b) shows the result of Algorithm 1 when applied to the online shop model. It discovers the hidden choice modeled by transitions t_1 and t_2. These transitions can be used as a starting point to fix the online shop. If, for example, the outcome of the internal decision would be communicated to the customer (e. g., by adding two output places premium and standard which are connected to t_1 and t_2, resp.), the shop would be controllable.

4.7   Implementation of the Diagnosis Algorithm

The diagnosis algorithm is based on the partner overapproximation TS_0 which can be infinite if the net under consideration has no message bound (e. g., Fig. 2(a)). We already required that a message bound k is given for the analysis, so instead of first calculating TS_0 and then removing states with exceeded message bound, TS_1 can be calculated in the first place. In fact, this is exactly the way the controllability decision algorithm is implemented in the tool Fiona [20].

The diagnosis algorithm can be implemented straightforwardly. The set $blacklist_{DLL}$ can be calculated in a preprocessing stage. During the calculation of TS_1, $blacklist_{EMB}$ can be built whenever the currently calculated state contains a marking with exceeded message bound. Whenever a state with a covered final marking is detected, $blacklist_{CFM}$ can be filled according to the criteria of Lemma 1.

5   Conclusion

The concept of counterexamples greatly boosted the acceptance of model checking [14] in the field of computer-aided verification. However, the decision algorithm for controllability [3,15] does not give such counterexamples in case of uncontrollability. In this paper, we investigated uncontrollable service models and presented a variety of reasons why a service does not have any partners that interact deadlock and livelock freely. We presented an algorithm to analyze an uncontrollable service model to give diagnosis information *why* the model is uncontrollable. This diagnosis information can be a starting point for corrections [4] of the model towards controllability to meet this fundamental correctness criterion for service-oriented computing.

In future work, we plan to implement the diagnosis algorithm in the tool Fiona [20]. Fiona already implements some reduction techniques [21] to efficiently decide controllability. We will investigate whether these techniques can be combined with the diagnosis algorithm. As service models usually stem from industrial specification languages such as WS-BPEL, the retranslation of (Petri net-related) diagnosis information back into WS-BPEL is subject of future work. Together with the translations [9,10] from and to WS-BPEL, the diagnosis algorithm can be directly applied to industrial service specification languages.

Acknowledgements. The author wishes to thank Karsten Wolf for advice on the relationship to classical model checking and the anonymous referees for their valuable comments. Niels Lohmann is funded by the DFG project "Operating Guidelines for Services" (WO 1466/8-1).

References

1. Papazoglou, M.P.: Agent-oriented technology in support of e-business. Commun. ACM 44, 71–77 (2001)
2. Alonso, G., Casati, F., Kuno, H., Machiraju, V.: Web Services: Concepts, Architectures and Applications. Springer, Heidelberg (2003)
3. Schmidt, K.: Controllability of open workflow nets. In: EMISA 2005, GI. LNI, vol. P-75, pp. 236–249 (2005)
4. Lohmann, N.: Correcting deadlocking service choreographies using a simulation-based graph edit distance. In: Dumas, M., Reichert, M., Shan, M.-C. (eds.) BPM 2008. LNCS, vol. 5240, pp. 132–147. Springer, Heidelberg (2008)
5. van der Aalst, W.M.P.: The application of Petri nets to workflow management. Journal of Circuits, Systems and Computers 8, 21–66 (1998)
6. Verbeek, H.M.W., Basten, T., van der Aalst, W.M.P.: Diagnosing workflow processes using Woflan. Comput. J. 44, 246–279 (2001)
7. Massuthe, P., Reisig, W., Schmidt, K.: An operating guideline approach to the SOA. Annals of Mathematics, Computing & Teleinformatics 1, 35–43 (2005)
8. Reisig, W.: Petri Nets. EATCS Monographs on Theoretical Computer Science edn. Springer, Heidelberg (1985)
9. Lohmann, N.: A feature-complete Petri net semantics for WS-BPEL 2.0. In: Dumas, M., Heckel, R. (eds.) WS-FM 2007. LNCS, vol. 4937, pp. 77–91. Springer, Heidelberg (2008)
10. Lohmann, N., Kleine, J.: Fully-automatic translation of open workflow net models into simple abstract BPEL processes. In: Modellierung 2008, GI. LNI, vol. 127, pp. 57–72 (2008)
11. Alves, A., et al.: Web Services Business Process Execution Language Version 2.0. OASIS Standard, April 11. OASIS (2007)
12. Lohmann, N., Massuthe, P., Wolf, K.: Operating guidelines for finite-state services. In: Kleijn, J., Yakovlev, A. (eds.) ICATPN 2007. LNCS, vol. 4546, pp. 321–341. Springer, Heidelberg (2007)
13. Massuthe, P., Serebrenik, A., Sidorova, N., Wolf, K.: Can I find a partner? Undecidablity of partner existence for open nets. Inf. Process. Lett. (2008) (accepted)
14. Clarke, E.M., Grumberg, O., Peled, D.: Model Checking. MIT Press, Cambridge (2000)
15. Wolf, K.: Does my service have partners? In: Jensen, K., van der Aalst, W.M.P. (eds.) ToPNoC II. LNCS, vol. 5460, pp. 152–171. Springer, Heidelberg (2009)
16. Desel, J., Esparza, J.: Free Choice Petri Nets. Cambridge University Press, Cambridge (1995)
17. Dehnert, J., van der Aalst, W.M.P.: Bridging the gap between business models and workflow specifications. Int. J. Cooperative Inf. Syst. 13, 289–332 (2004)
18. Lautenbach, K., Ridder, H.: Liveness in bounded Petri nets which are covered by T-invariants. In: Valette, R. (ed.) ICATPN 1994. LNCS, vol. 815, pp. 358–375. Springer, Heidelberg (1994)
19. Lohmann, N., Massuthe, P., Wolf, K.: Behavioral constraints for services. In: Alonso, G., Dadam, P., Rosemann, M. (eds.) BPM 2007. LNCS, vol. 4714, pp. 271–287. Springer, Heidelberg (2007)
20. Lohmann, N., Massuthe, P., Stahl, C., Weinberg, D.: Analyzing interacting WS-BPEL processes using flexible model generation. Data Knowl. Eng. 64, 38–54 (2008)
21. Weinberg, D.: Efficient controllability analysis of open nets. In: Bruni, R., Wolf, K. (eds.) WS-FM 2008. LNCS, vol. 5387, pp. 224–239. Springer, Heidelberg (2008)

Proof Techniques for Adapter Generation

Arjan J. Mooij and Marc Voorhoeve

Department of Mathematics and Computer Science*
Technische Universiteit Eindhoven, The Netherlands
{A.J.Mooij,M.Voorhoeve}@tue.nl

Abstract. We study the composition and substitution of services from
a theoretical perspective. An important notion is the operating guideline
of a service y, which is defined as the set of services x such that the
result of connecting x and y has a certain desired property. We define
several related notions and derive results for them in a general context,
thus abstracting from the underlying formalism, be it process algebra,
Petri nets or something else. We then focus on the open Petri-net (and
oWFN) formalism, and address the automated generation of adapters.

1 Introduction

Service-oriented computing is a paradigm of computing that emphasizes composition and interaction. Prominent applications include web services, supported
by industrial languages such as WS-BPEL. Complex services can be composed
from simpler services. As, in turn, the simpler services may have been developed
independently, upon composition a certain gap may need to be bridged. Bridging
this gap is the functionality of an adapter (or mediator) service.

Adapters are closely related to controllers. A controller of a service y is a
service x such that the composition of x and y has a certain desired property,
e.g., deadlock freedom or weak termination. An adapter between two services
x and y is a controller for the disjoint composition of the services x and y. In
[MS05], a representation of all controllers is called an operating guideline, and
it induces a pre-order on the services, which is called accordance [vdALM+08]
(similarly, inheritance [CPT01], conformance [FHRR04], compliance [CCLP06],
or sub-contract [BZ07, CGP08]). Operating guidelines and accordance are key
concepts for reasoning about adapters.

Many different yet related formalisms, including Petri nets and process algebras, have been proposed for describing services and their composition. The
just mentioned concepts are typically studied for a specific formalism, and hence
very similar results are obtained. Although others, e.g., [ML06], aim to unify
the languages for web services, we propose a general framework that unifies

---

* This work has been carried out as a part of the Poseidon project at Thales under the
responsibilities of the Embedded Systems Institute (ESI). This project is partially
supported by the Dutch Ministry of Economic Affairs under the BSIK program.

R. Bruni and K. Wolf (Eds.): WS-FM 2008, LNCS 5387, pp. 207–223, 2009.

results that can be obtained independently of a specific formalism. The algebraic view from [RBF+07] has a similar style as ours, and compared to, e.g., [CPT01, BZ07, CGP08], we discuss more than just accordance.

Using just a few assumptions on composition, we prove many general theoretical results, and in particular we discuss dual approaches to automated adapter generation. Regarding the open Petri-net [Kin97] and open WorkFlow Net (oWFN) formalisms, we discuss the associativity of the composition operator, and we develop a proof technique for partial adapters. Finally, we apply these techniques to the adapter generation approach from [GMW08].

Overview In Section 2 we introduce basic concepts like operating guidelines. In Sections 3 and 4 we define two additional concepts. In Section 5 we treat associativity of the composition operator, and in Section 6 we discuss some applications to adapter generation. In Section 7 we focus on the open Petri-net formalism, and in Section 8 we discuss a certain approach towards adapter generation. Finally, in Section 9 we draw some conclusions.

2   Basic Concepts

We consider a universe of services with interfaces, although, in contrast to [LP07], we leave the interfaces implicit. The main operation on services is composition, for which we introduce a binary operator $\oplus$. Service composition is similar to parallel composition with communication. Our composition operator $\oplus$ is defined as a partial operator, so that we can model certain technical restrictions on the composability of services (see for example Section 7).

2.1   Operating Guideline

Let B denote a correctness property on any (composed) service, e.g., closed interface, deadlock freedom or weak termination. Like the notion of strategies in [RBF+07], we define the operating guideline of any service y, denoted by $OG.y$, as the (possibly empty, and possibly infinite) set of services x such that $x \oplus y$ (is defined and) has property B:

$$(\forall x, y :: x \in OG.y \equiv B.(x \oplus y))$$

Such a service x is typically called a controller (or a partner) of the service y.

Notice that we use '.' to denote function application, and that we often omit the domains of variables that are bound by quantifiers. We do use the standard set operations: element $\in$, subset $\subseteq$, intersection $\cap$, and union $\cup$.

The function OG is in fact an asymmetric representation of a relation on services, though this relation is more explicit in the notation for compatibility from [CPT01]. A related notion is controllability of a service y, which denotes the existence of a service x such that $B.(x \oplus y)$ holds, i.e., whether $OG.y \neq \emptyset$.

Like most related work on service composition, except [LP07], we assume service composition $\oplus$ to be commutative, and hence we have:

$$(\forall x, y :: x \in OG.y \equiv y \in OG.x)$$

2.2   Sets of Services

To obtain nicer equations, we also study the operating guideline of a set of services Y. We define this as the set of services X such that property B holds for the composition of each service $x : x \in X$ with each service $y : y \in Y$:

$$(\forall Y :: OG.Y = (\bigcap y : y \in Y : OG.y))$$

Sets of services are also useful for various applications. In a multi-processor environment, the incoming requests might be distributed over several, slightly different, (versions of) services. Also, if there is some unclarity about the details of a service, we might be able to model the various possibilities. In any case, a controller of the set of services should be a controller of each service in the set.

As a convention we will use lower-case variables for single services, and upper-case variables for sets of services. Notice that lifting the operating guideline is a generalization, as $OG.y = OG.\{y\}$. For sets of services, we lift the composition operator $\oplus$ as follows: $(\forall X, Y :: X \oplus Y = \{x \oplus y \mid x, y : x \in X \wedge y \in Y\})$.

2.3   Galois Connection

The lifted operating guideline is a Galois connection (see, e.g., [Bac02]) on sets of services in the following way:

$$(\forall X, Y :: X \subseteq OG.Y \equiv Y \subseteq OG.X)$$

This can be proved as follows, for every X and Y:

$\quad X \subseteq OG.Y$

$\equiv \quad$ { definition of $OG.Y$; set theory }

$\quad (\forall x, y : x \in X \wedge y \in Y : x \in OG.y)$

$\equiv \quad$ { commutativity of $\oplus$ }

$\quad (\forall x, y : x \in X \wedge y \in Y : y \in OG.x)$

$\equiv \quad$ { definition of $OG.X$; set theory }

$\quad Y \subseteq OG.X$

Given this Galois connection and the pre-order (i.e., binary relation that is reflexive and transitive) $\subseteq$, we obtain all kinds of standard properties. Function OG is anti-monotonic in the following way:

$$(\forall X, Y :: X \subseteq Y \Rightarrow OG.Y \subseteq OG.X)$$

Moreover, the function $(OG \circ OG)$, where $\circ$ denotes function composition, is a closure operator on sets of services, as it is:

extensive:	$(\forall X :: X \subseteq (OG \circ OG).X)$
monotonic:	$(\forall X, Y :: X \subseteq Y \Rightarrow (OG \circ OG).X \subseteq (OG \circ OG).Y)$
idempotent:	$(\forall X :: ((OG \circ OG) \circ (OG \circ OG)).X \subseteq (OG \circ OG).X)$

The property that $(OG \circ OG)$ is idempotent also follows from OG being a semi-inverse of OG:

$$(\forall X :: (OG \circ OG \circ OG).X \subseteq OG.X)$$

In the last two properties, we can use extensiveness to strengthen the set inclusion $\subseteq$ into set equality, which is the equivalence relation induced by the pre-order $\subseteq$. Nevertheless, these formulae just contain the pre-order $\subseteq$, because in Sections 3 and 4 we will study Galois connections for which similar properties hold, but where different equivalence relations are induced.

These results indicate that applying $(OG \circ OG)$ extends the set of services, but after applying OG at least once, applying $(OG \circ OG)$ has no more effect. Moreover, the ordering $\subseteq$ is inverted by every application of OG.

3   Accordance

In [vdALM$^+$08] the notion of accordance is introduced to reason about the public and private view of a service. Like the inverse of relation "generalizes" from [RBF$^+$07], we define the accordance relation $\leq$ on sets of services as follows:

$$(\forall X, Y :: X \leq Y \equiv OG.Y \subseteq OG.X)$$

That is, $X \leq Y$ denotes that each controller of Y is a controller of X, and hence the set X has more controllers than the set Y.

Since the relation $\subseteq$ on sets is a pre-order, the relation $\leq$ on sets of services is also a pre-order. The empty set is a bottom element of this pre-order, and any set of services with an empty operating guideline is a top element. These two extremes correspond to the sets of services for which respectively each service is a controller, and no service is a controller.

In turn, the pre-order $\leq$ induces an equivalence relation [RBF$^+$07] $\doteq$ that relates the services with an identical operating guideline:

$$(\forall X, Y :: X \doteq Y \equiv X \leq Y \wedge Y \leq X)$$

We will abbreviate $\{x\} \leq \{y\}$ into $x \leq y$, and $\{x\} \doteq \{y\}$ into $x \doteq y$.

Using anti-monotonicity of OG, the pre-order $\leq$ contains the pre-order $\subseteq$:

$$(\forall X, Y :: X \subseteq Y \Rightarrow X \leq Y)$$

Moreover, some occurrences of $\leq$ and $\subseteq$ are related by an equivalence:

$$(\forall X, Y :: X \subseteq OG.Y \equiv X \leq OG.Y)$$

This can be proved as follows, for every X and Y:

$$X \leq OG.Y$$
$$\equiv \quad \{ \text{ definition of } \leq \}$$
$$OG.(OG.Y) \subseteq OG.X$$
$$\equiv \quad \{ OG \text{ is anti-monotonic } \}$$
$$X \subseteq OG.Y$$

3.1   Galois Connection

The lifted operating guideline is a Galois connection on sets of services with the accordance pre-order in the following way:

$$(\forall X, Y :: X \leq OG.Y \equiv Y \leq OG.X)$$

This can be proved as follows, for every X and Y:

$$X \leq OG.Y$$
$$\equiv \quad \{ \text{ relation between } \leq \text{ and } \subseteq \}$$
$$X \subseteq OG.Y$$
$$\equiv \quad \{ \text{ Galois connection } \}$$
$$Y \subseteq OG.X$$
$$\equiv \quad \{ \text{ relation between } \leq \text{ and } \subseteq \}$$
$$Y \leq OG.X$$

Hence, we can replace $\leq$ by $\subseteq$ in the standard properties from Section 2.3. In addition, using the previous semi-inverse property, we obtain that $(OG \circ OG)$ is an identity function with respect to accordance equivalence:

$$(\forall X :: (OG \circ OG).X \doteq X)$$

We also obtain the following stronger anti-monotonicity property:

$$(\forall X, Y :: X \leq Y \equiv OG.Y \leq OG.X)$$

This can be proved as follows, for every X and Y:

$$OG.Y \leq OG.X$$
$$\equiv \quad \{ \text{ Galois connection } \}$$
$$X \leq (OG \circ OG).Y$$
$$\equiv \quad \{ (OG \circ OG) \text{ is an identity with respect to accordance } \}$$
$$X \leq Y$$

Using these two properties we obtain:

$$(\forall X, Y :: X \doteq OG.Y \equiv OG.X \doteq Y)$$

From this we can conclude that the domain and range of function OG are equal up to accordance, i.e., $(\forall X :: (\exists Y :: X \doteq OG.Y))$. All together, we can conclude that function OG inverts the entire accordance pre-order $\leq$ on sets of services.

3.2   Relating Sets of Services to Single Services

In this section we explore some rules for proving $X \leq Y$ in terms of the elements of the sets X and Y. Using the definition of OG on sets of services, we obtain the following rule:

$$(\forall X, Y :: X \leq Y \equiv (\forall x : x \in X : \{x\} \leq Y))$$

As $(\forall y : y \in Y : \{y\} \leq Y)$, we also obtain the following rule:

$$(\forall X, Y :: (\forall x : x \in X : (\exists y : y \in Y : \{x\} \leq \{y\})) \Rightarrow X \leq Y)$$

Notice that this rule is not an equivalence; a counter example consists of sets X and Y that are both uncontrollable, and although X contains an uncontrollable service, all services in Y are controllable (but somehow conflicting).

4   Maximal Controllers

Computing the operating guideline is not very practical, as it can be an infinite set. In some settings [LMSW08], a single service z can be computed that encodes the operating guideline of any controllable set of services Y using accordance:

$$(\forall Y : OG.Y \neq \emptyset : (\exists z :: (\forall x :: x \in OG.Y \equiv x \leq z)))$$

Notice that such a service z is an element of $OG.Y$, as $\leq$ is reflexive.

The existence of such a service z cannot be concluded from the algebraic properties we have seen so far, as we will demonstrate using a valid model in which it does not hold. Suppose we model a (deterministic) service by a bag of actions from a set A (of size at least three), and use bag union as the composition operator (which is commutative and associative). Let $B.y$ denote that the bag y consists of exactly two actions, and that these actions are different. Now we have $OG.\{a\} = \{\{b\} \mid b : b \in A \wedge b \neq a\}$, for every action $a : a \in A$. Given that the size of A is at least 2, the singleton bags from A are not related by $\leq$. As the size of A is at least 3, the size of the operating guideline of a singleton bag is at least two, and hence there exists no such z for $Y = \{a\}$ where $a \in A$.

In what follows we just assume that for each controllable set Y such a maximal controller z exists, and we use $mc.Y$ to denote some maximal controller:

$$(\forall Y : OG.Y \neq \emptyset : (\forall x :: x \in OG.Y \equiv x \leq mc.Y))$$

As $\leq$ is reflexive, we have that $(\forall Y : OG.Y \neq \emptyset : mc.Y \in OG.Y)$; so, if $mc.Y$ is defined, i.e., Y is controllable, then $\{mc.Y\}$ is a subset of $OG.Y$. Nevertheless, given any set Y of services, we have that if $mc.Y$ is defined, then the sets $OG.Y$ and $\{mc.Y\}$ are equivalent up to accordance:

$$(\forall Y : OG.Y \neq \emptyset : OG.Y \doteq \{mc.Y\})$$

We prove this result using indirect equality. That is, we prove the equivalent condition $(\forall Y : OG.Y \neq \emptyset : (\forall X :: X \leq OG.Y \equiv X \leq \{mc.Y\}))$ as follows for every X and Y such that $OG.Y \neq \emptyset$:

$\quad X \leq \{mc.Y\}$
$\equiv \quad$ { focus on elements of X; shorthand of $\leq$ for singletons }
$\quad (\forall x : x \in X : x \leq mc.Y)$
$\equiv \quad$ { definition of mc, use $OG.Y \neq \emptyset$ }
$\quad (\forall x : x \in X : x \in OG.Y)$
$\equiv \quad$ { set theory; relation between $\leq$ and $\subseteq$ }
$\quad X \leq OG.Y$

4.1 Galois Connection

Since the result of the function mc is a single service, we obtain a nicer theory for mc by focussing on single services instead of sets of services. So, let us define $mc.y = mc.\{y\}$. Notice that mc is an endo-function on controllable services, i.e., every maximal controller of a controllable service is also a controllable service:

$$(\forall y : OG.y \neq \emptyset : OG.(mc.y) \neq \emptyset)$$

Moreover, we have $(\forall x, y : OG.y \neq \emptyset : x \leq mc.y \Rightarrow OG.x \neq \emptyset)$, i.e., every service $x : x \leq mc.y$ is controllable if y is controllable (i.e., $mc.y$ is defined).

Using the equivalence between OG and mc, we can transform the Galois connection of OG into a Galois connection of mc on controllable services:

$$(\forall x, y : OG.x \neq \emptyset \wedge OG.y \neq \emptyset : x \leq mc.y \equiv y \leq mc.x)$$

Thus we obtain similar properties as in Section 3.1, but in terms of single controllable services. Hence we can conclude that the function mc inverts the accordance pre-order $\leq$ on controllable services.

5 Associative Composition

In this section we study an additional assumption on the composition operator, viz., associativity.

5.1 Trading Rules

By assuming $\oplus$ to be associative, we obtain trading rules like the following (see also an instance in [RBF⁺07]):

$$(\forall X, Y, Z :: X \subseteq OG.(Y \oplus Z) \equiv (X \oplus Y) \subseteq OG.Z)$$

This can be proved as follows, for every X, Y and Z:

$$X \subseteq OG.(Y \oplus Z)$$
$\equiv$ \{ definition of $\oplus$; set theory \}
$$(\forall x, y, z : x \in X \wedge y \in Y \wedge z \in Z : x \in OG.(y \oplus z))$$
$\equiv$ \{ definition of OG; associativity of $\oplus$ \}
$$(\forall x, y, z : x \in X \wedge y \in Y \wedge z \in Z : (x \oplus y) \in OG.z)$$
$\equiv$ \{ definition of $\oplus$; set theory \}
$$(X \oplus Y) \subseteq OG.Z$$

As a consequence, the controllability of $Y \oplus Z$ implies the controllability of Z, i.e., $(\forall Y, Z :: OG.(Y \oplus Z) \neq \emptyset \Rightarrow OG.Z \neq \emptyset)$, but not the other way around.

Using our earlier results, we obtain similar rules for OG and $\leq$ in terms of sets of services, and for mc and $\leq$ in terms of controllable services. The controllability assumptions of the latter could be simplified as follows:

$$(\forall x, y, z : OG.(y \oplus z) \neq \emptyset : x \leq mc.(y \oplus z) \equiv (x \oplus y) \leq mc.z)$$

5.2   Accordance Pre-congruence

Using the associativity of $\oplus$, the accordance pre-order $\leq$ is a pre-congruence with respect to the operator $\oplus$:

$$(\forall X, Y, Z :: Y \leq Z \ \Rightarrow \ X \oplus Y \ \leq \ X \oplus Z)$$

This can be proved as follows, for every X, Y and Z:

$$
\begin{aligned}
& X \oplus Y \ \leq \ X \oplus Z \\
\equiv \quad & \{ \text{ definition of } \leq; \text{ indirect inequality } \} \\
& (\forall W :: \ W \subseteq OG.(X \oplus Z) \ \Rightarrow \ W \subseteq OG.(X \oplus Y)) \\
\equiv \quad & \{ \text{ trading } \} \\
& (\forall W :: \ (W \oplus X) \subseteq OG.Z \ \Rightarrow \ (W \oplus X) \subseteq OG.Y) \\
\Leftarrow \quad & \{ \text{ set theory; definition of } \leq \} \\
& Y \leq Z
\end{aligned}
$$

Pre-congruence properties are important when composing services from some smaller services, which is at the core of service-oriented computing. As $\oplus$ is commutative, we also obtain that $\oplus$ is monotonic in both arguments:

$$(\forall V, W, X, Y :: V \leq W \ \wedge \ X \leq Y \ \Rightarrow \ V \oplus X \ \leq \ W \oplus Y)$$

Similarly, for isolating a term Y from terms like $X \leq Y \oplus Z$ and $X \oplus Y \leq Z$, we obtain four rules:

$$(\forall X, Y, Z :: \ X \ \leq \ Y \oplus Z \ \equiv \ (\exists W :: \ W \leq Y \ \wedge \ X \ \leq \ W \oplus Z))$$

$$(\forall X, Y, Z :: \ X \ \leq \ Y \oplus Z \ \equiv \ (\forall W :: \ Y \leq W \ \Rightarrow \ X \ \leq \ W \oplus Z))$$

$$(\forall X, Y, Z :: \ X \oplus Y \ \leq \ Z \ \equiv \ (\exists W :: \ Y \leq W \ \wedge \ X \oplus W \ \leq \ Z))$$

$$(\forall X, Y, Z :: \ X \oplus Y \ \leq \ Z \ \equiv \ (\forall W :: \ W \leq Y \ \Rightarrow \ X \oplus W \ \leq \ Z))$$

6   Application to Adapter Generation

In this section we apply our theory to some topics related to adapter generation. To discuss adapter generation, we assume that some (incompatible) services are given that need to be integrated. It is usually assumed that their interfaces are disjoint, and we use x to denote their (disjoint) composition. Basically, an adapter [RBF$^+$07] for these services is a controller for the service x. So, assuming that the service x is controllable, an adapter is a service y such that $y \leq mc.x$, or equivalently, $y \in OG.x$.

This construction of an adapter establishes that property B (e.g., deadlock-freedom or weak termination) holds for the composition of the given service x with the adapter y. However, usually there are more requirements, e.g., what the given service x aims to achieve, or what operations the adapter y is allowed (or able) to perform. Various specification languages have been proposed for this.

6.1   Dual Approaches to Generating Adapters

Most of the approaches to adapter generation first construct a huge controller, possibly $mc.x$. For the typically-used properties B, such a controller contains (is larger in the accordance pre-order than) the adapter that conceptually consists of two independent parts, each one establishing property B with one given service. Afterwards (possibly on-the-fly), the additional requirements are imposed by restricting the behavior of the generated controller; moreover, part of the controller generation algorithm is repeated in order to eliminate branches that cannot establish property B anymore. This last step guarantees that the resulting service y is indeed *smaller* than $mc.x$ with respect to accordance, and hence it is a proper adapter. Unfortunately, this approach usually leads to complex algorithms [BBC05, BP06], with a bad separation of concerns.

As we have seen that the function mc inverts the accordance pre-order on controllable services, there also exists a second approach; however, it has not yet received much attention. In this case, the additional requirements are imposed by first creating a service z that is *greater* than x with respect to accordance. That is, the requirements are integrated with the given services, and afterwards an adapter is obtained by generating the controller $mc.z$. Thus, existing controller generation algorithms can immediately be reused.

For a given controllable service x, these two approaches yield the sets of adapters $\{y \mid y : y \le mc.x\}$ and $\{mc.z \mid z : OG.z \ne \emptyset \wedge x \le z\}$ respectively. To show the duality between these approaches, we will prove that the elements in this set are equal up to accordance equivalence, i.e., for every service w, an accordance-equivalent service is in one set if-and-only-if an accordance-equivalent service is in the other set:

$$(\forall w :: (\exists y :: y \le mc.x \wedge y \doteq w) \equiv (\exists z : OG.z \ne \emptyset : x \le z \wedge w \doteq mc.z))$$

As services x and z are controllable, services y and $mc.z$ are also controllable. Thus, the case that w is uncontrollable holds trivially, and in the remainder of this proof we assume that w is controllable:

$\quad (\exists z :: x \le z \wedge w \doteq mc.z)$
$\equiv \quad \{ \text{ property of } mc \}$
$\quad (\exists z :: x \le z \wedge mc.w \doteq z)$
$\equiv \quad \{ \le \text{ is a pre-order } \}$
$\quad x \le mc.w$
$\equiv \quad \{ \text{ Galois connection } \}$
$\quad w \le mc.x$
$\equiv \quad \{ \le \text{ is a pre-order } \}$
$\quad (\exists y :: y \le mc.x \wedge y \doteq w)$

This result also gives a formal foundation for the oWFN-based techniques from [LMW07]. It is even a completeness proof under the assumption that all controllable services $z : x \le z$ can be obtained using their constraint automata. We have not studied the validity of the latter assumption, as it is likely to be formalism dependent.

6.2 Partial Adapters

Some kinds of additional requirements, e.g., limitations on the operations that an adapter can perform, can nicely be modeled as a partial adapter (see, e.g., [GMW08]). A partial adapter for a (composed) service x is a service y with two interfaces. The first interface is the one with service x, which enables it to enforce the additional requirements. The second interface is a fresh one, which allows another service to control parts of the behavior of the partial adapter. Some examples of partial adapters are discussed in Section 8.

To construct an adapter, the services x and y are composed, and a controller from the set $OG.(x \oplus y)$ is computed. Afterwards, this controller is composed with the partial adapter y, yielding an adapter from the set $\{y\} \oplus OG.(x \oplus y)$.

Although interfaces are hardly discussed in our framework, our introduction to partial adapters seems to focus on interfaces. This mainly turns out to be an example of its usage, as we can use the trading rules to show that the resulting adapters are indeed adapters for x:

$$\{y\} \oplus OG.(x \oplus y) \subseteq OG.x$$

6.3 Service Approximation

When building adapters in practice, not always a complete or accurate model of the given (composed) service x is available. Instead, suppose that property B holds for $x \oplus z$, i.e., $x \leq mc.z$. If only the model of z is given, we like to use $mc.z$ as an approximation of x.

To show the validity of this approach, we show that by making a service larger with respect to the accordance, the set of adapters becomes a subset. Hence, larger approximations are no problem for adapter generation. From the definition of $\leq$, we obtain for adapter generation without additional restrictions:

$$(\forall x, y :: x \leq y \;\Rightarrow\; OG.y \subseteq OG.x)$$

Using that $\leq$ is a pre-congruence with respect to $\oplus$, we obtain a similar result for adapter generation using a partial adapter z:

$$(\forall x, y, z :: x \leq y \;\Rightarrow\; \{z\} \oplus OG.(y \oplus z) \subseteq \{z\} \oplus OG.(x \oplus z))$$

6.4 Proof Technique for Partial Adapters

Suppose a service x is given together with two partial adapters y and z. It is a natural question to determine whether partial adapter y leads to an adapter for x that is smaller with respect to accordance than the one that would be obtained using partial adapter z, i.e., whether $\{y\} \oplus OG.(x \oplus y) \leq \{z\} \oplus OG.(x \oplus z)$.

Although $\leq$ is a pre-congruence with respect to $\oplus$, conditions like $y \leq z$ or $z \leq y$ do not suffice, as OG is anti-monotonic. We will show that it is sufficient to prove that service z can be used to mimic service y, i.e., there exists a service a such that $z \oplus a$ is accordance equivalent to y.

To increase the generality of this approach in case $x \oplus y$ and $x \oplus z$ share interface names, we want to be able to introduce fresh names for the interface of $x \oplus y$. To this end we introduce a service i that can perform a one-to-one transformation between the complement of the interface of $x \oplus y$ and a fresh interface.

Combining these ingredients, we consider the lemma:

$$(\forall x, y, z, i :: (\forall Q : Q \leq OG.(x \oplus y) : (\exists P :: Q \doteq \{i\} \oplus P)) \Rightarrow$$
$$((\exists a :: y \oplus i \doteq z \oplus a) \Rightarrow \{y\} \oplus OG.(x \oplus y) \leq \{z\} \oplus OG.(x \oplus z)))$$

which can be proved for every x, y, z and i as follows:

$\quad \{y\} \oplus OG.(x \oplus y) \leq \{z\} \oplus OG.(x \oplus z)$
$\equiv \quad$ { pre-congruence (twice) }
$\quad (\forall Q : Q \leq OG.(x \oplus y) : (\exists R : R \leq OG.(x \oplus z) : \{y\} \oplus Q \leq \{z\} \oplus R))$
$\equiv \quad$ { dummy transformation using $(\exists P :: Q \doteq \{i\} \oplus P)$ }
$\quad (\forall P : \{i\} \oplus P \leq OG.(x \oplus y) :$
$\qquad\qquad (\exists R : R \leq OG.(x \oplus z) : \{y \oplus i\} \oplus P \leq \{z\} \oplus R))$
$\Leftarrow \quad$ { choose $R := \{a\} \oplus P$; trading }
$\quad (\forall P : \{x\} \oplus P \leq OG.(y \oplus i) :$
$\qquad\qquad (\exists a : \{x\} \oplus P \leq OG.(z \oplus a) : \{y \oplus i\} \oplus P \leq \{z \oplus a\} \oplus P))$
$\Leftarrow \quad$ { pre-congruence }
$\quad (\exists a :: y \oplus i \doteq z \oplus a)$

The term $(\forall Q : Q \leq OG.(x \oplus y) : (\exists P :: Q \doteq \{i\} \oplus P))$ causes this lemma to look complicated. In typical applications, given services x and y, a service i satisfying this condition can easily be chosen based on only the interface of $x \oplus y$, as we will also see in Section 7.2. Afterwards, a service a is chosen such that $(\exists a :: y \oplus i \doteq z \oplus a)$ holds.

7 Open Petri-net / oWFN

In this section we relate open Petri-nets [Kin97] (similar to open WorkFlow Nets, oWFN) to our framework, and discuss some issues. To this end we need to introduce some details about the syntax and operational semantics of this formalism.

A Petri net consists of a set of places P, a set of transitions T and a set of arcs $F : F \subseteq (P \times T) \cup (T \times P)$. A marking is a mapping from P to the naturals; for any marking m and place p, it is said that there are $m.p$ tokens in the place p. A transition t is enabled in marking m iff $m.p > 0$ for all places $p : [p, t] \in F$. A marking m' is reachable from marking m iff there exists a sequence of firings from m to m'. Firing an enabled transition t in marking m leads to a marking m' such that $m'.p = m.p - W.[p, t] + W.[t, p]$ for all places p, where $W.[x, y] = 1$ if $[x, y] \in F$ and $W.[x, y] = 0$ otherwise.

An open Petri-net is a Petri net with two disjoint subsets of places that denote the input and output interfaces; if these two subsets are empty then the net is called closed. Input places only have outgoing arcs, and output places only have incoming arcs. Furthermore, there is an initial marking (which is 0 for the interface places) and a set of final markings (each of which is 0 for the interface places). The inner of an open net is the subnet that consists of the transitions and the places that are not on the interface, and the arcs between them. The inner of an open net is abstract in the sense that it can be consistently renamed; in this way an open net represents an equivalence class of isomorphic nets. Thus, only the interface places have static names, which are used for composition.

Basically, two open nets are composable if their input places are disjoint and also their output places are disjoint; otherwise composition is not defined. The binary commutative operator $\oplus$ composes two open nets that are composable, by taking the union of the two nets; to ensure that only the interface places can be fused, their inners are first made disjoint. Each place that is an input place of one net and an output place of the other net ceases to be an interface place and becomes an internal place.

In, e.g., [vdALM$^+$08], the correctness property B is defined as

$$(\forall x :: B.x \equiv \text{"x is closed and weakly terminating"})$$

Weak termination of a closed net denotes that a final marking is reachable from every marking that is reachable from the initial marking. A consequence of closedness is that all services in $OG.y$ have an identical interface. To illustrate the accordance pre-order for such a property B, a service that can start with a skip transition and a number of alternative branches becomes smaller with respect to accordance by removing some of these alternative branches.

If instead of weak termination we consider the weaker notion of deadlock freedom, then tools like Fiona [LMSW08] can be used to compute a compact representation of the OG and the mc (if it exists) in terms of a labeled service automaton. Basically, this is an automaton (consisting of nodes and edges) in which each edge is labeled with an action (send or receive one token) on an interface place. Furthermore, the nodes are labeled with predicates that indicate which combinations of outgoing edges may be omitted. Basically, this means that every time a node is reached, an internal step can first decide which outgoing edges will actually be available. Thus the mc is obtained by replacing every labeled node by a non-deterministic internal choice between all the valid combinations of outgoing edges from this node.

7.1 Associativity of the Composition Operator

In case the inner of a net is not considered to be abstract, [vdALM$^+$08] mentions that the operator $\oplus$ is associative. If the inner is considered to be abstract, as we do, [RBF$^+$07] mentions that the operator $\oplus$ is associative for open nets that do not share any interface place. Indeed, associativity is not guaranteed if the inner is abstract and some interface places are shared. For example, consider the following four open nets:

- X_1: output interface a, behavior: send one token to a, and terminate;
- X_2: input interface a, behavior: receive one token from a, and terminate;
- X_3: output interface a, behavior: terminate immediately;
- X_4: input interface a, behavior: terminate immediately.

If the inner is abstract, then $(X_1 \oplus X_2) \oplus (X_3 \oplus X_4)$ is well-defined. If associativity holds, then this expression should be equal to $X_1 \oplus ((X_2 \oplus X_3) \oplus X_4)$. As the second one contains deadlocks and the first one does not, associativity does not hold in this setting. So, although both an abstract inner and associativity of $\oplus$ are convenient properties to have, the existing definitions only give one of them.

The problem seems to be that the composition operator $\oplus$ is doing two things at the same time, viz., taking the union of the open nets, and hiding some of the interface places. Similar to CSP-style process algebra [Hoa85], we propose to separate them in a new composition operator $\oplus$ and a new hiding operator τ. Like before, two open nets are composable if they do not share input places, and they do not share output places. The new binary composition operator $\oplus$ composes two composable open nets, by just taking the union of the two nets, after making their inners disjoint. The new hiding operator τ makes from each place that is both an input and an output interface an internal place (i.e., no interface anymore).

As the new composition operator $\oplus$ is just computing the union of two nets, it is both commutative and associative. As $\cap$ distributes over $\cup$, associativity does not affect the composability. Our previous example should then be rephrased as $\tau.(X_1 \oplus X_2) \oplus \tau.(X_3 \oplus X_4)$, and hence we would not even expect any form of associativity. The the correctness property B should be rephrased as:

$$(\forall x :: \ B.x \ \equiv \ \text{``}\tau.x \text{ is closed and weakly terminating''})$$

Phrased in this way, it is natural to generalize the composition operator $\oplus$ such that the interfaces become single-reader multi-writer (compare the Murata rules [Mur89]). As this could change the accordance pre-order $\leq$, we leave this as further work. Similarly, the hiding operator could be generalized with a parameter that indicates a part of the interface.

7.2 Proof Technique for Partial Adapters

In Section 6.4 we have introduced a proof technique for partial adapters, which for generality purposes depends on a special service i such that

$$(\forall Q : \ Q \ \leq \ OG.(x \oplus y) : \ (\exists P :: \ Q \ \doteq \ \{i\} \oplus P))$$

Although this requirement looks complicated, for the open Petri-net formalism it can easily be simplified. (Similar results may hold for other formalisms.)

Given the rules for composition of open nets, and given that property B guarantees a closed interface, all services from the sets $Q : \ Q \leq OG.(x \oplus y)$ have an identical interface. We propose for i a service that just performs a one-to-one transformation between the complement of the interface of $x \oplus y$ and a

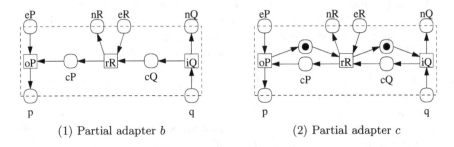

(1) Partial adapter b (2) Partial adapter c

Fig. 1. Two partial adapters

fresh interface. Using the Murata rules (fusion of series places), for every set Q a proper set P can be constructed by renaming the interface of the services in Q (which is the complement of the interface of $x \oplus y$) to the complement of this fresh interface.

So, for any service x, any partial adapters y and z, and the service i just described, we obtain the simpler proof technique:

$$(\exists a :: y \oplus i \doteq z \oplus a) \quad \Rightarrow \quad \{y\} \oplus OG.(x \oplus y) \leq \{z\} \oplus OG.(x \oplus z)$$

We will apply this proof technique to an example in Section 8.

8   Application to Some Specific Partial Adapters

In this section, we apply our techniques to the way of specifying and generating adapters from [GMW08]. The property B that we require is being closed and deadlock free. The additional requirements on the adapter are specified using transformation rules that describe the capabilities of the adapter. Each rule describes that a certain bag of messages can be transformed into a certain other bag of messages. The transformation rules are translated into a partial adapter, such that an adapter can be generated as described in Section 6.2.

In this section, we study two kinds of partial adapters that obey to these transformation rules, but with different properties. To this end we use the following example in terms of open nets. Let service x be any given service (or the composition of some given services) with an input interface p and an output interface q. Furthermore suppose the only transformation rule is $q \mapsto p$, which denotes that any token in q (sent by the service x) can be transformed into a token in p (sent to the service x). This is a representative example, as it turns out that our results can easily be copied to the general case.

Figure 1 contains two partial adapters. The places on the dashed border are the interface places. Each partial adapter has two series of interface places: the lower interface is used by the given service x, and the upper interface is used by the remaining generated controller. Interface nQ notifies incoming messages q, interface eR enables a transformation rule, interface nR notifies executions of

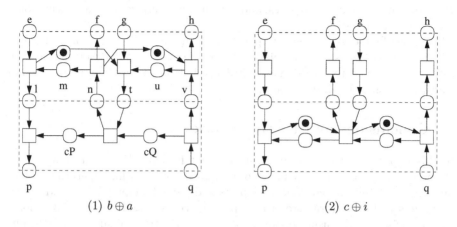

$(1)\ b \oplus a$ $(2)\ c \oplus i$

Fig. 2. Proof outline of $(\exists a :: c \oplus i \doteq b \oplus a)$

a transformation rule, and interface eP enables outgoing messages p; the only final marking is the initial marking, which is depicted.

Partial adapter b from Figure 1.1 corresponds to the conceptual partial adapter from [GMW08]. Partial adapter c is depicted in Figure 1.2, but in this case the internal places have been made bounded by adding complementary places with a token in the initial marking. These bounds are necessary for the tools that are used in [GMW08]. The resulting sets of adapters are $\{b\} \oplus OG.(x \oplus b)$ and $\{c\} \oplus OG.(x \oplus c)$ respectively.

8.1 Conceptual Versus Bounded

Given the partial adapters b and c from Figure 1, we want to conclude that the adapters $\{b\} \oplus OG.(x \oplus b)$ can behave like the adapters $\{c\} \oplus OG.(x \oplus c)$, i.e., replacing partial adapter b by c makes the adapters smaller with respect to accordance:

$$\{c\} \oplus OG.(x \oplus c) \quad \leq \quad \{b\} \oplus OG.(x \oplus b)$$

Using our proof technique from Section 7.2, this follows from $(\exists a :: c \oplus i \doteq b \oplus a)$, where i transforms the complement of the upper interface of c to a fresh interface. As b and c have equal interfaces, a will have the same interface as i.

Service $c \oplus i$ is depicted in Figure 2.2, but for service $b \oplus a$ we first need to choose an appropriate service a. As the difference between b and c is that c postpones the firing of certain transitions, we propose a service a that introduces these delays to b; see Figure 2.1.

To prove the accordance equivalence of services $c \oplus i$ and $b \oplus a$, we need to show that $OG.(c \oplus i) = OG.(b \oplus a)$, or equivalently, that for every service z we have $B.(c \oplus i \oplus z) \equiv B.(b \oplus a \oplus z)$. Therefore it is sufficient to show the equivalence of services $c \oplus i$ and $b \oplus a$ using common Petri-net techniques that maintain deadlock freedom, by considering the input interfaces as places with some invisible incoming arcs, and the output interfaces as places with some invisible outgoing arcs.

Thus we first observe the two place invariants $cP = l + m + n$ and $cQ = t + u + v$. This means that the places cP and cQ are redundant, and hence they can be removed. Afterwards, the equivalence follows by fusing some places and transitions using the Murata rules.

9   Conclusions and Further Work

In this paper we have introduced an abstract framework for reasoning about adapter generation. In particular we addressed concepts like operating guidelines, controllability, accordance, adapters and partial adapters. The underlying structures include several pre-orders, pre-congruences and Galois connections. In comparison to the usual operational characterizations of such concepts, our approach highlights the relations between these concepts, is independent of a specific formalism or language, and supports algebraic proofs. It is further work to include pre-orders like "can be made compatible" [CGP08].

We make just a small number of assumptions on the exact formalism and languages that are used to describe services and their interaction. Nevertheless, our results turn out to be strong enough for discussing real applications. For example, we have shown that two approaches to adapter generation have equal expressivity. While efficient implementations of the usual approach require modified controller generators, the dual approach can use existing controller generators. It is further work to expand this comparison with partial adapters.

Regarding the important property of associativity, we have proposed a variant of the composition operator for open Petri-nets, using ideas from process algebra. It is further work to explore the consequences of allowing interface places that are single-reader multi-writer interface places.

Finally we have contributed to adapter generation in the style of [GMW08]. To this end we developed a proof technique that allows us to show the formal relation between different partial adapters.

References

[Bac02]   Backhouse, R.: Galois connections and fixed point calculus. In: Blackhouse, R., Crole, R.L., Gibbons, J. (eds.) Algebraic and Coalgebraic Methods in the Mathematics of Program Construction. LNCS, vol. 2297, pp. 89–148. Springer, Heidelberg (2002)

[BBC05]   Bracciali, A., Brogi, A., Canal, C.: A formal approach to component adaptation. The Journal of Systems and Software 74(1), 45–54 (2005)

[BP06]   Brogi, A., Popescu, R.: Automated generation of BPEL adapters. In: Dan, A., Lamersdorf, W. (eds.) ICSOC 2006. LNCS, vol. 4294, pp. 27–39. Springer, Heidelberg (2006)

[BZ07]   Bravetti, M., Zavattaro, G.: A theory for strong service compliance. In: Murphy, A.L., Vitek, J. (eds.) COORDINATION 2007. LNCS, vol. 4467, pp. 96–112. Springer, Heidelberg (2007)

[CCLP06]   Carpineti, S., Castagna, G., Laneve, C., Padovani, L.: A formal account of contracts for web services. In: Bravetti, M., Núñez, M., Zavattaro, G. (eds.) WS-FM 2006. LNCS, vol. 4184, pp. 148–162. Springer, Heidelberg (2006)

[CGP08]   Castagna, G., Gesbert, N., Padovani, L.: A theory of contracts for web services. In: Proceedings of Principles of Programming Languages, pp. 261–272 (2008)

[CPT01]   Canal, C., Pimentel, E., Troya, J.: Compatibility and inheritance in software architectures. Science of Computer Programming 41, 105–138 (2001)

[FHRR04]   Fournet, C., Hoare, T., Rajamani, S., Rehof, J.: Stuck-free conformance. In: Alur, R., Peled, D.A. (eds.) CAV 2004. LNCS, vol. 3114, pp. 242–254. Springer, Heidelberg (2004)

[GMW08]   Gierds, C., Mooij, A.J., Wolf, K.: Specifying and generating behavioral service adaptors based on transformation rules. Preprints CS-02-08, Institut fur Informatik, Universitat Rostock (2008)

[Hoa85]   Hoare, C.A.R.: Communicating Sequential Processes. Prentice Hall, Englewood Cliffs (1985)

[Kin97]   Kindler, E.: A compositional partial order semantics for Petri net components. In: Proceedings of Application and Theory of Petri Nets. LNCS, vol. 1248, pp. 235–252. Springer, Heidelberg (1997)

[LMSW08]   Lohmann, N., Massuthe, P., Stahl, C., Weinberg, D.: Analyzing interacting WS-BPEL processes using flexible model generation. Data & Knowledge Engineering 64(1), 36–54 (2008)

[LMW07]   Lohmann, N., Massuthe, P., Wolf, K.: Behavioral constraints for services. In: Alonso, G., Dadam, P., Rosemann, M. (eds.) BPM 2007. LNCS, vol. 4714, pp. 271–287. Springer, Heidelberg (2007)

[LP07]   Laneve, C., Padovani, L.: The must preorder revisited — an algebraic theory for web services contracts. In: Caires, L., Vasconcelos, V.T. (eds.) CONCUR 2007. LNCS, vol. 4703, pp. 212–225. Springer, Heidelberg (2007)

[ML06]   Mazzara, M., Lanese, I.: Towards a unifying theory for web services composition. In: Bravetti, M., Núñez, M., Zavattaro, G. (eds.) WS-FM 2006. LNCS, vol. 4184, pp. 257–272. Springer, Heidelberg (2006)

[MS05]   Massuthe, P., Schmidt, K.: Operating guidelines — an automata-theoretic foundation for the service-oriented architecture. In: Proceedings of Quality Software. IEEE, Los Alamitos (2005)

[Mur89]   Murata, T.: Petri nets: Properties, analysis and applications. Proceedings of the IEEE 77(4), 541–580 (1989)

[RBF+07]   Reisig, W., Bretschneider, J., Fahland, D., Lohmann, N., Massuthe, P., Stahl, C.: Services as a paradigm of computation. In: Jones, C.B., Liu, Z., Woodcock, J. (eds.) Formal Methods and Hybrid Real-Time Systems. LNCS, vol. 4700, pp. 521–538. Springer, Heidelberg (2007)

[vdALM+08] van der Aalst, W., Lohmannn, N., Massuthe, P., Stahl, C., Wolf, K.: From public views to private views – correctness-by-design for services. In: Dumas, M., Heckel, R. (eds.) WS-FM 2007. LNCS, vol. 4937, pp. 139–153. Springer, Heidelberg (2008)

Efficient Controllability Analysis of Open Nets

Daniela Weinberg

Humboldt–Universität zu Berlin
Institut für Informatik
Unter den Linden 6
10099 Berlin, Germany
weinberg@informatik.hu-berlin.de

Abstract. A service is designed to interact with other services. If the service interaction is stateful and asynchronous, the interaction protocol can become quite complex. A service may be able to interact with a lot of possible partner services, one partner or no partner at all. Having no partner surely is not intended by the designer. But the stateful interaction between services can be formalized and thus analyzed at design time.

We present a formalization which is centered around a graph data structure that we call *interaction graph*, which represents feasible runs of a partner service according to the interaction protocol. As interaction graphs suffer from state explosion, we introduce a set of suitable *reduction rules* to alleviate the complexity of our approach. As our case studies show we are able to analyze the interaction behavior of a service efficiently.

Keywords: Business process analysis, Formal models in business process management, Process verification and validation, Petri nets.

1 Introduction

Complex inter-organizational business processes are more and more structured as a set of communicating elementary processes (services), which is one of the objectives of service-oriented computing (SOC) [1]. A service represents a self-contained software unit that offers an encapsulated functionality over a well-defined interface.

In practice, the language WS-BPEL [2] has become common for modeling services. WS-BPEL aims at describing the behavior of services by enhancing the service's underlying workflow by an interface description specifying the interactional behavior of this service with other services, its *partners*. The behavior of a service can become very complex due to the nature of the (asynchronous) interaction with its partners. The actions that are performed within a service usually depend strongly on the interaction that has taken place. Thus, analyzing the behavior of a service on the one hand and analyzing its interaction with other services on the other hand is by far not trivial.

R. Bruni and K. Wolf (Eds.): WS-FM 2008, LNCS 5387, pp. 224–239, 2009.
© Springer-Verlag Berlin Heidelberg 2009

With respect to SOC we are interested in whether every service instance will eventually terminate in a well-defined final state with no useless (dead) activities being pending. This idea has already been formalized as usability in [3]. We use the term *controllability* instead of usability to avoid misunderstandings w.r.t. other well established meanings of "usability". We analyze whether two services S and S' can interact properly, meaning that their composition $S \oplus S'$ is *deadlock-free*. Then S' is a partner that triggers S in a way that the composition $S \oplus S'$ is deadlock-free. In our approach, we model a service as an open net [4], which is a special class of Petri nets. In [5] we show that any WS-BPEL process can be translated into an open net.

In this paper, we introduce a technique for examining controllability of an acyclic open net. It is based on the *interaction graph*. The complete interaction graph exhibits all the communication that is possible between the net and its partner. The interaction graph contains, for open nets that indeed can interact with some partner, a subgraph that can be seen as the state space of a partner S'. This state space can subsequently be transformed into an open net by using the theory of regions [6], for instance. One such subgraph can be found by a repeated removal of those nodes of the original graph that are inconsistent with the goal that the composition of S and S' is deadlock-free.

The complete interaction graph is huge in size (comparable to the reachability graph of Petri nets). However, it is possible to apply specific reduction rules on-the-fly while building up the interaction graph. Thus, we compute a reduced graph, which is significantly smaller then the complete graph as our case studies show. Nevertheless, the reduction rules preserve the property that the resulting graph contains, for open nets that have partners, a subgraph that forms the state space of a partner S'. In [7] we already presented the interaction graph and showed that it is suitable for the analysis of controllability with the help of a case study. This paper focuses on technical details of the interaction graph and introduces reduction rules that we have developed in order to alleviate the complexity of the graphs.

The interaction graph along with the reduction rules we present in this paper has been fully integrated (by the author) into the tool FIONA[1]. In [7] we have shown a toolchain containing FIONA that starts out with a WS-BPEL process and transforms it into an open net. Then the computed net serves as an input of FIONA. That way any WS-BPEL process can be analyzed with respect to controllability.

This paper is structured as follows. We will first give a brief introduction of open nets. Then, in Sect. 2.2, we will present the interaction graph as a means of analyzing controllability of an open net in more detail. The second part of the paper, starting at Sect. 3, introduces techniques that reduce the interaction graph on-the-fly as it is calculated. We will further show case studies (Sect. 4) and conclude the paper with comparing our approach to related work (Sect. 5) and by presenting further work (Sect. 6).

---

[1] Available at http://www.service-technology.org/fiona

2   Background

2.1   Open Nets

As we aim at analyzing the controllability of services we need a formal model to represent those services. We use a special class of Petri nets – *open nets* [4].

We assume the usual representation of a (place/transition) Petri net $N = (P, T, F)$ (see [8], for instance). A *marking* is a multiset $m : P \to \mathbb{N}$ (graphically, $m[p]$ black tokens on place p). A transition t is *enabled* at a marking m if for each place p with $(p, t) \in F, m[p] \geq 1$. If enabled at m, the *firing* of t then yields the marking m' with $m'[p] = m[p] - 1$ if $(p, t) \in F$ and $(t, p) \notin F$, $m'[p] = m[p] + 1$ if $(t, p) \in F$ and $(p, t) \notin F$, and $m'[p] = m[p]$ otherwise. We denote the firing of t by $m \xrightarrow{t} m'$. The successive firing of a sequence of transitions is denoted by $m \xrightarrow{*} m''$. Note, $*$ indicates that no transition may fire at all, yielding $m = m''$. Throughout this paper we use the notation $m' = m - p$ ($m' = m + p$) if in marking m one token is removed from (put on) place p yielding marking m'.

Definition 1 (Open Net). *An open net* $N = (P, T, F, P_{in}, P_{out}, m_0, \Omega)$ *consists of a Petri net* (P, T, F) *together with (1) two sets* $P_{in}, P_{out} \subseteq P$, *such that for all transitions* $t \in T$ *holds: if* $p \in P_{in}$ ($p \in P_{out}$) *then* $(t, p) \notin F$ ($(p, t) \notin F$), *(2) a distinguished* initial marking m_0 *and (3) a set* Ω *of distinguished* final *markings of* N, *such that no transition of* N *is enabled at any* $m \in \Omega$.

The places in P_{in} (P_{out}) are called *input* (*output*) places and model channels to receive (send) messages from (to) another open net. This way we abstract from data and model the occurrence of messages just as undistinguishable tokens. We label a transition t connected to an input (output) place p with ?p and name it *receiving transition* (!p, *sending transition*). A place that is neither an input nor an output place is called *internal*. Figure 1(a) shows an example open net N_1. It has two input places, order and review, and one output place stats. Places p1, p2 and p3 are internal. The initial marking m_0 is [p1] denoted by one token on place p1 and all other places empty. The set of final markings of N_1 is defined by

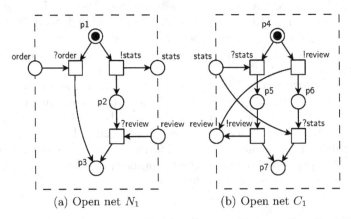

(a) Open net N_1 (b) Open net C_1

Fig. 1. Example open net N_1 (a) and a possible controller C_1 of N_1 (b)

$\Omega = \{[\mathsf{p3}]\}$. In m_0 the net either waits for the order message (receiving transition ?order) from a partner or it sends out a stats message (sending transition !stats). If the order message arrives, modeled as a token on input place order, transition ?order can fire and produces a token on place p3. If, however, the net sends out the stats message, transition !stats fires, yielding the marking [p2, stats]. If the partner consumes the message stats, the net reaches the marking [p2]. If the partner then sends the review message, the transition ?review of N_1 is enabled and fires, resulting in the marking [p3], which is the final marking of the net.

Since we aim at analyzing the controllability of an open net, we need a notion for the interaction of two open nets – the *composition* of open nets. Given two open nets N and C, their composition $N \oplus C$ is obtained by merging every input place of one open net with the equally labeled output place of the other net (if that one is present). Thereby, we demand that the nets only share input and output places such that an input place of N is an output place of C and vice versa. Merged places become internal to $N \oplus C$. For markings m_N of N and m_C of C let $m_N \oplus m_C$ be a marking of $N \oplus C$, defined for $p \in P_{N \oplus C}$ by $(m_N \oplus m_C)[p] =_{def} m_N[p] + m_C[p]$, where $m_N[p] = 0$ if $p \notin P_N$ and $m_C[p] = 0$ if $p \notin P_C$. Then, let $m_{(N \oplus C)_0} =_{def} m_{N_0} \oplus m_{C_0}$ and $m_{N \oplus C} \in \Omega_{N \oplus C}$ iff $m_{N \oplus C} = m_N \oplus m_C$ for some $m_N \in \Omega_N$ and some $m_C \in \Omega_C$.

As an example, Fig. 1 shows the open nets N_1 and C_1. We will now take a look at the composition $N_1 \oplus C_1$. Here we merge the output place stats of N_1 with the input place stats of C_1. Further the input place review of N_1 and the output place review of C_1 are merged. Both places become internal to $N_1 \oplus C_1$. That way the composition has just one input place order. The initial state m_0 of $N_1 \oplus C_1$ is [p1, p4] and the set of final states is $\Omega_{N_1 \oplus C_1} = \{[\mathsf{p3}, \mathsf{p7}]\}$.

A marking m of an open net is a *deadlock* if m enables no transition at all. An open net in which all deadlocks are final markings is called *deadlock-free*. So, for every reachable marking of a net, a final marking is reachable.

Throughout this paper we call a marking of a net a *state*. Further we only consider acyclic open nets, i.e. nets where the transitive closure of F contains no cycles, and we just permit those final markings that have empty input/output places. We currently adapt our approach to nets having final states that do not necessarily have empty input/output places.

Deciding controllability for a restricted class of cyclic open nets is shown in [9] by constructing a most permissive partner. Our reduction rules, however, have not yet been adapted to that class of open nets.

2.2 Controllability of Open Nets

Intuitively, controllability of an open net N means that N can properly interact with some other net. Like the *soundness* property for workflow nets (cf. [10]), controllability is a minimal requirement for the correctness of an open net. So, N is controllable, if there exists an open net C, such that the composed open net $N \oplus C$ is deadlock-free. Throughout this paper we will call C a *controller* of N.

We will take a look at the composition $N_1 \oplus C_1$ again. Here, C_1 (Fig. 1(b)) can be seen as a controller of N_1 (Fig. 1(a)). C_1 either waits for N_1 to send the stats message or it sends out the review message itself. No matter which path C_1 chooses, N_1 will eventually send the stats message. If C_1 has sent out the review message already the composition will reach its final state with a message pending on place stats. That message will be received by C_1 which leads the composition of both nets to its final state [p3, p7]. If, however, C_1 has received the stats message first, it will then send the review message to N_1. That message can be consumed by N_1 leading to the final state. Thus, we can conclude that $N_1 \oplus C_1$ is deadlock-free and therefore we know that C_1 is a controller of N_1.

We have developed the *interaction graph* (IG) in order to analyze the controllability property of an open net. The IG represents the controller's point of view. The edges of the IG represent the actions of the controller – sending and receiving messages. Each node v of the graph is the set of states of N, which can be reached by consuming and producing the messages along any path from the initial node of the IG to v. Basically, a node of the graph forms a hypothesis of the controller with respect to the state the net might be in. The controller only knows the set of states in which the net could be in after a certain sequence of communication steps. It does, however, not know the exact state of the net. Inside the set of states represented by a node of the interaction graph, we distinguish *transient* and *maximal* (deadlock) states. A state is transient if it enables a transition of N. Otherwise, it is called maximal. A node v contains, with a transient state m, its successor states in N as well. So we consider a node to be a set of states and write $s \in v$ with s being a state in node v.

The IG of the net N_1 of Fig. 1(a) is depicted in Fig. 2(a). The root node $v0$ of the graph contains all states that N_1 might be in if no communication between N_1 and its controller has taken place. State [p1] is transient, so the net can leave this state on its own by firing transition !stats yielding the maximal state [p2, stats]. Being in this state, N_1 needs the controller to either receive the stats message or to send the review message in order to reach another state.

The controller can actually control the net in a limited way by sending messages. Whereas by receiving messages from the net, the controller gets some knowledge about the state the net might be in. The actions of the controller (represented by the edges of the IG) are called *events*. We distinguish two kinds of events: (1) *sending event* means that the controller sends a message to the net (labeled by !) and (2) *receiving event* represents the receiving of a message (labeled by ?) by the controller. Each state of a node of the IG (and thus each node itself) can activate sending as well as receiving events.

Definition 2 (Activated Sending- and Receiving Events). *Let N be an open net. Let $v = \{s_1, \ldots, s_n\}$ be a set of states reachable in N and let $i \in \{1, \ldots, n\}$. The following sets are defined for v.*

- Activated sending events: $\mathcal{S}(s_i) = \{X \mid \exists s_i' : s_i + X \xrightarrow{?X} s_i' \wedge s_i[X] = 0 \wedge s_i'[X] = 0 \wedge X \subseteq P_{in}(N)\}$ *and* $\mathcal{S}(v) = \bigcup_i \mathcal{S}(s_i)$. *!X is a sending event.*
- Activated receiving events: $\mathcal{R}(s_i) = \{y \mid s_i[y] \geq 1 \wedge y \in P_{out}(N)\}$ *and* $\mathcal{R}(v) = \bigcup_i \mathcal{R}(s_i)$. *?y is a receiving event.*

In Def. 2 we use the notation $s_i + X \xrightarrow{?X} s_i'$. It says that state $s_i + X$ leads to state s_i' by firing transition $?X$. In this case X may be a set of input places. A receiving transition connected to multiple input places $X = \{x_1, \ldots, x_n\}$ is labeled with $?x_1, \ldots, ?x_n$ or simply $?X$. $s_i[X] = 0$ is defined element-wise: $s_i[x_1] = \cdots = s_i[x_n] = 0$.

Node $v0$ of the IG of Fig. 2(a) contains the set of states $\{[p1], [p2, stats]\}$. So, the sets of activated events are $\mathcal{R}([p1]) = \emptyset$, $\mathcal{S}([p1]) = \{order\}$ and $\mathcal{R}([p2, stats]) = \{stats\}$, $\mathcal{S}([p2, stats]) = \{review\}$. Therefore $v0$ activates the events: $\mathcal{R}(v0) = \{stats\}$ and $\mathcal{S}(v0) = \{review, order\}$.

At any given node v in the interaction graph we calculate the successor node v' with respect to the activated sending or receiving events of v. Since each node is a set of states, we define the successor state set of one particular set of states.

Definition 3 (Calculation of Successor State Set). *Let N be an open net and let v be a set of states reachable in N. The set of states v' is a successor state set of v and is calculated as follows.*

- *Sending event: $v' = \{s' \mid s + x_1 + \cdots + x_n \xrightarrow{*} s', s \in v, \{x_1, \ldots, x_n\} \in \mathcal{S}(v)\}$ denoted by $v \xrightarrow{!x_1, \ldots, !x_n} v'$.*
- *Receiving event: $v' = \{s - y_1 - \cdots - y_m \mid s \in v, \{y_1, \ldots, y_m\} \subseteq \mathcal{R}(v)\}$ denoted by $v \xrightarrow{?y_1, \ldots, ?y_m} v'$.*

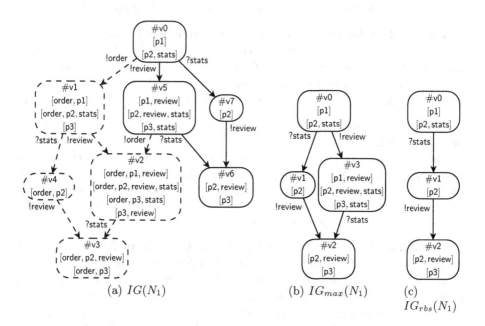

(a) $IG(N_1)$ (b) $IG_{max}(N_1)$ (c) $IG_{rbs}(N_1)$

Fig. 2. Interaction graphs of net N_1 of Fig. 1(a): (a) The complete $IG(N_1)$, (b) the reduced $IG_{max}(N_1)$ according to the *Maximal States* rule and (c) the reduced $IG_{rbs}(N_1)$ according to the *Receiving Before Sending* rule.

The notation $v \xrightarrow{!x_1,\ldots,!x_n} v'$ states that there is an edge labeled with $!x_1, \ldots, !x_n$ that leads from state set v to state set v'. In the following we will call v and v' nodes of an IG. As the communication between open nets is done asynchronously, a message being sent to a net may remain in the message channel, which is reflected by $\xrightarrow{*}$ in Def. 3.

We have already seen that the root node $v0$ of the IG of Fig. 2(a) activates three events, namely !order, !review and ?stats. We calculate the successor nodes of $v0$. We will start with the receiving event ?stats that is represented by the edge labeled with ?stats. There is only one state of $v0$ that activates the event ?stats, the state [p2, stats]. Receiving a message means we delete that message from the message channel. Formally, we subtract stats from state [p2, stats] yielding the state [p2], which is maximal. We add [p2] to the new successor node $v7$ of $v0$ (see Fig. 2(a)). Since there is no other state in $v0$ that activates the receiving event ?stats, state [p2] is the only state of node $v7$. Now we calculate the successor node of $v0$ that can be reached by the edge !order, in Fig. 2(a) this is $v1$. The controller sends a message order to the service. The message order might remain in the message channel. Thus, we first add the states [order, p1] and [order, p2, stats] to $v1$. Secondly we add those states to $v1$ that can be reached by firing transitions. Thus, we calculate the successor states of the transient state [order, p1]. Here, the transition ?order that activated the sending event !order fires, yielding the maximal state [p3], which is added to $v1$. Since state [order, p2, stats] is maximal we do not add any other state to node $v1$.

We will now define the complete interaction graph of an open net.

Definition 4 (Interaction Graph of an Open Net). *Let $N = (P, T, F, P_{in}, P_{out}, m_0, \Omega)$ be an open net and let $R_N(v) = \{v' \mid v \xrightarrow{*} v'\}$. The interaction graph of N is the directed graph $IG(N) = [R_N(v_0), E]$, with the root node $v_0 = \{m' \mid m_0 \xrightarrow{*} m'\}$ and the set of edges $E = \{[v, e, v'] \mid v, v' \in R_N(v_0) \wedge v \xrightarrow{e} v' \text{ with } e \in (\mathcal{R}(v) \cup \mathcal{S}(v))\}$. $v \in R_N(v_0)$ is a terminal node, iff $\mathcal{R}(v) = \mathcal{S}(v) = \emptyset$.*

For simplicity we will write $v \in IG(N)$ instead of $v \in R_N(v_0)$, meaning v is a node in $IG(N)$.

The interaction graph of an open net depicts all possible states the net can reach due to sending and receiving events. For analyzing controllability, we search for a subgraph of the IG that can serve as the state space of a controller. To this end, we label the nodes of the IG as *good* or *bad*. The desired subgraph is the one that consists of the good nodes only.

Definition 5 (Good/Bad Terminal Node, Good/Bad Node). *Let N be an open net and let $v \in IG(N)$. (1) If v is a terminal node, we classify v as a (i) good terminal node, iff $\forall s \in v : s \xrightarrow{*} \omega \in \Omega$ holds and (ii) bad terminal node otherwise. (2) If v is not a terminal node, we call v (i) a good node, iff for every maximal state $s \in v$ holds $\exists v' : v \xrightarrow{e} v'$ with $e \in \mathcal{S}(s) \cup \mathcal{R}(s)$ and v' is either a good node or a good terminal node and (ii) a bad node otherwise.*

Consider the IG of Fig. 2(a), which has two terminal nodes, $v3$ and $v6$. Node $v3$ is classified as a bad terminal node. It contains two states. Neither of them is a final state of the net N_1. Node $v6$, however, contains the final state [p3]. The state [p2, review], which is also contained in $v6$, is transient. That state enables transition ?review. By firing ?review the net reaches the final state [p3], which is part of the node. So we can conclude that $v6$ actually is a good terminal node.

Definition 6 (Control Strategy in the Interaction Graph). *Let N be an open net. Let $IG_c(N) \sqsubseteq IG(N)$ be a subgraph of $IG(N)$ with the set of nodes $V_c \subseteq V$. The graph $IG_c(N)$ is called* control strategy *of N, if it holds:*

1. *The root node v_0 of $IG(N)$ is the root node v_0 of $IG_c(N)$.*
2. *The terminal nodes of $IG_c(N)$ are good terminal nodes in $IG(N)$.*
3. *For every node $v \in V_c$ that is not a terminal node and every maximal state $s \in v$ there exists an event, which is activated in s and leads to a good successor node of v in $IG_c(N)$.*

The control strategy[2] is a subgraph of the IG. The root node is just the root node of the IG. The terminal nodes of the control strategy are good terminal nodes in the IG by Def. 6. For every maximal state of each node, which is not a terminal node, within the control strategy, we can find an event which leads to another node of the control strategy.

As an example, we consider Fig. 2(a) again. We know that $v6$ is a good terminal node and that node $v3$ has been classified as being bad. We now propagate these properties to the remaining nodes of the IG. We start with node $v3$ and classify its two predecessor nodes $v4$ and $v2$. Node $v4$ has one maximal state, [order, p2], that activates an event which does not lead to a good terminal node. So $v4$ is classified bad. Node $v2$ has a maximal state, [order, p3, stats], that activates the event ?stats which leads to $v3$ only. So $v2$ is also classified as bad. The predecessor nodes of $v2$ are $v1$ and $v5$. The two events that are activated by the maximal state [order, p2, stats] of $v1$ lead to a bad node, so $v1$ is bad as well. The maximal states [p3] $\in v1$ and [p3, review] $\in v2$ activate no event and therefore violate property 3 of Def. 6 as well. Node $v5$ contains the maximal state [p3, stats], which activates the event ?stats, that leads to the good terminal node $v6$. That is why, we classify $v5$ as good. We apply the same procedure to every other node of the IG. After we have reached the root node, we can conclude whether the net N_1 is controllable or not – if the root node is classified good we have found a control strategy. So the net N_1 is controllable. The control strategy $IG_c(N_1)$ is depicted by solid lines in Fig. 2(a).

We will now compare the controller C_1 of Fig. 1(b) and the control strategy $IG_c(N_1)$. The control strategy demands that a controller of N_1 being in its initial state has to be able to either receive the stats message or to send a review message. After having received the stats message it has to be able to send the review message. Or in the other case, if it has sent out the review message it then has to be able to receive the stats message. With this in mind we can easily see that C_1 models exactly the described behavior.

---

[2] In this paper the control strategy of an interaction graph is depicted by a solid line. Those nodes and edges that do not belong to the control strategy of the graph are drawn with dashed lines.

3   Efficient Calculation of Interaction Graphs

In this section, we will introduce reduction rules that reduce the number of events being considered for building up the IG, which leads to a reduction of the number of nodes (and edges) of the graph. The root node of each reduced graph, however, is the same as the root node of the complete IG. The rules preserve containment of at least one (not necessarily every) controller. We refer to [11] for the complete and formal description of the reduction rules as well as the complete correctness proofs.

The set of all maximal states of a node $v \in IG(N)$ will be called $\mathcal{Z}_{max}(v)$ with $\mathcal{Z}_{max}(v) = \{s \mid s \in v \land$ s is maximal$\}$.

3.1   Reduction by Maximal States

The nodes of an IG may contain transient states. Being in a transient state, the net can change to another state without letting its controller know. Consider node $v0$ of the reduced IG of Fig. 2(b). The transient state [p1] activates the sending event !order. Since the transition !stats is enabled in this state, N_1 may leave [p1] on its own. If the controller now sends the message order, there is no way of knowing that the net will ever consume this message. The net might just have switched to state [p2, stats] by firing transition !stats. State [p2, stats] does not activate the sending event !order anymore. Thus, in node $v0$ the reduction by *Maximal States* takes only those events into account that are activated by the maximal state [p2, stats], namely !review and ?stats. In node $v3$ the maximal state [p3, stats] activates the receiving event ?stats. So we add the edge ?stats to the reduced graph. Compared to the IG of Fig. 2(a) we do not add the edge !order to nodes $v0$ and $v3$ (which is node $v5$ in Fig. 2(a)) because this event is activated by a transient state only.

Definition 7 (Reduction by Maximal States). *Let N be an open net.*
$IG_{max}(N)^3$ is a directed graph $[V, E]$ with nodes V and edges E such that (1) $v_0 \in V$. (2) If $v \in V$, and there is an $e \in (\mathcal{R}(\mathcal{Z}_{max}(v)) \cup \mathcal{S}(\mathcal{Z}_{max}(v)))$, then $v' \in V$ with $v \xrightarrow{e} v'$ and $[v, e, v'] \in E$.

Fig. 2(b) depicts the reduced interaction graph $IG_{max}(N_1)$ of net N_1.

We prove in [11] that if the $IG(N)$ (for a given open net N) contains a control strategy, then we can find a control strategy in $IG_{max}(N)$ as well. So the reduced interaction graph $IG_{max}(N)$ (Def. 7) can be used for the controllability analysis. Therefore we will integrate this rule into every other reduction rule. Thus, we will only consider the maximal states of a node to compute the activated events.

3.2   Reduction by Receiving Before Sending

We turn our attention to those maximal states of the nodes of the IG that activate receiving events. Node $v0$ of the reduced IG of Fig. 2(c) contains one

---

[3] *max* stands for "**Max**imal States".

maximal state, [p2, stats], which activates the receiving event ?stats and the sending event !review. According to the *Receiving Before Sending* rule, we only consider the receiving event ?stats of that state to be activated. Therefore we only add one edge, ?stats, to node $v0$ and calculate the successor node. The successor node $v1$ still activates the sending event !review. It is the only event that is activated in $v1$. So we add an edge labeled with !review to the graph and calculate the next node $v2$, which is the good terminal node of the graph.

We will now define the reduced set of activated sending events of a node of the interaction graph.

Definition 8 (Receiving before Sending). *Let N be an open net and let* $v \in IG(N)$. *The set $\mathcal{S}_{rbs}(v)^4 = \{x \mid s \in \mathcal{Z}_{max}(v) \wedge x \in \mathcal{S}(s) \wedge \mathcal{R}(s) = \emptyset\}$ contains the activated sending events.*

For every maximal state of node $v \in IG(N)$ we check if it activates a sending event and no receiving event. If this is the case, we will add that sending event to the set $\mathcal{S}_{rbs}(v)$. Consequently, just those sending events are considered to be active that are activated by states that do not activate any receiving events.

Now we can define the reduced interaction graph based on this rule.

Definition 9 (Reduction by Receiving before Sending). *Let N be an open net. Let $\mathcal{S}_{rbs}(v)$ of node v be computed by Def. 8. $IG_{rbs}(N)$ of N is a directed graph $[V, E]$ with nodes V and edges E such that (1) $v_0 \in V$. (2) If $v \in V$, and there is an $e \in (\mathcal{R}(\mathcal{Z}_{max}(v)) \cup \mathcal{S}_{rbs}(v))$, then $v' \in V$ with $v \xrightarrow{e} v'$ and $[v, e, v'] \in E$.*

By letting the controller receive the message first, we make sure that the successor node will not increase in size (see [11]) and we only calculate one successor node even though both events are activated. The reduced interaction graph $IG_{rbs}(N_1)$ of net N_1 is shown in Fig. 2(c). It reflects the behavior of a valid controller of N_1 because $IG_{rbs_c}(N_1) \sqsubseteq IG_{rbs}(N_1)$.

In [11] we prove that the reduced $IG_{rbs}(N)$ can be used for analyzing controllability. In order to prove this property we need quite a few corollaries and lemmas. Since one of the lemmas plays a central role in the proof we want to at least mention it here. It states a fundamental property of a control strategy: every receiving event being activated in a (good) node v of the control strategy leads from v to a (good) successor node of v of the control strategy. In other words, it is always a good idea for the controller to receive as many messages possible, before sending messages out to the net.

3.3 Reduction by Combining Receiving Events

In order to show the effect of this reduction rule we extend the net N_1 of Fig. 1(a) by adding transition !note and place p_4 resulting in the net N_2 of Fig. 3(a). The initial state m_0 is [p1] and the set of final states of N_2 is $\Omega = \{[p4]\}$. The control strategy of N_2 is depicted in Fig. 3(b). The root node $v0$ of the reduced IG in

---

4 *rbs* stands for "**R**eceiving **B**efore **S**ending".

Fig. 4(a) is again the same node as the root node of the *IG* of Fig. 3(b). *v0* has one maximal state, [note, p3, stats], which activates the receiving events ?note and ?stats. To calculate the successor nodes of *v0* we will now combine both receiving events to one single receiving event. That way node *v0* has an outgoing edge labeled with ?note, ?stats. Since the same maximal state activates the sending event !review we will also add an edge labeled with !review to node *v0*. The same procedure is applied as we calculate the events of node *v1* (see Fig. 4(a)).

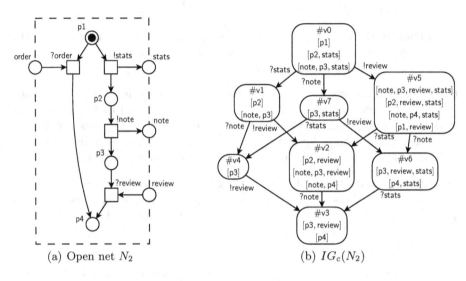

(a) Open net N_2 (b) $IG_c(N_2)$

Fig. 3. (a) Open net N_2 and (b) its control strategy $IG_c(N_2)$

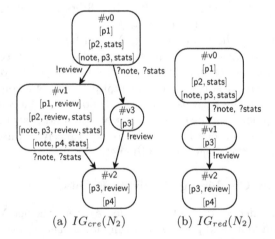

(a) $IG_{cre}(N_2)$ (b) $IG_{red}(N_2)$

Fig. 4. Two reduced interaction graphs of net N_2 of Fig. 3(a): (a) reduced $IG_{cre}(N_2)$ according to the *Combining Receiving Events* rule and (b) reduced $IG_{red}(N_2)$ combining all reduction rules.

The maximal state [note, p4, stats] activates the receiving events ?note and ?stats as well. Therefore we again add an outgoing edge labeled with ?note, ?stats to node $v1$.

We now define the reduced set of activated receiving events of a node in the interaction graph.

Definition 10 (Combine Receiving Events). *Let N be an open net and let $v \in IG(N)$. The set $\mathcal{R}_{cre}(v)^5 = \{\mathcal{R}(s) \mid s \in \mathcal{Z}_{max}(v) \wedge \neg \exists s' \in (\mathcal{Z}_{max}(v) \setminus \{s\}) : \mathcal{R}(s) \supset \mathcal{R}(s')\}$ contains the activated receiving events.*

The set $\mathcal{R}_{cre}(v)$ contains all receiving events activated in v. Hereby, all receiving events of one maximal state in v are combined to one single receiving event. If there are two states s_i and s_j in v, such that the set of receiving events of s_i ($\mathcal{R}(s_i)$) is a real subset of $\mathcal{R}(s_j)$, we just add $\mathcal{R}(s_i)$ to the set $\mathcal{R}_{cre}(v)$. Consider, for instance, two states $s_i = $ [y1, p0] and $s_j = $ [y1, y2, p1] with $\mathcal{R}(s_i) = \{y1\}$ and $\mathcal{R}(s_j) = \{y1, y2\}$. Adding both sets to $\mathcal{R}_{cre}(v)$ of node $v \supseteq \{s_i, s_j\}$ would result in two outgoing edges. The successor node v' of edge ?y1 would activate the event ?y2 which would then lead to the same node as the edge ?y1, ?y2 of node v. By Def. 10 we just add $\mathcal{R}(s_i)$ to $\mathcal{R}_{cre}(v)$.

Now we will define the reduced interaction graph.

Definition 11 (Reduction by Combining Receiving Events). *Let N be an open net. The set $\mathcal{R}_{cre}(v)$ is calculated according to Def. 10. $IG_{cre}(N)$ of N is the directed graph $[V, E]$ with nodes V and edges E such that (1) $v_0 \in V$. (2) If $v \in V$, and there is an $e \in (\mathcal{R}_{cre}(v) \cup \mathcal{S}(\mathcal{Z}_{max}(v)))$, then $v' \in V$ with $v \xrightarrow{e} v'$ and $[v, e, v'] \in E$.*

The reduced $IG_{cre}(N_2)$ of net N_2 is depicted in Fig. 4(a) and represents a valid controller of N_2 because $IG_{cre_c}(N_2) \sqsubseteq IG_{cre}(N_2)$. In [11] we prove that the reduced $IG_{cre}(N)$ can be used for the controllability analysis of an open net N.

3.4   Combination of Reduction Rules

The reduction rules shown in this paper can be combined. The rule of Sect. 3.1 has already been integrated into the rules of Sect. 3.2 and Sect. 3.3. Those rules define either a reduced set of activated sending events or a reduced set of activated receiving events. Thus, in order to calculate an IG that uses all reduction rules ($IG_{red}(N)$), we use exactly those reduced sets of activated events. The reduced $IG_{rbs}(N_1)$ (Fig. 2(c)) is actually identical to $IG_{red}(N_1)$ that combines all reduction rules. Fig. 4(b) shows the reduced $IG_{red}(N_2)$ of net N_2 (Fig. 3(a)).

4   Case Studies

The interaction graph as a means of analyzing controllability together with the reduction rules we have developed and presented in this paper has been fully

---

[5] *cre* stands for "**C**ombining **R**eceiving **E**vents"

Table 1. Experimental results running FIONA on a Linux machine with 2GB RAM and an Intel® Pentium® M 1.73GHz processor. The number of places (#P) and transitions (#T) of the respective open net are depicted. Further, the number of all nodes (#N) and all edges (#E) of the complete IG, of the reduced IG, and of the operating guideline (OG) for each service are shown. Column "T [s]" represents the time in seconds it took to calculate each graph. The reduced IG has been calculated by applying all reduction rules we have presented in this paper. The "red. [%]" column shows the percentage of reduction w.r.t. the number of nodes and edges.

Service Name	open net		complete IG			reduced IG			red. [%]		OG		
	#P	#T	#N	#E	T [s]	#N	#E	T [s]	#N	#E	#N	#E	T [s]
online shop	108	128	946	2111	11	56	60	1	94	97	7713	35010	242
order processing	789	1069	49	129	130	5	4	5	90	97	161	517	345
car breakdown	143	216	2728	10468	202	121	200	10	99	99	49313	295923	2776
deliver goods	116	156	1584	7473	302	31	41	1	98	99	12289	81054	1496

implemented and integrated into the tool FIONA [7]. At our group we maintain a quite complex repository of services. Most of them are modeled in WS-BPEL. The services were taken from the WS-BPEL specification, have been modeled at our group or were given to us from industrial partners. In order to analyze the services we use the tool BPEL2oWFN[6] to translate the WS-BPEL processes into open nets [5]. In Table 1 we summarize the results of our experiments on some case studies. Here, we also compare our approach to the operating guideline (OG) [9]. The OG represents *every* possible controller of a service and could therefore be used for the controllability analysis as well.

The "online shop" is the running example of [5] (Sect. 6). The "order processing" service is an industrial service that was given to us in WS-BPEL. The service has a quite complex net structure with 3 input places and 38 output places. The "car breakdown" service is also an industrial service modeling a part of a car rental service in case a rental car broke down. Even though the net structure (6 input places, 9 output places) is not as complex as the "order processing" service, it possesses a highly complex interaction behavior, which is reflected by its OG. Finally, the "deliver goods" service models the activities that are done after a customer has ordered products. It is also a service that was given to us from an industrial partner.

Comparing the complete IG and the reduced IG of every service we can easily see that the reduction rules we have developed indeed work very well for real life services. The percentage of reduction (of the number of nodes and edges) is more than 90% for each net. So, the number of nodes and edges that need to be calculated for the controllability analysis has decreased significantly resulting in a faster analysis result (see column "T [s]" of the reduced IG).

Due to the nature of the OG it is always significantly bigger than both the complete and the reduced IG. It even takes much more time to calculate the OG. Especially at design time, it is of great importance that the analysis is fast.

---

[6] Available at http://www.service-technology.org/bpel2owfn

There may be some constellations in which the reduction is not as significant. The reduction rules do not yet deal with sequences of sending events. Further, we do not examine conflicting sending events. Therefore, as we calculate the reduced set of activated sending events, we are not able to summarize sending events or set priorities regarding which event to consider first. Our reduction, however, works best in settings that contain sequences of receiving events and/or sending and receiving events that are in conflict to one another.

5   Related Work

For analyzing controllability of an open net, *communication graphs* have been introduced in [3]. The edges of those graphs represent communication steps of the controller. These steps are divided into an input phase and an output phase. In each phase, a number of messages is received (input phase) or sent (output phase). The approach is similar to the IG. However, if no receiving event can take place, for instance, the output phase will still be modeled in the graph. Therefore the communication graph tends to be more complex than our IG (cf. [11]).

In [12] different types of controllability notions are introduced – centralized, distributed, and local controllability. Further, the author shows algorithms to construct (whenever possible) the *most permissive* controller with respect to the notion of controllability. The construction of the IG is similar to those algorithms. One major difference is, that at any node of the most permissive controller *all possible* (not necessarily activated) sending events are considered. Our contribution is to apply reduction techniques to decide controllability more efficiently. We do not aim at computing the most permissive controller. So, even the complete IG does not necessarily represent the most permissive controller. As the IG is built up, just the activated sending and receiving events of each node are taken into consideration in order to calculate the successor nodes.

The notion of the most permissive controller has been formalized by the operating guideline [9]. Since the OG represents *all* controllers of a service, the graph tends to be too complex to be used for checking controllability (see Sect. 4).

In [13] the authors show that controllability is undecidable for general open nets. If the class of (cyclic) open nets is restricted, controllability can indeed be decided [9,13]. The restricted class of open nets consists of those nets, where the reachability graph of the inner net (that results from removing the input/output places and adjacent edges from the net) is finite. Further, they demand that the communication between two open nets is limited. So the controller never sends more then k messages to the net (for some $k \in \mathbb{N}$).

Our approach of deciding controllability with the help of the IG has already been introduced in [7]. The focus of that paper was to present a technology chain, to analyze WS-BPEL processes w.r.t. controllability and to calculate the operating guideline. The formal model of the IG and the reduction rules presented in this paper have only been mentioned rather briefly in [7].

6 Conclusion and Further Work

In this paper we introduced interaction graphs to analyze the controllability of an acyclic open net. By analyzing the graph, we have focused on one property of open nets – controllability. We have described how this property can be verified using interaction graphs. In order to make the analysis more efficient, we have defined reduction rules for the interaction graph. The IG and the reduction techniques have all been integrated into the tool FIONA. Our case studies show that the theoretical assumptions we have made while developing the reduction rules indeed work very well in practice. We currently adapt our results to a more liberal version of open nets. That is, we want to permit final states that do not necessarily leave the input and output places empty. We also adapt our techniques in order to be able to analyze cyclic nets as well.

Furthermore, we work on finding more reduction rules. We have ideas on how to reduce the number of states stored in each node. Here we aim at defining a certain set of generator states to represent each node. We also intend to use stubborn sets [14] to calculate the states of the net. Another major goal is to adapt the partial order reduction [15] to fit our needs in choosing the set of activated events. We intend to use this technique to decide which sending event to consider in case of conflicting sending events (see Sect. 4). Further, we study sequences of sending events in order to combine them in a way similar to our "Combining Receiving Events" rule (see Sect. 3.3).

References

1. Papazoglou, M.: Web Services: Principles and Technology. Pearson - Prentice Hall, Essex (2007)
2. Alves, A., et al.: Web Services Business Process Execution Language Version 2.0. Technical report, OASIS (2007)
3. Martens, A.: Analyzing Web Service Based Business Processes. In: Cerioli, M. (ed.) FASE 2005. LNCS, vol. 3442, pp. 19–33. Springer, Heidelberg (2005)
4. Massuthe, P., Reisig, W., Schmidt, K.: An Operating Guideline Approach to the SOA. AMCT 1(3), 35–43 (2005)
5. Lohmann, N., Massuthe, P., Stahl, C., Weinberg, D.: Analyzing interacting WS-BPEL processes using flexible model generation. DKE 64(1), 38–54 (2008)
6. Badouel, E., Darondeau, P.: Theory of Regions. In: Lectures on Petri Nets I: Basic Models. LNCS, vol. 1491, pp. 529–586. Springer, Heidelberg (1998)
7. Lohmann, N., Massuthe, P., Stahl, C., Weinberg, D.: Analyzing Interacting BPEL Processes. In: Dustdar, S., Fiadeiro, J.L., Sheth, A.P. (eds.) BPM 2006. LNCS, vol. 4102, pp. 17–32. Springer, Heidelberg (2006)
8. Reisig, W.: Petri Nets. EATCS monographs on theoretical computer science edn. Springer, Heidelberg (1985)
9. Lohmann, N., Massuthe, P., Wolf, K.: Operating Guidelines for Finite-State Services. In: Kleijn, J., Yakovlev, A. (eds.) ICATPN 2007. LNCS, vol. 4546, pp. 321–341. Springer, Heidelberg (2007)
10. Aalst, W.: The Application of Petri Nets to Workflow Management. Journal of Circuits, Systems and Computers 8(1), 21–66 (1998)

11. Weinberg, D.: Reduction Rules for Interaction Graphs. Technical Report 198, Humboldt-Universität zu Berlin (2006)
12. Schmidt, K.: Controllability of Open Workflow Nets. In: EMISA. LNI, pp. 236–249. Bonner Köllen Verlag (2005)
13. Massuthe, P., Serebrenik, A., Sidorova, N., Wolf, K.: Can I find a partner? Inf. Process. Lett. (2008) (accepted)
14. Schmidt, K.: Stubborn sets for standard properties. In: ICATPN 1999. LNCS, vol. 1639, pp. 46–65. Springer, Heidelberg (1999)
15. Valmari, A.: A stubborn attack on state explosion. Formal Methods in System Design 1(4), 297–322 (1992)

Author Index